26.50

JUBILATE!

Church Music in the Evangelical Tradition

Donald P. Hustad

HOPE PUBLISHING COMPANY
Carol Stream, Illinois 60188

Copyright © 1981 by Hope Publishing Company
International Copyright Secured. All Rights Reserved.
Printed in the United States of America
Library of Congress catalog card number: 80-85185
ISBN 0-916642-17-8

to DONNA, SONDRA and MARCIA

ACKNOWLEDGMENTS

Appreciation is expressed to the following publishers and other copyright holders for permission to use the following major quotations from their publications.

Abingdon Press: (1) for a selection from *God's Party* by David J. Randolph (Copyright © 1975 Abingdon Press. Used by Permission); (2) for a selection from *Hymns Today and Tomorrow* by Erik Routley (Copyright © 1964 Abingdon Press. Used by Permission); (3) for a selection from "The Educational Ministry of the Church" by Roger L. Shinn, in *An Introduction to Christian Education* (Copyright © 1966 by Abingdon Press. Used by Permission).

American Occupational Therapy Association, for a selection from "Psychological Foundations for Functional Music" by E. Thayer Gaston in *American Journal of Occupational Therapy,* Vol. 2, Feb., 1948.

Auburn Theological Seminary, for a selection from "The Revival Heard Around the World" by Richard Manzelmann.

Broadman Press, for a selection from *With My Song I Will Praise Him* by Claude Rhea (Copyright © 1977 by Broadman Press. Used by Permission).

Christianity Today: (1) for a selection from the editorial "The Christianity Today-Gallup Poll: An Overview," December 21, 1979 issue (Copyright 1979 by *Christianity Today.* Used by Permission); (2) for a selection from "Toward a Biblical View of Aesthetics" by Frank Gaebelein, August 30, 1968 issue (Copyright 1968 by *Christianity Today.* Used by Permission).

Concordia Publishing House: (1) for a selection from *God and Man in Music* by Carl Halter (Copyright © 1963 Concordia Publishing House. Used by Permission); (2) for a selection from "The Case for the Soloist in Christian Worship" in *Church Music 71-2* by Carl Halter (Copyright © 1971 Concordia Publishing House. Used by Permission).

Da Capo Press, Inc., for a selection from *History of American Church Music* by Leonard Ellinwood (Copyright © 1953 by Morehouse-Gorham Co. Da Capo Press reprint edition 1970. Used by Permission).

William B. Eerdmans Publishing Company: (1) for a selection from *The Evangelical Renaissance* by Donald G. Bloesch (Copyright © 1973. Used by Permission); (2) for two selections from "On Church Music" in *Christian Reflections* by C. S. Lewis (Copyright © 1967. Used by Permission).

First Baptist Church, Shreveport, Louisiana, for a selection from "In Praise of a Good Man" by Dr. William E. Hull in *The Church Chimes,* Vol. 58, No. 51, August 28, 1976.

Harper & Row, Inc., for a selection from *Leave It to the Spirit* by John Killinger (Copyright © 1971. Used by Permission).

Harvard University Press, for a selection from *Harvard Dictionary of Music* by Willi Apel (Copyright © 1964. Used by Permission).

The Hymn Society of America, for a selection from "HSA Convocations: Back to Basics" by Carlton R. Young in *The Hymn,* October, 1977.

Marshall, Morgan & Scott, Ltd., for a selection from *Worship in the Early Church* by Ralph P. Martin (Copyright © 1964. Used by Permission).

McGraw-Hill Book Company, for a selection from *Foundations and Principles of Music Education* by Charles Leonhard and Robert W. House (Copyright © 1959 by McGraw-Hill Book Company. Used by Permission).

The New York Times, for a selection from "The Electronic Church is Turning More People On" by Kenneth A. Briggs, Feb. 10, 1980 (Copyright © 1980 by the New York Times Company. Reprinted by Permission).

Newsweek, for a selection from "The Year of the Evangelicals," October 25, 1976 (Copyright 1976 by Newsweek, Inc. All Rights Reserved. Reprinted by Permission).

Oxford University Press: (1) for a selection from *New English Bible* (Copyright © The Delegates of the Oxford University Press and the Syndics of the Cambridge University Press 1961, 1970. Reprinted by Permission); (2) for a selection from "Early Christian Music" by Egon Wellesz in *The New Oxford History of Music,* Vol. II (Copyright © 1954. Revised in 1955, reprinted 1961. Used by Permission).

Radio Bible Class, for a selection from the October 2, 1979 devotional by Henry G. Bosch in the *Our Daily Bread* booklet.

Random House, Inc., for a selection from *The Random House Dictionary of the English Language, the Unabridged Edition* (Copyright © 1981, 1966 by Random House, Inc. Used by Permission).

Fleming H. Revell Company: (1) for a selection from *Then Sings My Soul* by George Beverly Shea (Copyright © 1968 by Fleming H. Revell Co. Used by Permission); (2) for a selection from *Because He Lives* by Gloria Gaither (Copyright © 1977 by Fleming H. Revell Co. Used by Permission); (3) for a selection from *Amazing Grace* by Anita Bryant (Copyright © 1976 by Fleming H. Revell Co. Used by Permission).

Time, for a selection from "Back to That Old Time Religion," December 26, 1977 (Reprinted by permission from TIME, The Weekly Newsmagazine; Copyright Time Inc. 1977).

The University of Chicago Press, for selections from *Dwight L. Moody: American Evangelist, 1837–1899* (Copyright © 1969 by University of Chicago. All Rights Reserved. Used by Permission).

Wheaton College, for a selection from "Toward a Biblical Perspective on the Arts" by Dr. Harold M. Best in *InForm,* Bulletin of Wheaton College, April 1979.

Word Books: (1) for a selection from *The Evangelical Heritage* by Bernard Ramm (Copyright © 1973. Used by Permission); (2) for a selection from *Billy Sunday* by D. Bruce Lockerbie (Copyright © 1965. Used by Permission); (3) for a selection from *Come and See* by Ken Medema (Copyright © 1976. Used by Permission).

Zondervan Publishing House: (1) for a selection from *Man in Black* by Johnny Cash (Copyright © 1975. Used by Permission); (2) for a selection from *The Miracle Goes On* by John W. Peterson (Copyright © 1976. Used by Permission).

FOREWORD

The Pilgrimage of a Schizophrenic Musician

No doubt some individuals will say that this book was written in an effort to establish once and for all my personal identity. For almost as long as I can remember I have functioned as a student and a performer in the two very different worlds of art music and traditional evangelical church music. Through the years, as my musical roles grew to include teacher, composer and editor, the tensions between those two worlds have occasionally produced an inner conflict that bordered on aesthetic schizophrenia. At the same time, in more than a half century of musical activity, there has been a large measure of satisfaction and many evidences of God's providence.

Ours was not a particularly musical family, though mother and father both played the guitar and sang Norwegian pietist hymns. Growing up in central Iowa, I began to study piano at age four and, while still in grade school, was playing the more difficult Czerny etudes, Beethoven sonatas and Liszt's transcription of the Second Hungarian Rhapsody. At the same time I was accompanying in church (beginning at age eight) and improvising on the gospel music that was common in fundamentalist worship in the 1920's.

It was at college that I first became conscious of the disparity between great music and typical church music. In theory classes, we identified the differences between strong and weak melodies, good and bad harmonic progressions. In choir I accompanied the classic oratorios and motets of choral literature. But on weekends I sang baritone in one of the college male quartets, with a repertoire that was partly in the southern Stamps-Baxter style and partly traditional gospel music, with a smattering of the pseudo-anthem material that was found in typical quartet books.

After graduation, with no clearly defined vocational goal, I drifted into Chicago and began to work as a musician in the Moody Bible Institute's radio station, WMBI. Their music programming covered a wide spectrum of styles—sacred and secular, serious and "gospel." In their studios I narrated music appreciation programs and taught creative hymn improvisation, played the music of Beethoven, Mozart, Schubert and Brahms, and arranged simple hymns for choirs. At the same time I continued to study, first at the American Conservatory of Music and later at Northwestern University, completing a master's degree in piano.

During the years that followed, teaching and professional performances seemed to get an equal share of attention. There was an eight-year tenure as director, arranger and organist for "Club Time"—a program of hymns on the American Broadcasting Company network, with George Beverly Shea as featured soloist; this was concurrent with a four-year stint as associate professor, teaching piano and musicology at Olivet Nazarene College, Kankakee, Illinois. I was also organist-director at the prestigious First Methodist Church in Park Ridge, Illinois and organist for the "Songs in the Night" broadcast from the Village Church in Western Springs.

In 1950 I became director of the Sacred Music Department of the Moody Bible Institute and simultaneously began what is now a thirty-year relationship with Hope Publishing Company. Moody's program sought to bring the two contrasting worlds of music together; with a long and distinguished heritage as the center of training in gospel music, they were now interested in offering bonafide credits in college-level education that could be transferred to any college or conservatory. Accordingly, the curriculum was updated to achieve that standard, and the Moody Chorale's repertoire ran the gamut from the motets of J. S. Bach and Johannes Brahms to my latest arrangements of religious "folk music." Working as an editor with Hope, it was my challenge to assist them in enlarging the scope of evangelical hymnody, and also to expand their publishing into a wide range of church music materials.

Through the years, I became increasingly aware of the tensions and prejudices that exist between individuals and groups based on differing tastes and concepts in church music. While still a radio musician at Moody, I learned that the teachers in the Institute's educational division frowned on the "show business excesses" perpetrated by those of us in radio. Actually, more "art music" was produced in the radio studios than in the school's recital halls, but at the same time, our "gospel music" styles were more *avant garde,* following rather closely the recent fashions in secular popular music. Later, when I became director of the Sacred Music Department, the "shoe was on the other foot" and I found myself guilty of the same critical attitude. This may demonstrate the differing viewpoints of musicians in academia and those in a performance ministry.

While teaching at Moody, I began work on a doctorate in church music at Northwestern University. On one occasion during that period of study, I was stopped in the hall by Grigg Fountain, member of the organ faculty and formerly a Southern Baptist. He said to me: "How can we get to this fellow Billy Graham to persuade him to change his music? I see him on television and his preaching gets to me. But the music is awful!" I wish I could report that I took time to communicate to him my own accommodation to a musical split personality. But, knowing that he just wouldn't understand, I passed it off quickly and hurried to my next appointment.

Actually, it was partly a conflict about music styles that persuaded me to leave Moody Bible Institute in 1963. Some time earlier the music department began to "get flak" from some of the "colonels" in the Institute staff, with the accusation that our program was more suited to a conservatory than a Bible institute. I am still convinced that the curriculum and emphasis were proper for that school. But, because I didn't have either the skills or the stomach for political jousting, and because I felt keenly that my work at the school was over, I resigned to accept a position with the Billy Graham evangelistic team, playing the organ in crusade services and in promotional concerts, and developing a male chorus for "Hour of Decision" broadcasts.

Both Dr. Graham and music director Cliff Barrows understood that being a crusade musician was a temporary activity for me. I had told Cliff so at the beginning, and a couple of years later while riding in a car across the Argentina *pampas*, Billy asked me, "Don, what do you really want to do?" I answered, "I believe God wants me to teach in a strong school of church music." The crusade schedule allowed me time to finish my doctoral study, prepare a number of hymnals and other publications for Hope Publishing Company, and do more organ practicing than ever before or since. Traveling with the team on four continents plus Australasia reminded us of the variety of music used in Christian worship the world around. At the same time, we learned that misunderstanding and conflict about church music styles exists in such places as Hong Kong, East Africa and West Germany, as well as in the United States.

The opportunity to teach again came in 1966 when I was called to the faculty of the School of Church Music of Southern Baptist Theological Seminary. Of all evangelical groups, Southern Baptists have made the most progress in church music in recent years. I am convinced that this is true, partly because the churches offer opportunities for fulltime, lifetime vocations in church music, and partly because they approach the ministry as both music education and Christian education, not as performance. Notwithstanding some frustrations (and what position doesn't have them?) these have been satisfying years at the seminary that have provided the opportunity to pull the disparate arts together, at least partially ameliorating the schizophrenia.

Now, about this book . . . . .

Except in matters of faith and theology, I suppose that I have always been something of a rationalist, wanting things to fit together to make sense. Admittedly, my early thinking about church music was subjective and empirical, based only on evaluation of my own experience. I was troubled about the gulf that seemed to exist between the music which I heard regularly in Chicago's Orchestra Hall and Opera House and the ordinary, even commercial expressions which dominated the gospel music programs of WMBI and the platform of a Billy Graham crusade. I was sure that I found meaning in both experiences, although increasingly there was evidently more creative enjoyment in serious music. Obviously, I was becoming "acculturated"—my musical tastes were changing from those I knew in younger years. And yet, I reasoned, this was happening because I had spent years in music study, and I could not expect it to be true of my family and friends who had not made the same aesthetic pilgrimage.

I reasoned also that history seemed to be on the side of traditional evangelical church music. Gospel hymns have been the norm for pietist Americans ever since the campmeeting movement began in 1800. What is the point of arguing for or against a musical style which has persisted for so long, and which has evidently sustained and nourished certain religious-cultural groups? Has not history itself validated it? Is there not evidently some genius in this music which meets the needs of the people with the doctrinal and liturgical heritage we call "evangelical"?

Most standard texts on church music approach these questions with the tools of historical musicology. As a result, such a book as Leonard Ellinwood's *The History of American Church Music* (New York: Morehouse-Gorham Company, 1953) sounds like one long jeremiad, bemoaning the primitive character of the art in this country; the few scant glimmers of hope emanate from the Oxford Movement in the Episcopal Church, the Cecilian tradition in Roman Catholicism, and the modern graded choir program which took shape at Westminster Choir College earlier in this century. The gospel song culture is not even mentioned in some treatises; in most others, it is presented as the worst scab on the "body musical."

My own more disciplined thinking and writing about church music began in 1959, when I was invited to give the W. Griffith Thomas Lectures at Dallas Theological Seminary, later included in the seminary journal *Bibliotheca Sacra*. The most significant lasting influence of that experience was derived from the study of biblical references to worship music.

In recent years I have become convinced that church music should be approached as a *functional* art, and judged by whether or not it fulfills its best function. This should not be understood to imply that it may be used for *unworthy* functions, such as excessive manipulation in worship or evangelism. It simply means that music in church is not a free art, an end in itself. It is art brought to the cross, art which is dedicated to the service of God and the edifying of the church. Again, this is not meant to deny the validity of music which *is* free, music which *is* an end in itself—art music. "All truth is God's truth" and all beauty comes from God, whether or not it is commonly experienced and understood.

It is also apparent that each culture and subculture worldwide has its own meaningful musical expressions, its own musical language or languages. This led me to approach church music as an aspect of ethnomusicology—music in relation to the culture which produces it. Although American evangelicals are by no means homogeneous culturally, they share a common heritage based on their theology and liturgical practice which is reflected in certain basic text/music patterns. Accordingly, I have examined the history, the doctrines, and the worship traditions of evangelicals, in the context of their distinctive musical expressions, in order to show the relationship between our identity and the church music we use.

Christianity Today, in the issue of December 21, 1979, reported on their use of the services of the renowned pollster George Gallup, Jr. to determine, among other things, the religious beliefs and attitudes of evangelicals.

> The hardest problem faced by the editorial staff in organizing the poll was how to determine who are evangelicals. After several weeks of serious consideration as to how this matter should be handled in the poll, the editor took the resulting definition home to his wife and discovered that by that definition she wasn't an evangelical. In the end the staff settled for two groupings, the first of which, for want of a better term, we called "orthodox evangelicals" and the second, "conversionalist evangelicals." The magazine's editors warn that neither of these should be construed as meaning that the term is the equivalent of "true Christian." They simply represent segments of the Christian community which for purposes of this study are described as "evangelical" on the basis of adherence to a specific set of standards and beliefs.
>
> . . . The editorial staff placed in the "orthodox evangelical" group all who identified themselves as holding that (1) Jesus Christ is the divine Son of God, or is both fully God and fully man; (2) the only hope for heaven is through personal faith in Jesus Christ; (3) the Bible is the Word of God and is not mistaken in its statements and teachings; and (4) those who read the Bible at least once a month; and (5) attend religious services at least once a month.

While acknowledging that "the overlap between 'orthodox evangelical' and 'conversionalist evangelical' was large, but by no means complete," the magazine editors offered this description of the second group.

> . . . The conversionalist evangelicals include those who read the Bible, attend religious services at least twice a month, and who have had a particularly powerful religious experience that is still important to them, which they understand as a conversion experience that included an identifiable point at which they asked Jesus Christ to become their personal Savior.

I have found the more detailed delineations of two contemporary theologians to be helpful, as found in the recent books, *The Evangelical Renaissance* by Donald G. Bloesch (Eerdmans, 1973) and *The Evangelical Heritage* by Bernard L. Ramm (Word, 1973). A summary of their findings is contained in this volume's Introduction and is generally accepted as the basis for this book. There is no desire to be discriminatory or to exhibit sectarian pride in this delimitation and analysis. It is simply a description of one group within the family of God—the group which has taught me much of what I know about things spiritual, and has permitted me to serve it with my own limited gifts—a group that has not been adequately considered in other books of this kind.

Even though the American evangelical tradition is less than three hundred years old, it has seemed to be necessary to survey the use of music in worship during the entire span of Christian history. Our roots lie in the New Testament church and the early church fathers. In addition, there have been many "greenings" of spiritual renewal throughout history, each of which exhibits certain similar evangelical phenomena. Finally, although our recent traditions are mostly those of reaction against the formalism and sacerdotalism of the middle ages, it is helpful to identify what we have reacted against, in order to separate our true identity from any indulgence in blind iconoclasm.

At the same time, it would be a mistake to surmise that this book has been written simply to justify the aesthetic choices of evangelicals throughout history. Notwithstanding the fact that each culture has validity simply because it represents the lifestyle of a people made in God's image, it is also true that every culture is corrupted by sin. H. Richard Niebuhr is correct in his argument that the world needs—not a "Christ of culture" or a "Christ against culture"—but a "Christ who transforms culture." Some will insist that the transformation wrought by Christ should result in a change in a culture's languages, of words or of music. But the church of the fifth century was wrong when it decreed that new converts in Gaul and Britain must worship in the Latin language rather than in the vernacular. Similarly, American and British missionaries of the 19th century were short-sighted when they imposed Anglo-American literary styles and hymn tunes on the nationals of each evangelized country. In the same context, although some evangelicals in America may not use the best text/music styles known to their particular culture, we should not expect conformity countrywide. It *is* important to ask whether each music and verbal language common to each culture and subculture has truly been "transformed"—brought to the cross—so that it makes the strongest possible contribution to the worship life of that culture.

It has often puzzled me that music—which Martin Luther described as a "noble, wholesome, and joyful creation," a gift of God—should so frequently be a source of conflict in the church. To be sure, such conflicts are sometimes caused simply by a failure to understand a particular musical language, and this possibility is discussed in the early chapters that follow. It must also be true that, while music which *is* commonly understood has great potential for profitable use, it also has potential for misuse. Undoubtedly, evangelicals have experienced both possibilities. In the first part of this book, I may seem to be preoccupied with establishing the positive contributions of our common cultural expressions, while listing the standards by which evangelical music should be judged. The reader who stays with me to the end will discover that there is a tightening focus on our weaknesses, and increasing emphasis on the areas in which we need to grow in spiritual-aesthetic maturity.

It is a familiar truism that music is not intrinsically sacred or secular; in our day, the only criteria by which it may be labeled are its lyrics and its avowed purpose. Just so, music performance in church is neither spiritual or unspiritual of itself. It is spiritual exercise by performers when their best is offered with humility and sincerity. It becomes spiritual food to the listener when it is perceived and assimilated as sincere, mature spiritual expression. Is it fair then to suggest that, while we are grateful for the gift of God in church music, we may be wise to harbor some lingering doubts about our use of it, both as performer and as listener? Even though redeemed, we are still (in the words of the hymnist) "prone to wander."

There is little that is really original in these pages. I am indebted to professors under whom I have sat, musicians and theologians whose books I have read, as well as to fellow teachers and church musicians who have shared their ideas with me. Thanks to my colleagues at Southern Baptist Theological Seminary—especially to Jay Wilkey, who encouraged me to believe I was on the right track in my approach; to Michael Hawn, who helped me update my thinking about church music education; and to music librarian Martha Powell, and other members of her staff.

Finally, thanks to my beautiful and understanding wife Ruth, who deserves much of the credit for anything I accomplish, and who helped in this project by typing, reading, correcting, encouraging, and retyping, ad infinitum.

It is my hope that this book may help fellow evangelicals understand and appreciate their best heritage of doctrine, worship habits and musical expression. May it also encourage them to constantly reexamine and reform their music—as well as their preaching and their liturgy—to be sure that it achieves its highest potential in God's kingdom.

Louisville, Kentucky   Donald P. Hustad
May 1, 1980

INTRODUCTION

Who Are the Evangelicals?

It was almost as challenging to find a name for this book as it was to write it. *Jubilate!*—"shout for joy!"—was a happy afterthought; it characterizes much of our Judeo-Christian musical heritage. I have settled on the more definitive subtitle, *Church Music in the Evangelical Tradition*, knowing that it will be offensive to some, partly because the common understanding of the word "evangelical" has changed through the years. At the time of the 16th century Reformation, all Protestants were "evangelicals," and the German (Lutheran) Church bears that name to this day. In recent years the word has tended to mean "not liberal" (rejecting late 19th century liberal theology), or "fundamentalist, but not obscurantist or cantankerous!"

The *Random House Dictionary of the English Language* gives these definitions:

> evangelical, *adj. 1.* pertaining to or in keeping with the gospel and its teachings. *2.* belonging to or designating the Christian churches that emphasize the teachings and authority of the Scriptures, esp. of the New Testament, in opposition to the institutional authority of the church itself, and that stress as paramount the tenet that salvation is achieved by personal conversion to faith in the atonement of Christ. *3.* pertaining to certain movements in the Protestant churches in the 18th and 19th centuries that stressed the importance of personal experience of guilt for sin, and of reconciliation to God through Christ. *4.* marked by ardent or zealous enthusiasm for a cause. *5.* evangelistic. —*n. 6.* an adherent of evangelical doctrines or a person who belongs to an evangelical church or party.

In the wake of the publicity given to President Jimmy Carter's "born again" faith, the media have accepted much the same meaning for the term, as demonstrated in the *Newsweek* cover story of October 25, 1976,

"Born Again." Calling 1976 "The Year of the Evangelicals," the authors[1] stated:

> Evangelicalism is the religion you get when you "get" religion. Its substance and style vary by region, denomination and theological tradition. But all evangelicals are united by a subjective experience of personal salvation, which they describe as being "born again," converted or regenerated.

> The term evangelical derives from the Greek word *euangelion,* meaning "good news," which American evangelicals are committed to spread through preaching and proselytizing. Unlike most other Christians, evangelicals insist that all people must be converted to Christ before they can do anything in their lives that is pleasing to God. They are Protestants who take a conservative view of Christian doctrine, emphasize personal morality rather than social ethics, look to the Bible as the sole authority in faith and practice and tend to regard themselves as the only true heirs of the New Testament church.

In a similar story, *Time* (December 26, 1977) extended the period of the "Evangelical Renaissance," even though some of their implications were somewhat negative.[2]

> In terms of sheer hoopla, 1978 promises to be one of the biggest years in recent history for the Evangelicals.

Time's characterizations of evangelicals were similar to those in *Newsweek:*

> Most Evangelicals . . . are basically conventional Protestants who hold staunchly to the authority of the Bible in all matters and adhere to orthodox Christian doctrine. They believe in making a conscious personal commitment to Christ, a spiritual encounter, gradual or instantaneous, known as the born again experience.

> Almost by definition (the Greek word *evangelion* means gospel), Evangelicals also believe in bringing the word of God to their fellow man, and today they are bringing it more exuberantly than ever.[3]

The validity of the secular press's description of an evangelical is borne out by contemporary theologians. In *The Evangelical Heritage,* Bernard Ramm identifies modern-day evangelicals by tracing their philosophical/theological roots:

1. They have the "mindset" of the West (Roman Catholic) rather than the East (Eastern Orthodox). Orthodoxy historically is *more mystical*

---

1. Kenneth L. Woodward, John Barnes and Laurie Lisle, "The Year of the Evangelicals," pp. 68-69.
2. Editors, "Back to That Old Time Religion," p. 53.
3. Ibid.

and views its doctrines and its liturgies as "mysteries" to be adored; the Western Church is *more rational* and has developed its philosophers/theologians/preachers from Tertullian, Augustine and Thomas Aquinas on down to those of the present day.[4] (See pages 11-21)

2. They are in the succession of the great reformers of the 15th and 16th centuries—Zwingli, Luther, Calvin and Cranmer. According to Ramm, the Reformers set the Word of God above the church and its traditions, and taught "justification by faith alone." They also reconstructed the doctrine of the Church so that it is seen as an "instrument (not a dispenser) of grace" and its pastors as "ministers of the Word of God," not as priests with the power to forgive sin and to change bread and wine into the body and blood of Christ. Furthermore, the Church effects its ministry, not through a monolithic, hierarchical organization but through the members of the local "body of Christ." It is therefore "congregational." (See pages 23-48)

3. They remained unmoved by (or have repented of) the heresies of the "Enlightenment" (17th and 18th centuries) and of "Modernism" (late 19th century). Ramm points out that evangelicals' strong reactions to the "modernist" movement included the establishing of Bible conferences and the founding of Bible institutes, the organizing of fellowships like the World Christian Fundamentals Association and the National Association of Evangelicals (countering the National Council of Churches and the World Council of Churches), evangelism (especially in mass meetings), publishing, religious radio, "faith" missions, etc. (See pages 64-102)

In a similar volume, *The Evangelical Renaissance,* Donald G. Bloesch succinctly lists and explains "The Hallmarks of Evangelicalism." They include both doctrinal tenets and emphases in ministry.

1. The sovereignty of God—"the living God of the Bible" who is both transcendent and immanent. (pp. 52-55)
2. The divine authority of scripture, "the infallible norm for faith and practice." (pp. 55-59)
3. Total depravity—"all of our goodness is corrupted by sin." (pp. 59-60)

---

4. This may be a bit difficult for some readers to accept, since Orthodox worship has traditionally been conducted in vernacular languages, and Roman Catholics universally worshiped in Latin until very recently. Nevertheless, it will be evident to anyone who compares an English version of the Liturgy of St. John Chrysostom with that of the contemporary Roman mass; the former is couched in flowery, abstruse, mystical language while the latter sounds very much like traditional Protestant expression. Furthermore, Orthodox liturgy and theology has remained static for more than 1000 years—since the second Nicaea council of bishops in 787 a.d.; as "mysteries to be adored," they are not subject to reform or development.

4. The substitutionary atonement—"Jesus Christ died in our place by His sacrifice on the cross." (pp. 60–62)
5. Salvation by grace—"Not by works of penance or deeds of mercy but by divine compassion are sinners justified and delivered." (pp. 62–64)
6. Salvation by faith alone. "Although our salvation is to be attributed to the grace of God alone, it must be received by faith if it is to benefit us . . . Faith consists of knowledge, intellectual assent and trust." (pp. 65–67)
7. Primacy of proclamation. "Evangelicals stress the preaching and hearing of the Word of God over audiovisual aids, rituals and symbols, though this is not to deny the rightful place of these things." (pp. 67–68)
8. Scriptural holiness. "While justification places us in a new relationship with God, sanctification makes us a new creation . . . The work of the Holy Spirit brings us into conformity with Christ in a life of holiness." (pp. 69–72)
9. The Church's spiritual mission. "To convert individuals . . . to instruct them in the way of discipleship . . . Social service (*diakonia*) done in the name of Christ." (pp. 72–75)
10. The personal return of Christ. "The visible coming again of Jesus Christ in power and glory to set up the kingdom that shall have no end." (pp. 75–77)

Bloesch insists that modern-day evangelicals are also inheritors of the European pietist movements which were especially significant in England, Germany and Scandinavia in the 17th, 18th and 19th centuries. He lists these salient features of pietist thinking:[5]

(1) An emphasis upon the "religion of the heart."
(2) The "doctrine of the new birth."
(3) The "new life in Christ."
(4) The "assurance of salvation."
(5) A close relationship between religion and personal ethics.
(6) The "preparation of the heart" for receiving Christ.
(7) A strong emphasis on missions.
(8) "Concrete embodiment" of the reformed doctrine of the "priesthood of believers."

These are the doctrinal emphases which, according to Bloesch, are held by today's "evangelicals." No doubt some individuals or groups will want to bear that name while adding some items to the lists and/or deleting others. Nevertheless, for the purposes of this volume, the theological characterizations of Ramm and Bloesch are acceptable.

---

5. Admittedly, this is a selective syncretism of Bloesch's material, and the reader is urged to examine his entire chapter, "The Legacy of Pietism" (pp. 101–157).

In our study, I will also tend to focus on the music of churches which are "non-liturgical"—those who do not have a fixed order and content of worship. This is not to say that all evangelicals are non-liturgical—that Lutherans, for instance, (who are liturgical in worship) may not be evangelical in theology; indeed, in our day, many Roman Catholics would want to claim that name! It is hoped that this book will have something to say to some within the liturgical fellowships.[6] However, in those denominations the musical traditions are rather clearly established by bishops and/or liturgical commissions. The worship theology is well stated by the church leadership and there is considerable uniformity of practice within each group. We are more concerned with the needs of churches which do not have either authoritarian direction or authoritative leadership in worship and music—"nonconformist" or "free" churches, as they are called in Europe.

Actually, I have considered calling this book *Church Music in the Evangelical, Free Church Tradition*. However, that title (without the comma) denotes a specific denominational fellowship in America and would be confusing to many. So I left it "Evangelical" with the understanding that the material will have particular relevance to those whose worship practice is "free" or "non-liturgical."[7]

In addition, because this volume is written for American free, evangelical churches, it presumes an understanding and an acceptance of our distinctive heritage of "revivalism." This historic and seemingly indestructible phenomenon has its roots in the preaching of Jonathan Edwards and George Whitefield in the 18th century, and its most recent flowerings in modern evangelistic crusades, a continuing emphasis on missions, and new expressions of outreach via radio and television.

Some of my students have objected to the use of the word "evangelical" because it "puts restrictive labels on people." This may reflect the current tendency to reject all "shibboleths" in expressing our faith, as well as the tensions created by the diverse theology and culture that is gathered together under the label! I use the word simply as identification; it should be just as valid to say "I am an Evangelical" as "I am a Christian" or "I am a Methodist."

On the other hand, there are probably some who will want a more sharply-drawn definition of "evangelical." Does it include Methodists, Baptists, Bible Church adherents, Presbyterians, Christian Church, Church of Christ, Mennonites, United Church of Christ, United Brethren, Church of the Nazarene, and the Assembly of God? The answer is "yes!" These are only a few of the denominational ties within evangelicalism. Some denominations might be described as "completely evangelical"; others will have evangelicals within their ranks. Within this

---

6. During the last two decades, pietist (experiential) religion has been emphasized in many liturgical churches, and they have tended to borrow traditionally-evangelical music for its expression.

7. Of course, it is true that some "free" churches (e.g., Unitarian groups) do not adhere to evangelical theology, and this volume may have little interest for them.

heterogeneous fellowship, the various denominational traditions and a wide spectrum of subcultures have developed many different patterns of worship and musical preference. In fact, some denominations (e.g., Southern Baptists) may contain as much variety as the total group. The distinctives common to them all is a basic adherence to evangelical concepts of theology, religious experience and ministry, and to free worship. It is my position that those who possess this common heritage should also hold certain attitudes about the use of music in worship, in Christian education, in ministry and in outreach. I have hoped to set forth those standards clearly, while allowing for the continuing authenticity of expression of each denomination and subculture.

No doubt some readers will anticipate my own lingering suspicion that it is impossible to span the evangelical culture spectrum in a book of this kind—from "primitive Baptist" groups in rural Kentucky (whose worship patterns have not changed much in 100 years) to a sophisticated Presbyterian church in suburban Washington, D.C. Nevertheless, I believe that in the relationship of theology and liturgical practice ("evangelical" and "free") to the *text* materials of worship music, I am on safe ground. My observations while visiting many different churches throughout the world has confirmed this to my satisfaction.

Music styles are another matter. In this area, I am probably communicating mostly to my own middle class American culture, which includes a growing number of evangelicals. The relevance of the musical examples I have used will probably be determined by readers on the basis of their own objective self-consciousness. If evangelicals are sufficiently interested in their worship/music practices to peruse these pages, they should find both affirmation and challenge. What seems to be irrelevant should not be taken as an affront. It can be an opportunity for them to better understand other believers who have somewhat different cultural traditions.

CONTENTS

Chapter I

MUSIC: GOD'S GIFT TO US

A number of years ago, a story was circulated among members of the recording industry which may or may not be true. As I heard it, the late Wanda Landowska was taping the preludes and fugues of Johann Sebastian Bach's *Well Tempered Clavier* on her harpsichord. The willowy Polish artist, with penetrating eyes and patrician nose, had completed a "take" and was listening to the "playback" in the production booth. The recording engineers and the producer watched her anxiously as the tape unwound and the music was revealed on huge loudspeakers. Would she be pleased with the results of their microphone placement and electronic adjustment?

Finally she spoke softly, almost to herself. "Wonderful! Superb! A masterpiece!" The men around her beamed in appreciation of her approval. But their smiles faded just a bit when it became apparent that Mme. Landowska was exclaiming mostly about the genius of the great Bach, and even about her own artistry in re-creating Bach's music on the harpsichord keyboards!

Even if the story is only "apocryphal," it reminds us of the self-approval of another artist-creator.

> In the beginning God created the heavens and the earth. The earth was without form and void, and darkness was upon the face of the deep; and the Spirit of God was moving over the face of the waters. And God said, "Let there be light"; and there was light. (Gen. 1:1-3)

There follows the record of God's creative acts, including the placing of sun and moon and stars in the heavens, and the creation of sea life, birds and animals.

> So God created man in his own image, in the image of God he created him: male and female he created them. And God blessed them, and God said to them, "Be fruitful and multiply, and fill the earth and subdue it; and have dominion over the fish of the sea and over the birds of the air and over every living thing that moves upon the earth." ... And God saw everything that he had made, and behold, it was very good. (Gen. 1:27-28, 31a)

1

Wanda Landowska's actions were inevitable. As a creature of God, made in God's image, she could love and think and create. Along with all other human beings, she shared something of God's compulsion to fashion something of beauty—in this instance, a performance of a 200-year-old musical work which was possibly different from every other performance of that piece. She had spent years preparing for this single creative act, practicing to master the instrument, and studying the music of Bach to learn just what he was trying to communicate. In so doing, she had obeyed the injunction to "subdue the earth" in which she was placed—the world of sound, the world of her own mind and body. When, after all the discipline of preparation, she had fulfilled her God-given self as creative artist and the music was heard in the production booth, she recognized that "it was very good." It is not hard to believe that her delight was accompanied by humility and reverence!

Anthropology supports these implications of the Genesis narrative by showing us that all persons are aesthetic beings. The cave dwellers of prehistoric Europe may not have had a written language, but they left drawings and paintings of rare beauty. Even in this 20th century, the "stone age" Auca Indians of Ecuador cavorted around in little clothing, freely spearing both the foreign missionary and their own neighbors, yet enjoyed a distinctive folksong.[1] The primitives' clothing, tools and weapons are invariably decorated with design and color. African tribe members often extend their artistry to their own bodies, carving lines with sharp rocks or rudimentary knives. No doubt this aesthetic expression is considered even more beautiful and meaningful, because it is the result of *painful* creativity.

Typical human beings may not see themselves in the same context as Johann Sebastian Bach or Wanda Landowska, but the God-given instinct for creating and enjoying beauty is universal. We share the art of others when we watch a motion picture or a television program, or listen to John Denver or to the Philadelphia Symphony Orchestra; when we read the work of columnists in the morning newspaper, or the Bible, or the "Peanuts" comic strip; or when we gaze at the Picasso statue in front of Chicago's City Hall or the ubiquitous Sallman's painting of Christ in the church's social room. We are artists when we put on cosmetics or choose a tie to match a suit, when we plan the redecorating of our home or office, when we teach a Sunday School class or write a term paper.

Some readers will not be comfortable with the argument that primitives are as truly artistic as sophisticated folk from western cultures, or that an "unbeliever" might possibly possess more creative talent than a confessing Christian. But no less an evangelical than John Calvin proclaimed that artistry is imparted by God promiscuously, to believers and unbelievers alike. The concept stems from what the theologian calls

1. One traditional ballad proclaimed that the Andes mountains were scooped up out of the plain by the beak of an enormous woodpecker. After the tribe had become Christian through the witness of foreign missionaries, the music of this folksong became the basis of their first Christian hymn of praise.

"common grace." Calvin even suggested that sinners sometimes seem to have more than their share of God's gifts, for he once wrote: "These radiations of Divine Light shone more brilliantly among unbelieving people than among God's saints."[2] This idea is confirmed by the late C. S. Lewis in a brief essay which is recommended to all church musicians as a "mind-blower."

> There is . . . a sense in which all natural agents, even inanimate ones, glorify God continually by revealing the powers He has given them. And in that sense we, as natural agents, do the same. On that level our wicked actions, in so far as they exhibit our skill and strength, may be said to glorify God, as well as our good actions. An excellently performed piece of music, as a natural operation which reveals in a very high degree the peculiar powers given to man, will thus always glorify God whatever the intention of the performers may be.[3]

The Place of Art (including Music) in Historical Culture

To primitive peoples, in ancient history or in unexplored corners of today's world, to live is to be artistic. The marking of the body, the gaudy robes and waving feathers, the carefully designed bows and spears, the handmade musical instruments, the dance and song and pantomime—all say that, for these cultures, art was (and is) a means of giving identity to the tribe or clan, of adding intensity to everyday life and toil, to the hunt, to religion, to family or tribal festivity.

Although each member of the group shares the art in everyday life, there have always been specialists who produce it. One of the first pages of scripture contains the name of "Jubal," who is described as "the father of all those who play the lyre and pipe." Jubal's brother was Jabal, "the father of those who dwell in tents and have cattle."[4] No doubt Jubal enjoyed the food produced by Jabal's toil, while Jabal shared Jubal's music! The establishment of a professional guild of music makers was well advanced by the time Israel built its temple for worship. As recorded in I Chronicles 15:22, "Chenaniah, leader of the Levites in music, should direct the music, for he understood it."

In ancient Greece, the arts were also central to life. A well-rounded education in that culture was one which integrated the letters, the sciences and the arts. Training in music was part of that education, and amateur choristers sang in the cult of the gods, at marriages and funerals, and in celebration of victory in athletics or in commemoration of famous men. As John Dewey has said:

> The collective life that was manifested in war, worship, the forum, knew no division between what was characteristic of these places and

2. Cited in Abraham Kuyper, *Lectures on Calvinism,* p. 216.
3. C. S. Lewis, "On Church Music," in *Christian Reflections,* p. 98.
4. Genesis 4:20,21.

operations, and the arts which brought color, grace and dignity into
them. Painting and sculpture were organically one with architecture,
as that was one with the social purpose that buildings served.[5]

During the Middle Ages, the Church was the dominant force in western society, and the art which has survived demonstrates this. By and
large, it sets forth biblical history, religious dogma, or ecclesiastical activity. The soaring Gothic cathedrals with the icons, stained glass and
sculptures which graced them, along with the masses and motets and the
illuminated choir books in which they were recorded, all give witness
that in this period most art was directed to God, and was planned to
benefit all persons, serf and noble alike.

Even so, during this long period of western history, there is evidence
that artistic expression existed on two levels, the professional and the
amateur. Though democratic education was unknown in the "Dark
Ages," the ordinary person—the amateur artist—produced things of
beauty, including "folksong." During the later Middle Ages, folk carols,
macaronic hymns (combining vernacular languages and Latin), and contrafacted hymns (parodies of secular forms) were common. And in the
16th century, the new forms of Protestant worship—German chorales
and French metrical psalms—were frequently based on secular folk
poetry and folk melodies.

With the coming of the Renaissance, the rise of humanism turned the
artist's attention toward ordinary people. The subject material of aesthetic expression is changed; in painting and sculpture, the secular scene is
no longer shunned, and in music, the texts and its uses could be temporal as well as spiritual. Beginning in the 16th and 17th centuries, the
serious artist composed music for concerts as well as for worship, and the
first setting was the salon of noblemen's palaces.

By the 19th century, recital performances by fine orchestras and brilliant soloists were also available to the *bourgeois,* the middle class. In
addition, especially in the frontier culture of America, "folk music" became a professional art devoted largely to entertainment. The American
minstrel show, the Viennese operetta, and the traveling ballad or gospel
singer were all indications that the ordinary person had gained sufficient
financial security to be able to spend money on "musical pleasure." In
the late 20th century, "popular music" has become the prevailing aesthetic of much of the western world. Particularly in the United States, it
is big business, with billions of dollars spent each year on printed music,
recordings, and public concerts.

To be sure, America also has a thriving "serious" musical community.
Admittedly, before the 20th century, our heritage as an emerging culture decreed that we would be inferior to Europe in producing and
performing musical masterworks. Today, we offer more music education in public schools than any country in the world. Our major sym-

5. John Dewey, *Art As Experience,* p. 7.

phony orchestras are the best anywhere, and every city with a population of 100,000 or more is expected to have a community orchestra. We have superb choirs in every major university and conservatory, and even in many secondary schools. Admittedly, serious music is still an elitist art, but it is probably doing better in the United States than anywhere else in the world.

It has been argued by some that western culture is not truly aesthetic because it is obsessed with industrialism and materialism. As compared with both primitive and ancient-Oriental standards, art has apparently been removed from the center of life for most people. Instead of being an organic part of the activity of our society, it has become an appendage that is either a status symbol or a diversion. It is only our modern society which is *consciously* aesthetic, and then tends to separate the beautiful and creative from the rest of life. "Tonight, after work, I'm going to a concert," we say. Once we get there—whether it's a symphony or a rock concert—instead of integrating the music to life, we seem to worship it! The atmosphere is hushed and quiet, almost like church. We are in the presence of something numinous—transcendent sounds or a transcendent performer.

Others will contend that 20th century electronics have allowed us to surround ourselves with music, albeit strictly as spectators. We may be one of the most musical cultures in the world's history, if you make the judgment on the basis of the music you may *hear* in the community via recording and radio—in the home, in the car, on the street (with pocket transistor radio and ear plug), in the restaurant and tavern, the supermarket, the office and the factory.

The Meaning of Music in Culture

Through the years, philosophers, psychologists, sociologists, musicologists and ethnomusicologists have explored the phenomenon of music. Their questions have been wide ranging: What is music? How does music communicate? What does music communicate? For the purposes of this volume, we are not broaching the subject of aesthetics (what makes art "beautiful"?) We are concerned only with the questions of music's communication and its meanings.

It has frequently been suggested that music is a universal language. It would be more accurate to say that music is a universal means of expression, and that there are many symbolic musical languages, each understood best by its own culture or subculture.[6] Our world has African music (usually termed "primitive"), Oriental music (ancient, but well developed) and western music. Furthermore, in the Orient, Japanese music is different from Chinese, which is yet different from Korean or Indian or Indonesian. West African musical systems will not be under-

6. Alan P. Merriam, *The Anthropology of Music,* p. 223.

stood by natives of East Africa. In our own country, the language of musical worship among most blacks will not be completely shared by the typical white congregation; furthermore, residents in rural Kentucky may scorn that which is commonly accepted in Louisville or Lexington.

It should be noted that it is not necessary to learn one's own musicultural language in any formal way; it has basic meaning to the members of that culture simply because they have grown up hearing it. It should also be remembered that, whereas the communication of words has rather precise meaning, that of music does not. The musical language of a culture may have more or less (and differing) meanings to individuals in that society, but it has *little or no meaning* to those outside it.

Music as Divine Expression

What then is the significance of music in a culture? What is its meaning? These questions have persisted from the earliest times of philosophical speculation. The ancient Hindu tradition suggests that the "discovery of music is . . . attributed to Sarasvati, goddess of eloquence and the arts."[7] The argument for the divine origin and significance of music has cropped up occasionally in evangelical preaching, and it is usually based on Job 38:4-7, "Where were you when I laid the foundation of the earth . . . when the morning stars sang together, and all the sons of God shouted for joy?"

Music as Ethos

The early Greeks, especially Pythagoras (sixth century B.C.), developed the first complete theory of music, and they saw a close relationship between music and mathematics. From quite a different perspective, the Greek philosophers Plato and Aristotle developed the doctrine of *ethos,* a concept that certain music (based on certain "scales") affected human behavior, for good or for evil. They expressed strong convictions about music education, based upon their concern for the State. Neo-Platonists like Plotinus (205-270 A.D.) also ascribed moral (and immoral) influence to music, but from a *spiritual* rather than a civic concern, and this concept was adopted by many of the early church fathers.

> The tune of an incantation, a significant cry, . . these too have a
> . . power over the soul, . . drawing it with the force of . . tragic
> sounds—for it is the reasonless soul, not the will or wisdom, that is
> beguiled by music, a form of sorcery which raises no question, whose
> enchantment, indeed is welcomed . .[8]

7. Louis Laloy, *La Musique chinoise,* pp. 38-39, cited in Jacques Chailley, *40,000 Years of Music.*
8. Stephen MacKenna, *Plotinus on the nature of the soul, being the 4th Ennead.*

Music and Emotion

Modern thinkers tend to explain music in natural terms, rather than supernatural. Most authorities agree that music has a markedly significant relationship to human emotions. Some feel that it expresses emotional feeling, hence the common expression "Music is the language of the emotions."[9]

Others contend that music does not express a "present emotion," but rather, a *recall* of previous emotional experiences.[10] (The singer of a "happy song" is not necessarily happy at the moment of singing, nor is the listener. One projects and the other receives a *recall* of a previous experience of happiness.)

Still others argue that music also has the power to *affect* the emotions, that it is a *revealer* as well as an expresser. As a rediscovered aesthetic concept applied to music, it is best articulated by Wilfred Mellers of the University of York, England in *Caliban Reborn*.[11] This revival of the ancient Greek *ethos* idea (shared by many other cultures, including the early Jews) that music has power to change personality, has been explored and exploited widely by modern music therapists. E. Thayer Gaston has said, "Art, including music, is the most certain mode of affective expression which mankind has achieved.[12] He says also:

> The common creative urge, desire for diversion, and search for expression of beauty exists in all peoples. Music, above all arts, guarantees the fulfillment of these elemental urges and therein lies its greatest value. It has been an emotional governor for every tribe, nation, and race of people. Today, this is still the chief function of music.

Of course, it may still be argued that music's revelation can have a negative influence upon personality, as well as a positive one. Pacifists would probably find this true of military music, especially when used during war time. Others have insisted that contemporary rock music has contributed to anti-social behavior through its manipulation of human personality.

Music as Pleasure

It is also apparent that music has meaning as *pleasure* in many, if not all, societies. Anthropologists have noted that primitive cultures begin to

9. Merriam, op. cit., pp. 219-222. See also Susan B. Langer, *Philosophy in a New Key*, p. 179. My esteemed colleague, Jay W. Wilkey, has given me this summation of Ms. Langer's theses: (1) music presents tonal symbols of feeling; (2) music expresses feelings symbolically; and (3) the tonal movement of music is symbolic of the flux of feelings (three attempts to say the same thing!)
10. See Hermann Helmholtz, *On the Sensations of Tone*, p. 250.
11. Wilfred Mellers, *Caliban Reborn*, see pp. 1-33, 151-182.
12. E. Thayer Gaston, "Psychological Foundations for Functional Music," in *American Journal of Occupational Therapy*, Vol. II, No. 1.

develop artistic expression after they have supplied the basic needs of their people for food, shelter, and protection from hostile forces. Some experts make a distinction between "aesthetic enjoyment" and "entertainment," while others argue that this is a difference of degree, not of essence.[13]

Music as Cultural Reinforcement

There is rather wide agreement among ethnomusicologists and anthropologists that music's most important function in any society is the support of that culture's value system.[14] This "meaning" is probably for most people the aggregate of all the meanings mentioned above—its "divine" or supernatural source and power, and its significance as ethos, as emotional expression or as pleasure. First of all, a unique musical expression gives identity to the entire culture. Furthermore, music is frequently used to accompany the society's most significant activities, and adds significance to those rituals. In this way, music tends to reinforce the ideals of that society, whether they be political, social, or religious.

In our own era, we have noted that various music styles support the identities of different age groups; teenagers are usually identified with rock-and-roll, while the college-age group may prefer folk music or jazz, and the middle-aged supports the "pop" music of Lawrence Welk. In Nazi Germany in the 1930's, the music of Wagner was used to promote the political and sociological ideals of Hitler's philosophy; in modern times, protest songs (e.g., "We Shall Overcome") support the concepts of reformers in our society. In all of the important activities of life—the worship service or a school football game, the Lions Club meeting or the political rally—music is used to *add meaning* to that activity. To some who participate, its only meaning may be its association with the activity. To others, there may be added meaning from pleasure, emotional expression (or impression) and even more profound experience, especially for those who have studied the art of music thoroughly. But the basic meaning lies in the association of musical sound with the significant activity of a particular culture or subculture, and each participant shares that.

Communication Gaps in Music's Meaning

Musical communication gaps exist between various cultures and subcultures, because the musical language distinctive to a particular group is

13. Merriam, op. cit., p. 223.
14. Ibid., p. 224. Professor Merriam lists at least three functions under this caption: (1) the function of enforcing conformity to social norms; (2) the function of validation of social institutions and religious rituals; and (3) the function of contribution to the continuity and stability of culture.

strongly associated with its identity and its community life. "Eastern" music is not shared by most westerners, and neither culture normally understands primitive music. "Country" music fans are often deaf to the communication of "bluegrass" groups, even though they share something of a common heritage.

One of the most serious communication gaps exists in western society between today's "serious" and "pop" cultures. Those who attend the symphony and the opera often have nothing but scorn for what goes on in the "rock music" festival or in the "Grand Ol' Op'ry" in Nashville. To their claim that art music is better, the country music fan responds "who says so?" and if it were put to a national referendum, the "folk-pop-country-rock" crowd would no doubt win. Perhaps in self defense, serious music enthusiasts have frequently adopted a snobbish attitude which suggests that they relish their elitist status. It is sometimes expressed in such statements as "It can't be good art if everybody likes it," or "the better art is, the fewer people will find meaning in it."

The passing of time creates other gaps in music's communication. In western society, the languages of music and/or their symbolic meaning are in a state of constant flux. In the world of "art music," the prevailing style changes frequently; in the 20th century, for instance, we have known post-romanticism, impressionism, expressionism, neo-classicism, atonality, aleatory techniques, and mutations of each. In the area of popular music, there has appeared ragtime, Dixieland, jazz, swing, folk, rock and country, to name just a few. Apparently, styles in art change almost as frequently as styles in clothing or in home decoration. At the moment of iconoclasm (down with the old!) there is a period of uncertain meaning until the new form is accepted, assimilated and given meaning. This type of communication gap exists within a specific culture, but it may be as wide as that between different cultures.

Summary

What then should be the Christian's attitude toward God's universal gift of creativity, and, in particular, the gift of musical expression?

It is to be expected that all persons will live up to their God-given instincts. Like Wanda Landowska, we are challenged to "have dominion" over the natural world God has given—to use, preserve, enjoy and develop it. God has given beauty as well as bread, ideas as well as machines, and the mature Christian will keep these gifts of life in proper balance. This does not mean that every believer is expected to be a performing musician or to create a meaningful painting. To enjoy—to find meaning in art—is itself a creative activity.

Evangelicals have often been accused of being anti-aesthetic, of not living up to their potential as creative "children of God." This is not too surprising since, in our heritage, we are the successors of iconoclasts who have rejected artistic symbolism in worship. Frank E. Gaebelein states this indictment rather categorically, but, by the end of his monograph, it is apparent that he is championing specific aesthetic tastes, and that evangelicals may be no different from typical Americans.

> Among the rank and file of evangelical Christians, aesthetic standards are generally low. The evidence is abundant. The pictures on the walls, the books on the shelves, the records played—so many of these things are products of a sentimental, pietistic dilution of the aesthetic integrity that should mark the Christian use of art. But, and this also must be said, evangelicals are not alone in their habituation to the mediocre in art and literature. A similar kind of cultural illiteracy runs through much of Protestantism, and indeed through most of American life today.[15]

It may be argued that, as believers in the transcendent Creator-God, evangelicals should do better than others. But this presumes that all churchgoers have learned that "good taste" in art is a Christian ethic. In our science-oriented culture, this is not apt to happen quickly. Furthermore, we musicians should be slow to judge a scientist's failure to see God's image in great music, so long as we fail to see God in the splitting atom or in the vast sweep of star-filled space!

It does seem that more and more evangelicals are making their mark in the arts today. There is no way to tell how many there are, but an increasing number are choosing to make a strong personal witness to their evangelical faith. These musicians will be easily identified, and they are only typical of a much larger group:

Debbie Boone, singer, recordings and films
Pat Boone, singer, recordings and films
James Buswell III, concert violinist
Johnnie Cash, country singer
Ernie Ford, country singer
Jerome Hines, Metropolitan Opera
Irene Jordan, soprano, Metropolitan Opera
Carol Lawrence, singer, motion pictures, concerts, etc.
Daniel Majeski, concertmaster, Cleveland Orchestra
Howard Nelson, baritone, Zurich (Switz.) Opera
John Nelson, conductor, Indianapolis Orchestra
Daniel Spurlock, assistant conductor, Louisville Orchestra
Norma Zimmer, singer, television, recordings, concerts

In our day it is increasingly popular for evangelicals in any profession to unite for fellowship and for witnessing. The operatic basso Jerome Hines heads Christian Arts, Incorporated, formerly known as the Fellowship of Christians in the Arts, Media and Entertainment, which claims the motto: "We put Christianity back into the arts and the arts

15. Frank E. Gaebelein, "Toward a Biblical View of Aesthetics," p. 2.

back into Christianity." This organization has membership categories in "radio, television, motion pictures, press, theater, records, audiovisuals, music and the arts, advertising and promotion; including artists, craftsmen, technicians and executives." They publish a newsletter, conduct an annual national meeting, and have planned certain regional meetings.[16]

The Fellowship of Christian Musicians includes mostly educators in the arts, and seems to specialize in instrumentalists (band and orchestra directors.) They meet annually in connection with one of the music education societies (MENC, MTNA, or the Mid-West National Band and Orchestra Clinic); they also publish a newsletter.[17]

The Christian requirement pertaining to artistic activity applies to the amateur as well as the professional. Every true believer is expected to offer to God his *best* creativity, in all of life. This is good stewardship of our talents—"a worthy sacrifice"—whether we are playing (or hearing) a recital, singing in the church choir or worshiping through its music, writing a business report, making a dress or cooking a meal. In music, God expects J. S. Bach's best, John Stainer's best, John Peterson's best, the Auca Indians' best, each Christian's best. Nothing less is acceptable, but our best is good enough!

Mature and informed Christians will not approach another culture with the arrogant insistence that their own cultural expression is superior. Every culture and subculture has validity simply because it exists. Furthermore, every individual, Christian or pagan, primitive or sophisticated, is capable of knowing truth and beauty, and of expressing it. Finally, every person's knowledge of truth and beauty is limited by our humanness, our sin. Though J. S. Bach was remarkably creative because he realized a high degree of the "image of God" with which he was born, his art never achieved absolute perfection, because we all "fall short" of the glory, the creativity of God.

It might also be argued that individuals are "more cultured" if they are at home in a variety of cultures, for example, if they understand a number of musical languages. We applaud the missionary musicians who find meaning in the music of Bach and Beethoven and also in the indigenous art of the people they serve. There is an increasing number of composers and conductors today (e.g., Leonard Bernstein and Andre Previn) who seem to be equally at home with the music of Broadway and of the Lincoln Center in New York City. In the context of this book, there is little point in broaching a discussion of the relative "worth" of serious music and popular. Obviously, both communicate meaning and both give pleasure. Possibly, art music is more profound in its delineation of "meaning"—though some would find it abstruse. At the same time, perhaps popular music gets through to "meaning" more directly—though some would call it simplistic.

16. Christian Arts, Inc., 1755 West End Avenue, New Hyde Park, NY 11040.
17. Fellowship of Christian Musicians; Ms. Jamie Bowell, secretary, 303 So. Gables Blvd., Wheaton, IL 60187.

In speaking of serious music, Carl Halter says that we should not think of it as tone and rhythm, or even as a portrayal of simple emotions, like happiness or sorrow. He suggests that the structure of music expresses such complex and weighty concepts as affirmation and rejection, tension and release, growth and decline, rise and fall.

> We find affirmation and rejection, unity and diversity, growth and decline in all of life . . The composer says implicitly: "Here is how the experiences of life sound. I cannot explain them to you, but I can make them sound. After you have heard how they sound, you will understand them better and have for all of life a sympathy which you did not have before and which you cannot get in any other way."
>
> Listen carefully to a recording of Beethoven's Ninth Symphony or to any of Bach's gigantic organ fugues, and within the music you will hear struggles which can only be described as titanic. The composer has set in motion gigantic forces of sound and time which clash and contend to a climax of fury. On listening to such music it becomes obvious to us that the composer did not manipulate these massive forces merely to show that they exist and that he has the skill and strength to control them. An attentive and expectant listener inevitably is convinced that the composer has grasped forces and meanings which relate to life. Indeed, such music convinces us that the grasp of music extends, however feebly, to the divine and the eternal. Such music gives us an apprehension of ultimate reality, ultimate values, and ultimate destiny.[18]

No doubt the ethnomusicologist could argue that the same exploration of life's meaning is present in the simple music of the primitive, or the "pop" burden songs of today's youth culture, and that in them the approach is less abstract and more direct, less ambiguous and more definite. Perhaps that too is a kind of profundity!

This possibility was brought to my attention rather vividly in a recent chapel service at the Southern Baptist Theological Seminary. Our guest lecturer was a professor from a Canadian Lutheran seminary. I was conducting the choir that day, and we sang a selection from Vaughan Williams' double-choir *Mass in G minor* with confidence that, whereas a Baptist speaker might be unhappy with our choice, this liturgically-oriented guest would be delighted. However, he soon announced that he was a country music fan, and his sermon was partly based on an expression of human experience contained in a song by the late Hank Williams! Actually, Hank Williams and Vaughan Williams both contributed to worship that day, for those who understood the communication of each!

Finally and above all, Christians should be creative in their relationship to God in all of life. One of Paul's descriptions of the life of faith is this: "Therefore, if anyone is in Christ, he is a new creation; the old has passed away, behold, the new has come."[19] It is just as valid to say "all

18. Carl Halter, *God and Man in Music,* pp. 36–37.
19. II Corinthians 5:17.

things keep on becoming new." This concept is expressed by William Dean, a young Lutheran professor in his little volume, *Coming To*. For Dr. Dean, as he expresses it in his "Theology of Beauty," "living aesthetically" is "coming to" or "being Christian," and vice versa. To live aesthetically is to share God's imagination as to what life should be, for ourselves and for the world around us, and to work with God's Creator Spirit to make it happen.

If all of life is creative, surely our corporate worship will be. It is important that the leaders of worship, our ministers and musicians, work together to make the worship hour an opportunity for a dynamic, life-changing encounter between God and people. Even more, it is imperative that the individual worshiper use creative imagination and dedication, so that even if the service materials are predictable and commonplace, the worship experience will still be fresh and exciting.

In the next chapter we will point out that church music is not a "free art"—it is functional. It is an art that has been brought to the cross of Christ, in order to achieve God's particular purposes for the Church. Even so, it too must be creative, because God is forever making things and people new!

Chapter II

CHURCH MUSIC: A FUNCTIONAL ART

In chapter one I pointed out that in primitive cultures, almost all music is "functional"; it is performed in connection with the many activities of ordinary as well as festive life, and adds significance and intensity to those activities. It was also noted that it is uniquely a phenomenon of Western sophistication that art is enjoyed "on its own," disassociated from other activities of life. This is not to say that western cultures, including our own, do not have functional music. We have marches to accompany both military and non-military processionals. Characteristic songs contribute meaning to the club meeting, the athletic event or the political rally. "Muzak" (recorded music) is played in factories, offices and department stores to increase the efficiency of the worker or to provide a favorable atmosphere for shopping. Music is used with television and radio "commercials"; once the tunes are familiar, they are immediate mnemonic reminders of the product being advertised, even if the listener can not hear the words!

Church music is also a functional art, though church musicians will certainly argue that its functions are more important than those mentioned above! It is created by human beings to serve the purposes of God and the church, particularly in the church's corporate expression of its worship, its fellowship and its mission. In this chapter, I will endeavor to prove that church music has the same "meanings" as other music. At the same time, I will suggest how its most important meaning can be safeguarded in the activities of the evangelical church.

In his essay, "The Arts, the Snobs, and the Democrat,"[1] Jacques Barzun contends that "consumer" or functional art requires a high degree of talent, creativity and diligence. He also says that there is no point in comparing a Sousa march with a Beethoven sonata, or a billboard advertising new Fords with the paintings in the Sistine Chapel in Rome; each has its own reason for existence and its own standard of excellence. Judging quality in "serious" or "pure" art is an aspect of the philosophy of *aesthetics,* and too complex a matter to be considered here. "Functional

1. See also Jacques Barzun, *Music in American Life,* pp. 65-92.

14

art," however, is judged by *how well it fulfills its function.* Following this principle, we may argue that there is no point in comparing a simple anthem or a fine hymn-and-tune with Mozart's opera, *Don Giovanni.* Each may be a masterpiece within its own *genre.*

Who Is An Evangelical?

As one examines the functional musics and texts[2] of various Christian groups, it is obvious that there are great differences between them; there are many different church music languages. It is possible to speak of an "eastern Orthodox" style and a "Roman Catholic" style. Lutheran traditions are different from Anglican (Episcopal), and typical Presbyterian worship contrasts sharply with that of black Baptists. It seems apparent that the theological, liturgical (worship practice) and cultural traditions of a particular Christian group determine how music "functions" in that fellowship. In turn, music's functions can be expected to determine the language or style of both music and lyrics.

In this volume, we propose to approach church music from the viewpoint of "evangelicals." Admittedly, that name has meant different things throughout the history of Christianity, and it may have uncertain meaning to various individuals and groups today. In the Introduction to this book, I have given my own definition of "evangelical," using principally the characterizations of theologians Bernard Ramm and Donald Bloesch. The following is a very concise statement of these evangelical distinctives.

1. Evangelicals accept the scriptures as authority, rather than tradition or ecclesiastical institutions.
2. Evangelicals believe that salvation is achieved through faith, rather than through the sacraments.
3. Evangelicals emphasize a personal experience of conversion; in this regard they may be called modern pietists.
4. Evangelicals are zealous in outreach, in which (2) and (3) are emphasized, often in the context of evangelistic services.
5. Evangelicals tend to worship in a non-liturgical, "free" tradition.

Music's Functions in Evangelical Church Life

In chapter one, it was noted that music is a symbolic means of expression, that there are many different musical languages in the world, and that each language has the most meaning to the culture which creates it and within which it functions. Certain specific meanings of music were given, as anthropologists have identified them within every culture. These same meanings or functions are to be found in church music.

2. In this book, the designations "music" or "church music" will often include both music and the text associated with it.

Pleasure in Evangelical Church Music.

It should be apparent that "pleasure" is one of the important meanings of functional evangelical church music. For unless individual
worshipers find some measure of enjoyment in a certain church music language, they will probably not be ministered to in a deeper way by either
the music or the words associated with it. Typical laypersons clearly
associate pleasure with their musical experiences in church, though they
would probably not use that particular word. More likely such a person
would say "I enjoyed the anthem (or the prelude, or the solo) today,"
and it is also probable that dislike of some musical item will be expressed
in the same straightforward manner!

It is more difficult to find church music authorities who will openly
admit that "pleasure" is one of the functions of their art in worship, in
fellowship or in outreach. Occasionally, however, the admission slips
through. St. John Chrysostom in the fourth century had this explanation
for the appearance of music in worship.

> When God saw that many men were lazy, and gave themselves only
> with difficulty to spiritual reading, He wished to make it easy for
> them, and added the melody to the Prophet's words, that all being
> rejoiced by the charm of the music, should sing hymns to Him with
> gladness.[3]

Adlung, a German organist of the baroque era, in a treatise offering
techniques for composing or improvising chorale preludes, which are
played before the singing of a hymn, gave three purposes for that musical experience:[4]

> 1. To prepare the congregation for the key.
> 2. To inform them of the tune.
> 3. To delight them "through fluent ideas" (*durch wohlfliessende
>   Gedanken*).

Recently, Carlton R. Young (principal editor of *The Methodist Hymnal,*
1964-66) stated that "a third function of congregational song (in addition to its relationship to preaching and teaching) is found at the inter-
section of the recreational and the devotional attitudes of the gathered
community." He continued:

> This is hard to explain, but as an example, the gathered community
> may just want to express through song its sense of togetherness and
> it can be led to share in the feeling through song. Further, the whole

3. MigneG LV, 156; WagE I, 10; cited in Gustave Reese, *Music in the Middle Ages*, p. 65.
4. *Anleitung zur musikalischen Gelahrtheit* (1783 edn.), 825 ff. Cited by Peter Williams, *Bach
Organ Music*, p. 10.

idea of recall of previous times of being together and of sharing as members of the family of God can be focused in corporate action such as (but not limited to) congregational song.[5]

On the basis of music's pleasurable appeal, many churches have developed their music programs for the purpose of church promotion. A pastor-friend of mine[6] once expressed it this way:

> Of the potential congregation we might attract on a Sunday, one-half are "God's faithful." They'll come rain or shine, whatever the preaching or the music. If the pulpit ministry is strong, we'll add twenty-five percent of the potential audience. And if the music is especially good, with a personable songleader, a good choir and "special music," we'll add another twenty-five percent.

In recent years, this same reasoning has abetted the argument for the validity of "youth musicals" and other forms of sacred folk/rock music. Because they enjoy performing the new popular music, young people are attracted to the church and may thus be evangelized and discipled.

Nevertheless, there are potential dangers in the element of pleasure in church music. St. Augustine once said: "When I am moved by the voice of him that sings more than by the words sung, I confess to have sinned."[7] In other words, it is wrong to find pleasure in the music as an end in itself, while missing its full significance as a spiritual exercise.[8] This is a danger which may be present in the use of any type of music in church, a Schütz cantata as well as a gospel folk song or a religious ballad. I find no distinction between purely "aesthetic" experience and simple musical pleasure, where church music is concerned; both fall short of their more noble, significant function as cognitive and emotional (as well as enjoyable) expressions of worship, fellowship or outreach. Tragically, many evangelicals fail to identify this as their truncated spiritual experience in church. They are entertained—they find pleasure in music—but little more has happened. Even if their appreciation is couched in the pious phrase "The solo was a blessing," the full spiritual experience may have been missed.

The dangers of unwarranted pleasure in church music may be most present when the performance of typical church music is detached from a clearly-defined experience of worship, fellowship or outreach. This may happen in some "sacred concerts," or in constant half-listening to

5. Carlton R. Young, "HSA Convocations: Back to Basics!"
6. Rev. H. B. Prince, for many years pastor of the Bethesda Evangelical Free Church, Minneapolis, Minnesota.
7. Paraphrased from Oliver Strunk, ed., *Source Readings in Music History,* Vol. I, p. 74.
8. This is not to say that there is no spiritual significance in an experience of this kind. Because the "pleasure experience" takes place in a service of worship, it may be interpreted by the listener to be "spiritual."

religious music over "gospel radio." These possibilities are dealt with
more fully in subsequent chapters.[9]

Emotion in Evangelical Church Music.

Beyond a doubt, the use of music as an expression of emotion is
common in all churches. In the evangelical tradition where personal
religious experience is emphasized, this is one of music's important
meanings. It is probably this function which is referred to when either
pastors or lay-persons identify "music that speaks to the heart." But this
is not a new experience for churchgoers. St. Augustine mentioned it in
the fifth century.

> How greatly did I weep in Thy hymns and canticles, deeply moved
> by the voices of Thy sweet-speaking Church! The voices flowed into
> mine ears, and the truth was poured forth into my heart, whence the
> agitation of my piety overflowed, and my tears ran over, and blessed
> was I therein."[10]

The emotional power of music is perhaps best realized in the life of
the church when that music is well coupled to appropriate text. In this
union, the music dramatizes, explains, underlines, "breathes life" into
the words, resulting in more meaning than the words themselves could
express. To read Isaiah 9:6 is itself a moving experience when one does
so with the conviction that it speaks of the advent of God's incarnate
Son, Jesus Christ.

> For unto us a child is born, unto us a son is given, and the govern-
> ment shall be upon his shoulder; and his name shall be called Won-
> derful, Counselor, The Mighty God, The Everlasting Father, The
> Prince of Peace. (KJV)

But, despite the too-frequent and sometimes faulty performances which
Handel's *Messiah* receives, the meaning of those words is undoubtedly
more dramatically and emotionally revealed when they are coupled with
the music of that chorus in the oratorio.

Indeed, it may be said that the right music intensifies the emotion of
the text, and at times even transcends it, resulting in an experience
which may be called "supra-rational." It is said that on one occasion a
recital-goer asked the great Marian Anderson to explain a song she had
sung. Her response was: "If I could have said it in words, I wouldn't
have sung it!" Or, as the mountaineer preacher said, "Some things are
better felt than telt!"

---

9. See Chapters XVII and XVIII.
10. Mignel. XXXII, 769; Nicene & Post-N. Serv. 1, I, 134. Cited in Reese, op. cit., pp.
    64-65.

It is interesting to observe that the Apostle Paul confessed that his worship experiences (praying and singing) were not all identical. Some were basically emotional ("with the spirit") and others were more rational ("with the understanding").[11] No doubt this is true of every worshiper. Music without words (as in the organ prelude) may evoke a worthy spiritual response ("I'm in God's house and I want to prepare to worship him") without a specific theological thought being present. It may be that this was the type of experience-response of the medieval serf who heard the Roman mass sung in Latin to Gregorian chant. But, for the mature evangelical, exclusively emotional worship will not suffice. Largely emotional experiences (like Paul's) must be balanced by others in which the mind is focused and active.

The effectiveness of musical worship may be most threatened when emotion is reduced to *sentimentality*—superficial emotion, or emotion not based on full reality. Sentimental response to music was illustrated for me at a dinner party on a seminary campus in 1965. The wife of an Old Testament professor was complaining that we church musicians frequently neglect and even criticize the congregation's "most significant hymns." "Take 'In the Garden', for instance," she said. "I've even heard some church musicians say that the words of that great old song are 'erotic'." It was too much of a temptation for me to see how well she knew the gospel song. "What garden?" I asked. She pondered for a moment and then retorted with some exasperation: "What garden? What difference does it make? It's my favorite gospel song."

The fact is that both the critic's evaluation of the song and my friend's understanding of it were not based on reality! The hymn is a musical setting of the experience of Mary Magdalene in meeting the risen Christ on Easter morning in the garden of the tomb. Unfortunately, for most people the meaning of the hymn is limited to enjoyment of a tune known from childhood, or at best, identification with the "experience" words, "And he walks with me and he talks with me, And he tells me I am his own." The remainder of the song is also potentially meaningful and follows closely the New Testament narrative on which it is based (without eroticism!), but it may be largely lost on most folk who sing it![12] For the professor's wife, the attachment was a sentimental one. I too had much the same quality of worship experience hearing my mother sing Norwegian pietist hymns with guitar accompaniment, without understanding a word of the text! That was emotion not based on full reality (the meaning of the words)—emotion for emotion's sake—and has to be labeled "sentimentalism."

These are some of the symptoms which indicate that sentimentality is a determining force in a church's music program:

---

11. See I Corinthians 14:15.
12. Words and music by C. Austin Miles. I have analyzed this hymn more fully in *Crusade Hymn Stories* (Cliff Barrows, ed.), pp. 49–50.

(1) A tendency to over-use certain favorite music.
(2) A lack of relationship between the music and the rest of the service in which it appears.
(3) The failure to sing "up to" the full theology and experience of the church.
(4) Resistance to new music selections, as well as to new forms of music.

No doubt persistent sentimentalism is fed by two of the otherwise-valid meanings in church music: (1) Pleasure (Enjoyment of the favorite music triumphs over more significant meanings); and (2) Identity definition (The sentimental favorite becomes a tradition.)

Lovelace and Rice[13] explain why the lack of a mature, cognitive experience is one of the "besetting sins" in church music. The emotional response is an *immediate* one; it occurs as soon as a familiar tune (or even a certain quality of musical sound) is heard, recalling earlier associations. The mental process of assimilating the text's meaning takes longer, and unfortunately, many worshipers do not even wait for the mind to get into gear. It may be argued that everyone is sentimental occasionally, and that America is peculiarly a "sentimental culture." Perhaps so, and possibly there should be room in church life for everybody's sentimental favorites. However, if worship, fellowship and outreach are to achieve their highest goals, they must be *primarily* served by music chosen for more significant reasons.

Ethos in Evangelical Church Music.

A modern-day adaptation of the Greek doctrine of musical *ethos* is not hard to find in evangelical church life. The 19th century evangelist D. L. Moody once stated: "I believe that music is one of the most powerful agents for good or for evil.[14] He did not elaborate on the implications of that statement, but evidently he was referring to certain forms of entertainment music as "agents for evil" and the music used in his evangelistic campaigns as an "agent for good." Because he held this conviction, Moody gave a large place to music in his mass meetings in England and America between 1873 and 1899; under the musical leadership of Ira D. Sankey the gospel songs of that era became firmly entrenched as one of the norms for evangelical outreach and worship. Moody also established training in "evangelistic music" at his Chicago school (later named Moody Bible Institute) in 1888, long before church music education was offered in major colleges, universities and seminaries in America.

We have recently heard the assertion that "rock music" has a debilitating influence on its listeners, and this has been argued at some length by Robert Larson in his little book, *Rock and the Church.*[15] This criticism of

13. Austin Lovelace and Wm. C. Rice, *Music and Worship in the Church,* pp. 19-20.
14. Cited by Bernard R. DeRemer in *Moody Bible Institute: A Pictorial History,* p. 30.
15. See also Mr. Larson's earlier book, *Rock and Roll: the Devil's Diversion.*

modern youth culture has also been voiced by Rev. Billy James Hargis, a radio preacher in Oklahoma, who has suggested that rock music was introduced into western culture by Soviet communism, in order to subvert our society and undermine our moral strength!

Most evangelicals today would probably hesitate to categorize as "agents for evil" the types of music which D. L. Moody evidently criticized; in fact, were he alive today, it is doubtful that he would retain his 19th century negativism. That pragmatic, down-to-earth lay preacher, who led a most significant revival movement in England and America, would probably approve of modern-day evangelicals' positive consideration of the values of well-chosen recreation and entertainment, including many kinds of music. He might even notice that Sankey's gospel music was not very different from the entertainment music of that day, except for the lyrics!

It is interesting to note that each new form of youth entertainment music is greeted with the charge that it is conducive to immoral and anti-social behavior, but those fears are usually forgotten when the next style is introduced and the earlier becomes "old hat." Only a few evangelicals are dogmatic enough to say that rock-gospel music was devil-inspired or even communist-oriented. In fact, many more have found some of the new forms to be effective media for communicating the gospel to today's young people. This subject will be dealt with more completely in later chapters.

On the positive side, it is apparent that musical sounds do tend to encourage certain kinds of activity in the church-going individual. Because of its long association with the church, the sound of the organ in the service prelude can assist people in preparing for worship. Certain types of vocal melodies and forms can remind folk that they are in the traditional place of worship, and encourage them to think about God and his self-revelation to human beings. Musical sounds are frequently used to signal a congregation to stand (as for the *Gloria Patri*), to sit, or to pray.

The concept of ethos—of affecting human behavior with music—is frequently expressed by some evangelical religious leaders who see music largely as a "conditioner," an attention-getter, or a persuader. I have frequently heard such statements as these:

> Music prepares the soil of the heart to receive the seed of the gospel.

> Music breaks down an individual's resistance to the message of the word of God.

Historically, a good deal of criticism has been leveled at the "ethos" use of hymns by evangelists at the time of the "appeal" or "altar call." In earlier days, the emotion of fear was often encouraged to elicit a positive response to the gospel, and this was evident in the sermon, in the words of the invitation hymn, and in the prolonging of the appeal by repeating the hymn over and over! It is difficult to criticize intelligently the actions and attitudes of a past age, unless we ourselves lived through it. Suffice it to say that the intensely-emotional appeal to conversion based largely on fear of God's judgment has been rejected by most contemporary evangelicals. No doubt it still occurs in some situations, perhaps to the detriment of a true understanding of the gospel of God's love and grace.

Recently the idea of "manipulation" has been discussèd in connection with the effort to get more personal, emotional involvement in worship. It has been suggested that jazz and/or rock music could help people be rid of their inhibitions in order to share the spirit of joy and freedom in worship. It should be mentioned that this new interest and activity is not restricted to those who want to be called "evangelical"; indeed, it did not originate with them. The liberal theologian John Killinger hit the issue head on, and incidentally, I believe he is quite right about this. "Manipulation is a fact of life," he says.[16]

> It cannot be avoided even in Christian worship. The best thing, then is to recognize this fact and to focus instead upon the question of which are the most legitimate aims of manipulation in Christian worship . . . If it is a manipulative gospel, it is so in terms of a manipulation to freedom, to a bondage *chosen,* not one bestowed.

I am convinced that church music falls short of its high purpose when "ethos" is its principal function, or when for "persuasion" purposes it resorts to excessive manipulation or gimmickry. The highly personal response of each individual to music should encourage restraint. One individual will be challenged to respond to the gospel message by the inevitable use of "Just As I Am";[17] another may be "turned off" by it. One person responds positively to the introduction of novel experiences that are highly provocative of emotional response. Someone else may be so angered that he looks for a new church home!

Church Music as an Expression of God.

It may be surprising that we consider the possibility that some individuals still think of music as "the language of the gods" or "the language of God." A vestige of this concept may be demonstrated by the minister who asks the organist to play during the invocation or the pastoral prayer. Evidently, it is thought that the sound of music can help the listener feel the presence of God and experience the reality of prayer. This may be true for some. For others, the music is a distraction which prevents them from hearing the words of the minister or from forming their own prayer in their thoughts.

The author is tempted to believe that the "language of God" idea may also be perpetuated by those who insist that only a certain style of music

16. John Killinger, *Leave It to the Spirit,* pp. 75-76.
17. Billy Graham's regular use of this hymn is said to result from his own personal experience; it was sung at the time he responded to the gospel call in a meeting conducted by evangelist Mordecai Ham in Charlotte, North Carolina in 1934. For another view of Graham's estimate of the significance of invitation hymns, see chapter eight.

(usually their own natural style or preference) is suitable for church use; in effect, they suggest that that style is "inspired by God." It seems probable that the early church fathers considered that the cantillation with which the Hebrews read the scriptures was as fully inspired as the words themselves; consequently, they attempted to perpetuate those melodies in Christian worship. This same fallacy was demonstrated by the early missionaries who insisted that the primitives must sing their faith to the music of western hymns and gospel songs. It is also supported by those who presume that we can match God in creativity, and insist that only the best art music is suitable for the church, whether or not it has meaning to the congregation. Each of these groups is attempting to deify their own music language or their own aesthetic preference.

This misconception is related to that of Calvin who (in promoting the exclusive singing of psalms) insisted that "only God's Word is worthy to be sung in God's praise," though what he referred to were 16th century French poetic versions of the psalms. Music, like words, may speak of God, or of evil, but it does so in symbolic languages created and used by human beings. We may say that God speaks through the sermon, or through the anthem or the congregational hymn; but if he does so, the communication is couched in symbols of language and of musical tone created by people. There may well be validity for our preference for a certain style, but that style may not be at all appropriate for other Christians in other cultures. There is reason for excellence in our use of both text and musical languages, but that excellence is not related to the standards of an elitist art, understood by only a minority of the congregation.

Music as Reinforcement of Evangelical Church Life.

As in all the world's musics, church music's principal function is a reinforcing of our culture's value system; indeed, it might be considered to be the most significant statement of our values—our corporate expression of faith. Along with the symbolism of church architecture, furniture and decoration, words and actions, the symbolic language of music adds identity, intensity and meaning to our faith and its expression. Functional church music should be judged by how faithfully it fulfills its functions, supporting the common beliefs (theology) and goals (worship, fellowship and ministry), as well as the identity (traditions) of each particular culture or subculture. It seems to me that evangelical church music's larger meaning or function is threatened when there is an improper balance of all the possible meanings in music, and particularly by an unhealthy emphasis on the meanings of "pleasure" and "emotion" (including ethos.) Typical examples of these imbalances were given in the preceding pages of this chapter.

Most thoughtful leaders agree that church music offers its strongest cultural/theological reinforcement when it serves as an effective medium of "revelation and response." For that is the essence of the Christian life in its entirety, and of Christian worship as a microcosm of that life: God has revealed himself to human beings and invites their response. Our worship, fellowship and outreach gatherings (with their music) may well be evaluated by how fully and clearly the true God is revealed and how complete and mature is the response.

The Implications of Evangelical Traditions for Church Music

Using the description of evangelicals by Bernard Ramm and Donald Bloesch set forth in this book's Introduction, we can now draw certain implications regarding the use of music in the evangelical church and its ministry. These general positions are suggested, and they will be amplified in later chapters.

1. Because their "mindset" is Western instead of Eastern, worship (including its music) will be more rational than mystical. Music with understandable text will be of primary significance.

2. Because of the Reformation emphasis on the "priesthood of each believer," worship (including music) will emphasize the personal involvement and participation of each member of the congregation. When the music is intended to be sung by the entire worshiping assembly, it should be simple enough for the musically-untrained and the theologically-unsophisticated to learn. Furthermore, *all* of a church's music should be in musical and textual languages that are potentially "understandable" by most people in that congregation.

"Believer-priesthood" implies not only that we approach God individually and directly for ourselves; we are priests also to our fellow believers. This implies a caring fellowship in the church which will be evident in the fellowship hymns that are used, and also in the effort to minister to everyone through the music program.

3. Because evangelicals believe in a sovereign God, both transcendent and immanent, their worship (with its music) will include both adoration of, and communion with God. It may also be expected that the suprarational expression of music may be used to reveal something of God's transcendence.

4. Believing in the "divine authority of scripture," worship and ministry activities and experiences (including music) will conform to biblical standards where these are set forth, and will be saturated with scripture truth. The actual words of scripture will be considered ideal for use with music.

5. In the context of the centrally important tenets relating to personal salvation—man's sinfulness, the substitutionary atonement, salvation by grace through faith alone—worship and outreach music will give proper emphasis to the expression of these doctrines. In addition, because "evangelical" also implies something of a pietist heritage, this emphasis may well include "experience hymns" which speak of "religion of the heart," "new life in Christ" and "the assurance of salvation."

6. Accepting the "primacy of proclamation," the evangelical church musician will remember that his worship structuring or improvising, while providing for a full-orbed experience of worship, will demonstrate

the "centrality of preaching." Some of the music will prepare for, or reinforce the reading and preaching of the Word of God in a particular service. Other music will offer an opportunity to respond to the total revelation of God.

7. Accepting the requirement of "scriptural holiness," there will be room in evangelical worship (and its music) for an emphasis on both crisis experience and "growing in grace" to the mature Christian life. Furthermore, "holiness" really means "wholeness" and this may well include growth to broader-based expressions of worship, in both text and music.

8. Understanding "the church's spiritual mission"—to convert, to instruct and to minister—these emphases will be safe-guarded in the church's activities, including its use of music. There will be consideration of the particular musical techniques and forms (music and text languages) involved in evangelism, Christian education and pastoring, both in the home church and in worldwide outreach.

9. Most uses of church music are associated with worship services. Since, for the purposes of this book, the word "evangelical" includes the concept of "free" worship, particular attention must be given by ministers and musicians to the planning of the congregation's worship experiences. In this regard, the evangelical minister's challenge is more demanding than that of a worship leader in a liturgical church. The latter has been taught the biblical, historical and theological principles upon which his worship order and rubrics (instructions) are based, and was then handed a book of liturgy to follow.

Free church ministers ("of the Word" or "of music") have no such pattern given to them and often receive little instruction in college or in seminary to prepare them for worship planning; they must find other authority for their worship patterns and other guidance for planning their services, including the music. It is one of the purposes of this book to make a modest contribution in an approach to evangelical worship content and design.

Summary

In this chapter, church music has been identified as a functional art, created and used by human beings to serve the purposes of God and the church. General and specific functions of music in evangelical church life have been listed, and some basic standards for the music (and especially the texts) which perform those functions have been suggested. These points will be further developed in the succeeding chapters, as they relate to specific services and activities in church life.

There remain, however, vast differences between the musical "languages" used by evangelicals, and those differences frequently result in communication gaps and even serious conflict between Christian groups. The next chapter will suggest proper approaches to this problem.

Chapter III

MUSIC LANGUAGES: COMMUNICATION AND CONFLICT

In the preceding chapter, evangelical distinctives in faith and in activity were listed, and certain related implications for church music were suggested. Insofar as churches support the distinctives named, they will probably concur with the implications drawn. Nevertheless, evangelical church music still exhibits a plethora of styles (languages) which are determined by geography, by social, educational and economic factors, and by denominational tradition. Music in the urban East may be expected to be different from that in the rural South. Canadian churches tend to be more conservative than their counterparts in the United States. Methodist worship in a working class community contrasts sharply with that in a university setting or in a "country club" church. Most black worshipers use a different musical speech from that of whites. Most Southern Baptists will not be at home with the hymnic diet that is common to Mennonites.

Obviously, the common language of each group is important to its members. It serves to establish their particular identity. Because they understand it best, it helps them to experience fully their own distinctive religious activities. It is not necessary for individual churchgoers to share in detail the rationale of their worship leaders, or to understand the musical techniques and forms that are used; their church music has *basic* associative meaning for them which they have learned from hearing it repeatedly. Episcopalians "understand" the sound of psalm chant, because they hear it every time they attend Morning Prayer. In the same way, evangelicals find meaning in their particular heritage of hymns, gospel songs, Christian folk music, or anthems (or a combination of these) because they are a regular part of their worship experiences.

It is my contention that, within certain expectations of healthy growth and change, each church culture has validity. It follows then that the functional music which gives it identity and which adds meaning to the experiences of the congregation, also has validity. In communicating

26

musically to a particular group, it must be remembered that they understand a particular musical language (or possibly a few languages), and that they may have quite a strong emotional resistance to "foreign" languages which tend to threaten the validity of their heritage.

It is true, as mentioned in chapter one, that every culture is affected by sin, and shows its weaknesses and immaturity in its life style, including its mode and expressions of worship. Nevertheless, as human beings, we tend to be convinced that our own way of life is superior, and to want to impose it on others. If healthy change is to come to a culture, it must be guided by those who are identified with it, who love and understand it. Actually, only they are really qualified to evaluate it.

In this chapter, it is my purpose to investigate the communication gaps which exist (some of which should be ignored and some which should concern us) in the use of church music. In conclusion, I will list some general standards for evangelical church music.

The "Good Church Music is the Best Art Music" Myth

American evangelical churches have often been criticized by outsiders for the quality of their music, usually on the basis of their preference for the "gospel hymns" which stem from our revivalist heritage. In recent years, talented and trained musicians who have grown up in the evangelical *milieu* have adopted the same negative stance. The general tenor of the argument seems to be that church music should be equal to (or even identical with) the best art music our generation can produce. Since we admit that evangelicals may need to make substantive changes in their musical worship, it should be helpful to consider the proposition.

This idea was once expressed in words of the noted conductor Robert Shaw at a conference at Wheaton College[1] (Illinois): "Ninety percent of the sacred music written since Beethoven (d. 1827) is not worthy of being offered in praise of God." Nobody is going to argue that, as pure art, the bulk of church music written in the 19th and 20th centuries can be compared with the music of Beethoven, Mozart or Bach. However, the argument is specious, because (1) it fails to differentiate between "sacred music" and "church music"; (2) it fails to consider church music as a functional art; and (3) it is based on erroneous assumptions about the glory of God and the edifying of human beings.

It is true that Beethoven wrote a Mass in C (Op. 86), the *Missa Solemnis* (Op. 123) and the oratorio *Mount of Olives*. The liturgical works were conceived as "festival masses" and the oratorio as a "sacred music" piece to be performed outside the church. Nowadays, save for a few perfor-

---

1. My memory is hazy about the date; it was sometime in the 1950's. On the occasion mentioned, Shaw identified his parents as ministers in an evangelical church, who sang such hymns as "The Way of the Cross Leads Home" (Pounds-Gabriel). He argued that Bach's *Crucifixus* from the Mass in B Minor is a more valid presentation of the theology of the cross.

mances in large churches (mostly the "Hallelujah" from *Mount of Olives*), the concert hall is the only place they may be heard. Mozart, as a Roman Catholic, wrote a large amount of church music, but only a very few individual mass movements and an occasional motet are adapted for Protestant use.

The argument is most often heard while naming J. S. Bach as the archetypical church music composer. While no one doubts his genius or his strong Christian faith, it is interesting to note that very little of Bach's sacred choral or vocal music is used or usable in churches today. The Passions, the Christmas Oratorio and the Easter Oratorio may be heard in some large churches, but only at the high festivals of the year. The six motets are certainly worthy of use, but they require choral forces and abilities that are not often available; they also are longer than modern worshipers will tolerate on a typical Sunday. The same arguments could be advanced regarding Bach's three hundred cantatas which are almost never sung in worship; in addition, many would insist that their texts are not relevant to the modern church.[2]

The Historical Perspective.

It may be that Johann Sebastian Bach (1685–1750) is considered to be the ideal church music composer because he was the last of a long line of master composers to give his attention largely to writing and performing church music. For this reason, we should consider this argument from an overview of history.

Admittedly, for the long period from 392 a.d. (when Emperor Theodosius made Christianity the official religion of the Roman Empire) until the Renaissance, church music and "great art" were essentially one and the same, because all arts were under the control of the clergy, and were expected to support and enhance the church. From our viewpoint today, it would be presumptuous to try to evaluate the quality of the worship of the individual, whether serf, tradesman, or nobleman, while listening to the medieval masses of Perotin or Okeghem or the motets of Josquin des Prez or Guillaume Dufay. We do know that most worship services were conducted in a language which few understood, with little or no verbal participation by the congregation. We tend to presume that the music was a part of the "mystery" experience of medieval worship.

Under the leadership of Martin Luther, John Calvin and Thomas

2. It is interesting to note that Erik Routley judges that Bach transcends the limitations of his "pietist texts." See his *Church Music and the Christian Faith*, pp. 54–58. Actually, today's evangelicals would not have too much difficulty with the theology of the cantata lyrics, if they were available in a good modern translation. Many would find it a greater challenge to try to understand Bach's musical language. (Incidentally, the little cantata *Unto Us a Child Is Born* is a delightful and practical work in baroque style, but I judge that, like the *Eight Little Preludes and Fugues* for organ, it is not really J. S. Bach's.)

Cranmer in the 16th century protestant reformation that spawned the Lutheran, Reformed and Anglican traditions, a functional church music began to evolve based on a commitment to congregational participation. If the non-musical or amateur-musical laypersons were to take part in the hymns and the liturgies, the material would have to be simple enough for them to perform. In addition, the growing evangelical conscience dictated that the choral and instrumental music should also be "shared" by typical worshipers; it should be their "sacrifice of praise" and they should enter into the meaning of both the words and the music, even though it was performed by musical specialists.

It is interesting to note that few "master composers" (except perhaps Hans Leo Hassler, 1564–1612 and Ralph Vaughan Williams, 1872–1958) have written successful tunes for congregational song. The few tunes credited to Mozart, Haydn, Beethoven and Schumann were "borrowed" by later church musicians from ostensibly secular, usually-instrumental compositions. Though a few of J. S. Bach's chorale harmonizations still persist in some hymnals, none of his own melodies are simple enough to be adapted for congregational use. In the earlier Lutheran tradition, Martin Luther himself (a talented amateur musician, but not a composer) wrote chorale melodies or adapted secular tunes for the church. The later Lutheran hymn tune writer Melchior Vulpius (ca.1560–ca.1615) also wrote secular music, but he is remembered chiefly for his contributions to the church. In the Calvinist reformation, Louis Bourgeois did the musical spadework, basing his psalm tunes on German and French secular sources; he was a musician by profession, but appears in history only because of his association with Calvin.

It should also be remembered that, in the reformed liturgical traditions, there has always been a pluralism of musical language. The cathedrals, collegiate churches (e.g., Westminster Abbey) and certain others (like Bach's St. Thomas' parish in Leipzig) were known as "high church," enjoyed a high degree of symbolism in worship, and supported a choir that sang settings of the liturgy by serious composers. The typical parish church, however, existed on simpler fare—often sparse symbolism and little more music than congregational singing—and was called "low church" in worship. In fact, there is even a third category of worship style: Anglican hymnals and others frequently have a section of "gospel hymns" for what is called the "mission church."

The trend toward "common" worship with "popular" music was intensified with the emergence of the pietist and "free church" movements in the 17th century. German pietists opposed all "artistic" forms of church music, used only congregational song, and lived in constant tension with the traditionalists, including J. S. Bach. Puritans in England (including both rebelling Anglicans and "Separatists"), in reaction against what they saw as the impotent formalism of the state church, abolished choirs and sometimes destroyed priceless church organs and hand-copied choir books; their own music consisted of unaccompanied psalms and chants sung by the congregation. The first Baptists in England had no music whatsoever; when it later appeared, it was limited to congregational singing from the psalter.[3]

It seems obvious that, beginning with the Reformation, the church was moving away from "art music." Serious composers were also shifting their loyalty away from the church. Beginning with the Renaissance, they gave increasing attention to secular music, and in the 19th and 20th centuries this was essentially their only interest. By 1850, most large churches in Europe and America had returned to the use of choirs; the literature of that day, largely written by gifted musical craftsmen, tended to imitate the forms of the masters, but was more popular in its appeal. At the same time in history, many evangelical groups, inspired by the experience of mass revivals, used choirs to sing expanded hymns that were sometimes called "chorus choir" selections (e.g., "Awakening Chorus" by C. H. Gabriel or "Hallelujah for the Cross" by Bonar-McGranahan). Beyond a doubt, a "popular" approach to music had taken over in the typical church, largely due to the rising tides of humanism, of democracy, and of "religion of the heart." Church music was now expected to be functional in the evangelical sense that everybody should share it. Consequently it moved to the level of the worshiper who rarely frequented the concert hall.

The situation has not changed drastically up to the present time. As an aesthetic concept, 19th century Romanticism is now judged to be unsuited to church music and many feel that popular 20th century styles offer better media for the Christian message. Even so, our churches use essentially the same basic practical materials which they have always favored. Though many denominations have become increasingly sophisticated by virtue of education (including the arts), what is performed in ninety-nine percent of American churches today is functional church music that should not be confused with great art.

To be sure, "great art" and functional church music coincide occasionally. Most choirs aspire to sing the "Hallelujah" chorus from Handel's *Messiah,* even if they have to transpose it to a lower key, and then achieve a performance that does not measure up to the quality of the score! A very few churches in metropolitan centers (and they may be considered to be the cathedrals of American church life) sing a consistent diet of composers of the stature of Byrd, Schütz, Bach, Mozart, Mendelssohn, Brahms, Vaughan Williams, Britten and Distler. The more-typical large church which considers itself to be musically sophisticated hears mostly choral music by such individuals as David McK. Williams, Dale Wood, Austin Lovelace, Gordon Young, Eugene Butler, Hal Hopson and Maxcine W. Posegate, with occasional works by the historic art composers. With all due respect and admiration, these individuals named write good church music that uses much the same techniques as the "masters," but it

---

3. Indeed, in many European "free" churches today, a choir is considered to be unnecessary and even undesirable, especially if it tends to replace the congregation in singing and thus deny, even momentarily, the priesthood of the individual believer.

will not be acknowledged by critics to be serious art music, and probably will not outlive the next generation.

Still the conflict goes on, and it is not limited to those who espouse "art music" (however mistaken they may be in labeling it) and criticize "gospel," "folk" or "popular" music in church. Every group has "communication gaps" between itself and others who use different music. Frequently we reveal our failure to understand another musical language by labeling it "too romantic," "too cold," "too emotional" or "too austere," or, even worse, "less spiritual" than ours!

At this point, it may be helpful to list the principal streams of congregational and choral music in common use in America's evangelical churches. Of course, all churches use more than one "style" and some combine certain diverse styles, while shunning others.

Congregational Styles

Gregorian Melodies

Chorales

Metrical Psalms

Standard Hymns
 17th century
 18th century
 19th century
 20th century

Spirituals (White and Black)

Gospel Songs

"Southern" gospel songs
 (Stamps-Baxter)

Historic Folk Hymns

Contemporary Popular Hymns
 Gospel
 Folk
 Country
 Rock
 "Soul", etc.

Choral Styles

Historic Art Music
 Renaissance
 Baroque
 Classic-Rococo
 Romantic
 Twentieth Century
 Avant garde

Traditional Anthems
 (Dudley Buck, John
 Stainer to Leland
 Sateren, John Ness
 Beck, Eugene Butler,
 etc.)

"Chorus Choir" Selections
 (Expanded hymns)

Hymn Anthems
 (Hymns arranged for choir)

Gospel Song Arrangements

Contemporary Arrangements
 Gospel
 Folk
 Country
 Rock
 "Soul", etc.

The few "purists" who favor Bach, Schütz, Praetorius, etc. are frequently scornful of those who patronize Clokey, Christiansen, or other "traditional anthem" composers. The latter are often critical of the churches which specialize in "gospel" or "folk" music. Frequently the communications gap exists in both directions—e.g., the gospel music enthusiast shuns the "traditional anthem" as "too formal" and the "country" or "Stamps-Baxter" style as "too undignified" for church use.

Indeed, the tension often exists within a confessional or a denominational structure. There is marked difference in taste between Missouri-synod Lutherans and other Lutheran groups; this is demonstrated in the stylistic contrasts between the publications of Concordia and those of Augsburg, and in the internecine struggles which went on during the preparation of the new *Lutheran Book of Worship* (1978). There is also quite a cultural gap between "high church" and "low church" adherents in the Episcopal (Anglican) tradition, and these terms are borrowed by Methodists and Baptists for the purpose of making disparaging remarks about each other! The continuing debate includes discussion of all the forms of church music—the hymns, the choral and organ literature, and even the types of instruments used. In some churches, only a "baroque" organ is acceptable; others prefer a more eclectic "American classic" design, and in still others a "theater style" electronic instrument is selected.

It should not be difficult to understand the human factors underlying this cross-cultural tension, even though they may point to sociological and spiritual immaturity. A church's musical style is tied up with its identity; when it is *our* church, and because we consider ourselves to be theologically correct, we believe that our music is the "best" spiritual expression of God's truth. We react negatively to "strange" church music because it threatens our identity and therefore our truth; our reaction may be more intense because music is an emotional language. Again, artistic achievement tends to deal in absolutes of excellence, and we want to be assured that we already have the "best."

The Perspective of "the Glory of God."

It is easy to understand how trained musicians who are committed Christians may tend to equate "good church music" with western culture's best art. They believe in a transcendent God and have experienced transcendent art as a gift of God. We have already admitted that God is glorified by the work of his creatures, whether or not they acknowledge him as God. Does it not then follow that God is more glorified with "great art" (e.g., a Bach motet) than he is with something "less" (e.g., a gospel folk song)? Is not music a "sacrifice of praise" and wasn't the sacrifice in Old Testament times required to be the best available?

To be sure, our words and melodies and actions in church are all offerings to God, but we are not accepted by him according to the quality of our texts and our music. In both old and new covenants, people are reconciled to God on the basis of Christ's own perfect sacrifice of himself on their behalf; the only offering we can bring relative to our salvation is *penitence*—the "sacrifice of a broken spirit." As the Hebrews brought their best offerings, so God asks that Christian believers bring their best selves (Rom. 12:1) and their most excellent "sacrifices of praise" (Heb. 13:15) as expressions of love—their "reasonable service" or "spiritual worship." We should bring him *our best*—not someone else's—because that is good stewardship of the talents he has given us, as well as our faithful response in devotion and dedication.

The New Testament contains a poignant reminder of God's grace in his expectations concerning our offerings, in the story of Mary's sacrifice for purification (Luke 2:22-24). According to Leviticus 12, for such an occasion a well-to-do family would bring a lamb, but a poor household (like that of Joseph) was allowed to offer two pigeons. Of course, they were expected to be the best pigeons in the dovecote, but they were only pigeons! Accordingly, if a church and its leadership decides (after considering the possibilities) that its best offering of praise includes a Brahms motet or a Robert Powell anthem or a John Peterson cantata, it should select the best of those types suitable for the occasion, should present it in the very best manner possible, and most of all, with "pure hearts"—with sincerity.

It would be foolish for us to insist that one of these sacrifices is more acceptable, or brings more glory to God than another. To do so is to be guilty of an idolatrous anthropomorphism which reduces God's aesthetic perspective to ours. To be sure, God's ears are not tickled by great music in church; he is not impressed with the artistic gifts of any of his creatures. It is more realistic to see him (and here I paraphrase a sentence of C. S. Lewis[4]) as a loving father whose toddler brings him a page of childish scribblings. "Look, daddy, isn't it pretty?" "Yes, darling, it's lovely; we'll fasten it on the refrigerator so everyone can enjoy it!" That may be a little picture (hopefully not too irreverent for one who loves great music) of God's indulgent concern for all his creative children, whether John Peterson or J. S. Bach!

Finally, it is important to clarify the difference between glorifying God and pleasing him. According to the rationale of C. S. Lewis (quoted in chapter one), even Satan's power (as a creature of God) eventually glorifies God. The humblest believers please God when they bring their best offerings with sincerity.

The Perspective of the Edifying of the Congregation.

But isn't Bach (or other great music) really better? As Robert Shaw intimated, isn't there greater spiritual potential in the *Crucifixus* than in "The Way of the Cross Leads Home"? Let's say there is *great* spiritual potential, if we are looking for it, and if we understand the theological and musical languages of the great Bach! The unbeliever may be impressed with the musical craftsmanship and even possibly comprehend Bach's expression of his theology, without accepting that theology or

---

4. "All our offerings, whether of music or martyrdom, are like the intrinsically worthless present of a child, which a father values indeed, but values only for the intention." The quotation is from "On Church Music" by C. S. Lewis, in *Christian Reflections*, p. 99.

being converted to Bach's faith. On the other hand, the profundity of both musical and theological expression are so great that its meaning can easily be missed, even by evangelical music-lovers. The historian Paul Henry Lang declares that during the last years of his life, Bach's music was not even understood by his own congregation in Leipzig![5]

"Great art" in our culture, as in Bach's Leipzig years, tends to be elitist. One of the requirements of the art music composer is that he must be *free*—free to communicate anything that is in his mind and heart, *free even to fail to communicate* (if that is his choice) so long as the work is his honest expression. Church music cannot be so "free." It must communicate the truth of God and express the response of the body of believers by whom it is used, and this means that it must have the potential to be understood by that particular community of faith. When it is so used and so understood, whether it be Palestrina or Felciano or Medema or Gaither, it is functional church music.

Again, music written for the recital hall may be evaluated by how deeply it stimulates the imagination of the listeners. A diversity of response is expected and welcomed. Music planned for communal worship cannot be so esoteric and abstruse that it is misunderstood by many of those present. Ideally, there should be a united understanding of, and a common response to, the communication.

An example of a communication gap caused by the failure to distinguish between "art music" and "functional church music" came to public attention with the release of the *Armed Forces Book of Worship* (1974).[6] The hymnal included the Sydney Carter song "It was on a Friday morning"[7]—a narrative of the experience of the two thieves who were crucified with Christ. In his agony and frustration, the unrepentant thief addresses Jesus and curses, "To hell with Jehovah . . It's God they ought to crucify instead of you and me." The casual reader or worshiper judges that the hymn is blasphemous; as a result, protests from chaplains and from armed forces families caused the song to be removed from later editions of the book. Actually, Carter's song is a powerful and provocative presentation of the profound mysteries of Calvary. It is an art work (though in folksong style) with which a thoughtful evangelical would have little theological quarrel. But it is not common and simple enough (even with a reasonable explanation) to be a good congregational hymn. It is not functional church music, at least for most congregations.

Communication Gaps within a Culture

Communication gaps related to music styles also occur within a culture. A culture may adopt a new style as its norm (1) because of a change

---

5. Paul Henry Lang, *Music in Western Civilization*, p. 700.
6. It was my privilege to serve as a member of the group of churchmen and hymnologists who were consultants to the Armed Forces Chaplains Board in compiling this book.
7. The song appeared as no. 286 in the first edition; words and music copyright 1960, 1969 by Galliard, Ltd., with Galaxy Music Corporation, New York the U.S. agent.

in the economic and cultural level of the congregation, (2) because of the influence of effective music leadership, or (3) because, in the passing of time, there are regular changes in communication languages. Frequently, a sizable number of people within the culture find that their religious identity and the significance of their experiences are threatened by the change of musical language. For at least a period of time there is a gap in effective music communication.

I have already suggested that there is little *intrinsic* meaning in the expressions of a musical language; however, very specific meaning may be assigned to certain music by the culture which uses it. This is why we can say (at least for a period of time) that certain music "sounds" happy or sad, solemn or flippant, sacred or secular. However, these meanings may (and probably will) change over a period of time; when they do, at least temporary confusion exists.

During the late 18th and the 19th centuries, music in the minor keys was often said to sound "sad" or doleful; for those who met in church settings, the minor was expected to express the ideas of doubt, of temptation or of sin, while the major mode characterized the joy and serenity of the victorious Christian life. Within the last fifty years, however, the great Welsh hymn tunes have been discovered by all Christians, and those in the minor have tended to alter the previous image. Even more recently, the rediscovery of American "folk hymn" tunes (like "Wondrous Love" and "Wayfaring Stranger"), together with the use of the minor and the modal in new gospel-folk songs, has completed the transformation in music's meaning.

Again, during the 19th century, a type of hymn tune was written in England and America that was understood by worshipers to express piety, devotion and communion with God; a good example is H. Percy Smith's MARYTON, commonly sung in this country to "O Master, let me walk with Thee." While some may feel that the music says the same things today, there are many others who find that style of hymn tune only "romantic and sentimental," lacking strength and conviction.

It is also true that a music style is intrinsically neither "sacred" or "secular."[8] Handel frequently used the same music for both religious and "profane" texts; Verdi's *Requiem* is constructed of the same music materials as his operas. However, for a certain period of history, through its persistent association with a culture's acts of worship, a particular musical language or expression may become "sacred." Later, in a period of renewal in the church, old symbols of worship (including word and music languages) are discarded for new; invariably the new will be an adaptation of a "secular" (outside the church) language. So it was that Martin Luther developed chorale tunes from secular German folk songs, Charles Wesley adapted opera airs for his new hymn tune meters, Ira Sankey wrote gospel songs in the style of Stephen Foster, and modern

8. It might be argued that Gregorian chant (and other historic chants) used in worship for some 1500 years, are undeniably and permanently "sacred." However, the roots of these forms are in the secular music of the period when each was first developed. They are "sacred" simply because they have always been associated with certain worship acts.

worship/outreach uses folk, rock, jazz and "country" styles, to name only a few. At the moment of the "switch" in meanings, communication tends to be confused, because many folk cannot believe that "secular" music can communicate "sacred" truth. In time, after it has been associated with church activities for a period, the "old secular" becomes the "new sacred" and communication is restored. This particular phenomenon in changing meanings in musical languages is dealt with more completely in a later chapter.

A recent example of this metamorphosis should be fresh in the minds of many readers. In the mid-1960's, evangelicals began to toy with the new secular-becoming-sacred styles which had already been used by Christians in Britain. The new sounds were greeted with a storm of protest by evangelical leaders, who heard in them a tidal wave of secularism that would engulf and weaken the church. In less than five years, the new music (at least some form of it) was common language in the church, and hailed by many to be a symbol of spiritual renewal.

About Grace and Judgment.

What then should be the evangelical attitude about styles in church music? First of all, we should show *grace* toward those whose tastes and practices are different from our own. Unless we are a part of a particular culture, there is very little possibility that we can evaluate whether or not it is using its best possible functional church music, whether or not it is pleasing to God (as a sacrifice) or edifying to man (as communication).

> The danger exists . . . of assuming that the other audience, the audience one does not converse with, is more passive, more manipulated, more vulgar in taste than may be the case. One can easily forget that things that strike the sophisticated person as trash may open new vistas for the unsophisticated; moreover, the very judgment of what is trash may be biased by one's own unsuspected limitations, for instance, by one's class position or academic vested interest.[9]

The above comment by David Riesmann was made in the context of a purely anthropological approach to differences between art music lovers and secular "pop" fans. The Christian has an added incentive to show grace, because of God's grace extended to him; none of us measures up to God's expectations, yet he accepts us. It is not for us to judge the worship or musical practices of other religious cultures, even when our own aesthetic sensibilities are offended.

With regard to our own practices in church music, our own "sacrifices of praise," the individual Christian should live in *judgment*. Even as we should constantly evaluate whether or not our "offering of self" is complete, we should judge whether or not we are giving God our best sac-

9. David Riesmann, *Individualism Reconsidered,* p. 184. Quoted by Jacques Barzun, *Music in American Life,* pp. 88–89.

rifice of praise. In all my defense of the validity of the expressions and experiences of each culture, I may seem to understate the sins which beset evangelicals, particularly in our use of the arts in worship. In keeping with my encouragement to "live in grace," I list only the flagrant offenses which I believe are a part of my middle-class evangelical culture. If others identify them as their own, they are invited to join in the confession.

1. The sin of pride. While acknowledging the significance of forms which confirm our own identity, we must flee the temptation to believe that our worship practices are more acceptable to God than those of others. Again, whereas we strive for excellence as good stewards, the achieving of it should not be self-conscious. Admittedly, this is a very difficult standard, but it is biblical!
2. The sin of hedonism. I am afraid that for many evangelicals, the most central meaning in church music is "pleasure." Few of our people use the expressions in hymns, anthems and instrumental music for their maximum "spiritual" benefit.
3. The sin of spectatorism. Most evangelicals would rather be sung to than to sing for themselves. True, there is involvement and even meaning in "listening music"; it need not be given up, so long as there is full and meaningful participation in the congregation's own music.
4. The sin of sentimentalism. This is related to (2), and is shown by our predilection for "favorite hymns," cantatas, anthems or solos, or for a favorite musical style. Undoubtedly, this sin is encouraged by the commercialism which prevails in much of our affluent American culture, including evangelical publishing and recording. Of course, an artist and a composer must be compensated for their workmanship, and a company must make a business profit; but the net result in recent years is the creation of an evangelical "hit parade." Such conformity stifles creativity and cannot be called ideal.

In a broader and possibly more significant sense, evangelicals are guilty of sentimentalism in their tenacious hold on their traditions, especially the heritage of reaction. Our forefathers first parted company with the Roman church during the Reformation, and later left the established liturgical Protestant churches to become "free." Many of the prejudices which encouraged violent iconoclasm in those early days (e.g., the destruction of artistic symbolism) are still with us. Having left the bondage of a required liturgy, we find ourselves denying the validity of worship by failing to approach it with any amount of serious thought. As evangelicals, we have been too long captives of reaction. It is time for positive leadership (both in our schools and in local churches) so that the arts may fulfill their highest calling as "handmaidens of theology" and servants of the church.

Finally, the leaders of a church should show *both judgment and grace* toward the members of their congregation. The minister and music leader should judge whether the traditional musical expressions best serve that particular culture, and whether or not they are fully apprehended as "spiritual experiences." If it appears that changes should be made either in the worship literature or in its presentation, they will endeavor patiently and lovingly to lead the congregation to make those changes.

Within every congregation, there are different musical tastes, and communication gaps may be intensified by the increasing mobility of our population. At the same time, there is probably a common spectrum of music and worship style on which most people agree. Wise church musicians will choose most of their music within that spectrum, while occasionally moving to either side of it (1) to satisfy the extremes of taste, (2) to increase the musical literacy of everyone, and (3) possibly to give folk (including themselves) a chance to "grow in grace."

That last challenging possibility has been discussed by C. S. Lewis.

> There are two musical situations on which I think we can be confident that a blessing rests. One is where a priest or an organist, himself a man of trained and delicate taste, humbly and charitably sacrifices his own (aesthetically right) desires and gives the people humbler and coarser fare than he would wish, in a belief (even, as it may be, the erroneous belief) that he can thus bring them to God. The other is where the stupid and unmusical layman humbly and patiently and above all silently, listens to music which he cannot, or cannot fully, appreciate, in the belief that it somehow glorifies God, and that if it does not edify him this must be his own defect.[10]

Evangelical Standards for Church Music

These then are standards suggested to those who are concerned about maturity in the use of music in evangelical church life:

1. It should communicate and express the gospel in a text language and a music language that are richly understandable by the culture for which they are intended.
2. It should offer a worthy "sacrifice of praise," for the individual and for the corporate body, in worship experience. It should be "our best"—our best performance of the most meaningful text and music that is shared by all. It should be offered in love, humility, gratitude and grace, without arrogance or shame in comparing it to the offering of other persons in the same culture or in other cultures.

10. C. S. Lewis, op. cit., pp. 96–97.

3. It should express and enhance the best Christian theology of each particular culture or subculture, supporting all tenets of that faith in proper balance.
4. It should express and support the best Christian activities related to the group's beliefs—worship, fellowship and outreach—with due consideration of the musical needs of each.
5. It should speak from the "whole person" to the "whole person," carefully balancing the physical, intellectual and emotional, while avoiding the sentimental.
6. It should be genuinely creative, shunning the hackneyed and trite as well as the elitist and abstruse.

No doubt some readers will be disappointed with the lack of specifics in this statement. Obviously, a heavy burden of responsibility still rests on individual pastors and musicians to develop criteria for evaluating a congregation's response to various kinds of musical communication.[11] I will recommend just one specific goal. It is usually thought that the criteria listed above imply "raising the standard" of musical aesthetic experiences. I suggest rather that evangelicals should be open to a *broader* experience in musical expression. For one thing, we will increase our understanding of fellow Christians in other cultures if we can share their worship experience, whether it be more or less sophisticated than ours, more or less cerebral, more or less emotional, more or less physical. Beyond this, in sharing music with others, whether it be in a cathedral with Britten's *Festival Te Deum,* in a rural Alabama church with "Sacred Harp" music or in a Thailand mountain village singing to the accompaniment of an *angklung,* we will get a new glimpse of God and his truth.

Harold M. Best, dean of the Conservatory of Music at Wheaton College, and one of evangelicalism's leading spokesmen, defines excellence in church music as "stretching and yearning for the unexpected."

> What is excellence, anyway? We often confuse it with perfection and end up frustrated. Failing this, we equate it with snobbery or assume it to be the sole property of someone better trained than we are. Or, in this age of valuelessness, we might assume excellence to be totally irrelevant—a thing of the past. But to the biblical perspective, excellence is, simply put, a commandment. It is both absolute and relative; absolute, because it is the norm of stewardship and cannot be avoided or compromised; relative, because it is set in the context of striving, wrestling, hungering, thirsting, pressing on from point to point and achievement to achievement. Moreover, we are unequally gifted and cannot equally achieve. Consequently, some artists are better than others. But all artists can be better than they once were. This is excelling.

11. Some additional standards are suggested by Erik Routley in *Church Music and the Christian Faith,* pp. 6-20, 77-99.

We should be no more impressed with congregation "x" preferring great art than we are appalled by congregation "y" preferring bad art, as long as both are stretching and yearning for the unexpected. Taste by itself is useless. In fact, it is often one of the forms of idolatry which overcome us. However, if God senses faith at work— faith which makes us creatively discontent and eager to live in the surprises of creation—He smiles, whatever the level of achievement *at the time.* And the important words are *at the time,* because God ever expects us, as He did Abraham, to be on the move.[12]

12. Harold M. Best, "Toward a Biblical Perspective on the Arts," p. 7.

Chapter IV

AUTHORITY AND LEADERSHIP IN EVANGELICAL CHURCH MUSIC

The two preceding chapters set forth some of the standards by which evangelical church music can be evaluated. It is now proper to ask "who has the authority and responsibility to see that music measures up to its high potential in supporting worship, fellowship and ministry?"

The Authority of Scripture.

All evangelicals recognize the authority of God as expressed in scripture, for life as well as for faith. However, looking to the Bible for complete directions in worship and its music has caused some historic confusion, because the scriptures do not claim authority or speak definitively in these matters. One noteworthy example—the question of the validity of instruments in church—has persisted for almost two thousand years!

The early church fathers understood that no instruments were used by the Christians of the first century, and they deduced that this was a New Testament standard. It is said that Clement of Alexandria (ca.150–ca.220) "tolerated the lyra and kithara because King David had allegedly used them . . (but) disapproved of most other instruments."

> The one instrument of peace, the Word alone by which we honour God, is what we employ, . . no longer . . the ancient psaltery, the trumpet, the timbrel, and aulos, which those expert in war and contemners of the fear of God were wont to make use of also in the choruses at their festive assemblies; that by such strains they might raise their dejected minds.[1]

Another early theologian insisted that the instruments mentioned in the Old Testament were actually symbols of Christian grace!

> We sing God's praise with living psaltery . . For more pleasant and dear to God than any instrument is the harmony of the whole Chris-

---

1. MigneG VIII, 443; transl. from Ante-Nicene II, 249. Quoted in Gustave Reese, *Music in the Middle Ages*, p. 61.

tian people.. Our cithara is the whole body, by whose movement
and action the soul sings a fitting hymn to God, and our ten-stringed
psaltery is the veneration of the Holy Ghost by the five senses of the
body and the five virtues of the spirit.   (Eusebios, ca.260-ca.340)[2]

St. Augustine also followed this line of reasoning.

> Nor must we keep back the mystical meaning of the "timbrel and
> psaltery." On the timbrel leather is stretched, on the psaltery gut is
> stretched; on either instrument the flesh is crucified.[3]

Upholding this tradition, Eastern Orthodox worship for the most
part[4] continues to use only vocal music. In the Western church as well,
the use of instruments has been opposed from time to time, both before
and since the 16th century Reformation. Until recently, a fairly large
number of evangelical groups in America (e.g., the Free Methodist
Church, "primitive Baptists," "old Mennonites," and certain Presbyterian bodies) perpetuated the "no instrument" practice, but the antagonism is waning. At the present time, the prohibition is most
conspicuously continued and defended by certain Churches of Christ,
whose leaders argue that they must adhere strictly to what the New
Testament authorizes.

Even in the Old Testament tradition of Jewish liturgy, we do not find
any rubric of music practice. We do read that in the Mosaic period, God
gave specific instructions regarding the sacrificial offerings and other
liturgical acts. In Numbers 10:1,2 it is recorded:

> And the Lord spoke unto Moses, saying, Make thee two trumpets of
> silver; of a whole piece shalt thou make them, that thou mayest use
> them for the calling of the assembly, and for the journeying of the
> camps. (KJV)

We presume that these trumpets were more loud than lovely; their purpose, like the trumpet in ancient warfare, was to get the attention of the
entire nation of Israel, who were encamped over a large area. The full
vocal-instrumental glory of formal Hebrew worship seemed to emerge
with the musician-king David (see I Chron. 13:1–8), and the record
simply says, "And David spake to the chief of the Levites to appoint their
brethren to be singers with the instruments of music . . ." (I Chron.
15:16). Evidently there was no divine command or permission, just
David's own creative initiative!

It is difficult to find a negative word about musical art in the Bible.
The prophet Amos does utter scathing words about pleasure-loving

2. MigneG XXIII, 1171; WagE I, 12. Quoted in Reese, ibid., p. 62.
3. MigneL XXXVII, 1953; Nicene and Post-N, Ser. 1, VIII, 678. Quoted in Reese, ibid.,
    p. 64.
4. Recently, the Greek Orthodox Church in America has begun to use the organ.

leaders of Israel in the eighth century B.C., who evidently included some musicians.

> Woe to them that are at ease in Zion . . that lie upon beds of ivory, and stretch themselves upon their couches, and eat the lambs out of the flock, and the calves out of the midst of the stall; that chant to the sound of the viol, and invent to themselves instruments of music, like David; that drink wine in bowls, and anoint themselves with the chief ointments; but they are not grieved for the affliction of Joseph.   (Amos 6:1a, 4-6, KJV)

This might be construed to be an indictment of entertainment music, except that it is also negative about other normal actions like eating and drinking and anointing the body. We know from other Old Testament passages that the Hebrews used music to accompany the ordinary and the festive occasions of secular life[5] (if any lawful activity in a theocracy can be called "secular"). It seems obvious then that Amos's condemnation is for indolence, living in luxury and not caring for God's people.

Those who look for scriptural authority for church music usually point to the New Testament and the activities of the early Christian Church. Here again we find no regulations—only a few sketchy references to music's use. Jesus apparently participated in all the normal Jewish worship customs of his day, including the singing of psalms (Mark 14:26). The Apostle Paul speaks positively of the singing of "psalms, hymns and spiritual songs" in early Christian gatherings (Eph. 5:18, Col. 3:16).

It is true that *instrumental* worship music is not mentioned in the New Testament. Paul speaks disparagingly about "sounding brass" and a "tinkling cymbal" (I Cor. 13:1) which may have been the same "loud cymbals" and "high sounding cymbals" which are apparently authorized for worship of Jehovah in Psalm 150:5. These instruments which had played a large part in early Hebrew history were gradually eliminated from use during the period of the Second Temple; they were prominently associated with the practice of idolatry in Mesopotamia and even by heretical Jewish sects, and were therefore considered to be "unclean." Furthermore, since instruments were used only in connection with the sacrificial offerings, they had no place in the worship of the Jewish synagogue. We do know that after the destruction of the Second Temple (A.D. 70), Jews ceased the practice of sacrificial worship and banned the use of all instruments; some authorities see the latter as a symbol of national mourning, and others cite a growing suspicion of instrumental music, because it figured prominently in the rituals of the mystery cults of the middle-east.

---

5. For instance, a song for the digging of a well (Num. 21:17-18), a war song from the conquest of Canaan (Judges 5:19-31), David's lament over the deaths of Saul and Jonathan (II Sam. 1:19-27), a song of harvest celebration (Psa. 4:7 and Isa. 9:3), and a song for wine making (Jer. 25:30).

For all these reasons, first century Christians simply did not consider the possibility that instruments could be functional in their worship life. However, the scriptures neither approve the introduction of instruments or their banishment from worship. And John the Divine sees both trumpets and harps in his eschatological vision recorded in the Revelation (8:2; 14:2).

In all of scripture, the idea of "beauty" is never associated with music; it is, in fact, limited to visual experiences (e.g., "beautiful" face). Music is obviously important in its functioning but it is described as "pleasant" and "agreeable"—words which connote almost more ethics than aesthetics. It is interesting to note that in the long description of the First Temple and its ritual (I Kings, chapters five through eight) the word "beautiful" is never used.

It seems clear that any argument about the specifics of church music style that is based on biblical authority is extremely tenuous—there is simply no definitive or consistent word. The Bible clearly sets forth a theology of worship and of ministry. But it does not defend any particular culture, nor is it a manual of acceptable worship aesthetics. There are no more divine directions for musicians (the successors of Jubal) than there are for those who practice animal husbandry (the successors of Jabal) (Gen. 4:20). As noted before, the scriptures give sketchy reports of man's use of music over a period of thousands of years. It is remarkable to note that our experiences of worship music are not too different from those in ancient times.[6] To me, this says that God has given creative gifts to all peoples throughout history, and with those gifts a common wisdom for their use.

The Authority of the Individual Believer.

Where then lies the authority for church music? We could argue that in a non-hierarchical, non-liturgical, evangelical tradition, it rests with individual worshipers. Because meaningful listening and participation are also creative acts, believer-priests are the "final artists" who take the available materials (hymns, choral and instrumental music, sermon, scripture and prayers) and fashion for themselves a worship experience. The individual exercises authority when choosing a church on the basis of its style of worship—whether "high church," "low church" or charismatic, structured or improvised, choral or congregational, spectatorist or "involved." We may add (and this is an implied scriptural standard) that we have an obligation to find a church within our cultural norm that offers an opportunity to worship "in spirit and in truth." But this involves a degree of cultural knowledge, self-knowledge and spiritual discernment which is rare. Most people will argue that they "know what they like" when the truth is "they like and accept what they know." The tendency then is to look for a church which offers "familiar" worship experiences rather than one which will present opportunities for

6. See Chapter VI.

growth. Mature believers will find a fellowship which is "open" in spirit, and allow it to enlarge their own horizons in music experiences.

The Authority of Church Leadership.

In fellowships where adherence to a prescribed liturgy is expected, the planning of worship standards and materials is assigned to a liturgical commission, and administrative decisions are made by a bishop or some similar official. In most evangelical churches, authority in church music is vested in the leadership of each congregation. Within this authority and responsibility, the pastor and church music director choose the hymns, plan and lead worship services, and develop the congregation's musical talents. To do this well, it is necessary that both pastor and music leader understand the traditions of that church in theology and worship practice, and their relationship both to scripture and to the customs of other Christian communions; they should also be familiar with the fundamental issues of "musicultural" communication. The musicians, in addition, must possess adequate resources in talent and training, to prepare them to select proper music materials and to train the congregation, as well as the vocal and instrumental specialists, to perform it.

In an evangelical church with congregational polity, the individual church member still retains final authority. It is best exercised through a music (or a worship) committee who are chosen on the basis of their ability to understand the perspectives and goals of the church leadership and to evaluate their progress toward those goals.

The Professional Ministry of Music

In our own day, the concept of a professional ministry of music has been adopted by many evangelical churches. While choir singers and incidental instrumentalists are usually unpaid talented volunteers, music directors are often compensated for their tasks of planning, supervising, training and conducting. In some instances, the leadership is part-time; in others it is full-time. Because of evangelicalism's unique emphases, the music ministry usually encompasses "spiritual" (pastoral, prophetic and pedagogical) leadership as well as musical. It also emphasizes the role of the congregation as well as that of the choir and other musical specialists.

In the remainder of this chapter, I will review briefly the history of "professional music ministry" in the Christian heritage and discuss the roles of the "minister of music" today, considering some of the problems faced in filling those roles.

History.

In the sacrificial temple worship of the Old Testament, music was professional—the work of talented, trained and "ordained" directors, singers and instrumentalists of the Levitic tribe. Later in history, in the synagogue tradition both in Old and New Testament times, musical worship was still largely professional, though usually soloistic and always vocal. The early worship music of the Christian Church was completely congregational, so far as we can tell. However, following the spread of Christianity throughout the Western world, the increasing power and sophistication of the church was accompanied by the development of trained choirs and music leaders.

Church history records that about the fifth century congregational singing was largely eliminated in Christian worship, and the music was given to choirs made up of the clergy, in the interest of orderly procedure and to prevent the introduction of heretical hymns[7] in worship gatherings. This was only one indication of the transformation of the church from a small group of persecuted believers who engaged in simple worship and a simple life style, to a powerful political organization which represented the official religion of the Roman empire, and adopted the outward symbols of authority which were previously associated only with the emperor and his governors. Theologically, the Church returned to much of its Jewish heritage, particularly in adopting a hierarchy of priesthood, in viewing the Eucharist as a sacrifice, and using the symbols of worship common to the Hebrews—vestments, sanctuary design and furniture, and liturgical actions. It is believed that the *Schola Cantorum* was founded (or possibly reorganized) by St. Gregory (590–605) as the papal center for propagating and teaching the official church chant. From Rome the musician-priests were sent to churches and monasteries throughout the Christian world.

At the time of the Reformation, Calvin abolished church choirs, and they have never returned to a position of significance in French protestant worship. However, in the Lutheran tradition, and partly because Martin Luther loved the historic Church's music, the choir was retained to sing the main parts of the service and to lead the congregational chorales. Choral training was provided in the parochial and the cathedral schools, and also in the secular Kantorei choirs.

Anglicans tended to follow the Lutheran standard. Once the Book of Common Prayer was established (1549), the 16th century composers (e.g., William Byrd, Thomas Tallis and Orlando Gibbons) composed settings of the services of Morning and Evening Prayer as they had previously composed masses and motets for Roman Catholic worship. Although many parish churches had only congregational song, the choir schools continued without much change in the cathedrals, the collegiate chapels and the Royal Chapel. As the "principal" in another school was called "master of the boys," the head of the music school was known as the "choirmaster."

For many years of the "free church tradition"—the groups which left the established state churches beginning in the late 16th century—choirs

7. The use of "Arian" hymns in the third and fourth centuries contributed to the theological battle concerning the personhood of Christ, which led to the formulation of the Nicene Creed.

and their leaders were shunned as "popish." The only musical leadership—as it was in early Calvinist worship—was the "precentor" who announced the psalms (and later, the hymns), set the pitch, and sometimes "lined them out" phrase by phrase, to be repeated by the congregation. The one notable exception to such musical austerity was provided by the Moravians. Originally a pietist movement within the established churches of Europe, it eventually became a separate church which is recognized as one of the early sponsors of missionary activity. Particularly in the late 18th century, their composers developed a large body of fine choral music. They were also noted for their use of *posaunenchöre* (trombone choirs) in worship.

Early American churches followed much the same patterns as their European forebears. The precentor was a familiar figure in lining out the psalms, and later, the hymns of Watts and Wesley. In the 19th century, the Protestant Episcopal church led in the development of a professional ministry, possibly because their liturgy necessitated the use of choirs to lead the congregation in singing the psalms and canticles in Anglican chant.[8] In major cities, most large congregations followed the Episcopalian example in the use of a choir to lead the hymns and to sing an anthem in the service. In all except the largest churches, the "music director" was "part-time" though often compensated. In the later 19th century, a "quartet-choir" became the "pattern of prestige"— professional soprano, alto, tenor and bass soloists struggled to lead the congregation in the hymns, and frequently seemed to try to outsing each other in the anthems and responses!

In the late 19th century, the evangelistic campaigns which centered in the ministry of Dwight Lyman Moody and his soloist/song leader Ira D. Sankey had a marked influence on the groups which supported them. Many churches adopted the revivalist pattern for worship, with a "songleader" who physically directed the congregational hymns as well as the choir selections, and often sang a solo, usually just preceding the sermon. By this time, public school music education was helping to improve the singing of amateur choirs in the larger towns and cities. In rural America, "singing schools"—often conducted by itinerant musicians—contributed largely to the training of singers and the development of church music leadership.

With the 20th century, the popularity of the quartet-choir waned. A few of the largest-and-richest churches employed a full professional choir, but most returned to a "volunteer" chorus, possibly with a "paid quartet" to lead the sections and sing the solos. In the early years of this century, the concept of "graded choirs" appeared, generally associated with the founding of Westminster Choir College by John Finley Williamson. (Actually, children's choirs had appeared much earlier, even in such unsophisticated surroundings as the Moody Tabernacle in

---

8. This was especially true after the Oxford Movement in England (ca. 1840) brought a revival of interest in the liturgical heritage of the mother church.

Chicago.[9]) The graded choir program became the basis of a full-time ministry of music in many "free" churches, and Westminster supplied many of their musicians. Several other schools developed professional church music curricula, notably Union Theological Seminary (N.Y.) and Northwestern University. For the Episcopal communion, Canon Charles Winfred Douglas established the annual Evergreen Conference in Colorado, and provided both motivation and instruction through his many writings and lectureships. For the church which emphasized the evangelistic, gospel-song tradition, religious schools like Moody Bible Institute set the pattern and offered training, mostly for laypersons.

The strongest impetus for evangelicals to move to a professional ministry of music came at the end of the Second World War. Professional organizations dedicated to the improving of church music were formed and remain active in various denominational bodies; they usually publish educational materials or conduct a periodical church music conference, or both. The Fellowship of United Methodist Musicians has published *The Music Ministry* and meets annually. The Fellowship of American Baptist Musicians convenes at Green Lake, Wisconsin every summer; they also receive a newsletter which is a part of a special FABM edition of *Journal of Church Music,* published by Fortress Press, a subsidiary of the Lutheran Church in America. The Lutheran Society for Worship, Music and the Arts releases a periodical bulletin and publishes the magazine *Response. Church Music* is another Lutheran magazine, published by Concordia. Presbyterians conduct a national church music conference annually at Montreat, North Carolina; the Presbyterian Association of Musicians cooperates with the two largest Presbyterian bodies in publishing the journal, *Reformed Liturgy and Music.* The National Church Music Fellowship was organized in 1952 by leaders in Bible schools and colleges who were concerned with the church music needs of smaller conservative denominations and of churches which consider themselves to be nondenominational; they too conduct an annual convention and distribute a newsletter. All of these organizations give significant help and guidance to both full and part-time directors of church music activities. Together with the impact of the burgeoning church music curricula in Bible schools, colleges, universities and seminaries, they encourage more and more churches to move toward engaging a full-time professional minister of music.

Perhaps the most dramatic growth and development in church music during the last generation has been experienced by Southern Baptists. In 1952 their Church Music Department was organized as a part of the Sunday School Board of the Southern Baptist Convention. The department regularly publishes eight magazines: *The Music Leader, Music Makers, Young Musicians, Opus One, Opus Two, Gospel Choir, Choral Praise,* and *The Church Musician.* It also conducts annual Church Music Leadership

9. The New Orleans Baptist Theological Seminary owns a reed organ which was played by the late teacher-author E. O. Sellers in accompanying the children's choir in the Moody Tabernacle between 1910 and 1920.

Conferences at the denomination's assemblies at Ridgecrest, North Carolina and Glorieta, New Mexico, as well as many other specialized conferences at their headquarters in Nashville, Tennessee. The Church Music Department also assists in the development of local church music activities, working through state music secretaries. These individuals plan music institutes, workshops and festivals, and generally assist churches in obtaining musical leadership and in improving the contribution of each individual musician. Much of their work is done through local Baptist associations, headed by local ministers of music.

Baptist seminaries in Wake Forest (N.C.), Louisville (Ky.), Fort Worth (Tex.), New Orleans (La.) and San Francisco (Calif.) are at present training some eight hundred graduate music students each year, most of whom are preparing to be ministers of music in Southern Baptist churches. Baptist colleges and universities train many more in graduate and undergraduate programs. At the present time, according to the records of the Church Music Department, 3500 of the 33,000 Southern Baptist Churches employ a full-time Minister of Music. In addition to all this, the Southern Baptist Church Music Conference brings together representatives of the Church Music Department, institutional music educators and local ministers of music in an annual conference, and releases papers presented at their meetings.

The Minister of Music: a Professional Musician.

Since the ministry of music is comparatively a new profession, many church members have little understanding of what the work entails. The average churchgoer sees a music director in action from one to three hours a week, and may wonder how there can be enough activity to warrant a full-time appointment. On the other hand, active ministers of music complain that there are not enough hours in their normal six-day work-week to accomplish what needs to be done. The musician who serves in the church fills not just one, but many professional roles.

Ministers of music are *professional musicians,* leaders and promoters of music in the church and in the community. They are *performers,* sometimes serving as church organist, sometimes as a vocal soloist, or playing the piano or some other instrument. They are always conductors, capable of working with singers and instrumentalists of all ages, and in the music of many different styles. Increasingly, they are also expected to understand the use of dramatic action and staging and to be able to relate both to the production of sacred music drama, opera or musicals.

It may be helpful to see music ministers principally as *music educators* who work in the context of the church. Like their counterpart in public school education, they teach (or supervise the teaching of) young children to produce good vocal sounds and to read musical symbols; frequently the internationally-recognized Orff and/or Kodaly techniques are the methods used for earliest music education. The training aspect of church music continues at every age level. Older youth learn proper techniques of vocalization, plus intonation; some music ministers give private voice lessons to choir members. Both youth and adults learn to understand and to sing music of many different styles with proper blend and variety of tone color, and with precision of ensemble.

The Minister of Music: a Professional Administrator.

In the context of our growing churches, ministers of music must also exercise the skills of an *administrator*. They will have an office and a music library, and ideally, their own budget for music and performance costs. They work with other ministers in the church, and frequently with church committees. They supervise the activities of a secretary, of assistant directors (if one person cannot conduct all the groups), and of choir "parents" or sponsors.

One of the principal tasks of a music minister is the marshaling and developing of all the musical talent in a church family. It is necessary to constantly recruit new members for all the choirs, and also to develop instrumental groups, insofar as that capability is present in the church. Individuals who have had little training but who are instinctively musical can develop a new instrumental skill through handbell choirs, which are becoming increasingly popular.

Ministers of music also plan the music for all the regular and special services of the church. They may be expected to choose congregational hymns for Sunday services; hopefully the preaching minister will also share that task, so that each service will be integrated and move with dramatic unity and effectiveness toward its particular goals. Special musical presentations (cantatas, hymn sings, hymn festivals, musicals, music dramas, recitals, festival services) have long been a part of a music ministry, and they must be planned, rehearsed and presented. In our day, some churches send their youth choirs on tour, often with a missions goal; music ministers must usually assume the booking and financing responsibilities for such ventures. Finally, they must enthusiastically support the very-important social activities for choirs of all ages.

The Minister of Music: a Professional Minister.

The term "minister of music" first appeared earlier in this century, but its high popularity came with the burgeoning of church music programs about 1945–1950. Even now, its implications may not be fully understood. In the early 1950's one of my former students, who was serving a church in such a capacity, wrote me: "In Ephesians 4:11–12 Paul lists the ministries God has given his church. Where does music fit in?" It is a good question, and it sent me back to study the passage.

> And his gifts were that some should be apostles, some prophets, some evangelists, some pastors and teachers, for the equipment of the saints, for the work of ministry, for building up the body of Christ.

No doubt the titles "apostle," "prophet," "evangelist" and "pastor-teacher" denoted specific roles in the first century church. With the possible exception of "apostle," they also represent ministries common in today's churches, all of which can be shared by a church music program. If musicians use their talents in these ways and feel called of God to serve in the church, they may well be called "ministers of music."

In the general New Testament sense, a *prophet* is not a foreteller—a divine Jeanne Dixon!—but rather a "forth-teller," one who brings the Word of God to others. The best church music has always been saturated with the holy scriptures and frequently quotes them verbatim. This means that musicians should consider themselves to be "musical prophets" who are as concerned with the words of hymns and anthems as they are with their music. To be true to their calling, they must choose texts that bring the *whole Word to the whole person,* and they will equip themselves theologically to do this. They will use every means at their disposal to increase the knowledge of the musical Word in the congregation. This probably means that they will occasionally "break the bread of life" in the anthem text, explaining it verbally in the choir rehearsal (sometimes even in the corporate worship service), or in writing in the church bulletin. Again, as worship leaders, they will ensure that the services they plan offer the opportunity for a "whole response" to the "whole Word."

Thoughtful musical prophets will also understand that music, like speech, is a language; it should be intelligible to those who are expected to participate and respond. They will remember that languages change from generation to generation, and that just as we need new versions of Scripture and new phrases and modes in preaching, we need new expressions of music. If they are realistic, they will not bow too long at the shrine of any current style, for what we praise today we may ridicule tomorrow and reclaim the day after. Finally, if they feel that the hymn texts common to their fellowship do not provide a healthy singing diet, or that their musical settings do not really help to make the words more meaningful, they will speak to their people as prophets, and help them find alternatives.

An *evangelist* is a prophet with a specific message—of our sin and estrangement, and of God's love and grace which provides salvation. Some musicians have felt constrained to dedicate their talents exclusively to traditional or contemporary modes of witnessing and evangelism; their ministry is dealt with elsewhere in this volume. Today's ministers of music in the local church should also see themselves as evangelists. They should be prepared to address another person with a simple, personal witness to "the old, old story." Furthermore, the solo or the invitation hymn may be the direct tool of the Holy Spirit in achieving a positive response and a decision that leads to Christian discipleship.

The graded choir program, too, contributes to evangelism and church growth. Young children are attracted by the musical activity, learn to sing the truths of God, and often come rather easily and naturally to personal faith. The recent acceptance of contemporary youth musicals by skeptical adults was no doubt due in part to the music's potential in attracting young people to the church. There is strong appeal in the opportunity of amateur "show-business," in which many teens see themselves in the image of John Denver, Joan Baez, or Jimmy Brown. Faithful music ministers will see that the deeper message is not lost in the music or in its performing, and that each singer and instrumentalist (as well as each member of the audience) is confronted with the claims of Christ.

In the evangelical sense all believers are priests, because they speak to God directly for themselves, and also because they pray for others. Similarly, every Christian is in a sense a *pastor*—a shepherd—caring for the needs of others. Ministers of music have a responsibility to show love and special concern for the members of their musical groups, giving counsel when it is needed, visiting them in their homes or in the hospital, and standing by them in the occasions of celebration as well as in the times of crisis and sorrow. In a larger sense, because music is said to be "the language of the emotions," they minister to the spiritual/emotional needs of the whole congregation through hymns, anthems, solos, and instrumental music. Music helps to heal the human spirit; the church musician can learn something of this ministry from the science of music therapy, using the art in working with children or with geriatrics, with the physically and emotionally handicapped or with comparatively healthy persons.

We have already said that a central role for today's ministers of music is that of a *teacher*. They are involved in *Christian education* as well as in music education. They achieve the same satisfaction as the public school or college music teacher in developing the musical gifts and tastes of others. But they also affect young lives in a more significant way when they teach worship and churchmanship. In choosing music with strong scriptural texts, they teach theology and discipleship. They dramatize the Christian challenge to live and to worship creatively, and perhaps most importantly, they teach stewardship of life and of talent. God has a prior claim on a Christian's musical gifts; he expects us to develop them to the utmost, and to use them for his glory. This lesson should be taught in the home, but also in the church, the family of God.

Nowhere in the New Testament is there specific authorization for a Christian to serve God in the professional ministry of music. But if musicians respond to the challenge to give their time and their talents to the service of God in the church, they will find themselves challenged to function in four of the roles mentioned in Ephesians chapter four—as a prophet, an evangelist, a pastor and a teacher.

Moreover—if I may be permitted to reconsider my exegesis—there are some in our day who serve musically in foreign lands, and they may be said to "follow in the train" of the *apostles*, the first missionaries! In this latter half of the 20th century an increasing number of musicians have chosen missions as their field of service. They function in all the ways mentioned in this chapter. In addition, they help the emerging churches around the world to develop their own indigenous expressions of musical worship. We have given space to a discussion of this specific ministry in another part of this book.

Full-time or Part Time?

For many years in most churches of the evangelical movement, it was commonly held (and was consonant with "lay priest" theology) that the ministry of music was performed by laypersons, without compensation[10] and "in their spare time." This was as true of choir leaders and organists as it was of individual choir members. After all, Sunday School teachers are not paid—not even the Sunday School superintendent—so why should musicians be compensated? We can have no quarrel with that arrangement if the "spare" time available is enough to meet the needs of the church. Many part-time music directors are giving extraordinary, effective leadership. All of the principles expressed in this chapter (regarding music and ministry) are the same, whether the individual is paid or not, whether the full week is given to the work or only a few hours evenings and on Sunday.

More recently it has been generally agreed that competent music leadership requires special expertise (and special education—at considerable expense) that merits compensation. Moreover, no individual can contribute as much—either as a musician or as the preaching pastor—if his time is limited by the necessity of making a living in another vocation. In our day, many churches have felt that the potential "music ministry" was significant enough to engage a full-time individual to give it leadership. That person is able to fulfill most completely the challenge to be an effective prophet-evangelist-pastor-teacher-musician and deserves to be called a "minister of music."

Short Term or Life Time?

Not all churches who engage a minister of music are fully aware of the perameters of a "complete" ministry or of their responsibility in calling a trained musician. Sometimes the action is a desperate effort to solve the problem of obtaining competent, dependable choir leadership. Often the candidate is a young person, just graduated from college or Bible school. In many situations, the music service is tacitly understood to be a sort of an "internship" in preparation for another, more significant ministry. The church has only enough budget money to support a 25-year-old; in a very few years another young person is sought for the same low compensation. The problems this procedure creates should be obvious. First, the church fails to receive the *mature* ministry of trained and experienced musicians—because they are forced to move into other fields which offer more adequate compensation. Second, the young persons (whose principal preparation was in music) must enter other voca-

10. In some fellowships, even today, the "preacher" too is unsalaried!

tions for which they are not adequately trained. The investment in music education is at least partially wasted and it is rather late in life to prepare for other forms of work.

How then can the evangelical community meet this challenge? What is a fair salary for a music minister? First, compensation should be geared to the needs of a person in the economic culture of the church involved. A full-time minister of music should certainly receive as much salary as a comparably trained public school music teacher who is employed eleven months a year. Second, within the available positions in a denominational fellowship, it should be possible to serve without undue hardship over an entire lifetime, including the years in which the minister may have children in college. Finally, a church musician should be treated as a "professional" who has certain special needs of continuing education.

Combining Ministries.

No doubt there are some evangelical church musicians who are not convinced that they should be "ministers" as well. However, in evangelical theology every Christian is a minister—a prophet (witness), a priest (intercessor) and a pastor (expressing concern and help) to all persons with whom he or she comes in contact. Recently a number of churches have added a new listing to their outdoor bulletin boards: Ministers—All the Congregation. Certainly it will be expected that "ministers of music" will fulfill these functions even more fully than the average Christian, especially in their relationship to the singers and instrumentalists who serve with them. The amount of time one spends, and the specific ministries which one may want to emphasize, should be determined by agreement with the senior minister and the personnel committee of the church. Ideally, that agreement will be based on each person's gifts and interests.

In some instances, the church position is acknowledged to be a dual ministry, in which the musician has administrative responsibility in a second area. Frequently this arrangement is indicated in the job title— Minister of Music and Education, Minister of Music and Youth, Associate Pastor and Minister of Music (if the individual has major responsibilities in visiting, counseling or preaching), Minister of Music and Evangelism, or even Minister of Music and Administration.

It must be admitted that, particularly in a large church, it is difficult to fill two administrative posts well. The time one spends to develop Christian education cannot be used in developing music, and vice versa. Besides, a musician has unusual pressures because of the need to keep performance skills sharp, and to stay abreast of the ever-changing trends in church music literature and activity.

Challenges Relating to a Philosophy of Church Music.

Because of the distinctive heritage of evangelicalism, there are a number of problems relating to a philosophy of church music which will impinge on the happiness and the success of the professional minister of music.

I believe it is important to understand the concepts of church music as "ministry" and as "functional art," as outlined here and in the earlier chapters of this book. Still, church musicians may find that they live in a sort of perpetual schizophrenia, because they use music to meet the needs of a congregation that does not fully meet their own aesthetic standards. We might remind ourselves that foreign missionaries live in this same tension—they are not really a part of the culture in which they work. It may also help to remember that we are more *educators* than performing artists, and that public school music teachers may experience the same type of frustration. Like the school teacher, our objective is the personal and musical development of our choir members—as well as communication to the worshiper in the pew. The mature minister will evaluate music "performances" in that light.

Even when they possess a dedication to ministry and a willingness to "bring to the cross" their own aesthetic desires, ministers of music should carefully read the "frame of mind" of the church in which they are asked to serve. Unfortunately, few of our "free" church seminaries give future pastors training in music, to help them understand the challenges and frustrations faced by a minister of music. In a time of tension that may occur in a "growth through education" situation, the pastor may possibly align himself with the critical congregation against the musician. Prospective music ministers should discuss their philosophy and goals thoroughly with the senior minister and/or the personnel committee to whom they are responsible. Some congregations see church music as "entertainment," others as "service performance." If ministers of music feel that their primary challenges are ministry and education—the personal, spiritual and musical development of all the individual church members—they should come to that agreement with the individuals to whom they are responsible.

Just as there are many different cultures among Christians worldwide, there are many different subcultures among American evangelicals. Again, some congregations (and pastors) are more open to change and growth than others. It would be wise for music ministers to accept the call of a church in which they would be most at home, and in which they may expect to serve as "agents for change."

Administrative Relationships.

There are always potential pitfalls for ministers of music in staff (or team) relationships. In candidating for a position, they will soon learn that there are several different administrative "styles" common to evangelical churches. In some, the "senior minister" (the preacher/pastor) sees himself as *the* minister, with all other members of "the staff" appointed as "assistants" to him, contributing to his goals in doing the work of the church. This individual usually runs the church in military style,

with important decisions often made unilaterally and in a rather authoritarian fashion.

This type of minister usually looks for a musician to "solve the music
problems" in the church—which generally means to provide talent for
all the services, and to enroll as many people as possible in the church
choirs. Although (and possibly because) he has not been trained in
church music or in worship, this pastor is not willing to sit down with the
music minister to discuss music's full contribution to the church, or the
format and details of the Sunday worship services. As long as things go
smoothly, he leaves the musicians alone to "do their own thing." But
when someone in the congregation complains about the hymn choices or
the "strange" new anthem, he will be quick to mention this to the music
minister, with the inference that it would be better to "play safe." At the
same time, he may mention his personal musical preferences and prejudices!

Another type of senior minister communicates the idea of a "shared
ministry" to the members of his "team." They are all ministering to the
congregation and community, each in areas of special expertise. There
are frequent times of free discussion so that each might understand the
basic philosophies and practices of the others. Of course, the senior
minister is *captain* of the team; in most churches, one administrative
individual must be finally responsible to the deacons, the trustees or the
"session." But he also works with other ministers in a *peer* relationship
which engenders the spirit of "sharing." In times of tension due to congregational criticism, this pastor supports his team members until he is
thoroughly convinced that their positions are unwise.

It seems to me that the latter style of administration should contribute
most to a healthy church as well as to the serenity and fulfillment of each
member of the ministry team. It should also have a strong positive impact on the planning of worship experiences. This preacher/pastor and
the minister of music will share their concepts of worship, and agree on
common goals for each service. There will be careful planning be-
forehand, and thorough evaluation afterward. In this relationship, each
learns from the other, and the congregation can expect that worship will
be spiritually "whole"—healthy and fruitful.

It may be that some music ministers prefer to work with an authoritarian pastor; I have several acquaintances who seem to thrive in such
situations. In any case, the prospective minister of music should ascer-
tain the administrative style of the senior minister, before accepting a call
to a church. If it does not become apparent in casual conversation, there
should be frank discussion. It is not likely that established patterns of
administration will change after the music minister arrives at the new
post.

The Challenge of Continued Personal Growth.

It is also very important that professional church musicians work to
keep their consciences alert and their minds open in all aspects of their

ministry. Occasionally individuals will grow in one aspect of the role and will "lose faith" in another. One person may neglect "musical growth" and settle for just "pleasing" the congregation; the argument that this demonstrates a fuller commitment to "ministry" may be an honest (if misguided) rationalization. Another will become completely engrossed in the musical chores, to the neglect of personal spiritual growth and a full spiritual ministry to the congregation. All Christian ministers need to keep their own worship life fresh and renewed. Church musicians may also need to take additional studies in ministry areas in which they are most involved—perhaps in counseling, in group dynamics, in youth work or in Christian education.

The temptation may be even stronger to relax in the area of one's musical development, particularly if the prevailing church culture places no great demand on the individual's resources. It is easy to settle into a routine that requires little discipline—hurriedly preparing an anthem for the following Sunday, or repeating one that has been sung too many times before, because the "audience likes it." Music ministers must continue to improve their specialized skills—as conductors and/or singers or instrumentalists—if they are to be happy with themselves, and fulfill their responsibility as Christian stewards of talent and of training. There needs to be regular time to study and practice, as well as to survey new literature and hear great music performances, both in person and by recording. No doubt it will also be necessary to continue investigating the theology and structure of corporate worship as well as the philosophy and practice of church music in all its various expressions.

Ministers of music can determine their own growth and effectiveness partly by measuring the growth of their congregations. It may be wise to take an annual (or bi-annual) inventory based on these questions:

1. Is our worship mature, with preaching and music that covers the full spectrum of Christian truth? Is it fresh and vital each week? Is it being received "with grace?" Is it resulting in more mature Christian discipleship?
2. Is our church truly evangelistic? Are we bringing the children and youth in the congregation and choirs to Christian decision? Are we reaching the uncommitted in our community? Is music making its own unique contribution to "winning the lost?"
3. Is the congregation singing better—with full participation, learning new hymns regularly, and with evident comprehension of the hymns' texts?
4. Are the choirs and congregation finding meaning in a constantly broader range of church music, enjoying new styles as well as new works in the old styles?
5. Are choirs singing with better tone than before? Do they sightread a little better? Have they grown in other aspects of musicianship?
6. Are we utilizing all the potential musical resources in the church? Are we developing the musicianship of each person?

It is safe to say that enthusiastic, dedicated music ministers can achieve any reasonable goal within their musical horizons if they begin with love of the people and of the work of God, and if they pursue their dream with optimism, humility, some persistence and a little talent!

The Question of Ordination.

One question which has increasingly arisen in interviews with prospective ministers of music is whether or not they should be "ordained to the ministry." (Of course, the same issue is often raised with ministers of education, or ministers of any other specialization in the church.) The answer is usually based on theological opinion, and many denominations or individual congregations have their own beliefs and established polity in the matter. This discussion will set forth my own convictions, and may be helpful to those whose churches have freedom in this regard.

The significance of ordination in "free" churches is not so weighty as it is in liturgical communions, where the minister is a "priest" who administers sacraments.[11] Evangelical groups—while maintaining the idea that each believer is a priest—follow New Testament practice in "laying hands" on individuals who are devoting themselves full-time to "ministry." The action signifies "setting the minister apart"—acknowledgment by a church or a denomination that the individual is "called by God" to do the work of ministry. Admittedly, in New Testament times "ministry" was apparently limited to "preaching, teaching and pastoring, as set forth in Ephesians 4:11,12. In our day of increasing specialization, there are many who feel that ordination need not be so limited. Others want to *define* the ordination clearly, setting apart one person "to the gospel ministry" and another to the "ministry of music" or the "ministry of Christian education."

The issue also brings into focus the questions of whether or not a woman may serve as a "minister of music" and whether or not a woman might be ordained. Traditionally, there has been considerable resistance among some evangelicals to both possibilities and probably for one reason—there is objection, on personal or on scriptural grounds, to a "woman minister." It is interesting to note that some pastors have no problem working with a part-time "director of music" who is a woman, but they would not consider her as a candidate for a full-time position as "minister of music!"

Without delineating the theological rationale, and while confessing some entrenched male-chauvinist prejudice, I must declare my kinship with those who believe that a person may be active in the ministry of the church who is called of God and is dedicated to that ministry, whether man or woman. Furthermore, if that person is a musician who senses the full spiritual significance of the calling and is personally challenged to such a

---

11. The famed English Baptist preacher C. H. Spurgeon spurned ordination for himself. Some evangelical fellowships (like the Plymouth Brethren) never practice it.

ministry, he or she may truly be called a "minister of music" and be ordained.

Preparation for the Ministry of Music.

It is apparent that the challenges of fully-prepared ministers of music are both many and large. They must be well-trained *musicians* and music educators, and must know the principles of administration. They must also be prepared as *church* musicians, understanding fully the essential contribution of this functional art to the service of God and the church. Finally, they must be *ministers* who know the basics of theology, and of the scriptures and their interpretation, and who understand the roles in which they serve the church family.

Training for such a demanding ministry must be both varied and comprehensive, and will probably require at least six years beyond high school. These are the disciplines which must be mastered:

Music—learning the basic art in its theory, its history and literature, and its performance (both in solo and in ensembles).

Music Education—learning the principles and practices of teaching music to various age groups.

Church Music—learning the philosophy and administration of church music, worship, hymnology, church music literature and history, conducting, service playing, Bible, theology and ministry.

Ideally a master's degree[12] should be achieved in the process of covering these study areas. Church musicians who have received that level of preparation and recognition will be assured that they are competent to serve with seminary-trained pastors, and will be less likely to consider leaving the ministry when the going gets difficult.

There are several educational routes commonly followed to this goal: (1) a Bible college education terminating in a B.Mus. in church music, followed by a master's program at a university; (2) a bachelor's in music followed by a M.Div. with a major in church music; or (3) a bachelor's in music, followed by a M.C.M. or M.S.M. in church music.[13]

Fortunately there are many means through which the ministers of music may amplify their training and improve their skills while continuing in the ministry year by year. These opportunities are particularly important for the individuals who have had less than optimum institutional schooling. Some of these are:

12. Some schools offer a doctorate with an emphasis on local church music ministry.
13. Each of these possibilities is available at different schools in America. The first (1) might be followed at Philadelphia College of Bible and then Temple University, and at many similar schools. The terminal study of the second (2) was formerly offered at California Baptist Theological Seminary (Covina, CA) and is being developed at Southeastern Baptist Theological Seminary (Wake Forest, NC). The last possibility (3) is the norm for graduates of Southern Baptist seminaries at Fort Worth, Louisville, New Orleans and San Francisco, as well as of Yale University's sacred music division (formerly located at the Union Theological Seminary in New York City.)

1. Short term courses or workshops at colleges, universities and seminaries, or conducted by church music organizations.
2. Conventions of professional organizations: denominational church music societies, American Choral Directors Association, Hymn Society of America, American Guild of Organists, Choristers Guild (children's church music), etc.
3. Periodicals released by the above organizations.
4. New books published in all the pertinent areas.

Summary

According to the accounts in today's books and journals, evangelical churches are enjoying a high degree of affluence, both in adherents and in financial income. Many more churches are able to consider the possibility of engaging a professional minister of music. However, it is also reported that many young Christian musicians are more interested in the possibility of a ministry in religious "show business," as a traveling performer and in the growing "electric church" whose congregations meet in front of the television set. I dare to suggest that their talents might be more completely used in the local church, that there might be better "job security," and that they might experience greater personal fulfillment, especially if they enjoy working with people "up close."

To the churches which may consider calling full-time ministers of music, I reiterate that they must give those persons full and enthusiastic support. They need *economic security* for themselves and their families throughout a lifetime of service. They also need *emotional security* in a mutually-open peer relationship with fellow ministers. Most of all, they need *professional security* in a mutual understanding of the type of ministry they are expected to lead. It is our conviction that the church is best served by a music program (1) which encourages optimum participation by the whole congregation, (2) which emphasizes the ministry *to* the singers and instrumentalists as fully as that which results from their performances, and (3) which gives priority to the principal meanings of functional church music rather than to its promotional value in providing pleasure and nostalgic emotional fulfillment for the congregation.

Young musicians tend to look for a ministry within their own fellowship or denomination. They will probably hesitate to consider a local church opportunity, unless there are a reasonable number of related churches to which they might be called during a lifetime of service. Even though evangelical churches are "free," they tend to follow their denominational leadership; consequently, the possibility for growth and effectiveness in church music is strongest when it has the full support of that larger fellowship. Such support is ideally centered in a church music department or commission, which would plan regular activities and publications and assist in the placement of musicians.

Hopefully, if evangelicals continue to flourish, we can look forward to the day when more of our seminaries will provide training in worship and related arts for all pastors. Perhaps some schools will also initiate graduate curricula for the preparation of professional church musicians.

Chapter V

CHRISTIAN WORSHIP: A DEFINITION AND SOME IMPLICATIONS FOR CHURCH MUSIC

In the preceding chapter, foundations were laid for understanding the perameters of a ministry of music in evangelical churches. It is appropriate now to center our attention on specific activities in which music has an important role, beginning with that which occupies the central "Christian hour" of the week—the worship service.

We cannot escape the probability that the acts of Christian worship are not meaningful to most Americans in our day. This is demonstrated by the fact that the majority of people never participate in worship from week to week, and also by the declining church rolls of established denominations. It is also revealed by the criticism of worship practices with which we are frequently confronted. A young Methodist theologian, in a book which espouses radical revision of traditional worship, begins with this story:[1]

> A circus parade was moving gaily through the streets of Milan, Italy. Suddenly one of the elephants veered from the line and marched into a church. This visitor wandered up the center aisle, trumpeted a bit, swung her trunk around and headed back to the parade.
> Unfortunately, many humans seem to imitate this pious pachyderm. On a Sunday morning we lurch into church, make a few noises, observe the congregation, then step out to resume our place in the parade. The great drama of worship is played out, but it is lost on us. We are elephants in church!

Recently, when a young person was asked to give an appraisal of his church's customary services, he said that "they seemed to him to be

1. David J. Randolph, *God's Party*, p. 40.

constantly-repeated rehearsals for a performance that never comes off!"
A few months ago, the front cover of a Presbyterian church bulletin in
Greenville, South Carolina carried this motto: "Too many Christians
worship their work, work at their play, and *play at their worship.*"

To be sure, in the last few years a great number of remedies have been
recommended and tried, most of them aimed at revising the forms of
worship. We have updated the language of scripture and hymns and
prayers, introduced a contemporary musical language, and substituted
"celebration" for the old atmosphere of awe and solemnity. But, with all
the modernization, many would-be worshipers find themselves left with
the same empty feeling. In the tradition of the wandering elephant, they
may have trumpeted with more syncopation and moved around with
better choreography, but they still resume their places in the daily
parade with no awareness that anything significant has happened to
them.

Certain evangelicals seem almost to be afraid of the word "worship."
In service style, they still live in the "revivalist" era which began about
1800; for them, worship is evangelistic preaching to "reach the lost." The
building where they meet is the "preaching place" and the service is the
"preaching service" even if it is called "worship." Others may have sermons which include *didache* as well as *kerygma,* yet still miss much of what
worship is intended to be—a full confrontation with the self-revealed
God of the scriptures, with ample opportunity to respond to him.

It is time once again to re-examine the scriptural and theological (as
well as anthropological and sociological) bases of our worship. If we do
so, we may be better prepared to reshape its forms and language, including its music, or to leave them as they are.

The Anthropological Need

Anthropology tells us that every person worships. Primitive societies
engage in ritual and sacrifice to something or someone that is transcendent
(*mysterium tremendum et fascinans*),[2] hoping to share in the life and power
of the transcendent entity and to prevent misfortune. Modern pagans
may not bow down to images of wood or stone, but they are fascinated
and dominated by other gods—possessions, pleasure, power, themselves
or their families—an extension of themselves. As I have often heard
Billy Graham say, "There is a God-shaped void in our hearts, but many
people try to fill it with other things."

The Christian Response

Christians have chosen to worship the God revealed in the Bible, responding affirmatively to his ancient command repeated by Christ,

---

2. The phrase is used by Rudolf Otto in *The Idea of the Holy.*

".. you shall love the Lord your God with all your heart, and with all your soul, and with all your mind, and with all your strength." (Mark 12:30) To aid us in such a consuming worship, God has revealed himself comprehensively. In the works of creation and in his mighty acts in history, he shows his power and sovereignty. In the God-man Jesus Christ, he reveals his goodness and his love for his creatures. In the written Word of God, through the witness of the Holy Spirit, he gives us a rationale upon which our faith rests.

Christian worship is our affirmative response to the self-revelation of the Triune God. Unlike the primitives, we are not seeking to know an obscure, frightening being in order to placate him. God makes and always continues to make the first move, showing himself in power and in love, inviting our response. In fact, worship is *any* and *every* worthy response to God. There is no point to a question raised by some evangelicals, whether it is more important to "express adoration of God" or to "witness and evangelize" in our communal gatherings. One act gives corporate voice to our inner commitment; the other is our outward expression of our love in obedience to Christ's second great command, ".. You shall love your neighbor as yourself." (Mark 12:31)

To worship is to think about God and to converse with him. To worship is to preach God's good news, and to minister to a hungry and hurting world in the name of Christ. To worship is to enjoy God's world with gratitude, since he made it for us. For the Christian, each act of life is an act of worship, when it is done with love that responds to the Father's love. For the believer, living should be constant worshiping, since worship may be said to provide the metabolism for spiritual life.

In this chapter we are principally concerned with the expression of worship which occurs when members of the "body of Christ" meet together in a church building—the *worship service*. That title itself witnesses that our distinction between ritual and service is artificial. A comparison of various scripture translations also demonstrates that the Bible shows no semantic distinction between "worship" and "service."[3] Worship is service. Service is worship.

It has been said that we meet together on Sunday morning to give one hour to God, as a token that all of life is his. That is the human part, but the worship service is even more. It is a microcosm of all salvation history, of the centuries of God's self-revealing and the invitation of our affirmative response.

A Biblical Example

Most worship theologians find a picture of worship in the Vision of the prophet Isaiah.

---

3. The Authorized Version of Romans 12:1 reads "present your bodies a living sacrifice, holy, acceptable unto God, which is your reasonable service." The New International Version (and most other new versions) translates it "which is your spiritual worship."

In the year of King Uzziah's death I saw the Lord seated on a throne, high and exalted, and the skirt of his robe filled the temple. About him were attendant seraphim, and each had six wings; one pair covered his face and one pair his feet, and one pair was spread in flight. They were calling ceaselessly to one another,
> Holy, holy, holy is the Lord of Hosts:
> the whole earth is full of his glory.

And as each one called, the threshold shook to its foundations, while the house was filled with smoke. Then I cried,
> Woe is me! I am lost, for I am a man of unclean lips and I dwell among a people of unclean lips; yet with these eyes I have seen the King, the Lord of Hosts.

Then one of the seraphim flew to me carrying in his hand a glowing coal which he had taken from the altar with a pair of tongs. He touched my mouth with it and said,
> See, this has touched your lips;
> your iniquity is removed, and your sin is wiped away.

Then I heard the Lord saying, Whom shall I send? Who will go for me? And I answered, Here am I; send me.

He said, Go and tell this people . . .

Then I asked, How long, O Lord? . . .
> (Isaiah 6:1-8, 9a, 11a, NEB)

Check this account of a single individual's worship experience against the anticipated events in a Sunday morning service, and also with the macrocosm of God's self-revelation and human response in all history.

1. The revealing of a transcendent God, all holy (v.3, "Holy, holy, holy," which is the basis of the historic church song, *Sanctus*), all powerful (v.4, "the threshold shook to its foundations") and still mysterious, inscrutable and incomprehensible ("the house was filled with smoke").
2. Seeing God as he is, we see ourselves as sinners—people "of unclean lips"—and confess the same (v.5).
3. God removes the sin and guilt, and individuals are reconciled to the holy One.
4. God calls for volunteers who will do his work in the world (v.8).
5. The cleansed and reconciled believers respond affirmatively (v.9).
6. The volunteers are commissioned to "Go and tell"; in doing so, they have a part in continuing the self-revelation of God.
7. In the continuing reality of the difficulties of life, the witnesses call on God for help (v. 11, "How long, O Lord?").

It is obvious from this passage that the central figure of the drama is not the worshiper, but the God who is worshiped. For the God of scripture is above all his creation, whose holiness is the standard against which we recognize our sinfulness, whose power is the answer to our impotence, and whose inscrutability challenges our best efforts to rationalize and to comprehend, and finally asks us to "accept by faith." "For as the heavens are higher than the earth, so are my ways higher than your ways, and my thoughts than your thoughts." (Isa. 55:9) In the ancient Anglo-Saxon tongue the word "worship" was "woerth-scipe" (later "worthship")—meaning to "ascribe supreme worth to God." The Christian chooses to worship the God of biblical revelation because he alone is "worthy."

Paul Hoon has pointed out that the concept of God's worth should not be the primary "point of departure" in expressing motivation for worship, because "the category of value in biblical thought is secondary to the categories of being, decision and action." Besides, he says, it is not a distinctively *Christian* idea; it is shared by other religions and philosophies. Finally, it denies the transcendence of God because it implies that the "initiative to worship lies with man .. who 'recognizes' and 'ascribes worth'."[4]

Each of us will agree that we can only know God's worth through his self-revelation in the Living Word, of whom the written word bears witness, and then only insofar as we have personally experienced Christ through the Holy Spirit. As Hoon says, "It is precisely the recital of, and engagement with, a particular history bound up with a particular Jew, in a particular land, at a particular time, that is the basis of Christian worship."

Evangelicals then may seem to be worshiping authentically when they emphasize God's redemptive work through Christ. However, we must contend that too much of our expression of redemption (especially in song) is man-centered rather than God-centered. It frequently speaks of our personal experience of God in salvation, without adequately revealing the God whom we may know and his purposes for us in the world. Worship is not a self-centered obsession with our sins, our experiences of God's grace or even with our holy desires. Worship is "preoccupation" with God, whose attributes qualify him to forgive and to cleanse, and enable him to regenerate and to transform!

Worship as Response

The character of our response to this "wholly other" God may be represented in the imagery of the six heavenly beings of Isaiah six. Some scholars have discerned them to include *reverence* ("one pair covered his face"), *humility* ("and one pair his feet") and *willing service* ("one pair was spread in flight.") Certainly these should be present in evangelical worship.

In this chapter we will consider corporate worship in terms of three actions of human response: *speaking, giving* and *becoming.*[5] And because

4. Paul Hoon, *The Integrity of Worship*, pp. 91-94.
5. These human responses are cited by many students of worship. I am especially indebted to the insights of Stephen Winward, as set forth in *The Reformation of Our Worship.*

the worship service is a microcosm of the relationship of revealing God to responding man throughout life, we offer a rebuttal to the argument that "worship is a repeated rehearsal for a performance that never comes off." Actually, the worship service should be a rehearsal for the continuing "performance" of the Christian life!

Worship is *conversation* between God and man, a dialogue that should go on constantly in the life of a Christian. The worship service is the beginning of that conversation; it should help us anticipate what God may communicate in the days ahead, and remind us what our continuing response should be.

Worship is also *giving* to God; the worship service is practice for a lifetime of giving God the "sacrifice" he asks for—our total selves.

Finally, worship is *becoming* like God in our total selves—body, emotions, mind and will. In the Sunday worship service we rehearse the use of body, of emotions, of intellect and will in order that our bodies may truly be the temple of God, that our spirit may be moved by his Spirit, that our minds may be as the mind of Christ, and that our will may be one with God's.

Worship as Dialogue.

Recall for a moment the dialogue of Isaiah six:

    God: I am that I am—all holy, all powerful, yet mysterious.
    Isaiah: Woe is me! I am a man of unclean lips!
    God: Be forgiven! Be cleansed! Be reconciled!
        (Pause)
    God: I need you to do my work in the world.
    Isaiah: Here am I, Lord; send me.
    God: Go then, and tell this people . . .
        (After the going gets rough)
    Isaiah: O Lord, how long?
    God: Until cities fall in ruins and are deserted . . . (to the end of
        time.)

In chapter ten we will argue that this passage not only suggests all the basic experiences of worship, but also puts them in a logical order. Notice that the scripture records the responses of confession, of dedication of self, and of petition. These are only a few of the human words of worship, and many of them are carried on the wings of music. God may show himself to us and we could respond—in a quiet personal confession of need or expression of adoration—during the organ prelude or the offertory. God speaks to us through the reading of scripture and the sermon; we respond through the hymns, expressing our praise, our thanksgiving, and also our confession, our dedication, our petition and intercession.

It may be that some worshipers are confused about the identity of the conversational participants. Sometimes it appears that the minister and the choir are engaged in some sort of antiphony, or perhaps the congregation and the minister (as in the responsive reading). When Søren Kierkegaard speaks of worship as a drama,[6] he insists that the congregation are the actors and that God is the audience. The minister and the choir, he says, are "prompters" who stand offstage to remind us when we forget our lines!

When the minister preaches, he should bring us a message from God, and at the same time remind us what our response to God should be. When he prays, he does so vicariously on our behalf, speaking to God the congregation's praise, thanksgiving, confession, and petition. It would be good if American evangelicals would follow the example of their fellow Christians around the world, by responding with a unison "Amen" at the end of the prayer. For that is the congregation's way of affirming that it was not the minister's prayer alone, but theirs.

The choral anthem or the solo or ensemble piece is not planned principally for the pleasure of the congregation, or the gratification of the singers. Hopefully, the latter are speaking their own praise of God, but they are also expressing it for each non-choral worshiper. As "prompters" they are putting words of response to God in our minds and underlining them with the emotional language of music. Our challenge then is not to express our like or dislike of the musical style, but to endeavor to make it our own expression of response to God. Nevertheless, evangelicals have traditionally been jealous of the congregation's right to speak its own praise. As Calvin expressed it in stressing the priesthood of every believer, the congregation is the church's *first choir!*

But how do we represent that it is *God's* voice which we hear, not just that of the minister or the choir? Obviously, we begin by guarding the texts which are used, to be sure they are true to our best understanding of God's Word, the scriptures. But is that enough? How do we communicate his omnipotence, his holiness and his mystery? Throughout the centuries, this challenge and responsibility has often been given to artists, including musicians.

The ancient Hebrews sensed that God was present in the fiery cloud which hung over the tabernacle and in the curtained Holy of Holies where stood the ark of the covenant, holding the tablets of stone (the Decalogue) and Moses' rod. They understood that the furniture within the tabernacle (the candlestick, table of shewbread, altar of incense) had symbolic meaning in their understanding of God. They saw and shared in the drama of sacrifical offerings, accompanied by the shouts of the priestly choir, with trumpets and other musical instruments, and sometimes even by dance. With all this to stimulate the senses of sight, sound, and even touch and smell, the presence of God was not difficult to apprehend.

In the Middle Ages, this example was copied by Christians who created magnificent, soaring cathedrals whose space and design had theological significance and whose spire fairly reached out to touch the

---

6. Søren Kierkegaard, *Purity of Heart Is to Will One Thing,* pp. 160-166.

transcendent. They filled the windows with stained glass telling the stories of our faith. God's presence and his revelation to them was suggested by vestments, candles and other ornamentation, in the sound of a choir and organ and in the pageantry of procession and worship drama. It is important to remember that in the Middle Ages these physical sensory images could communicate something of God, even when no word of the liturgy was understood by most of the congregation.

All of these artist-created elements are what we call *symbols*. According to the late Evelyn Underhill, "a symbol is a significant image, which helps the worshiping soul to apprehend spiritual reality." We use symbols, she says, because we are men and God is God.

> It is only by . . . reference to the things that are seen, that we can ever give concrete form to our intuition of that which is unseen . . . Though it be true indeed that faith makes good the defects of the senses, it is no less true that the senses must play their part in making good the limitations of faith, bringing into focus within our field of vision the far-off objects she discerns.[7]

Evangelicals tend to disassociate themselves from this understanding of the significance of symbolism in worship. Our forefathers built plain "meeting houses", proclaiming that God no longer dwells in "temples made by hands" but in the human heart, and that we do not expect to see him in phenomena of nature (as the Hebrews did) or in the symbolism of a sanctuary (as in the medieval church). We sense God's presence, they said, in the individual believer's "witness of the Spirit"; beyond that, we are expected to take it by faith. It may be that in our modern day that is expecting too much! Our people respond affirmatively to the idea that worshiping in an outdoor setting helps them feel the presence of God, as in an Easter sunrise gathering, a service at the seashore or in the mountains. For "the heavens are telling the glory of God" (Psalms 19:1). Liturgical artists are simply trying to do what the Supreme Artist has done in nature.

Mrs. Underhill suggests that the most transcendent aspect of "free church worship" is our congregational hymn singing.[8] The rhythm, rhyme and imagery of a great text set to music—especially if it is sung and played magnificently—can remind us that the numinous God is speaking. Consider for a moment these two examples which are rather commonly known in many evangelical churches. Read them aloud, dwelling on the images which the words suggest, and the scriptures which are referred to.

> O worship the King, all glorious above,
>   O gratefully sing his power and his love;
> Our Shield and Defender, the Ancient of Days,
>   Pavilioned in splendor and girded with praise.

---

7. Evelyn Underhill, *Worship*, p. 37.
8. Ibid., p. 107 and p. 305.

O tell of his might, O sing of his grace,
  Whose robe is the light, whose canopy space.
His chariots of wrath the deep thunder clouds form,
  And dark is his path on the wings of the storm.

Thy bountiful care what tongue can recite?
  It breathes in the air, it shines in the light;
It streams from the hills, it descends to the plain,
  And sweetly distills in the dew and the rain.

Frail children of dust, and feeble as frail,
  In thee do we trust, nor find thee to fail;
Thy mercies how tender! how firm to the end!
  Our Maker, Defender, Redeemer and Friend.
                    William Kethe, 1561, based on Psalm 104
                    Adapted by Robert H. Grant, 1833

In a hymn by Walter Chalmers Smith based on the doxology in I Timothy 1:17, the author is emphasizing that the mystery of God derives from his glory, a glory comparable to the sun. Consider also the possibility that Smith is suggesting (verse three) that as nature receives its life from the sun, we receive ours from God.

Immortal, invisible, God only wise,
  In light inaccessible hid from our eyes,
Most blessed, most glorious, the Ancient of Days,
  Almighty, victorious, thy great name we praise.

Unresting, unhasting, and silent as light,
  Nor wanting, nor wasting, thou rulest in might;
Thy justice like mountains high soaring above
  Thy clouds, which are fountains of goodness and love.

To all, life thou givest, to both great and small,
  In all life thou livest, the true life of all.
We blossom and flourish as leaves on the tree,
  And wither and perish—but naught changeth thee.

Great Father of glory, pure Father of light,
  Thine angels adore thee, all veiling their sight;
All praise we would render; O help us to see
  'Tis only the splendor of light hideth thee!
                    Walter Chalmers Smith, 1867

Although our earliest evangelical heritage is that of unaccompanied congregational singing, we have learned to understand and to hear other music as distinctively "the voice of God." The organ was possibly chosen as the logical instrument for "setting the intonation" and eventually accompanying the congregation because it provided a *lot of sound* and needed only one person to play it. Simply because of its longtime association with the church, it has come to communicate "God" and "worship." It may also be said that the grandeur as well as the variety of organ tone express to many people the presence and the voice of God.

The same may be said of any group of musical instruments played well—a brass ensemble, for instance.

A good choir can also have the same function. For a few moments in the service they lead in a quality of worship that is not possible with simple congregational hymns. Admittedly, the listeners must avoid the pitfalls of idolatry; they must not hear a "transcendent" choir for music's sake, nor enjoy a transcendent experience solely as pleasure. But if the attitude is right, the imagination can soar on the wings of music and text, which help to reveal a numinous God. The psalmist encourages us to "Sing the glory of his name; give to him glorious praise." (Psalm 66:2) When we do so, we help to make God's presence real.

In approaching worship as conversation, we must also be sure that the congregation *understands* a particular expression as "from God." The musical style which communicates God's transcendence in one culture may not do so in another. The text-style which is understood by one group to contain "the word of God" will not be so understood universally.[9] Each congregation must find its own best languages.

If a congregation matures in its understanding of God, or in its understanding of languages (musical and/or textual), their worship expressions should communicate this. When in the passage of time, there are basic changes in the meanings of languages, worship should also reflect those changes, so that it may continue to be vital, not sentimental or romantic. The latter has been illustrated recently in the use of new translations of scripture, new ways to address God in prayer ("You," not "Thee," etc.) and new styles (both in lyrics and in music) in contemporary hymnody.

Finally, effective worship of God will endeavor to bring the *whole* Word of God to the congregation in languages which they understand. The problem with "revivalist worship" is that it communicates only the gospel of "sin, grace and initial salvation." It is directed almost completely to the uncommitted; the believers present can do little more than recall their own conversion experience. I am convinced that we must hear the "total Word" and encourage a total response.

Worship as Offering to God.

The life of the worshiping believer is also a life of giving to God. The service of worship is fundamentally a rehearsal of that offering, giving God the sacrifice which he requires—nothing less than the total self.

From earliest times, sacrifice has been the central act of worship. Primitives worldwide understand this from their God-given instincts; they bring something of great value to offer to their gods, sometimes

9. It will be remembered that the Roman church evangelized pagan Europe using the Latin language, because the undeveloped vernacular tongues were judged to be inadequate to properly express the theology and liturgy of the church. Modern evangelical missions would reject such an approach, insisting rather that the theology and worship forms should be adapted to the limitations of the known languages.

even their own flesh and blood. The ancient Hebrews had a complex system of sacrifices which is set forth in the book of Leviticus. Dr. Stephen Winward reminds us that Jewish sacrifices were of three types, and each has its counterpart in Christian worship.[10]

The *peace* offering was a primitive act of worship, which reached back into the nomadic period of Jewish life. It was sacrifice followed by an agape, a communal meal, a "love feast." In this practice, the blood and the fat of the animal were offered to God, and the rest was eaten together. It was essentially a joyful social occasion, at which the worshipers ate and drank before God, and also shared the feast with God! Fellowship with God and with each other is a prominent part of our worship services, and should reach its highest level in the service which we call "Communion" in which we also eat and drink the Lord's Supper, or Eucharist. This then is the Christian peace offering: we *offer ourselves* to God and to our neighbors, in fellowship.

In the typical Hebrew *sin offering*, the Jewish priest took some of the blood of a slain animal into the holy place, sprinkled it with his finger seven times before the veil, and applied some of it to the horns of the altar of incense. The blood signified "the life released by death"; it had cleansing and sanctifying power and was an expiation for involuntary or inadvertent sin. In Roman Catholic theology, it is believed that worshipers offer to God (through the priest) the sacrifice of the mass—the body and blood of Christ in the bread and wine—for the forgiveness of sins. Evangelicals understand that Christ "was offered once to bear the sins of many . . ." (Heb. 9:28). Nevertheless, believers continue to offer their confession ("a broken and a contrite heart," Psa. 51:17). Even if they are not aware of specific wrongdoing, they know that they have "fallen short" of God's glory, involuntarily or inadvertently; yet they also have the confidence expressed in I John 1:9, "If we confess our sins, he is faithful and just, and will forgive our sins and cleanse us from all unrighteousness."

As Anglicans begin the service of Morning Prayer (Matins), they confess in unison, "Almighty and most merciful Father; we have erred and strayed from thy ways like lost sheep," etc. and then hear the minister give assurance that God "pardoneth and absolveth all them that truly repent, and unfeignedly believe his holy gospel." Evangelicals may do this quietly and personally as they pray during the organ prelude. Because many may not do so, there should be an opportunity for all to offer the sacrifice of contrition and confession early in the worship service, in order to free the conscience from guilt,[11] and to prepare to worship God with pure hearts.

The *burnt offering* in Jewish worship was an oblation given wholly to God, completely consumed upon the altar. The sacrifice of the evangelical Christian is the same total offering; as Paul said, "I appeal to you

---

10. Winward, op. cit., pp. 35-36.
11. Paul Hoon lists some of the reasons contemporary persons inevitably feel guilt when they come to worship. See Hoon, op. cit., p. 304.

therefore, brethren, by the mercies of God, to present your bodies as a living sacrifice, holy and acceptable to God, which is your spiritual worship" (Rom. 12:1). Christian worshipers give money in church, give their attention to God's word, their response in song, in prayer and in willing service, in token of the fact that they are completely God's.

The question of the "acceptability" of a sacrifice has always been fundamental; it was at the root of the clash between Cain and Abel, underlies all the instructions to the Hebrews, and remains valid for the Christian. In tabernacle and temple worship, animals chosen for sacrifice were required to be the best of the lot, without blemish or disease. Paul's call to Christians is "to offer your very selves . . . a living sacrifice, dedicated and fit for his acceptance" (New English Bible).

This quality of sacrifice is a costly act, demanding our dearest treasure. In the Middle Ages, landless peasants gave their coppers, as well as their bodies in back-breaking toil, to build soaring cathedrals in praise of God. The great composer Johann Sebastian Bach labored tirelessly on a cantata or an organ piece "*soli Deo gloria,*" only for the glory of God. Modern church musicians—organists, directors, choir singers and instrumentalists—rehearse carefully and painstakingly to prepare for our worship leadership, and our motivation should be the same—to offer our best "sacrifice" to God.

In the Old Testament, music was closely connected with the offering of sacrifices.

> I will offer in his tent sacrifices with shouts of joy; I will sing and make melody to the Lord. (Psa. 27:6b)

> There shall be heard again . . . the voices of those who sing, as they bring thank offerings to the house of the Lord. (Jer. 33:10b, 11a)

In the new covenant, sacrifices of material things are no longer required; but words of praise are acknowledged to be one of the offerings the Christian continues to bring to God through Christ.

> Through him then let us continually offer up a sacrifice of praise to God, that is, the fruit of lips that acknowledge his name.
> (Heb. 13:15)

Admittedly, concern for musical excellence in church can lead to a distortion of the concept of acceptability that is a form of idolatry. Some church musicians seem to be convinced that the numinous God must be worshiped only with the most exalted art which man can create. To insist on this is to commit the same sin as Cain (Gen. 4:1–7), worshiping the symbols of expression we have fashioned, rather than God himself. In such a moment of pride, we may well learn the truth of I Corinthians 1:27, 29: "God chose what is foolish in the world to shame the wise, God chose what is weak in the world to shame the strong . . . so that no human being might boast in the presence of God."

All of which does not negate our obligation to bring God our best sacrifices of praise, as emphasized in a previous chapter. In this connection, we may be challenged by the poignant story of King David's offering in worship of God conducted on the threshing floor of Araunah the Jebusite, as retold in II Samuel 24:20-24.

> And when Araunah looked down, he saw the king and his servants coming on toward him; and Araunah went forth, and did obeisance to the king with his face to the ground. And Araunah said, "Why has my lord the king come to his servant?" David said, "To buy the threshing floor of you, in order to build an altar to the Lord"... Then Araunah said to David, "Let my lord the king take and offer up what seems good to him; here are the oxen for the burnt offering, and the threshing sledges and the yokes of the oxen for the wood. All this, O king, Araunah gives to the king."... But the king said to Araunah, "No, but I will buy it of you for a price; I will not offer burnt offerings to the Lord my God which cost me nothing."

It is a common misconception of evangelicals that worship is evaluated by whether or not one "gets a blessing." Worship is first *giving* to God; any really significant "blessing" we may receive will be the result of that self-giving. It is proper to ask the people of God, the full congregation as well as the "appointed" musicians: What has it cost you to offer to God your "sacrifice of praise?"

Worship as Becoming.

It is hardly necessary to argue the proposition that as persons we tend to be changed by what we idolize, what we worship. In effective Christian worship we become like God, who is the object of our worship, in our total selves—body, emotions, mind and will. The service of worship then is a rehearsal in becoming godly. We use our body, our emotions, our mind and our will, in order that our body might truly be "the temple of the living God" (II Cor. 6:16), that our spirit might be moved by God's Spirit, that we might "have the mind of Christ" (I Cor. 2:16), and that our will might be one with God's will.

For this reason, our worship should "exercise" the total person. As the British Baptist Stephen Winward has said in speaking of this "incarnational" aspect of worship:

> Both as revelation and response, it (worship) should involve the whole personality of man, the body and senses as well as thoughts and words, movement and action as well as listening and understanding.[12]

Are we really to worship with the *body?* Does that mean genuflecting? "crossing" oneself? religious dance? a march to a sacred shrine? Perhaps

12. Winward, op. cit., p. 7.

not for many evangelicals, but it is fair to admit that these can be sincere expressions of worship for those who perform them. They are all symbolic physical actions, and evangelicals can have their own! How about standing for the reading of scripture, to express its authority? Some Christians regularly kneel for prayer, both before and during the service, or possibly at an "altar service" after the invitation. Black believers often clap their hands during worship music, taking their cue from David's choir (Psa. 47:1). Hebrews have traditionally prayed with their hands stretched upward as though reaching toward God, and recently some Christians have picked up the habit. Some of our recent youth musicals have featured a certain amount of physical action which some have called "choreography." I remember a "witness march" in connection with a Graham crusade in Copenhagen, Denmark in 1965; thousands of believers carrying torches marched through the streets to totally surround a small lake, in witness to God's work in that city during those days.

Some evangelicals need to be reminded that the Puritan concept that the body is intrinsically sinful does not coincide with the biblical theology of either the Jews or the early Christians. It is a vestige of the philosophy of Plato and of neo-Platonist theology. Paul specifically exhorts us to present our bodies "as a living sacrifice" (Rom. 12:1), with the inference that if God has our bodies, the whole person is dedicated to him.

Worship with body action has special relationship to church music. Of course, it is conspicuously a part of the work of the director, the organist and the handbell choir, but it also includes the congregation. However, in some evangelical churches (including Southern Baptists) a fairly large percentage of the congregation seem to have picked up the idea that "singing in church is for singers" or "singing is for women and children." When a hymn is announced they do not even open the hymnal; they will stand with the rest of the congregation, but remain mute throughout the hymn. This is conspicuously a sin of American evangelicals; it would never happen in a liturgical church or in a mission church overseas. Part of worship is using the body—the lungs, the tongue and the vocal cords—in singing the hymns in church. The truth is, singing is for believers. The relevant question is not "Do you have a voice?" but "Do you have a song?"

Then too, singing leads to believing. From time to time, some church leaders have expressed fear that certain members of an audience might sing something which they do not really mean; I recall hearing ministers ask an audience not to sing if they didn't really believe what they were singing. Fortunately, this restrictive idea has just about died out, for it denies the validity on which we base much Christian education. As William James has said,[13] physical impression (going through the motions) leads to emotional response and then to physical expression (meaning it). Then again, perhaps most believer-singers rarely experience fully the words they repeat in a worship service. If we are honest,

13. See William James, *The Principles of Psychology*, Vol. II, 449 ff.

we will frequently say even while we sing: "Lord, I believe; help my unbelief" (Mark 9:24).

The progression of experience in William James' maxim is significant: physical impression leads to emotional response . . . Modern behavioral scientists have recently focused our attention on the emotional self, and worship leaders have placed new emphasis on the appeal to the *emotions* in full-orbed worship. For many years, evangelicals who perpetuated the revivalist image were accused of being "too emotional" in church. However, with the growing sophistication of many evangelical groups—and partly because we do not share the colorful and dramatic symbolism of our liturgical neighbors—much evangelical worship has become very proper, and frequently very dull! Time was when histrionic preaching contributed to the excitement of going to church, but nowadays music is usually expected to supply the emotional force in worship.

In chapter three, we considered both the strength and the potential weakness of music as an expression of religious emotion. The contemporary scene of religious emotionalism will be considered more fully in later chapters. My judgment is that most evangelicals are not in serious danger of "too strong emotion" in worship; we could well plan more intense emotional experiences, using all our resources of speech and music and drama, so long as they are associated with coherent truth. Our more serious threat, it seems, is too much "weak emotion" in church—emotion for its own sake (without relationship to cognitive experience) or emotion that is mere sentimentality.

As evangelicals, we have been trained to use the *mind* in worship, if only during the sermon. It's at that point that typical churchgoers open their textbook (the Bible), get their pencils ready (to take notes), and put their brains in gear. You can almost hear the idea passed from mind to mind, "Now the action really begins!"

Music too should be heard *with the mind*. A hymn, a solo, an anthem or a cantata is first of all a theological concept expressed in words. Consequently, all musical worship should involve and transform the mind, as well as the body and the emotions. This must begin, of course, with the worship planners. They should select a piece of music on the basis of its conceptual ideas, and place it in the total worship experience so that it has maximum meaning. Furthermore, the worshiper should hear it with the expectation of "understanding it." It is staggering to contemplate the possibility that university graduates, who regularly plow through abstruse technical journals with full comprehension, will sing hymns in church with little concern that the words they are mouthing should have meaning for them. This illustrates one of the besetting worship sins of evangelicals, and the clergy (including the music minister) are perhaps more to blame than the layman-worshiper. It remains then for them to take steps to remedy the situation, and we will offer suggestions in a later chapter.

The relationship of emotion to understanding is most important in the totality of worship. Each by itself may constitute an aborted experience.

God's truth may be comprehended by the mind; but if there is no emotional involvement, nothing more happens. Another individual may have an emotional experience; if it is not based on biblical concepts, it is soon forgotten in the quest for an even more intense emotive episode. But when truth is apprehended, and it is accompanied with strong emotion because the individual realizes its ultimate significance, then there can be an action of the *will*. This is the final step in the "James process" when true "expression" takes place.

It is also the final and definitive test of the effectiveness of our services, for worship is finally "submission." Its basic posture is kneeling. Its one necessary word is "Yes"—"Amen" ("Here am I; send me.") When this standard is applied to music in church, it is usually expressed in the overworked word "sincerity." This is "singing and making melody to the Lord *with all your heart*" (Eph. 5:19)—worship that springs from the seat of our affections—and should be the goal of all believers each time they meet with fellow Christians in God's house.

In the liturgical tradition, worship leaders follow a liturgy of confession and preparation before the public service begins, to insure that their hearts are pure before God. With the same motivation, an evangelical minister usually meets with his fellow ministers, or possibly with the session or the deacons, for informal prayer. A minister of music (meeting with the choirs and organist) should occasionally remind himself of the thundering words of Amos, who speaks for God (chapter 5, verses 21–23).

> I hate, I despise your feasts, and I take no delight in your solemn assemblies. Even though you offer me your burnt offerings and cereal offerings, I will not accept them, and the peace offerings of your fatted beasts I will not look upon. Take away from me the noise of your songs; to the melody of your harps I will not listen.

Some might guess that Amos was speaking as a music critic, and that he was condemning the ancient prototype of the southern quartet "gospel sing" or the rock-gospel musical. The chances are better that he was criticizing the well-rehearsed, traditional song of the Levite priests, every one a talented, trained and formally-consecrated professional. Culturally, the music was the best that the Hebrews could produce, and it was performed in all solemnity and with great technical care. Amos's condemnation was not for musicological or aesthetic reasons, but spiritual. The voices were singing gloriously, no doubt, but the hearts of the singers and of the listening congregation were mute and cold. We know this from the next sentence of the prophet's challenge.

> Take away from me the noise of your songs; to the melody of your harps I will not listen. But let justice roll down like waters, and righteousness like an everflowing stream.   (vss. 23, 24)

Summary

Worship is based on the inexhaustible excellences of the eternal God, and the never-ending need of mortal humanity. It is the relationship between God and persons, a continuing relationship of self-revelation and response. It is the normal activity—the normal relationship—of the Christian life, and it is expressed in conversation with God, giving one's self completely to God, and becoming like God in the total person— body, mind, emotions, and will.

The worship service is a *rehearsal for life.* It outlines the *dialogue* which goes on constantly between God and believers, giving God's word and suggesting the response he wants to hear—response which includes our adoration, our confession, our thanksgiving, our dedication and our petition. Worship also offers us an opportunity to *give* ourselves to God in all of life; in token of this, in the worship service we give him our attention as he speaks to us, we give him our praise and adoration, we give him our offerings of money and also of our service in ministry. Finally, worship is *becoming like God* in our total personhood—body, emotions, mind and will. The worship service allows us to exercise every part of ourselves, in order that our bodies might be God's temple, that our spirit might be moved by his spirit, that our mind might be the mind of Christ, and that our will might be one with the will of God.

True worship then is really all there is to being a Christian, and the worship service is important because of what it represents as a microcosm. As the late Archbishop William Temple said:

> The world can be saved by one thing and that is worship. For to worship is to quicken the conscience by the holiness of God, to feed the mind with the truth of God, to purge the imagination by the beauty of God, to open the heart to the love of God, to devote the will to the purpose of God.[14]

---

14. William Temple, *The Hope of a New World,* p. 30.

Chapter VI

MUSIC AND WORSHIP IN THE BIBLE

To the evangelical, scripture is supremely important, because it is the infallible record of God's acts in human history. It is God's Word, our "rule of faith and practice," so what it says about worship should be a guide to us in our service planning. For Christians, people of the "new covenant," the New Testament is understood to be most relevant in its statements about worship theology and practice. Yet the New Testament may be said to "fulfill" the Old, and there are threads which tie ancient Jewish cultic acts to modern evangelical practice.[1] Both Jews and Christians revere a transcendent God and both give honor to scripture; for these reasons and others, Jewish synagogue worship and modern Christian services (without communion) are similar in content and spirit.

Through almost three thousand years of Hebrew-Christian history, music has been associated with worship, and the Bible contains much of our early heritage of worship song. In early Jewish life, music expressions seem to have been spontaneous and ecstatic in nature; later music-making was formalized and became part of the professional responsibility of the worship leaders, the Levites. The Old Testament psalms come from many periods of the ancient Jewish culture and they were augmented by canticles that date back to Israel's deliverance from Egypt.

Synagogue worship probably developed among the Jews as a result of their Dispersion in the fifth century before Christ. With its emphasis on the reading and discussion of scripture, prayers and the singing of psalms and canticles, it was very significant in the framing of early Christian worship. Music in the synagogue was probably led by cantors—soloists who may have been trained in the temple Levitical ministry—and may have included some congregational participation.

The New Testament era began with a paean of praise song at Christ's birth. Later, when Christian churches were formed, singing was unmistakably and appropriately congregational. The new faith and its expres-

1. See Chapter V, "Worship as Offering to God."

79

sion were supported with several types of music—"psalms and hymns and spiritual songs" according to the Apostle Paul. Although the Old Testament gave specific directions for Hebrew worship, early Christians were apparently free to devise their own forms. The epistles do contain some general principles: the scriptures were to be read and the gospel was to be preached; certain types of prayer were encouraged, and believers were expected to "remember their Lord" in the eucharist, or communion. Beyond this, it appears that people were expected to use their God-given intellects and artistic gifts to devise modes of expression which would glorify God and edify man. It is interesting to note that the basic needs, and consequently the solutions, of first century worshipers were not unlike our own. Where evangelical worship practices (including our use of music) do not measure up to their full potential today, it will probably be evident that we are not following the standards of the leaders in the first century church.

The Early Traditions

The first biblical reference to musical experience is a narrative of musical thanksgiving, led by Moses and his sister Miriam, after the Israelites had been delivered from the Egyptians.

> Then Moses and the people of Israel sang this song to the Lord, saying, "I will sing to the Lord, for he has triumphed gloriously; the horse and his rider he has thrown into the sea.."
>
> Then Miriam, the prophetess, the sister of Aaron, took a timbrel in her hand; and all the women went out after her with timbrels and dancing. And Miriam sang to them: "Sing to the Lord, for he has triumphed gloriously; the horse and his rider he has thrown into the sea." (Exodus 15:1, 20, 21)

This performance was both instrumental and vocal, involved both men and women, and was accompanied by expressive movement. The song was a prototype of the expressions of praise to Yahweh that are found throughout the Old Testament, particularly in the Psalms.

Erik Routley has reminded us[2] that there are two musical worship traditions in the Old Testament: one was spontaneous and ecstatic, the other formal and professional. The first of these is mentioned as part of Saul's preparation to become king of Israel; the prophet Samuel was giving the instructions.

> After that you shall come to Gibeathelohim, . . . and there . . . you will meet a band of prophets coming down from the high place with harp, tambourine, flute, and lyre before them, prophesying. Then the spirit of the Lord will come mightily upon you, and you shall prophesy with them and be turned into another man. (I Sam. 10:5, 6)

2. Erik Routley, *Church Music and the Christian Faith*, p. 6.

In this early period, music was apparently expected to transport the worshiper into a supernatural experience of God. The same idea is expressed in connection with an occasion when the prophet Elisha foretold God's judgment (II Kings 3:15,16a).

"But now bring me a minstrel." And when the minstrel played, the power of the Lord came upon him. And he said, "Thus says the Lord..."

The expectation that music can affect human behavior (ethos) was common in scripture times, and has persisted throughout history. The Bible also records an early use of music in therapy.

And whenever the evil spirit from God was upon Saul, David took the lyre and played it with his hand; so Saul was refreshed, and was well, and the evil spirit departed from him. (I Samuel 16:23)

Music in the Temple

The Appointment.

The second Old Testament musical tradition—the music for the temple—was formal and professional, and was initiated by Israel's shepherd-king who was himself a musician and hymn composer.

David also commanded the chiefs of the Levites to appoint their brethren as the singers who should play loudly on musical instruments, on harps and lyres and cymbals, to raise sounds of joy. (I Chron. 15:16)

As priest-musicians, these performers gave full time to their musical service. They were chosen on the basis of their talent (I Chron. 15:22) and were thoroughly trained, serving five years of apprenticeship before being admitted to the regular chorus. The Jewish choir was organized under at least three composer-conductors—Asaph, Heman and Jeduthun (II Chron. 5:12). The singing was accompanied by many kinds of instruments—"lyres," "pipes," "harps," "trumpets," and "cymbals"— and was also associated with dance (Psa. 150:4).

The Musical Sound.

In ancient Hebrew worship, the words of scripture were never spoken without melody; to do so was considered to be a minor sacrilege. They were always sung in a lusty cantillation. ("Shout to God with loud songs of joy!" Psa. 47:1). They were accompanied by instruments in what is believed to have been a sort of *heterophony,* in which the instruments provided embellishments of the vocal melody. Like most early cultures, Hebrew instruments were of three basic types:[3]

3. See *The New Oxford History of Music,* Vol. 1, pp. 295–296, and footnote references.

(1) String — *kinnor* ("lyre," related to the Greeks' *kithara*) and *nebhel* ("harp" with up to ten strings, sometimes called "psaltery" in KJV)

(2) Wind — *shophar* (a ram's horn), *halil* (a double-reed, like the oboe), *hazozerah* (a metal trumpet), and *ugabh* (a vertical flute, used mainly in secular music).

(3) Percussion — *toph* (tambourine, or hand drum), *zelzelim* (cymbals), and *mena an im* (a sistrum).

We believe that in Old Testament worship antiphonal singing was possibly the norm, partly because the psalms are couched in a responsory pattern. In modern liturgical church practice, each verse would be divided into a "versicle" and "response."

V: God be merciful unto us, and bless us;
R: And cause his face to shine upon us. (Psalm 67:1, KJV)

V: O give thanks unto the Lord; for he is good:
R: For his mercy endureth for ever.   (Psalm 136:1, KJV)

It is natural for us to try to guess what this ancient music sounded like. Some Jewish worship musicians insist that they still retain much of the original character of their chants, even though they may have been originally preserved only by oral tradition. Recent musicologists have reasoned that the early Christian chant styles were patterned after Jewish antecedents; so it is possible that certain traditions in Eastern Orthodox worship chant carry some remnants of the original sounds. Eric Werner says that all the foremost authorities (Curt Sachs, A. Z. Idelsohn and R. Lachman) agree that the chants were based on four-note (tetra-chordal) melodic motives, and that

the archetype of chant was similar to ancient Gregorian tunes, which means that they were based upon small melodic patterns of a rather narrow range, usually not exceeding a fourth or a fifth.[4]

In the last few years, a French musician and scholar Suzanne Haik Vantoura has released a book, *La Musique de la Bible Reveleé*[5] (The Music of the Bible Revealed), which is the result of four years' research. She is convinced that mysterious signs scattered through the Hebrew scriptures, both above and below the letters, are actually a system of musical notation, not punctuation or accent marks as has been traditionally held. Furthermore, she has reduced these signs to a system of notation, and has transcribed and recorded the melodies for approximately three hours of Bible music. The following is an example.[6]

4. Eric Werner, "Jewish Music," p. 623.
5. Suzanne Haik Vantoura, *La Musique de la Bible Reveleé*.
6. Ibid., p. 364.

The Lord of hosts (is) with us;   Our   refuge (is)

ʾA.da.nay tse.ba.ʾôth ʿim.ma.noû   mis.gab - la - noû

the God of Jacob.   Selah.   Psalm 46:11

ʾe.lo.hê ya- ʿa.qob   se.lah   :

Werner also describes the musical performance in the Jews' Second Temple.[7]

> The morning sacrifice was accompanied by three trumpet blasts; the cymbals clashed, signalling the beginning of the Levitical chant. At the end of each portion the trumpets joined the singing to indicate to the congregation the moment to prostrate themselves. Every song was probably divided into three portions . . .

Most scholars agree that music in the temple was almost completely professional and sacerdotal (performed by priests). The Jewish layman participated principally as a spectator and a listener. It is reasoned that he may have frequently joined in the traditional responses "Amen" and "Alleluia," and possibly in an antiphonal refrain like "for his steadfast love endures for ever" (Psalm 136).

The Songs of Hebrew Worship.

The book of Psalms has been called the "hymnal" of Israel. The psalms were sung in regular sequences following the morning and evening sacrifice on specified days of the week, and were accompanied by instruments which occasionally indulged in an interlude indicated by the word "Selah."

Psalms offered three types of worship expression:

> (1) *Praise.*
>   Praise the Lord!
>   For it is good to sing praises to our God;
>   for he is gracious, and a song of praise is seemly. (Psa. 147:1)
>
> (2) *Petition.*
>   Give ear, O Shepherd of Israel,
>   thou who leadest Joseph like a flock!
>   Thou who art enthroned upon the cherubim, shine forth
>   before Ephraim and Benjamin and Manasseh!
>   Stir up thy might, and come to save us! (Psa. 80:1,2)

7. Werner, op. cit., p. 623.

(3) *Thanksgiving.*
    I love the Lord, because he has heard my voice
    and my supplications. (Psa. 116:1)

There were special psalms associated with festival occasions—royal psalms to honor the king (21, 45, 101), processional psalms (24, 95, 100), and penitential psalms for periods of national repentance (130). The "Egyptian Hallel" psalms (113-118) were very significant in the observance of the Passover and other times of national penitence.

There were probably at least four[8] different modes of presentation:

1. A simple psalm (46:1), sung by one person alone.
2. A responsive psalm (67:1,2), in which a choir answers the solo chant.
3. An antiphonal psalm, with several lines beginning or ending with the same phrase (103:1,2,20-22), sung by two choirs in alternation.
4. A litany (80:2,3, 6,7, 18,19), which included a repeated refrain.

Eric Werner also gives four design types:[9]

1. The plain, direct psalm—no strophic arrangement.
2. The acrostic psalm—phrases in alphabetical sequence. (119)
3. The refrain psalm—each verse ending with the same refrain. (136)
4. The Hallelujah psalm—begins or closes with the ecstatic exclamation. (145-150)

In addition to the psalms, a number of important biblical Canticles were used regularly by the Hebrews in worship, and have been carried over into many Christian traditions as well. These are the best known:

1. Moses' (and Miriam's) song of victory over Pharaoh (Exo. 15).
2. Moses' prayer before his death (Deut. 32).
3. The song of Hannah (I Sam. 2), a prototype of Mary's song in Luke 1:46-55.
4. The song of Habakkuk (Hab. 2).
5. Isaiah's song (Isa. 26).
6. The prayer of Jonah in the fish's belly (Jonah 2).
7. The prayer of Azariah—*Benedictus es, Domine* (Daniel 3, Douay version; Vulg. 3:26-49, Apocrypha).
8. The song of the three Hebrew children in the furnace—*Benedicite omnia opera Domini* (Dan. 3, Douay version; Vulg. 3:52-90, Apocrypha).

8. Ibid., pp. 621-623.
9. Eric Werner, *The Sacred Bridge*, p. 133.

Worship and the Calendar.

Historic Jewish worship acknowledged that Yahweh is the God of times and seasons in the ebb and flow of life. The sacrifices were observed both morning and evening every day in the tabernacle and later, in the temple; in addition, the Jewish family regularly offered prayers at home at stated hours and at mealtime. The sabbath was a time for more exacting expressions of worship; it commemorated God's rest from the acts of creation and was observed in obedience to his command. Finally, there were times of intensely celebrative or penitential worship: Passover, to commemorate their deliverance from Egypt; the Day of Atonement, at the beginning of the New Year; Pentecost, associated with the giving of the Law, at the corn harvest; and the Feast of Booths (tabernacles) as "harvest home." As we will see later, most of these practices based on the calendar have been carried over into Christian worship.

Worship Music and the Experience of God.

We have already observed in chapter five that the Hebrews shared a richly symbolic worship that appealed strongly to the senses. The music which accompanied the sacrifices was a conspicuous part of the sensory experience. Musical sound was frequently associated with a sense of the presence of God, as evidenced in the accounts of the ecstatic moments of Saul and Elisha, and also in the requirement that song-chant would always be the vehicle of the holy scriptures.

One occasion when God was pleased to reveal his presence through musical performance was the dedication of Solomon's temple.

> Now when the priests came out of the holy place (for all the priests who were present had sanctified themselves, without regard to their divisions; and all the Levitical singers, Asaph, Heman, and Jeduthun, their sons and kinsmen, arrayed in fine linen, with cymbals, harps, and lyres, stood east of the altar with a hundred and twenty priests who were trumpeters; and it was the duty of the trumpeters and singers to make themselves heard in unison in praise and thanksgiving to the Lord), and when the song was raised, with trumpets and cymbals and other musical instruments, in praise to the Lord, "For he is good, for his steadfast love endures for ever," the house, the house of the Lord, was filled with a cloud, so that the priests could not stand to minister because of the cloud; for the glory of the Lord filled the house of God.   (II Chron. 5:11-14)

Worship in the Synagogue and the Jewish Home

The tradition of synagogue worship is of uncertain origin. Some scholars surmise that laymen gathered in remote parts of Palestine at the time of the regular sacrifices in the temple at Jerusalem; others guess that the practice may have begun among Jews who were captives in other lands. Because the traditional sacrifices could only be offered in the temple, "sacrifices of praise and prayer" were substituted for offerings of animals and grain. Synagogue worship was in full flower during the lifetime of Jesus and the early days of the Christian church. It is not surprising then that early Jewish Christians modeled their worship partly on what they had experienced in the synagogue.

Synagogue worship was essentially a Service of the Word; it centered in the ceremonial reading of the scripture, especially the Torah and the prophets, followed by discussion. It should be understood that the synagogue service was essentially congregational; though the position of the rabbi (teacher) developed in its context, it was essentially a meeting of laymen, who probably participated in the prayers, and also in the free discussion which might follow the scripture lection. (See Acts 17:17)

These then are the component parts of synagogue worship, most of which have come down to us from the earliest traditions.

Scripture Readings (Torah; the Prophets)
Homily, followed by discussion
Psalmody
The *Kedusha*, "Holy, Holy, Holy," (Isa. 6:3)
Prayers (The *Yotzer* and the *Ahabah*, emphasizing the creative acts of God and his love for his people, ending with the *Shema*—"Hear, O Israel; the Lord our God is one Lord" etc., a declaration of faith and a glad benediction, from Deut. 6:4-9, 11:13-21; Numbers 15:37-41)
The Eighteen Benedictions (expressions of praise, petitions for material and spiritual blessings, and intercessions for many people, concluded with a united "Amen.")

It is not known when music entered synagogue worship, but it is surmised that certain Levitical singers may have continued to practice their art in the lay-oriented gathering. We do know that only one or two solo singers (cantors) were involved in a service. They chanted the scripture readings, the psalms, the post-biblical prayers (Benedictions) and, according to some scholars, certain "melismatic" songs which may have been similar both to the ecstatic music of earlier days and to the "spiritual songs" mentioned in Colossians 3:16 and Ephesians 5:19. The musical style must have been related to that of temple worship, though presumably no instruments were involved, since they were associated only with animal sacrifices. It is also surmised that, in the congregational character of this gathering, all the worshipers joined in the psalms which they knew, and very frequently in a repeated refrain, a "Hallelujah" and an "Amen."

We make this latter assumption partly on the witness of Mark (14:26): "And when they had sung a hymn, they went out to the Mount of Olives." On the occasion of the last supper of our Lord with his disciples, the hymn sung was no doubt one of the "Egyptian Hallel" psalms (113-118), traditionally used in the observance of Passover. In the custom of a typical Jewish home, Jesus pronounced a blessing over a loaf of bread, broke it and gave portions to all those around the table. Similarly, at the end of the meal, a Jewish host would take a cup of wine mixed with water, give thanks, and then pass it around for all to drink. So it was that at the "upper room" supper, Jesus gave new meaning to a traditional act of thanksgiving (eucharist), and instituted the "Lord's Supper," which many Christians believe to be the most significant single act of worship. The full order of historic Christian liturgy was developed by uniting the pattern of Jewish synagogue worship with the "Lord's Supper."

Modern Jewish worship of Jehovah continues in the synagogue, without significant change in the basic elements. (In the orthodox tradition, the singing is still largely cantoral, and unaccompanied.) The feasts are still observed as in ancient times, with one significant addition—hanukkah, "the festival of lights," is celebrated in December to commemorate the rededication of the temple in the 2nd century B.C., following the victory over the Syrians under Antiochus IV. In connection with the cycle of annual worship centering in the festivals, a regular schedule of Scripture readings (the lectionary), psalms and prayers was developed to support the emphasis of each season.[10] This tradition has been passed on to the Christian church in the shape of the Christian (or Liturgical) Year, centering in the festivals of Christmas, Easter and Pentecost, and their corresponding periods of penitence and preparation, Advent and Lent.

Early Christian Worship

It is not just coincidence that the birth of Christ was announced by an outburst of song which is recorded in the first two chapters of Luke. Since that time, the Christian faith has been expressed with joyful music that has not been matched by any other religion in history. The four Lukan canticles are psalmodic in style, and are traditionally known by their first words in Latin.

Magnificat. And Mary said, "My soul magnifies the Lord, and my spirit rejoices in God my Savior . . . " (Luke 1:46-55)
Benedictus. Zechariah was filled with the Holy Spirit, and prophesied, saying, "Blessed be the Lord God of Israel . . ." (Luke 1:67-79)
Gloria in excelsis Deo. And suddenly there was with the angel a multitude of the heavenly host praising God and saying, "Glory to God in the highest, and on earth peace among men with whom he is pleased!" (Luke 2:13,14)

10. The close relationship between Jewish and early Christian activity in the developing of "propers" for daily worship is related in Werner, ibid., pp. 50-101.

> *Nunc dimittis.* . . . he (Simeon) took him up in his arms and blessed God
> and said, "Lord, now lettest thou thy servant depart in peace, ac-
> cording to thy word; for mine eyes have seen thy salvation . . . "
> (Luke 2:28-32)

The Song of Mary, the Song of Zechariah (father of John the Baptist),
the Song of the Angels, and the Song of Simeon have been used more in
historic Christian worship than any other Biblical passages, outside of
the psalms.

After the resurrection and ascension of Christ, the disciples (and including the apostle Paul) continued to meet in the synagogues on the
sabbath as was their custom, giving witness to their faith in the risen
Christ as the Jewish Messiah. At the same time, they met on the first day
of the week to "remember their Lord" in a simple observance of the
eucharist, sometimes held at the conclusion of an agape meal, a love
feast. Eventually, it became apparent that their presence would no
longer be tolerated in the synagogues, and they began to meet for their
own "Christian synagogue" service. In the final evolution of full Christian worship, the synagogue and the upper room experiences were
united in one two-part service.

When we begin reading about worship activity in the infant Christian
community, we are immediately impressed with the changes that had
taken place since the days of the tabernacle and the temple, and even of
the synagogue.

> What then, brethren? When you come together, each one has a
> hymn, a lesson, a revelation, a tongue, or an interpretation. Let all
> things be done for edification.   (I Cor. 14:26)
>
> . . . addressing one another in psalms and hymns and spiritual
> songs . . .   (Eph. 5:19a)
>
> . . . and sing psalms and hymns and spiritual songs with thankfulness
> in your hearts to God.   (Col. 3:16b)

Worship is no longer the work of ordained priests or professional cantors, with the congregation largely spectators, in awe of the transcendent
God. It is now social and congregational, with all worshipers aware of
their neighbors as well as of God, and each person taking part and even
assuming some leadership.

The unstructured, Spirit-led worship mentioned in the letter to the
Corinthians had retained three elements from the synagogue: psalms (a
hymn), scripture lections and discussion (a lesson). There were some
new ecstatic activities that were evidently emphasized in the Corinthian
church (revelations, tongues and interpretations) and they prompted
special instructions from Paul, including the final admonition "Let all
things be done for edification." Prayers are not mentioned; they must be
taken for granted.

It seems clear that, in the use of music, first century Christians had completely abandoned the professionalism of both the temple and the synagogue. Paul wrote these strong (and repeated) words about worship singing to the whole congregation both at Colosse and at Ephesus, not to a small musical clique.

And what were "psalms and hymns and spiritual songs"? It is little short of amazing that the Apostle delineates three different *genre* of music for worship, mentioning them in two different letters to young churches. We must believe that they were contrasting—in origin, in subject matter, and possibly even in performance practice. This is substantiated by Egon Wellesz, one of the leading authorities on the music of this period.

> St. Paul must certainly have been referring to a practice well known to the people to whom he wrote. We may therefore assume that three different types of chant were, in fact, in use among them, and we can form an idea of their characteristics from the evidence of Jewish music and later recorded Christian chant:
>
>   1. Psalmody: the cantillation of the Jewish psalms and of the canticles and doxologies modelled on them.
>   2. Hymns: songs of praise of a syllabic type, i.e., each syllable is sung to one or two notes of the melody.
>   3. Spiritual songs: Alleluia and other chants of a jubilant or ecstatic character, richly ornamented.[11]

Whether or not Wellesz is correct about the musical character of these forms, the nature and source of the texts seem well established. "Psalms" no doubt included all the psalms and canticles that were common to Jewish worship, in the tabernacle, the temple, and the synagogue. "Hymns" were probably *new* expressions in song, presenting the new Christology on which the new sect was based. There are a number of these hymns in the letters of Paul, written in the patterns of classical Greek poetry, and it is reasonable to assume that they were quickly adopted as "Christ songs" by the churches which read the epistles. One is in the form of a simple creed, or statement of faith:

> Great indeed, we confess, is the mystery of our religion:
>   He was manifested in the flesh,
>   vindicated in the Spirit,
>   seen by angels,
>   preached among the nations,
>   believed on in the world,
>   taken up in glory.   (I Tim. 3:16)

The poetic (and possibly antiphonal) form is obvious in another:

> The saying is sure:
>   If we have died with him, we shall also live with him;

11. Egon Wellesz, "Early Christian Music," *The New Oxford History of Music*, Vol. 2, p. 2.

> if we endure, we shall also reign with him;
> if we deny him, he also will deny us;
> if we are faithless, he remains faithful—
> for he cannot deny himself.   (II Tim. 2:11-13)

The *koine* Greek phrase for "spiritual songs" is "odaes pneumaticaes"—
"pneumatic odes," possibly "odes upon the breath" since the same word
was used for "breath" and "spirit." Some have conjectured that these
were "wordless" songs like a vocalise, or possibly that they used a single
super-word such as "alleluia." It has been suggested that they may have
been soloistic, and possible improvised in an experience of ecstatic
worship—"singing in tongues." Pentecostalists in our day claim to reproduce this biblical phenomenon, which may also have been related to
the ecstatic music experiences mentioned in the Old Testament.[12] Wellesz connects it with the common practice of most near-east cultures at
the beginning of the Christian era. Furthermore, he suggests that it was
perpetuated in later Christian worship in the *jubilus* of the mass, the
(originally improvised) melismatic prolongation of the final syllable of
the "Alleluia." As St. Augustine said of this type of Jewish-Christian
song:

> It is a certain sound of joy without words . . . it is the expression of a
> mind poured forth in joy . . . A man rejoicing in his own exultation,
> after certain words which cannot be understood, bursteth forth into
> sounds of exultation without words so that it seemeth that he . . .
> filled with excessive joy cannot express in words the subject of that
> joy.[13]

We presume that early Christian worship was strictly vocal, since instrumental music was primarily associated with Hebrew temple sacrifices, was probably not used in synagogues, and was abandoned even
by the Jews when the temple was destroyed in 70 A.D.

The Functions of Music in the Early Church.

The New Testament emphasizes both the human and the divine
springs of song. Music flows from human experience, and it no doubt
also affects that experience. James seems to suggest that it is most logically associated with the emotion of Christian joy.

> Is any one among you suffering? Let him pray. Is any cheerful? Let
> him sing praise.   (James 5:13)

12. I have heard wordless humming or vocalizing in pentecostal gatherings that might be
    compared to the sound of an Aeolian harp, produced by wind blowing through free
    strings.
13. MigneL XXXVII, 1272; Nicene & Post-N, Ser. 1, VIII, 488. Quoted in Gustave Reese,
    Music in the Middle Ages, p. 64.

In Paul's first letter to Christians at Corinth, one verse (when read alone) seems to be saying that all musical worship should be equally emotional and cerebral.

> ... I will sing with the spirit and I will sing with the mind also.
>
> (I Cor.14:15)

However, the scriptural context reveals that he is talking about two different experiences. Relating the verse to Ephesians 5:19 and Colossians 3:16, it may be Paul is suggesting that he would sing "hymns" with the mind and "spiritual songs" with the spirit. In any period of worship, no doubt our minds are engaged at different levels at different times; on occasion, perhaps most persons hear music more emotionally than rationally.

All of these functions of music in the early Christian community may be seen to support the *expression* of Christian faith. One passage in the Authorized Version—"teaching and admonishing one another in psalms, etc." (Col. 3:16), seems to be a clear biblical injunction to use song to indoctrinate and to teach Christian ethics. But the 17th century translators misplaced some punctuation, and it has been corrected in the New Scofield Reference Edition (1967) of the KJV:

> Let the word of Christ dwell in you richly, in all wisdom teaching and admonishing one another, in psalms and hymns and spiritual songs singing with grace in your hearts to the Lord.

We now have it in the Revised Standard Version:

> Let the word of Christ dwell in you richly, as you teach and admonish one another in all wisdom, and as you sing psalms and hymns and spiritual songs with thankfulness in your hearts to God.

The Bible does not clearly direct that song should be *impressive* as well as *expressive,* and most modern translations have clarified this verse. However, as a matter of simple fact, all expression may also be impression. The early church sang of the divinity and the work of Christ to express their new faith; at the same time, they were teaching those doctrines to the catechumens, those who were still being trained in the faith but had not yet been baptized.

Finally, and perhaps primarily, we should see Christian song as an offering to God in worship. Paul mentions this specifically in Hebrews 13:15.

> Through him (Jesus) then let us continually offer up a sacrifice of praise to God, that is, the fruit of lips that acknowledge his name.

This is affirmed when we remember that in the Hebrew temple, music was associated with sacrificial offerings, and in the synagogue, hymns of praise (along with prayer) were substituted for sacrifices of material things. Someone has said that in Old Testament worship God asked for the best "ewe" as an offering; in the New Testament, it is the best "you" that is required—our total selves with our best motives, thoughts and actions, in worship as in life. This is also emphasized in the two verses in which Paul says so much about musical worship:

> ... singing and making melody to the Lord *with all your heart.*
>
> (Eph. 5:19b)
>
> ... sing ... with thankfulness *in your hearts to God* ...   (Col. 3:16b)

Beyond a doubt, God is not impressed with the musical sounds which strike human ears in a worship experience. The true measure of our sacrifice of praise, then, is the sincerity with which we offer our best adoration to God.

Worship Elements Mentioned in the New Testament.

Even though the New Testament gives us only one liturgical outline and that was most informal (I Cor. 14:26), worship "bits and pieces" are mentioned throughout the epistles, showing us that early Christian practices included most of those which we consider to be important today. These then were the elements of first century worship, according to the New Testament witness, and the clarification of later history:

The New Christian Synagogue (Service of the Word)

Scripture readings (especially the prophets, and including letters from Paul.) "Till I come, attend to the public reading of scripture ... " (I Tim. 4:13). "And when this letter has been read among you, have it read also in the church of the Laodiceans ... " (Col. 4:16)

Homily (exposition). "On the first day of the week, when we were gathered together to break bread, Paul talked with them ... and he prolonged his speech until midnight." (Acts 20:7)

A Confession of Faith. " ... take hold of the eternal life to which you were called when you made the good confession in the presence of many witnesses." (I Tim. 6:12) The earliest form of an actual creed may have been as simple as "Jesus Christ is Lord," similar to the Ethiopian eunuch's confession, "I believe that Jesus Christ is the Son of God." (Acts 8:37 KJV)

Singing (of various types). " ... psalms and hymns and spiritual songs ... " (Col. 3:16), probably without instrumental accompaniment.

Prayers. "And they devoted themselves to ... prayers." (Acts 2:42)

Congregational Amen. " ... how can any one in the position of an outsider say "Amen" to your thanksgiving when he does not know what you are saying?" (I Cor. 14:16)

Collection (alms). "Now concerning the contribution for the saints . . . On the first day of every week, each of you is to put something aside and store it up, as he may prosper, so that contributions need not be made when I come." (I Cor. 16:1,2)

Physical Action. "I desire then that in every place the men should pray, lifting holy hands . . . " (I Tim. 2:8).

The Continuing Upper Room (Service of the Table)

Thanksgiving (eucharist). "And he took bread, and when he had given thanks . . . " (Luke 22:19)

Remembrance (*anamnesis,* Gr.) "Do this, as often as you drink it, in remembrance of me." (I Cor. 11:25)

The Anticipation of Christ's Return. "For as often as you eat this bread and drink the cup, you proclaim the Lord's death until he comes." (I Cor. 11:26)

Intercession (following the example of Christ in the Upper Room.) "When Jesus had spoken these words, he lifted up his eyes to heaven and said, . . . I am not praying for the world but for those whom thou has given me . . . " (John 17:1a, 9b).

The Kiss of Peace (evidently a Jewish practice, continued by early Christians). "So if you are offering your gift at the altar, and there remember that your brother has something against you, leave your gift there before the altar and go; first be reconciled to your brother . . . " (Matt. 5:23,24). The phrase "kiss of love" or "holy kiss" is found in Rom. 16:16, I Cor. 16:20, I Thess. 5:26, and I Pet. 5:14.

Summary

One of the Bible's most significant contributions to church music is the broad spectrum of texts it has left for Christian worship. The psalms and canticles of the Old Testament and of Luke 1 and 2 have been the basis for liturgical expression for almost two thousand years. In addition, the acknowledged New Testament "hymns" and many other passages in both Testaments have been used verbatim in anthems, motets and cantatas, and have provided the inspiration for many of our extra-biblical hymns and Christian songs. The scriptures will always be our best source for worship material; that which is not directly quoted or paraphrased is rightly expected to conform to Bible truth.

Because of the scriptural tradition in historic Judeo-Christian worship, certain segments of the church have at times rejected "songs of human composure." For almost three hundred years after the 16th century Protestant Reformation, Christian groups influenced by John Calvin held rigidly to the use of metrical psalms for congregational worship music, with the stated conviction that "only God's Word is worthy to be sung in God's praise." But even in biblical times *new hymns* "of human composing" were added. It is apparent that worship for the early church included traditional literature as well as contemporary, professional as well as amateur performances, carefully-designed as well as improvised compositions—psalms of praise, hymns of doctrine and spiritual songs of Christian experience.

By inference, the scriptures also suggest proper functions for today's church music. Both Old and New Testaments reveal a transcendent God who is the object of our vocal (and sometimes, instrumental) adoration. From the New Testament, we understand more of the believer's personal relationship with God through Christ, and also of his fellowship with other saints. This suggests that evangelical musical worship will be both objective and subjective. From the examples of worship music in both parts of the Bible, we learn that it may also be both cerebral and highly emotional, and not necessarily at the same time!

In the area of liturgical practice, there is marked and significant contrast between the Old and the New Testaments. Some have argued that the Hebrew system of Levitical choirs is a logical pattern that modern New Testament churches should follow. One writer, directing the argument to congregations that might resist the use of choir robes, insisted that the Levites' use of vestments was sufficient authorization! It is fair to ask whether on the same authority he would limit congregational participation, require the minister (as the "high priest") to wear an ephod (Exo. 39:1-7) along with bells and pomegranates (Exo. 39:24-26), and revive animal sacrifices?! We are people of the New Covenant, and the spiritual experiences of the New Testament church are typical of those which evangelicals should expect in any age. This is not to say that either choirs or instruments (or robes) are denied to us for our worship gatherings. However, as believer-priests, each Christian should be personally involved in all the experiences of worship, and the most significant music is that which is performed by the whole congregation, the church's *first* choir.

Today, most Christian groups defend their worship traditions on the basis of New Testament authority. (In addition, Catholic and Orthodox groups have retained Old Testament concepts of the priesthood, of repeated presentation of sacrifice for sin, and of symbolism.) The evangelical worships the God of the Old Testament through the Christ revealed in the New, and his worship practices should be expected to be similar to those mentioned in the early record of the church in the Acts and the Epistles. When the elements we have noted are all present and used in the power of the Holy Spirit, worship may be expected to please God and transform the members of the congregation!

Chapter VII

CHRISTIAN WORSHIP FROM THE SECOND CENTURY THROUGH THE REFORMATION

Music in the church has little valid function of its own, except as it contributes to such significant actions as worship, proclamation, evangelism, teaching and pastoring. For this reason, our study must explore these acts—especially worship—in their historic evolution both in theology and in practice. In this chapter we will trace in broad strokes the patterns of Christian worship, beginning with the early post-biblical period and ending with the decimation of the monolithic medieval church, caused by the Reformation and the emergence of "free churches" in the 16th and 17th centuries.

Evangelicals will identify most closely with the beginning and the close of this long period. Nevertheless, we consider that it is important to tell the full story, at least briefly. Historically, we are inheritors of all Christian history, even of the periods when the Church may have failed to live up to its divine calling.[1] It is important also to identify the theological and liturgical errors which led to the Reformation and the "Separatist" tradition, so that we may better understand our "heritage of reaction."

It will be seen that, in its basic outline, worship in the middle ages retained the New Testament essentials in content, but lost its evangelical spirit in a distortion of the theology of the eucharist. It also lost its spontaneity and congregational nature in the development of a fixed, complex liturgy performed by priests, with minimal congregational involvement. Furthermore, as the church spread westward in missionary expansion, the official Latin language was used universally in worship, because the vernacular tongues were considered to be "too vulgar," too

---

1. Bernard Ramm has said, "The church is the body of Christ not only for the first centuries but for all centuries." (*The Evangelical Heritage*, p. 15.)
   Since, as Ramm has also stated, evangelicalism stands in the tradition of the "Roman West," we will observe the evolution of worship and its music in Roman Catholicism, rather than the Eastern Orthodox heritage. See Introduction to this book, and *The Evangelical Heritage*, pp. 16-21.

undeveloped to carry the message of the liturgy. Consequently, the average untutored Christian understood few of the words he heard in church.

The Reformation was an effort to return to primal New Testament authority and practice, while retaining the concept of "established" religion, in which each protestant country has its official faith, whether Lutheran, Anglican or Calvinist. Because many leaders felt that Luther, Cranmer and Calvin did not go far enough in reform, certain groups of "nonconformists" began to separate from the "established" churches. From this movement comes the evangelical tradition in Congregational, Presbyterian, Baptist, Moravian, Mennonite and Methodist bodies.

The Early Church

The records of worship forms in the patristic church are few, but it is evident that a set pattern of liturgy emerges at a very early date. In a letter to the Corinthian church (A.D.96), Clement of Rome included a long, noble prayer which is closely related to eucharistic prayers of later centuries; it also refers to the *Sanctus* (Holy, holy, holy, Lord of hosts, etc.) which was a common feature of both Jewish and early Christian worship. The *Didache* (ca.100 A.D.) records that the Communion celebration was combined with a common meal (an *agape* or love-feast), and that it was preceded by the confession of sins; it also gives the "set prayers" that were to be used, along with the encouragement to the "prophets" to improvise prayer "as much as they desire."[2] At about the same time, the pagan historian Pliny (governor of Bithynia ca.111-13), in a letter to the Roman emperor Trajan, referred to Christians as "meeting on a fixed day before daylight and reciting responsively among themselves a hymn[3] to Christ as a god, and that they bound themselves by an oath not to commit any crime ... When they had performed this it was their custom to depart and to meet together again for a meal, but of a common and harmless kind."

The Second Century.

The first definitive worship order is contained in Justin Martyr's *Apology* to the Emperor Antoninus Pius (ca.150) in which he describes a typical Christian worship service "on the day called the Feast of the Sun." This outline can be clearly traced:[4]

2. *Didache* X, 7. Quoted in T. S. Garrett, *Christian Worship*, pp. 41–42, and in Wm. D. Maxwell, *An Outline of Christian Worship*, pp. 9–10.
3. Cited by T. S. Garrett, *Christian Worship*, p. 47. This may well have been one of the New Testament Christological hymns (Col. 3:16) mentioned in chapter six, or an extra-biblical hymn of the same type.
4. See Garrett, ibid., p. 47; and Wm. D. Maxwell, op. cit., pp. 11–14.

The Service of the Word (The Christian Synagogue)
  Readings from the Prophets, and "memoirs of the Apostles" (Gospels and Epistles)
  A Sermon (instruction and admonishing)
  Common prayers (the congregation standing, all participating)
The Service of the Lord's Supper (The Continuing Upper Room)
  Kiss of peace
  Offertory (Alms, bread and wine)
  Prayer of Thanksgiving ("at great length" and improvised "according to his ability") followed by a common "Amen"
  Communion

Music is not mentioned, but we have no reason to believe that the service did not contain psalms and hymns, and possibly "spiritual songs." Indeed, we may guess that the practice of chanting the readings and the prayers carried over from Jewish into Christian practice, without a break.

The Third Century.

Beginning with the third century, we have much more information about worship practice in the church; it may be found in the writings of Clement of Alexandria (d. ca.220), Tertullian (d. ca.240), Origen (d. 251), Sarapion of Thmuis (ca.340) and Cyril of Jerusalem (ca.313-ca.386). One of the most significant records is by Hippolytus of Rome (d. ca.236) in a Greek document known as *The Apostolic Tradition.*

The significant feature of this compilation is a complete Eucharistic Prayer which is suggested as a model for Christian worship, though each leader is encouraged to "pray according to his ability." It is interesting to note that the prayer begins with the Salutation and the *Sursum corda,* which were traditional Jewish forms long before they were used by Christians. The *Sanctus* (Holy, holy, holy) is not indicated, though it may have been in common use by this time. Music (psalms and hymns) are also not mentioned, but were probably included.

This then is the outline of worship as recorded by Hippolytus, including the biblical concepts mentioned in the eucharistic prayer:[5]

Service of the Word

  Lessons
  Sermon
  Psalms (?)
  Intercessory Prayers
  Kiss of Peace

5. See Garrett, ibid., pp. 51-55; and Maxwell, ibid., pp. 21-25.

Service of the Table

Offertory—the elements are brought to the table

Eucharistic Prayer

Salutation (responsory, between leader and people)

The Lord be with you: And with your spirit.

Sursum corda

Lift up your hearts: We lift them up to the Lord.

Let us give thanks to the Lord: It is meet and right to do so.

Thanksgiving

Salvation history (The incarnation; Jesus' life,
death and resurrection)

Words of Institution ("He took bread, and giving thanks, etc.")

Remembrance (Gr. *anamnesis*) "Remembering therefore his death
and resurrection, etc."

Oblation ("We offer to thee the bread and the cup, etc."

Invocation of the Holy Spirit (Gr. *epiclesis*) "We beseech thee that
thou shouldst send thy Holy Spirit, etc."

Doxology to the Trinity, with congregational Amen.

The Communion

Presbyter's post–communion prayer; people's Amen.

Bishop's benediction and dismissal

It is interesting to note that the service would be considered "evangelical" by modern standards, though also sacramental. According to the presbyter's closing prayer, the "holy Mystery" was received, "not for guilt or condemnation, but for the renewal of soul and body and spirit." The supper is an "offering" but the idea of transubstantiation[6] is not suggested.

The Fourth Century

We shall look at one more early worship form, recorded in *The Apostolic Constitutions* (ca.380 A.D.). It is called the Clementine Liturgy, since the anonymous book is written "in the name of" Clement, Bishop of Rome at the end of the first century. From Books II and VIII of the *Constitutions*, this complete service may be reconstructed.[7]

The Service of the Word

Scripture Readings (several, from Old and New Testaments, especially
the Epistles and Gospels)

Psalms, interspersing the above (some sung by cantors, some with
responses by the congregation)

Sermons (by several of the "presbyters")

6. The belief that, with the act of consecration, the bread and wine are miraculously
changed into the body and blood of Christ.
7. See Garrett, op. cit., pp. 59-65; and Maxwell, op. cit., pp. 26-34.

Dismissal of non-communicants (those not yet baptized) with a litany
  and people's response ("Lord, have mercy")

The Service of the Table

Prayers of the Faithful
Salutation and Response (a trinitarian benediction, or "The Lord be
  with you, etc.")
Kiss of Peace
Offertory
  Washing of hands of the bishop and presbyters
  Offering of the elements and of alms
  "Fencing" of the table (to forbid participation by the unworthy)
  Robing of the bishop in "a splendid vestment"; he then makes the
    "sign of the cross" on his forehead.
The Eucharistic Prayer
  Sursum corda ("Lift up your hearts, etc.")
  Preface: Thanks for all of God's providence, beginning with crea-
    tion.
  Sanctus ("Holy, holy, holy, Lord God of hosts, etc.")
  Thanksgiving for the incarnation and redemption.
  The Words of Institution (*Anamnesis* and Oblation) "That the Lord
    Jesus the same night in which he was betrayed took bread, etc."
    Includes a reference to Christ's return.
  Epiclesis (". . . send upon this sacrifice thy Holy Spirit . . . that he
    might reveal this bread as the body of Christ and this cup as the
    blood of Christ and that all we who partake of it may be
    strengthened in godliness."
  Prayer of Intercession (ten sections)
  The Lord's Prayer (?) (It was commonly used both earlier and later)
  Doxology and people's "Amen"
  "Bidding prayers" led by the deacon, and Bishop's Prayer
  The Call to Communion ("Holy things for holy people" with response)
  Gloria in excelsis (Luke 2:14, not the later expanded form)
  Hosanna and *Benedictus (qui venit*, Matt. 21:9)
Communion, with the singing of Psalm 34
  ("O taste and see that the Lord is good.")
Bishop's "after communion" thanksgiving and intercession followed
  by prayer and blessing.
Dismissal

It is evident that by this time Christian worship was already highly developed. The new religion was no more forbidden by the Emperor, and
was free to develop its practices openly and to record them in detail for
future posterity. It is apparent also that the "Service of the Table" was a
highly significant part of public liturgy, although it may not have taken
as long to perform as the "Service of the Word" (with multiple scripture
readings, psalms and sermons!) Worship at the end of the fourth cen-

tury was no longer spontaneous, but it was still strongly congregational with unanimous participation in the hymns, the prayers and the Amens. At the same time, there is the beginning of a professional hierarchy with specified activities by "the bishop, the presbyters, the deacons, sub-deacons, readers and singers."[8]

The change from the simple improvised worship of New Testament times to the glorious ceremony outlined above took place gradually. In the early decades after Christ, the Christian religion was practiced in secret, in adherents' homes or even in underground catacombs, for fear of persecution by Roman authorities. Once the emperor Constantine decreed (313 A.D.) that Christianity should be tolerated throughout the empire, the new faith spread like wildfire. Congregations were established so rapidly that it was impossible to train the new converts adequately to serve as pastors; consequently, bishops simply wrote down acceptable worship materials for the untutored (but ordained) leaders to read. Large and larger buildings had to be erected for the growing congregations, and worship was organized and disciplined to meet the challenge. More and more of the activity (including all the singing) was given to the clergy, partly to control the occasional outcroppings of heresy. Furthermore, when church bishops became the new nobility of the empire, they adopted the symbolism of the state which was now available to them because of their power and wealth—vast buildings and properties, glorious furnishings and vestments, and impressive pageantry.

Both in worship symbolism and liturgical action, it is apparent that the church fathers increasingly based their theology on Old Testament traditions more than on the New Covenant, and, fused with the Roman state cult, this led to serious distortions of first century worship concepts, particularly in relation to the Lord's Supper. The worship leader now became the priest who repeatedly offered the sacrifice of the body and blood of Christ (transubstantiation) for the forgiveness of sins and for identification with Christ in salvation. Instead of sharing a meal of thanksgiving, as they had done in the early years, believers came to witness the offering of the sacrifice, and to worship the communion bread itself. A spirit of awe and dread connected with this veneration discouraged worshipers from actually receiving communion. Eventually, most folk participated only once a year, as they were obliged to do.

The Church Year.

All liturgical worship is conceived as a re-enactment of the drama of God's self-revelation to man. In the Divine Liturgy of Eastern Orthodoxy and the mass of Roman Catholicism, God is revealed through scripture and sermon in the Service of the Word, and through sacrament in the Eucharist (Service of the Table). Furthermore, the macrocosm of

---

8. Maxwell, ibid., p. 32.

God's revelation throughout history is shown in the shape of the *liturgical year,* or *liturgical calendar.* As we have stated before, this concept was borrowed directly from Hebrew practice, and the Christian festivals are frequently parallel with Jewish antecedents.

In the western church, the church year starts with *Advent,* (beginning four Sundays before Christmas), a time of penitence in anticipation of the coming of Christ, a time when believers remember God's acts in creation, in the history of the Jewish people, and in the prophecies and the events leading up to Christ's incarnation. *Christmas* and *Epiphany* (January 6) celebrate God's self-revealing in Christ; the first of these is undoubtedly related calendar-wise to the Jewish Feast of Lights (Hanukkah) and the pagan celebration of the winter solstice, the beginning of the end of winter darkness. The season of *Lent* (forty days before Easter) begins with Ash Wednesday, is a high period of penitence to prepare for Holy Week, and recalls Christ's forty days of temptation, and Israel's forty years of wandering in the desert. *Holy Week* (Palm Sunday through Easter) follows the last days of Christ's life, his "triumphal entry," death and resurrection; *Easter* is often called the "Christian Passover" because it parallels the Jewish holiday and symbolizes the Christian's deliverance from the bondage of sin and death. *Pentecost* (the name is taken directly from the Jewish festival of "first fruits") commemorates the sending of the Holy Spirit and the establishing of the Church, and initiates the second half of the church year. In this final season (called variously "Trinity Season," "The Season of the Holy Spirit," "The Church Season" or simply "Ordinary Time") the emphasis is on God's purposes for the Church in this "age of grace" and through the empowering of the Holy Spirit.

In each period and on each particular day of the church year, the scripture readings (lections), the prayers, and the sermons are different, to match the theological emphasis of that season and day. The changeable parts of the Roman Mass are called the *Propers;* the rest is basically constant from day to day throughout the year and is called the *Ordinary.*

The Standardizing of Worship.

In the early years following Christianity's recognition, each metropolitan center developed its own liturgy and practices within the sphere of its cultural influence, and under the leadership of the bishops of Antioch, Alexandria, Byzantium, Jerusalem, Milan and Rome. Later developments of the Mozarabic liturgy in Spain, the Gallican liturgy of northern Europe, and the Celtic liturgies in Britain resulted from the missionary expansion of the Western church centers. Each liturgy was sung with its own traditions of cantillation, so that we have historical records of the development of Antiochian chant, Coptic chant, Mozarabic chant, Ambrosian chant (Milan), etc. All the early churches used the Greek language in worship, even the church at Rome. Latin began to be used in the fourth century, and eventually displaced the Greek in the western churches.

After the year 400, the Roman Empire was permanently divided into eastern and western empires. The imperial court at Byzantium exerted strong influence toward conformity in doctrine and worship practice in the eastern churches, in order to strengthen the political bonds of that empire. By the seventh century this control was quite complete and two Byzantine liturgies became standard throughout the domain: the Liturgy of St. Basil (used during part of Lent, on Christmas and Epiphany and on St. Basil's Day), and the Liturgy of St. Chrysostom (a shortened form, most commonly used). Orthodox liturgies have not changed essentially since that time, except that there was no hesitation to translate them from the Greek into the vernacular. Orthodox liturgy is always sung, partly in chant and partly in more contemporary music forms (e.g., Russian Orthodox music). Because Reformed and evangelical traditions stem directly from the Western church, we will not give further consideration to Eastern worship. Eastern and western churches were divided by a schism in the ninth century which was formalized in 1054 and became permanent.

The Roman Mass

In the west, Rome was the center of the Church and the Roman (Gregorian) rite eventually became the universal liturgy. Early important revisions were made by Pope Gelasius I (492–496), Pope Gregory the Great (590–604) (who also founded the *Schola Cantorum* which standardized western chant), the emperor Charlemagne (742–814) and his associate Alcuin (ca. 735–804). Even so, there were many differing practices throughout the Middle Ages, until the Council of Trent (1562) and the resultant *Missale Romanum*, 1570 (*Roman Missal*) brought liturgical uniformity.

The following is an outline of high mass[9] as it was celebrated about 1500. The parts sung by the choir are designated with an asterisk. The sections which are inaudible to the audience are marked "secretly." On the right, a counterpart from modern evangelical worship will help the uninitiated to identify some of the material.

The Liturgy of the Word

*Introit and	Call to Worship
*Kyrie eleison (ninefold)	Prayer of Confession
Entry of ministers	
Private preparation of ministers (secretly)	
Invocation	
Psalm 43, with *Gloria Patri*	
Psalm 124:8	

9. The word "mass" comes from the phrase "*Ite missa est*" (You are dismissed) at the end of the service. A "missal" is a book containing the mass liturgy. For a better understanding of the complete ritual see: Jones, Wainwright and Yarnold, eds., *The Study of Liturgy*, pp. 220–240; Garrett, op. cit., pp. 99–116; and Maxwell, ibid., pp. 54–71.

Confiteor and *Misereatur* (between
    ministers and celebrant)
Versicles and responses from psalms
Collects (prayers)
Blessing of incense, and censing of al-
    tar, etc.

**Gloria in excelsis Deo*	Choral Praise
Salution and collects of the day	Invocation
Epistle, sung by subdeacon, with response	Scripture Reading
*Gradual (psalmody)	Choral Psalm

*Tract or Sequence, during which are said:
    Prayers and Preparation for the Gospel
    Salutation, announcement of Gospel,
        with response
    Gospel recited (low tone) with response

Gospel (with lights and incense, sung by deacon with response)	Scripture Reading (from gospels)

Preacher goes to pulpit
    Intimations

Bidding Prayers	Prayers
Epistle and Gospel read (vernacular)	
Sermon (vernacular)	Sermon
*Credo (Nicene Creed)	Creed

Salutation and bidding to prayer

The Liturgy of the Upper Room

*Offertory: Psalms verses sung while cele-
    brant proceeds secretly

Offering of bread, with collect	Preparing of Commu-
Water mixed with wine, with collect	nion Table

    Offering of wine, with collect
    Prayers
    Blessing of incense, and censing of ele-
        ments, altar, and ministers
    Washing of celebrant's hands, while recit-
        ing the *Lavabo,* Psalm 25:6–12, with
        Gloria Patri
    Oblation, with prayers
    Collect (secret)
Salutation and *Sursum corda**

Prayer of Consecration (The Roman Ca-non)	Prayer over the bread and cup

    Preface and Proper Preface
    *Sanctus (while celebrants continue with
        the prayer, in secret)
    Request for acceptance of the offering
    Beginning of intercessions for the
        Church

The remembrance of the living
The remembrance of and intercession
  through the saints
The second request for acceptance
The third request for acceptance
The words of institution, with elevation   Words of Institution
  and *Benedictus**   ("The same night Jesus
Anamnesis and Oblation (Remembrance   took bread, etc."
  and Offering)
Further pleas for acceptance
The remembrance of the dead
The fellowship of the saints
The Doxology
The Lord's Prayer
The Peace (Fraction and mixing of the   Greeting One Another
  elements)
**Agnus Dei*
Celebrant's Communion, with collects, etc.
Communion of the People   Passing the bread
*Communion Hymn (psalm)   and the cup, with
Salution and post-communion prayers   hymn sung
Salutation and dismissal
Blessing of Congregation   Benediction
Last Gospel (John 1:1–14) and response

Historically, before Vatican II (1962) there were three modes of mass celebration: (1) The Low Mass (*Missa Lecta*) was spoken only, and it became most popular in the Middle Ages when it was traditional for every priest to celebrate once a day, and many individuals celebrated in the same church (at different altars) at the same time; (2) The Sung Mass (*Missa Cantata*) was the principal Sunday or holy day celebration in a parish church; and (3) High Mass (*Missa Solemnis*), sometimes called a Festival Mass, which included assisting celebrants, and frequently a choir.

The musical masses were commonly sung in Roman (Gregorian) Chant, which included Psalm tones (basically the use of a single reciting tone, followed by prescribed cadences). In addition, the high masses could feature composed settings of the five great prayer-songs of the mass (*Kyrie, Gloria in excelsis Deo, Credo, Sanctus et Benedictus, Agnus Dei*). The oldest extant settings of these mass forms are from the 12th century composers Leonin and Perotin in Paris. Through the centuries, mass settings (the five songs only) have been written by such great composers as Machaut, dés Prez, Palestrina, Haydn, Mozart, Beethoven, Schubert, Bruckner, Vaughan Williams and Stravinsky, each in his own distinctive musical style.

No doubt early Christian singing was principally, if not completely, congregational. After the fourth century, when Christianity began to grow rapidly, and particularly as worship became sacerdotal (priest-oriented), the singing was given over to a priest-choir. For all practical purposes the congregation's voice was stilled for 1000 years of Christian history.

The *Schola Cantorum* was established by Gregory the Great (ca.540–604) to standardize and to teach the official chant of the Church. As Christianity spread throughout the Western world, and as the various cultures developed during the Middle Ages, the cathedrals, monasteries, abbeys and collegiate churches developed choir schools where boys received their general education and were trained in music for the church's worship. The tradition of all-male music stems from the concept that worship is conducted only by priests; consequently the lower voice parts were supplied by men in minor priestly orders.

The early church fathers forbade the use of instrumental music in worship. Rudimentary organs began to appear in churches by the sixth century and their use in the Mass was wide-spread by the 12th century. In the 15th century, some German churches boasted organs with all the essential tonal resources of modern instruments. Evidently the use of the organ was limited, however. Basically it was a means of setting the pitch ("intonation") for the unaccompanied chant or choral setting. It was also featured in what is known as an *alternatim* practice, in which portions of liturgical music were shared by choir and organ, with the instrument performing sections (or stanzas) in alternation with the choir.

Non-Eucharistic Worship Through the Medieval Period

During this long period of Christian history, certainly for the millenium 500 to 1500, eucharistic liturgy was considered to be the highest form of worship. But it was not the only mode.

The Offices.

The "Services of the Hours" constituted another form of worship designed to dedicate time to God. It probably stemmed from the Jewish custom of regular prayer at stated hours of the day. Early Christians commonly prayed privately at the third, sixth, and ninth hours (Acts 3:1) and eventually this became a public practice, following the Roman division of the day into "hours" (*prima, tertia, sexts* and *nona*) and the night into four "watches." Office[10] worship was developed and perpetuated in the monasteries, but also observed in cathedrals and collegiate churches.

The full cycle of eight "Offices" consisted of Matins (between midnight and dawn), immediately followed by Lauds ("cockcrow"), Prime (6:00 a.m.), Terce (9:00 a.m.), Sext (noon), None (3:00 p.m.), Vespers (6:00 p.m.) and Compline (before retiring). The principal component of

---

10. Participation was the duty ("office") of the celebrants.

Office worship consisted of the reading and chanting of scripture; thus in the total "Hours" the Psalms were completed (sung responsively) once each week, the New Testament was read through twice in a year, and the Old Testament once. In addition, special place was given to the biblical Canticles,[11] especially the Song of Zacharias, father of John the Baptist (*Benedictus Dominus Deus Israel*), The Song of Mary (*Magnificat*), The Song of Simeon (*Nunc Dimittis*), The Song of the Three Hebrew Children (*Benedicite,* from the Apocrypha), and the fourth century extra-biblical hymn attributed to Niceta of Remesiana, *Te Deum laudamus.* Finally, this form of worship also included hymns, versicles and responses, prayers, and sometimes a homily. The offices of Matins and Lauds in the morning, and Vespers and Compline in the evening, were the major services in which the most music was featured. In the Roman tradition, the psalms, canticles and hymns were sung in Gregorian chant exclusively, except in the office of Vespers when contemporary, "composed" settings might be used. It is in this latter tradition that the Monteverdi "Vespers of 1610" was produced.

One office characteristic has been carried over as a conspicuous part of evangelical worship to the present day. Beginning in the second century it was the custom to follow each psalm (and later each canticle) with the *Gloria Patri*; this ascription of praise to the eternal trinity served to bring the Old Testament psalm into a "New Testament" context.

> Glory be to the Father, and to the Son and to the Holy Ghost; as it was in the beginning, is now, and ever shall be, world without end. Amen.

Preaching Services.

It has often been pointed out that, although preaching was allowed in the medieval mass, it was rarely included. Occasionally, throughout history, a sermon was featured in the Office of Lauds. Furthermore, "preaching missions" were common throughout Christian history. Congregations met in the naves of the cathedrals and large churches; this explains the location of a pulpit in the middle of a sanctuary far from the altar, as modern tourists will observe in historic European churches. From this tradition, a basically-vernacular worship form developed, known as the Prone, first inserted as a part of the mass and later featured as a separate service. It is significant because of its resemblance to the worship form adopted by John Calvin in the 16th century which has carried over into common evangelical worship. The following is an advanced form of the Prone which was used in Basel.[12]

11. The "Greater" Canticles are those which come from the New Testament (Luke, chapters 1 and 2). The "Lesser" (Old Testament) Canticles include those mentioned in Chapter VI; in the early centuries, they were especially featured in the office of Lauds in Eastern churches.

12. Eberhard Weismann, *"Der Predigtgottesdienst und die verwandten Formen," Leiturgia,* III, pp. 23-24; cited by Eugene L. Brand, "The Liturgical Life of the Church," in *A Handbook of Church Music,* Carl Halter and Carl Schalk, eds.

Call to worship (*"In nomine Patri,* etc.")
Sermon scripture in Latin (for the intellectuals)
German Votum with congregational "Amen"
Sermon text in German
Invocation of the Holy Spirit
Sermon
Parish announcements
Prayer of the Church
Lord's Prayer and "Ave Maria"
Apostles' Creed
The Ten Commandments
Public Confession
Closing Votum

Christian Worship in the Reformation

From an evangelical point of view, the service of the medieval eucharist considered earlier in this chapter was quite unbiblical, and urgently needed reform. From the simple, informal meetings of the first century, worship had developed into an elaborate ritual which evidenced serious distortions of New Testament standards, both in theology and in practice.

(1) The Liturgy of the Word had little significance. Though there was provision for scripture reading and a homily in the vernacular, the lections were often omitted in favor of readings from the lives of the saints. A sermon was rarely heard, since most local priests were too illiterate to be capable of preaching.

(2) Typical worshipers understood little of what was being said or sung, since the service was in Latin. Their own vocal participation was almost nil.

(3) The Lord's Supper was no more a joyful action of the whole congregation; it had become the priestly function of the celebrant alone. The congregation's devotion (mixed with superstition) was focused on the "host" (the bread) itself, on *seeing* the offering of the sacrifice, or on private prayers (e.g., the rosary).

(4) Each celebration of the mass was regarded as a separate offering of the body and blood of Christ. The emphasis was limited to Christ's death, with scant remembrance of his resurrection and second coming. Furthermore, the custom of offering "votive" masses for particular individuals and purposes became common.

(5) The Roman Canon was not a "Prayer of Thanksgiving," but rather a long petition which voiced repeated pleas that God would receive the offering of the mass, generating a spirit of fear lest it not be accepted. As a result, most of the congregation took communion only once a year. On many occasions, only the officiating priests received the bread and the cup.

Our look at the worship of the Reformation churches will include a consideration of the German, English and French-Swiss traditions. However, none of these was the first expression of rebellion against Rome. The *Unitas Fratrum* (United Brethren), which began under John Hus in Bohemia, had its own liturgical and musical expressions. However, that movement is not immediately pertinent to our narrative, since the reforms it began were aborted because of the death of Hus, who was burned at the stake in 1415.

The Lutheran Reformation.

Martin Luther's quarrel with Rome had more to do with the sacerdotal interpretation of the mass and the resultant abuses which accompanied it, than with the structure of the liturgy itself. For him, the Communion service was a sacrament (God's grace extended to man), not a sacrifice (our offering to God.) A musician himself, he loved the great music and the Latin text which graced the mass. Consequently, in his first reformed liturgy—*Formula missae et communionis* (1523)—much of the historic mass outline remains. Luther (1483-1546) is remembered as the individual who gave the German people the Bible and the hymnbook in their own language, to implement the recovery of the doctrine of believer-priesthood; he also restored the sermon to its central place in communion-worship. But in the *Formula missae,* only the hymns, scripture readings and sermon are in the vernacular; the rest continued to be in Latin. He achieved his theological purposes relating to the communion by removing the Offertory (offering the bread and wine to God) and much of the Roman canon; the Great Thanksgiving of the prayer was gone, and all that remained was the Preface and the Words of Institution.

The German Mass (*Deutscher messe,* 1526) was more drastic in its iconoclasm and may have been encouraged by some of Luther's more radical associates. In it, many of the historic Latin songs were replaced by vernacular hymn versions, set to German folksong melodies. This was the outline of its worship form:

Hymn or German Psalm (Introit)
Kyrie (In Greek, chanted to a psalm tone)
Collect (Short introductory prayer)
Epistle (chanted)
German Hymn (replacing the Gradual/Alleluia)
The Gospel (chanted)
The Creed (in the German hymn "We All Believe in One True God")
Sermon
Lord's Prayer (in paraphrase)
Admonition to Communicants re: the Lord's Table
Words of Institution
Communion, during which the German forms of the *Sanctus* (Isaiah,

Mighty Seer in Days of Old) and the *Agnus Dei* (O Christ, Thou Lamb of God) or other German hymns might be sung.
The Collect
The Aaronic Benediction

Throughout the 16th century, most Lutheran worship used a variant of one of these two liturgies. The *Formula missae* was the norm for cathedrals and collegiate churches, and the German Mass was common in smaller towns and rural churches. (20th century Lutherans tend to agree that Luther was excessively ruthless in the excisions made in the Communion service. Consequently, in recent service orders, they have recovered much of the historic eucharistic prayer, while still retaining their Reformation theological emphasis.)

We have already mentioned Luther's love of the historic music of the church. In the *Formula missae,* the choir sang the traditional psalms/ songs/prayers in Latin to Gregorian chant or in polyphonic settings. They also functioned in leading the congregation in the new unaccompanied chorales. Later, they sang alternate stanzas of the chorales in four and five-part settings by Johann Walther, published in 1524 in *Church Chorale Book.* In the 17th and 18th centuries, the choir made significant new contributions to worship, in the singing of motets, passions and cantatas.

The treble parts of the choral music were sung by boys who were trained in the "Latin" (parochial and cathedral) schools. The lower parts were sung by Latin school "alumni" or by members of the *Kantorei*—a voluntary social-musical organization that placed its services at the disposal of the church. Where there was no choir, the congregation was led by a "cantor"; that title ("singer") was also given to a musical director of large churches, as J. S. Bach was called in Leipzig from 1723-1750.

Luther seems to have been indifferent to (and occasionally critical of) the organ in divine worship, as were most Roman Catholic leaders of that period. As in the Roman church, the organ gave "intonations" for the unaccompanied liturgical singing and also continued the *alternatim* practice in the chorales. The "intonation" for the congregational chorales developed into what we know as a "chorale prelude." Later, as composing techniques moved toward homophonic styles with the melody in the soprano, the organ took over the responsibility of leading the congregation in the chorales.

Luther felt that the multiple services of the medieval offices had become an "intolerable burden." Since monasteries had been abolished, he prescribed that only the most significant morning and evening "hours"—Matins and Vespers—would be observed daily in local churches. However, office worship never really caught on among Lutherans; the practice soon died out and has only recently been revived, with moderate success. For non-eucharistic worship, Luther's followers have preferred a shortened mass, called an "ante-communion," which simply omits the Lord's supper observance from the regular liturgy.

The Reformation in England.

The early impetus for the Reformation in England was more political than spiritual. This was partly evident in the fact that for years after Henry VIII broke with the pope (1534) and assumed himself the leadership of the English (Anglican) church, the Latin Roman mass continued to be used without change. However, during the ensuing years, evangelical thought became more widespread and after Henry's death in 1547, Archbishop Cranmer (1489-1556) set about to devise a truly reformed English liturgy.

The first *Book of Common Prayer* was released in 1549, the title indicating that worship was now to be "congregational," not sacerdotal. This vernacular mass retained much of the form of the Roman rite, with drastic revision only in the Canon (Eucharistic Prayer), because of the rejection of the concepts of transubstantiation and "sacrifice." A significant number of Anglicans (especially Anglo-catholics) still express regret that this rite never became the norm for the Church of England. As was true in Lutheran Germany, popular opinion seemed to demand even more drastic revision, and three years later another prayer book was published. Much of the influence for the more radical trend came from the Calvinist movement in Strasbourg and Geneva.

In the Prayer Book of 1552 the word "mass" was dropped as the title of the worship form, vestments were forbidden, and altars were replaced by communion tables. The *Agnus Dei*, the *Benedictus,* and the Peace were all excised from the liturgy and the *Gloria in excelsis Deo* was placed near the end of the service. Thus the beginning of the ritual became basically personal and penitential, losing the corporate expression of praise and thanksgiving. The introit, gradual, offertory song and communion song were replaced by congregational psalms in metrical versions and later by hymns. In comparison with the "Liturgy of the Upper Room" which Roman Catholics used ca.1500, the greatest difference lies in the very-much shortened eucharistic prayer.

During the brief reign of "Bloody Mary" (1553-1558) the Roman Catholic faith and worship were reinstated, and many Protestant leaders were burned at the stake or beheaded. Others fled to such European refuges as Frankfort and Geneva, where they came under the influence of John Calvin and John Knox. When they returned to their native country, they brought with them an even more-radical revisionist attitude which eventually showed itself in the Puritan movement within the Church of England and the emerging of non-conformist churches (Presbyterian, Independent and Baptist). With the death of Mary, Queen Elizabeth I sought to heal the wounds of her broken country, and to bring Papists, traditionalists and Puritans together. Under her leadership, the Prayer Book was revised in 1559. The trend was back to the 1549 version, though the changes were slight; for one thing, vestments were once again permitted.

The Puritan movement gathered increasing momentum during the close of the 16th century and the beginning of the 17th. In worship, its emphasis was on "scriptural simplicity"—no choral or instrumental music, no written liturgy, and no symbolism (vestments, liturgical movement, etc.), much in the pattern of John Calvin in Geneva. Eventually, the group developed enough political strength to overthrow the king and set up a republic. In 1645 the Prayer Book was replaced by the *Directory for the Plain Worship of God in the Three Kingdoms*. For a brief period the choral and instrumental worship of the church went into complete limbo.

In 1660 Charles II was restored to the throne. He immediately brought the Prayer Book back into use. Soon a new revision (1662) was brought out; it made no substantial changes in the old version, retaining basically the 1552 worship outline, and that book became the norm for the Church of England for the next 300 years. It remains basically the same today, though there is considerable sentiment for a thorough revision.

This then was the outline of the Holy Eucharist as found in the *Book of Common Prayer*, 1662.

The Liturgy of the Word

The Lord's Prayer (minister alone)
Prayer (collect) for purity
Ten Commandments, and *Kyries* (in English)
Collects (Prayers)
Epistle
Gospel
Creed (Nicene)
Sermon

The Liturgy of the Upper Room

Offertory (Scripture sentences; collections; elements prepared)
Intercessions
Exhortation and Invitation
General Confession and Absolution: "Comfortable Words"
Sursum corda ("Lift up your hearts, etc.")
Consecration Prayer
   Preface and Propers; *Sanctus;* "Prayer of Humble Access"; Commemoration; Words of Institution
Communion
Lord's Prayer
Post-communion prayer of thanksgiving
Gloria in excelsis Deo
Peace and Benediction

We have already noted Luther's purpose pertaining to the continuance of the two "offices" Matins and Vespers as public, daily services of non-eucharistic worship. This practice was also adopted by Archbishop Cranmer for the English church, and liturgies for these services appeared in each of the prayer books mentioned above. As in the old Roman tradition, the emphasis was on the reading and singing of scripture; the Psalter was to be sung through each month, the Old Testament read through each year, and the New Testament twice each year. In making this service completely "English," the revisions of 1552 and 1662 had changed the titles of the services to "Morning Prayer" and "Evening Prayer," placed a general confession and absolution (assurance of pardon) at the beginning, added the *Jubilate Deo* (Psalm 100) as a regular canticle plus an anthem, with four collects and a general thanksgiving as the prayers. In common practice a sermon is also included, and this service has been for many Anglicans the "preferred" option for typical Sunday worship.

Morning or Evening Prayer (1662 prayer book)

(Hymn)
Scripture Sentences: Exhortation
Confession of sins and Absolution; Lord's Prayer
Psalms of the Day, each followed by *Gloria Patri*
Old Testament reading
Canticle (e.g., *Te Deum* for Matins, *Magnificat* for Vespers)
New Testament reading
Canticle (e.g., *Benedictus* for Matins, *Nunc dimittis* for Vespers)
Kyries; Lord's Prayer; Suffrages; Collects
Anthem
Prayer of Thanksgiving; Prayer for Grace
(Hymn)
(Sermon, followed by Ascription of praise)
(Collection)
(Hymn)
(Benediction)

The 1549 Prayer Book had stressed the requirement that Communion was not to be celebrated unless communicants were present and participating, and specified that members in good standing would receive Communion at least three times a year. The 1552 prayer book indicated that "Ante-communion"—the same service but omitting the eucharistic prayer and Communion—would also be observed on Sundays and "holy days." Because, like Lutherans, most Anglicans retained the medieval sense of awe and fear in receiving communion, non-eucharistic services tended to be the most popular in Anglican worship, until recent times.

We have already noted that congregational hymns became the norm of Protestant musical worship under Luther. In the early development of the English reformation church, this possibility was considered, and Bishop Myles Coverdale made an English translation of certain German and Latin hymns together with metrical versions of psalms and other liturgical material in a volume *Goostly psalmes and spiritual songs* (1543), intended for use in private chapels and homes. But, eventually the

Lutheran example was rejected in favor of the Calvinist standard—metrical psalms. In 1549, a Thomas Sternhold[13] published a small collection of nineteen psalms without music and by 1562, with the help of J. Hopkins the entire psalter was completed and named for its compilers; "Sternhold and Hopkins" remained in use (along with others) for more than two hundred years.

Psalm singing received added impetus during the exile of English protestants in Geneva during the reign of Mary, Queen of Scots, There they produced a number of versions of the Anglo-Genevan Psalter, with tunes, beginning in 1556; this book was based on Sternhold and Hopkins with certain additions of texts (and especially tunes) from the French psalters of Calvin. In the early 18th century, English nonconformists began to write and sing psalm paraphrases and "hymns of human composing," beginning with Isaac Watts (1674–1748). But free hymns were not widely accepted in Anglicanism until well into the 19th century.

Particularly in the services of Morning and Evening Prayer, the psalms were regularly sung in prose version; this was also true of the Canticles (*Benedictus, Te Deum, Magnificat, Nunc dimittis*). For this purpose, in the 17th century a new "Anglican chant" was produced, based on small snatches of Gregorian melody and sung in four-part harmony.

Despite its rejection of Luther's "hymns," the English church followed the example of the Lutherans in adapting the choir to its new Protestant patterns, particularly in the "cathedral tradition." From almost the beginning of Anglicanism, the choir was retained to lead the congregation, but also to sing alone, as in a "Choral Eucharist." In the 16th century the Tudor composers who had produced Latin masses (e.g., William Byrd, John Merbecke, Thomas Tallis, Richard Farrant) began to set portions of the new Prayer Book services. A complete "Service" included music for Holy Communion as well as for the canticles of Morning and Evening Prayer. Anglican "Services" have been written by British (and other) composers in every generation. These services are not performed in concert as is the Latin mass, but they are published together for liturgical use in larger Anglican (including Episcopalian) churches.

In addition, the Anglican heritage made a unique contribution to church music in the *anthem*—originally an English motet, whose name is derived from "antiphon." So-called "anthems" existed before 1550, but they were in disfavor until the Restoration. In the Prayer Book of 1662 they are acknowledged to be a regular part of worship in churches which boasted a choir.

In the English tradition it may be said that provision is made for a wide variety of musical tastes. In the parish church, congregational singing is central even though a modest choir may in some instances be available to sing an anthem and to lead the hymns and chants. In the cathedral setting, certain services are essentially choral, with less congregational

---

13. He is identified as robe-keeper to Henry VIII in Albert E. Bailey, *The Gospel in Hymns*, p. 7.

participation. These services give opportunity for the very finest examples of the choral art to be used.

Both Anglicans and Lutherans continued to observe the liturgical calendar with its festivals and "holy days." In both the eucharistic services and the offices, the "Ordinary" remained fairly constant throughout the year. The "Propers" provided scripture readings, prayers, responses and "sermon emphases" which changed according to the season and the day involved.

Worship in the Calvinist Tradition.

In Reformation times, the most severe reaction to traditional Roman Catholic worship came in the Calvinist tradition; for this reason, it is closely related to modern evangelical practice. But first, we must look briefly at some of John Calvin's predecessors.

Ulrich Zwingli (1484-1531), whose reform leadership centered in Zurich, was more a rationalist-humanist than Luther or Calvin, who stemmed from the medieval scholastic tradition. Consequently, Zwinglian worship tended to be more didactic than devotional. His typical morning service resembled the ancient Prone liturgy, consisting of scripture reading (Epistle and Gospel), preaching and a long prayer. In the first German liturgy of 1525, music was eliminated completely (although Zwingli himself was an accomplished musician); however, psalms and canticles were recited responsively. The communion service was celebrated four times a year, with the congregation seated as for a family meal. The eucharist service had no true eucharistic prayer and no prayer of intercession; it consisted of an Exhortation, Fencing of the Table, The Lord's Prayer, Prayer of "humble access," Words of Institution, Ministers' communion, Communion of the people, Psalm, Collect, Dismissal. According to Zwingli, the eucharist was only "the congregation confessing its faith in obedience to our Lord's command."

Martin Bucer (1491-1551), a follower of Zwingli, developed quite a different tradition when he was put in charge of Reformed worship in Strasbourg in 1535. Prior to that time, the city had been dominated by Lutheranism, consequently Bucer's liturgy of 1537 seems to combine Lutheran and Zwinglian elements. He retained the optional *Kyries* and *Gloria in excelsis,* though in time these were replaced by psalms or hymns. The Communion service included intercessions as well as a Prayer of Consecration.

When John Calvin (1509-1564) first preached and taught at Geneva, he evidently followed no set form of worship, and the service was entirely without music. When he was banished from Geneva in 1538, he went to be pastor of the French exiles in Strasbourg. He was quite impressed with Bucer's German rite and, according to his own admission, "borrowed the greater part of it" for his own French liturgy of 1540.[14]

---

14. See Wm. D. Maxwell, *John Knox's Genevan Service Book, 1556,* pp. 95-96, 188-198.

Later when he returned to Geneva, this liturgy was simplified slightly, became the Geneva rite of 1542 and the basis for Calvinist worship in all of Europe—Switzerland, France, Germany, Netherlands and Scotland.

Calvin's Geneva Liturgy (1542, etc.)
The Liturgy of the Word

Scripture Sentence: Psalm 124:8
Confession of sins; Prayer for pardon
Metrical Psalm
Prayer for Illumination
Sermon

The Liturgy of the Upper Room

Collection
Intercessions
Lord's Prayer, in long paraphrase
Apostle's Creed (elements prepared)
Words of Institution
Exhortation
Consecration Prayer
Communion (with psalm sung or scriptures read)
Post-communion prayer
Benediction (Aaronic Blessing)

Calvin's purpose was to return to the simple cultic practices of the early church; insofar as he failed to do so, it must be acknowledged that he did not have complete historical information. The medieval eucharistic vestments were discarded; the traditional black cassock now worn by Presbyterian ministers is essentially a reminder that Calvin preached in his overcoat because the cathedral at Geneva was unheated! Indeed, all the traditional Roman symbolism was stripped from the building; a Calvinist "processional" (particularly in Scotland) is headed by a deacon carrying the Bible into the sanctuary to place it on the pulpit. Calvin ignored the church calendar (except for the principal feast days) and with it the lectionary of readings; the scripture was read only to serve as a basis for the sermon. Finally, the prayers were allowed to be improvised in the ancient (and New Testament) practice.

Calvin's ideas about the eucharist were not radically different from those of Luther, though he rejected the idea of "consubstantiation."[15] He too saw the service as a "sacrament" and desired that it would be celebrated weekly as part of a full service of Word and Table, in the tradition of the early church. But this was not to be, because many of the French reformed leaders (including the magistrates at Geneva) had a more narrow view of Communion. Indeed, they restricted its observance to four times a year, despite Calvin's persistent objections.

---

15. This is the Lutheran view: that the body and blood of Christ are mystically "joined with" the bread and wine.

Calvin is most frequently criticized for his actions restricting music in worship. He discarded the choir and its literature completely, and Calvinist iconoclasts removed the organs from the formerly-Catholic churches. As mentioned earlier, the first worship at Geneva had no singing at all, and Calvin complained about the resultant "cold tone" in the services. When he went to Strasbourg, he was pleased with the German psalm versions he found in the congregations there, whereupon he set several psalms himself in metrical French to tunes of Mattheus Greiter and Wolfgang Dachstein. These were included with his Strasbourg service book, *The Form of Prayers and Manner of Ministering the Sacraments according to the Use of the Ancient Church* (1640). Later he commisioned the French court poet Clement Marot to set all the psalms in meter, which resulted in the historic Genevan Psalter (1562). The psalms were sung by the congregation in unison and without accompaniment.[16] Music editor for the volume was Louis Bourgeois (ca.1510-ca.1561) who adapted tunes from French and German secular sources, and no doubt composed some himself. This is not the place to debate Calvin's decision for psalms and against hymns, in the light of his dictum "Only God's Word is worthy to be used in God's praise." No doubt he was reacting strongly to the complex, verbose Roman liturgy, with its many "tropes" and "sequence" hymns. He did not have all the writings of the early church fathers at his disposal, from which he might have learned the significance of the New Testament "hymns and spiritual songs" (which at that time were not part of the biblical canon) and of the successors of those forms in the early church; no doubt the Apostle Paul and the earliest Christians understood that "human words" were also worthy to be the vehicle of God's praise! The Calvinist tradition of singing psalms was also inherited by the Anglican church and by early "free" churches in both England and America, and has persisted in some places to the present day.

Worship in the Free Church Tradition

In the closing years of the 16th century, the passion for religious reform was most intense in the English groups who were the most radical of the Puritans. They are known historically as the Separatists, since they intended to part company with the established Anglican church. When they did so, they were more iconoclastic than Calvin himself, reducing worship to something less than the essentials! They rejected all established liturgical forms; when they met together (in barns, in forests and fields, or in houses on back alleys, since such gatherings were forbidden by law), their services included only prayer and the exposition of scripture. Prayer was always spontaneous; not even the Lord's Prayer was used, since it was considered to be only a "model" for Christian

---

16. Four-part settings of the Marot psalms were composed by Sweelinck, Jannequin and Goudimel, but they were heard only in the home and in educational circles.

improvising. The early Separatists evidently had no music, but eventually they began to sing unaccompanied metrical psalms. When it was possible for them to celebrate communion, the appointed pastor broke the bread and delivered the cup which was then passed to every member of the group, while the leader repeated the words of I Corinthians 11:23-26. There is also record that on such occasions an offering was received at the end of the service, by men who held their "hats in hand."

The Separatists followed several traditions under a number of dynamic leaders, and eventually formed the churches known as Presbyterian, Independent (Congregational) and Baptist. Their negative attitude about earlier music is expressed in a quote from John Vicar in 1649, who was speaking as a convinced Puritan, but still an Anglican![17]

> ... the most rare and strange alteration of things in the Cathedral Church of Westminster. Namely, that whereas there was wont to be heard nothing almost but Roaring-Boys, tooting and squeaking Organ Pipes, and the Cathedral catches of Moreley, and I know not what trash, now the Popish Altar is quite taken away, the bellowing organs are demolisht and pull'd down; the treble or rather trouble and base singers, Chanters or Inchanters, driven out, and instead thereof, there is now a most blessed Orthodox Preaching Ministry, even every morning throughout the Week, and every Week throughout the year a Sermon Preached by the most learned grave and godly Ministers.

Anabaptists ("re-baptisers," who insisted that baptism was only for adult believers) appeared both on the continent and in Great Britain in the late 16th century. Records of a group in Holland in 1608 indicate that a typical service consisted of the following:[18]

Prayer
Scripture (one or two chapters, with a running commentary on its meaning)
Prayer
Sermon (one hour, on a text)
Spoken contributions by others present (as many as would)
Prayer (led by the principal leader)
Offering

It is not surprising that such a service often lasted as long as four hours. Sunday worship ran from about 8 a.m. to noon, and again from 2 p.m. to 5 or 6 o'clock.

English Baptists were by no means of one mind theologically. They divided into General Baptists (more Arminian in theology), Calvinistic Baptists (e.g., John Bunyan), Seventh Day Baptists (worshiped on Satur-

17. Cited by Jocelyn Perkins, *Westminster Abbey: Its Worship and Ornaments*, p. 111.
18. See Horton Davies, *Worship and Theology in England*, Vol. II, p. 89.

day) and Particular Baptists (radically Calvinist). For all of them, the typical worship consisted of Ministry of the Word (reading and exposition), extemporized prayer (lengthy—no collects) with a congregational "Amen," and possibly metrical psalms sung to open and to close the service.

There is evidence that in some churches the only music was sung by a single individual "who had a special gift." John Bunyan once argued that open congregational singing could not fulfill the standard of Colossians 3:16 because some might participate who did not have "grace in the heart." As late as 1690, Benjamin Keach (1640-1704) had difficulty persuading his own congregation to sing in unison. However, he did prevail and it is said that he was the first to introduce hymns (in addition to psalms) to an English congregation. He wrote the first hymn to be sung at the conclusion of the Lord's Supper, "following the example of Christ and his disciples in the upper room." Beyond this, we have little indication of how Baptists celebrated communion, except that it was a weekly occurence!

Evangelicals are in large part the successors of the Separatist movement, and in many instances have inherited the anti-Romanist, anti-liturgical, anti-aesthetic attitudes of their forebears. It may help us understand why these prejudices are so deeply ingrained, when we remember that our forefathers were moved by a strong spiritual commitment to evangelical theology and worship. Furthermore, as dissenters they endured constant persecution by the Puritan Anglican regime (or the Lutheran or Calvinist) under which they lived. To disobey the law by leading in clandestine worship was to be in danger of a heavy fine and lengthy imprisonment.

Summary

This chapter has traced our worship-practice roots, from New Testament times through 1600 years of the history of the Christian Church, ending with the Reformation and finally, the emergence of "free" churches. The purpose has been to show our universal Christian heritage, as well as the unique tradition of each individual fellowship.

To be sure, there is a common, universal heritage. We have seen that material from scripture was the basis of musical worship in all medieval services. We have also traced the evangelical emphasis on preaching from New Testament times and the early church fathers, through the medieval Prone, the reformed services of Luther and Calvin, and the worship of the Separatists. All Christians continue to experience a "Service of the Word" and a "Service of the Table," though most reformed and free churches have perpetuated the medieval reluctance to participate in communion on a frequent basis. Furthermore, particularly in the free church tradition, "occasional" observance tends to give the impression that the Lord's Supper is an appendage that is not central to full-orbed worship. Most evangelical scholars agree that the early Church celebrated the eucharist each Lord's Day. It may be that we should face up to the question as to whether or not, in this matter, we are living up to our claim to be a first century church.

All the changes brought by the Reformation were responses to the sincere desire to be more "evangelical." Obviously, the reaction of the "free" (Separatist) bodies was the most radical, and it tended to be tempered (as in the matter of the use of music) within a few years. Nevertheless, some of the attitudes and practices which began at that time have haunted certain free church groups ever since. It is important that we distinguish true evangelical reform from blind iconoclasm. In recent years, many Christian groups have taken a new look at their heritage and have tended to reinterpret those reforms. Some of the resulting enrichment of worship will be discussed in chapter nine, "Worship and Music in America." But first, we will take a look at the evangelical heritage of renewal in the church, and its distinctive musical expressions.

Chapter VIII

MUSIC AND RENEWAL IN THE CHURCH

At the close of the preceding chapter, we took notice of one of the most widespread movements of renewal—the 16th century Reformation and the emergence of the "free" churches. But this was not the first or the last revival movement. Because America has been uniquely the culture which encourages revivalism and because it has profoundly affected our worship, we will interrupt our narrative to present something of an apologetic for the accompanying music forms which have so frequently been the cause for controversy among church musicians. Actually, it is a little surprising that such an explanation is needed. From an anthropological viewpoint, the passing of time has validated the phenomenon far beyond our ability to add to, or detract from it!

The Nature of Renewal and Its Musical Expressions[1]

From time to time throughout its history, on a schedule determined by a sovereign Holy Spirit, the Christian church has been visited with spiritual renewal, or revival. Sometimes the emphasis has been on the purifying of dogma. Frequently it has included a concern for personal piety. Almost always there has been an accompanying outreach in evangelism and ministry. Consequently, in the context of this book's definitions, renewal must be seen to be closely related to evangelism.

Invariably these revival periods have been graced and supported by a flowering of new hymns, which quickly became very popular. The lyrics have carried the church's message of salvation, personal Christian experience and discipleship in poetic styles and images that were borrowed from non-ecclesiastical sources. The music of the new hymns has ignored traditional sacred symbols, taking on the characteristics of secular forms of the day. Generally speaking, these new "secular" forms and

---

1. Some of the material in this chapter first appeared in my essay, "Music and the Church's Outreach," in *Review and Expositor*, Vol. LXIX, No. 2, pp. 177–185.

sounds have remained in the church and have become part of a new "sacred" worship language. A generation—or perhaps centuries—later, these "new" symbols have been displaced or transformed by yet another renewal movement. A prototype of the subjective song to which we refer is the opening part of Psalm 40 and is entitled "To the choirmaster. A Psalm of David."

> I waited patiently for the Lord; he inclined to me and heard my cry. He drew me up from the desolate pit, out of the miry bog, and set my feet upon a rock, making my steps secure. He put a new song in my mouth, a song of praise to our God. Many will see and fear, and put their trust in the Lord.

Black slaves in America identified with the witness of the psalmist, since it expressed their hope for both spiritual and social salvation. This was their paraphrase:

> He took my feet from the miry clay. Yes, He did.
> And placed them on the rock to stay. Yes, He did.
> I can tell the world about this;
>   I can tell the nations I'm blessed.
> Tell them that Jesus made me whole,
>   And He brought joy, joy to my soul.[2]

I recall another version from my boyhood days, reminding us that biblical songs tend to outlive others in their usefulness.

> He brought me out of the miry clay,
>   He set my feet on the rock to stay,
> He puts a song in my soul today,
>   A song of praise, hallelujah![3]

It should be apparent that this type of text has important meaning to both singer and listener. It is a ballad, a narrative of human experience which speaks to every person who has shared the same experience. The psalmist is in serious trouble and is rescued—saved. His joy expresses itself in song, because music is a language of the emotions. Furthermore, emotional expression is contagious and may result in a change in the listener. As the psalm passage concludes, "Many will see (and hear the witness) and fear, and put their trust in the Lord." Such is the genius of experience song in renewal and outreach.

Renewal Music in History

We have already pointed out that the New Testament church sang "psalms and hymns and spiritual songs" and that the last-named may not

---

2. See "He Took My Feet from the Miry Clay," *Hymns for the Living Church,* p. 243.
3. Source unknown.

have had intelligible words, but was a compelling ecstatic expression of human Christian experience. "Hymns" on the other hand were probably doctrinal songs of the new Christology, possibly created by early European converts, and evidently shared by the Apostle Paul in his letters to the churches. An example is:

> He reflects the glory of God
>   And bears the very stamp of his nature,
> Upholding the universe by his word of power.
> When he had made purification for sins,
>   He sat down at the right hand of the Majesty on high . . .
>   (Hebrews 1:3)

Some of the songs also had a challenge to response which modern evangelists would call an "invitation."

> "Awake, O sleeper, and arise from the dead,
>   and Christ shall give you light."   (Ephesians 5:14)

The Early Christian Era.

Post-biblical writings of the early Church Fathers suggest that Syrian churches may have been first to develop a corpus of Christian hymnody, some of which was later declared to be heretical. The Gnostic teacher Bardesanes (born 154), together with his son Harmonius, evidently wrote a large number of lyrics which propagated a false gospel. In the conflict over the teaching of Arius (ca.250–366), both orthodox and heterodox used popular hymns to support their arguments. In the East, Ephraem Syrus (born ca.307), in northern Mesopotamia, so successfully advanced the anti-Arian cause that he was called "the cithern[4] of the Holy Spirit." In the West, Ambrose of Milan (ca.340–397) countered the Arian hymns with his own doctrinally-pure texts. He also developed a simple, rhythmic and syllabic chant which had strong appeal to the masses of unsophisticated worshipers, and probably had a secular antecedent.

Perhaps the only overt reference to musical evangelism in the early church is a statement about Niceta of Remesiana (ca.335–ca.414), a missionary to Dacia (now part of Yugoslavia), who is given credit for writing the immortal Latin hymn *Te Deum laudamus.* Jerome (ca.340–420) says that Niceta spread the gospel among fourth century European pagans "chiefly by singing sweet songs of the cross."[5]

The Middle Ages.

History records that by the sixth century congregational singing was suppressed in official Christian worship, partly to prevent any further

---

4. Evidently the kithara, the foremost stringed instrument of ancient Greece.
5. Cited by A. E. Bailey, *The Gospel in Hymns,* p. 214.

threats from heretical songsters and partly to stamp out the vestiges of "degenerate" music which had developed from a vulgarization of the Ambrosian chant. In the next few centuries the church spread westward throughout Europe and the British Isles, where the vernacular languages were considered unsuitable for the sacred message of the church. Wherever converts were won, by preaching or by military conquest, they were introduced to sacerdotal worship in the Latin tongue, with melodies in Gallican, Mozarabic or Gregorian chant. Eventually both the liturgy and the chant conformed to the Gregorian tradition, which centered in Rome.

It is a mistake, however, to believe that congregational singing disappeared from all corporate worship. It continued to be important in the extra-liturgical acts of devotion that have flourished from time to time throughout church history. In the early 13th century, for instance, Francis of Assisi (1182–1226) led a reform movement in his native Italy, preaching a simple gospel of "Christ first, Christ last, Christ all and in all." Singing was such a large part of his mission that Saint Francis billed himself as "God's gleeman." His hymns of praise and devotion were called *laude* and showed the influence of the secular French troubadour song. *Laude* flourished in informal Italian religious life for six centuries. Musical styles changed through the years but retained an affinity for the contemporary secular sound. In describing the late 16th century *laude* of Fra Serafino Razzi, *Harvard Dictionary of Music* (second edition) says:[6]

> Frequently folk songs and dance melodies were used for the religious texts, a procedure which shows a striking similarity to the methods of the Salvation Army. The numerous publications of the 17th century are important sources of early Italian folksong.

The Middle Ages boasted many examples of popular sacred song which flourished without ecclesiastical sanction. "Macaronic" hymns and dance-related carols combined the vernacular language with certain Latin phrases. "Contrafacted" hymns were written in the 13th century by Heinrich von Laufenberg and thereafter by many others; their texts were sacred parodies of secular songs, and the tunes were those commonly used with the secular antecedents.

The German church in the Middle Ages showed extraordinary independence of Rome in the matter of congregational participation in worship. In addition to the forms already mentioned, the *Geisslerlieder* were sung during the penitential processions of the 14th century flagellants. Even earlier, first in the ninth century, *Leisen* were sung in connection with processional litanies. The title derives from the common refrain "Kyrie eleison" corrupted to "kyrleis" or "leis." Each of these musical forms stemmed from some movement of spiritual renewal, and each drew its inspiration from popular, secular sources.

---

6. *Harvard Dictionary of Music*, 2nd ed., p. 394.

The Reformation.

It fell to the 16th century reformers to reestablish congregational participation as the foundation of official liturgical worship. Calvin went the route of vernacular "psalms in meter," set to tunes that were derisively called "Geneva Jiggs." For years the authorship of the melodies has been the subject of research and debate. It now seems obvious that many were adapted from folk music of German or French origin. A biographer of Louis Bourgeois, music editor of the *Genevan Psalter* (1562), explains:

> A composer of that day employed his talents on harmony rather than on melody, and used for his subjects any material that suited his purpose. A difference in style between sacred and secular music hardly existed, and "composing" was often literally "compounding."[7]

The secular origins of the Lutheran chorale tunes are much easier to verify. Luther himself borrowed the melody of *Wach auf, wach auf, du schöne* (Wake up, wake up, you beauty) for his own words, *Nun freut euch, lieben Christen g'mein* (Dear Christians, one and all, rejoice). Similarly, *Innsbruck, ich muss dich lassen* (Innsbruck, I now must leave you) lent its tune for *O Welt, ich muss dich lassen* (O World, I now must leave you) and *Ich hört ein Fraülein klagen* (I heard a girl weeping) became *Herr Christ der einig Gott's Sohn* (Lord Jesus Christ, God's only Son). Other chorale lyricists used or adapted melodies of earlier religious folksong (e.g., *leisen*), which in turn had secular origins. No doubt some of the chorale melodies had plainsong roots, and perhaps some were completely original. But they were all finally cast in the same "popular" style. The purposes of Martin Luther (1483-1546), as demonstrated in his chorale texts, were strongly pedagogical. He versified the principal songs of the Mass—*Kyrie, Gloria, Credo, Sanctus* and *Agnus Dei*—for use in his *Deutsche Messe* (1526). He also wrote hymns to parallel the salient emphases of Lutheran doctrine—Baptism, Communion, Penance and the Ten Commandments. Generally speaking, hymns of Christian experience in the pietist tradition do not appear until the late 17th century. But one text of Luther's is a noteworthy exception that bears strong resemblance to a later hymn of Charles Wesley.[8]

> Fast bound in Satan's chains I lay,
> Death brooded darkly o'er me,
> Sin was my torment night and day,
> In sin my mother bore me;
> Yea, deep and deeper still I fell,
> Life had become a living hell,
> So firmly sin possessed me.
>
> But God beheld my wretched state
> Before the world's foundation,
> And, mindful of His mercies great,

7. G. A. Crawford, "Louis Bourgeois" in *Grove's Dictionary*, Vol. I, p. 848 (footnote).
8. See "And can it be that I should gain" in *Methodist Hymnal* (1964), no. 527.

He planned my soul's salvation.
A father's heart He turned to me,
Sought my redemption fervently;
He gave his dearest Treasure.[9]

The Pietist Movement in Germany.

In the late 17th and early 18th centuries, an important movement flowered in the German Lutheran Church, known as Pietism. Its first leader was Philipp Jakob Spener (1635-1705), who called the church from its obsession with dry scholasticism, cold formalism and dead orthodoxy to an emphasis on personal study of the scriptures and experiential "religion of the heart."

Pietists rejected all art music in worship because of the "operatic tendencies" of the time. Johann Sebastian Bach was in constant conflict with the Pietists, though his cantata texts show the influence of their theology. The movement inspired a flood of subjective hymnody, much of which was set to tunes in dancelike triple meter, in sharp contrast to the older, rugged chorale style. Some of the best-known hymnists were Johann Freylinghausen (1670-1739), Ludwig von Zinzendorf (1700-1760), Benjamin Schmolck (1672-1737) and Erdmann Neumeister (1671-1756). It is interesting to note that the last-named wrote cantata texts used by J. S. Bach and also the original version of the gospel hymn "Sinners Jesus Will Receive" (Christ Receiveth Sinful Men).

One of the favorite images of pietest hymnody—the relationship of Christ (the bridegroom) to the church, and to the individual believer (the bride)—appears in even earlier hymns, such as "Jesu, meine Freude" by Johann Franck (1618-1677). The following is a rather literal translation of the first stanza and part of the last.

Jesu, meine Freude,	Jesus, my joy,
Meines Herzen's Weide,	My heart's longing,
Jesu, meine Zier,	Jesus, my beauty.
Ach, wie lang, ach lange	Oh, how long, how long
Is dem Herzen bange	Is the heart's concern
Und verlangt nach dir!	And longing after you.
Gottes Lamm, mein Bräutigam,	Lamb of God, my bridegroom,
Ausser dir soll mir auf Erden	May nothing on earth become dear
Nichts sonst Liebers werden.	To me except you.
Weicht, ihr Trauergeister,	Get out, spirit of sadness!
Denn mein Freudenmeister,	For my Lord of gladness—
Jesu, tritt herein.	Jesus, enters in.
Denen, die Gott lieben	To those who love God,
Muss auch ihr Betrüben	Even their sorrows
Lauter Zucker sein.	Are purest sweetness ("sugar").

Franck had modeled his hymn on the love song of H. Alberti, "Flora, meine Freude" (Flora, my joy). English translations have ignored much

---

9. These are the second and fourth stanzas of Richard Massie's translation of *Nun freut euch, lieben Christen g'mein*. See *The Lutheran Hymnal* (1941), no. 387.

of the original anthropomorphic imagery, and current German versions have changed the word *Zucker* (sugar) to *Freude* (joy). Nevertheless, it is interesting to observe this preview of Charles Wesley's "Jesus, Lover of My Soul" and the more-recent song, "In Love with the Lover of My Soul" by Phil Kerr, which scandalized many of us when it appeared in the 1940's!

Dissenters in England.

We have already noted that it was a Dissenter—Benjamin Keach, Baptist—who first introduced a hymn of "human composing" into the psalm-singing culture of 17th century England. Isaac Watts (1674–1748), a Congregational minister, had the most profound influence on his country's transition to hymn-singing and thus became known as the "father of English hymnody." It is significant that hymn singing flourished in the "renewal-born" free churches (Congregational, Baptist and Presbyterian) for a hundred years while it was still being rejected in the established Church of England. Watts has been said to combine most successfully the expression of worship with that of human devotional experience, and it is best illustrated in his well-known hymn "When I Survey the Wondrous Cross," of which the first and last stanzas are quoted here.

> When I survey the wondrous cross,
>   On which the Prince of glory died,
> My richest gain I count but loss,
>   And pour contempt on all my pride.
>
> Were the whole realm of nature mine,
>   That were a present far too small;
> Love so amazing, so divine,
>   Demands my life, my soul, my all.

The Wesleyan Revival.

"Evangelistic hymns" in the modern sense were one of the glorious by-products of Britain's "Great Awakening" in the 18th century. It was the preaching of John (1703–1791) and Charles Wesley (1707–1788), and the underlying tenets of the Dutch theologian Jacob Arminius (1560–1609), which led to the creation of the first "invitation" songs. Hard-line, hyper-Calvinism based on "covenant theology" and the doctrine of predestination has rarely generated widespread, enthusiastic evangelism. The Wesleys' Arminian theology emphasizes that an individual may say either "yes" or "no" to a seeking God. To press the claims of Christ while still admitting man's "free will," Charles Wesley wrote:

> Come, sinners, to the Gospel feast:
>   Let every soul be Jesus' guest;
> Ye need not one be left behind,
>   For God hath bidden all mankind.

> This is the time; no more delay!
> This is the Lord's accepted day;
> Come thou, this moment, at his call,
> And live for him who died for all.[10]

Musically the Wesleys must be credited with rescuing hymn singing from the bondage of the two-line meters—common, long and short. Their sources were the newer psalm tunes, opera melodies, and folk songs of German origin. An example of this type of tune is "Mendenbras" (which was actually first used with a hymn text by Lowell Mason in 1839); we commonly sing it to "O day of rest and gladness," but it may still be heard with its historic secular words in the "beer gardens" of Germany! The Wesleys' texts were fundamental for early Methodist theology. They also covered almost every conceivable aspect of Christian devotional experience and may be said to be the progenitors of the modern gospel song.

Pragmatically there is little mystery about the cycle of secular-sacred-secular-sacred symbolism recounted in this narrative. "Common" church music—that which is intended for congregational participation—must always be "popular," which is to say, simple and non-professional. When used in worship, this music assumes by association a *sacral* symbolism. It becomes a "sacred" music language. In any period of spiritual renewal, old symbols frequently lose their meaning and new ones must be sought. Obviously, they will be found outside the church, and because they must be "common" or "popular," they will come from secular folk song and even from commercial entertainment music. In the evangelistic thrust of renewal, the fresh "secular-become-sacred" song becomes an effective vehicle for witness to the uncommitted. The newly-adopted secular language eventually gains a new sacralization and becomes the norm for divine worship. It remains so until another spiritual revival displaces it.

In a theological rationale, one might say that this process demonstrates the church's willingness to be forever *incarnational,* to identify with "the world" and to transform it for Christ. It is certainly not a new concept in church music. As the late British musicologist Charles Sanford Terry said of the music of the German Reformation:

> In their action . . . the early Lutheran compilers were moved also to purify popular art by substituting—to quote a Frankfurt title-page dated 1571—"*geistige, guete, nuetze Texte und Worte*" (spiritual, pure, profitable lyrics) for the "*boese und aergerliche Wese, unnuetze und schampare Liedlein*" (evil and irritating style of the useless and shameful ditties) in popular use.[11]

In other words, worthy lyrics sanctify the secular melody!

---

10. *Methodist Hymnal* (1964), no. 102.
11. *Grove's Dictionary,* Vol. II, p. 271.

The American Scene

The same secular/sacred cycle continued in the early colonies, which largely took their worship and evangelism cues from Mother England. America's first worship music consisted of metrical psalms, and these were still the norm during the thundering revival preaching of Jonathan Edwards, best remembered by the title of one of his famous sermons, "Sinners in the Hands of an Angry God." When the Great Awakening came to America in the mid-18th century—largely through the preaching sorties of the Wesleys' associate George Whitefield—singing broke the bonds of strict psalmody and the hymns of Isaac Watts came to these shores. In the late 1700's, rural Baptists in New England were singing "Watts and Wesley" to modal folk melodies they had brought from the "old country"; the tunes were perpetuated through such books as *Kentucky Harmony* (1825) and *The Sacred Harp* (1844), and have come to be known as "white spirituals" or "Appalachian folk hymns." In this tradition, the folk tune associated with Samuel Stennett's "On Jordan's stormy banks I stand" strongly resembles one associated with "I'll go and enlist for a sailor" in Sharp's *Morris Dances*. [12]

The Campmeetings.

In 1800 the campmeeting movement began with an outbreak of revival in an outdoor encampment in Caine Ridge, Logan County, Kentucky. The music which characterized the campmeetings was very simple with much repetition, evidently very emotional and frequently improvised. These are typical texts which are little more than refrains:

> Come to Jesus, come to Jesus, Come to Jesus just now,
>   Just now come to Jesus, Come to Jesus just now.

> He will save you, he will save you, He will save you just now,
>   Just now he will save you, He will save you just now.
>   (*The Revivalist*, 1872, p. 142)

> O get your hearts in order, order, order,
>   O get your hearts in order for the end of time.
> For Gabriel's going to blow, by and by, by and by,
>   For Gabriel's going to blow, by and by.
>   (*Evangelical Harp*, 1845, p. 40)

Much has been said about the relationship between black spirituals and campmeeting music, with the general impression that the latter may have copied the former. However, at that time in history, particularly in

---

12. Cited in a lecture, "The Persistence of the Primitive in American Hymnology" by Ellen Jane (Lorenz) Porter, delivered at Southern Baptist Theological Seminary, Louisville, KY in October, 1978 with accompanying duplicated examples.

the revival context, blacks and whites worshiped together. It is possible that both cultures contributed to the spontaneous singing in the "brush arbor" meetings, and that blacks continued the tradition after the interest of the whites had diminished and they had moved on to new forms of more traditional, "composed" music. The similarity between campmeeting songs and black spirituals is shown by Ellen Jane (Lorenz) Porter in her lecture, "The Persistence of the Primitive in American Hymnology." She points out that the song "Where Are the Hebrew Children?" is found in both the north and the south, and among the blacks.[13]

> Where, O where are the Hebrew children,* (repeat)
>   Who were cast in the furnace of fire?
>   Safe now in the promised land.
>
> By and by we'll go home to meet them, (repeat)
>   By and by we'll go home to meet them,
>   Way over in the promised land.
>
> (Oriola, 1862, p. 236)
>
> *2. good Elijah, 3. prophet Daniel, 4. weeping Mary,
>   5. martyred Stephen, 6. blessed Jesus, etc.

Many of the campmeeting songs also used "secular" melodies. According to Mrs. Porter, "Where Are the Hebrew Children?" has many parodies, including the Ozark song, "Where, O Where Is Pretty Little Susie?" and the college song "Where, O Where Are the Verdant Freshmen?"

It is evident that refrains were the most important element in campmeeting music, and some songs were little more. In other instances, favorite refrains were attached to many different hymns. In *Companion to Baptist Hymnal*,[14] William J. Reynolds cites a quotation of P. P. Bliss in which "I will arise and go to Jesus" is identified as "one of the old-fashioned campmeeting spirituals" which could be sung as a response to Joseph Hart's "Come, ye sinners, poor and needy" or after each stanza of an anonymous paraphrase of the prodigal son story, "Far, far away from my loving Father." Note also that the refrain "Blessed be the name of the Lord" appears with Charles Wesley's "O for a thousand tongues to sing"[15] and with William H. Clark's "All praise to Him who reigns above."[16] In the same tradition, Ralph E. Hudson added the lilting testimony refrain "At the cross, etc., where I first saw the light" to the sober, devotional "Alas! and did my Savior bleed?" of Isaac Watts. In another example, the final stanza commonly sung to John Newton's "Amazing Grace" is by an unknown author and has some horrendous grammar, but it was also appended to Isaac Watts' "When I can read my title clear" and to the 16th century anonymous hymn "Jerusalem, my happy home."

13. Ibid.
14. P. 48.
15. *Baptist Hymnal* (1975), no. 50.
16. *Hymns for the Living Church* (1974), no. 81.

When we've been there ten thousand years
    Bright shining as the sun;
We've no less days to sing God's praise
    Than when we first begun. (sic)

The Finney Revival.

The Second Great Awakening was an urban phenomenon in Eastern seaboard states in the early 19th century. Charles Granville Finney, a Presbyterian with a pronounced Arminian theological bent, was the central preacher and he frequently worked with the music educator-composer, Thomas Hastings. Their association marks the first recorded instance of a "songbook" published specifically for a revival campaign. The following hymn was reputed to have been in one of Hastings' compilations and to have been used by Finney at the conclusion of the sermon as part of a protracted, emotional "altar call."

Hearts of stone, relent, relent,
    Break, by Jesus' cross subdued;
See his body, mangled—rent,
    Covered with a gore of blood.
Sinful soul, what hast thou done!
    Murdered God's eternal Son.

Yes, our sins have done the deed,
    Drove the nails that fixed him there,
Crowned with thorns his sacred head,
    Pierced him with a soldier's spear;
Made his soul a sacrifice,
    For a sinful world he dies.

Will you let him die in vain,
    Still to death pursue your Lord;
Open tear his wounds again,
    Trample on his precious blood?
No! with all my sins I'll part,
    Savior, take my broken heart.[17]

Sunday School Hymns and the Gospel Song.

Beginning in the 1840's, the Sunday School hymns of William B. Bradbury and others had the same musical form as campmeeting songs—catchy melody, simple harmony and rhythm and an inevitable refrain. Eventually these children's hymns were picked up by adults and the "gospel hymn" or "gospel song" was born, so named by Philip Phillips, "the Singing Pilgrim." It was the evangelistic missions of Moody and Sankey in Great Britain and America which launched the gospel song on its century-long career, and it is still going strong. No doubt it also

17. From "The Revival Heard Around the World," by Richard L. Manzelmann.

received a great impetus by its association with the "singing schools" conducted by itinerant music teachers in the middle of the 19th century. The most successful of the teachers—J. G. Towner, P. P. Bliss, and George F. Root, and many others—wrote and published both sacred and secular music, and in much the same style as Stephen Foster, composer of "My Old Kentucky Home" as well as many sacred selections. The hallowed Fanny Crosby, author of perhaps 9000 gospel song texts, had achieved earlier success writing popular secular songs in collaboration with George F. Root, an associate of Lowell Mason in public school music, who taught at New York's Union Theological Seminary and also supplied music for the original Christy Minstrel Singers!

It should not be thought that these were unlettered, uncultured individuals who lacked recognition in their own society. Phoebe Palmer Knapp, composer of the music for "Blessed Assurance," was married to the president of the Metropolitan Life Insurance Company. William Howard Doane, the most frequent collaborator of Fanny J. Crosby was an extremely wealthy industrialist and civic leader. William Bradbury, George F. Root, and Charles Converse (What a Friend we have in Jesus) all studied in Europe, and were acquainted with the Robert Schumanns, Franz Liszt and Louis Spohr. Fanny Crosby was well known by five American presidents and many other government leaders. The music these individuals wrote was highly successful in 19th century America, and often made a great deal of money for them and their publishers.

We must also note that "experience hymns" continued to appear in evangelical settings the world around. For one thing, American hymns in this style were translated into every language in which Protestant worship was conducted, both in Europe and in mission lands. In addition, other countries produced their own versions. In Sweden, for example, a renewal movement developed in the Lutheran church during the 1840's under the lay-preacher Carl Rosenius (1816-1868). Lina Sandell (1832-1903) supported the movement with her hymns to such an extent that she became known as the "Swedish Fanny Crosby." Music for many of her songs was written by Oscar Ahnfelt, who was called the "Swedish Troubadour" because of his itinerant ministry, singing and playing his own accompaniments on a guitar. The Sandell/Ahnfelt songs were published in a series of books, with the help of the famous coloratura soprano, Jenny Lind, "the Swedish Nightingale." This is the first stanza of one of Lina Sandell's best-known hymns, many of which were brought to America by Swedish immigrants and are now sung by many evangelicals.

> Day by day and with each passing moment,
> Strength I find to meet my trials here;
> Trusting in my Father's wise bestowment,
> I've no cause for worry or for fear.
> He whose heart is kind beyond all measure
> Gives unto each day what He deems best—

Lovingly, its part of pain and pleasure,
Mingling toil with peace and rest.
                              (Lina Sandell, 1865
                              Trans. by A. L. Skoog)

There have been many attempts to define a "gospel song" in order to differentiate it from more traditional hymn forms. Frequently, it has been argued that hymns are "objective" (about God, the "object" of our thought) and gospel songs are "subjective" (about the thinking "subject" and his/her experience of God.) However, many historic hymns are simultaneously both "objective" and "subjective" (e.g., Watts' "When I Survey the Wondrous Cross") and some acknowledged gospel songs are quite thoroughly objective (e.g., "Praise Him, Praise Him, Jesus Our Blessed Redeemer," by Fanny J. Crosby.) Even metrical psalms have been set to gospel song music (e.g., E. O. Sellers' adaptation of Psalm 119, "Thy Word Is a Lamp to My Feet.")

The title gives some cue as to the norm. "Gospel" suggests that it is usually concerned with the *basic* gospel, the message of sin and grace and redemption, and man's experience of them; "song"[18] indicates that it is *secular* of origin—not a hymn. Basically, the poetry was simpler than that of a hymn—less theological and less biblical, less challenging to the imagination, sometimes even innane. The musical structure was characterized by a refrain—a novelty in hymns, a simple lyric melody, inconsequential harmony and a sprightly rhythm.

The Moody-Sankey Campaigns.

Early in his ministry in the slums of Chicago, the untutored lay-preacher Dwight L. Moody (1837–1899) sensed the power of the new songs to motivate men and women to spiritual action. When he embarked on a wider ministry, he chose Ira D. Sankey (1840–1908), a civil servant and amateur musician, to accompany him. Sankey led the congregational hymns and sang his solos while seated at a little reed organ. He was also a prominent composer and publisher of gospel songs. The story of Sankey's experience as he accompanied Mr. Moody to Scotland in 1873 is told in his own book, *My Life and the Story of the Gospel Songs*. On one particular occasion, he was concerned because the illustrious hymn writer Horatius Bonar was in the audience.

> Of all men in Scotland he was the one concerning whose decision I was most solicitous. He was, indeed, my ideal hymn writer, the prince among hymnists of his day and generation. And yet he would not sing one of his beautiful hymns in his own congregation ... because he ministered to a church that believed in the use of the Psalms only.

18. Note that the phrase "spiritual songs" from Col. 3:16 and Eph. 5:19 has frequently been used for various kinds of hymnody; the form originally referred to was probably very free, possibly ecstatic and improvised. Many German hymnals have been titled "Geistliche Lieder" (spiritual songs).

With fear and trembling I announced as a solo the song, "Free from the law, Oh, happy condition." Feeling that the singing might prove only an entertainment and not a spiritual blessing, I requested the whole congregation to join me in a word of prayer, asking God to bless the truth about to be sung. In the prayer my anxiety was relieved. Believing and rejoicing in the glorious truth contained in the song, I sang it through to the end.

At the close of Mr. Moody's address, Dr. Bonar turned toward me with a smile on his venerable face, and reaching out his hand he said: "Well, Mr. Sankey, you sang the gospel tonight." And thus the way was opened for the mission of sacred song in Scotland.[19]

In the Moody-Sankey meetings, England and America witnessed the advent of "Jesus" preaching and singing. Along with the biblically-strong "Free from the law" which was a good choice for the theologically-minded Scots, there were many simple expressions of the love of God through Christ:

> I am so glad that our Father in heaven
>   Tells of His love in the book He has given;
> Wonderful things in the Bible I see:
>   This is the dearest, that Jesus loves me.
>
> (P. P. Bliss)

It is characteristic of the best witness songs, that they will always be couched in *contemporary* language. In Moody's day the idea of "being lost" or "saved" was often expressed in nautical terms:

> Pull for the shore, sailor, pull for the shore,
>   Heed not the rolling waves, but bend to the oar;
> Safe in the lifeboat, sailor, cling to self no more;
>   Leave that poor old stranded wreck, and pull for the shore.
>
> (Author unknown)

> I've anchored my soul in the haven of rest,
>   I'll sail the wide seas no more;
> The tempest may sweep o'er the wild, stormy deep,
>   In Jesus I'm safe evermore.
>
> (H. L. Gilmour)

The idea of conflict and challenge in spiritual living probably took images from the Civil War.

> Ho, my comrades! See the signal waving in the sky!
> Reinforcements now appearing! Victory is nigh!
>
> Hold the fort! for I am coming;
>   Jesus signals still.
> Wave the answer back to heaven:
>   "By thy grace, we will!"
>
> (P. P. Bliss)

---

19. Ira D. Sankey, *My Life and the Story of the Gospel Songs*, pp. 61-62.

Since the days of Sankey, the solo singer has been a distinctive part of musical mass evangelism in America. Philip Phillips (1834-1895) was perhaps the first in a long line of illustrious soloist-songleader-publishers, which includes Sankey's contemporaries Robert Lowry (1826-1899), P. P. Bliss (1838-1876), James McGranahan (1840-1907), P. P. Bilhorn (1865-1936) and Homer Rodeheaver (-1880-1955). The strong contribution of the gospel singer is the "person to person"—often layperson to person—witness of Christian experience. In this ministry, the gospel message acquires an intensity of emotional communication that is acknowledged by both its proponents and its detractors. This was true, even in the earliest days when the songs were not characteristically soloistic, but were sung by soloists and congregations alike. It is even more so, now that styles of writing and performing solo music are fully developed. The gospel singer's appeal and popularity may be surpassed only by the singer of secular "pop" music—whether Rudy Vallee, Bing Crosby, Frank Sinatra, Elvis Presley, Johnny Cash or Olivia Newton John. It was this same personal, emotional communication of common human experience that gave Sankey equal billing with Moody. A century later, history still speaks of the Moody-Sankey meetings!

"But that music is not only emotional," the critics complain; "it is *physical,* appealing more to the feet than the mind and heart." Rhythmic it is, and "physical music" has long served the church! In the middle ages, the penitential processions were the occasion of some of the first congregational singing after the long silence of severely-sacerdotal worship. We have already acknowledged that the 13th century *laudi spirituali* were based on earlier dance forms and that Calvin's psalm tunes were scorned as "Geneva jiggs." In the 19th century, the Anglican church expanded its processional hymn tradition to include outdoor Sunday school marches that were the inspiration of such hymns as "Onward, Christian Soldiers." The Salvation Army added the crowning touch, to reach the working man on the street—a full brass band. After performing on the street corner to attract a crowd, the cornet, trombone, tuba and cymbal led the way back to the meeting hall, playing "Are you washed in the blood of the Lamb." Inside the building, the big bass drum continued to be used to accompany the invitation hymn! All of this happened, not in frontier America, but in historic Europe and Great Britain. It remained for our country to contribute the "two-step" or "polka" gospel song, the "waltz" songs of C. H. Gabriel (1856-1932) and even the "rock gospel" beat of Tedd Smith and John Wilson.

"Charlie" Alexander and Gospel Choirs.

In the early 20th century, it was Charles Alexander (1867-1920), songleader for evangelists R. A. Torrey and J. Wilbur Chapman, who brought the "gospel choir" to its nadir. Not an outstanding soloist himself, Alexander specialized in the leading of massed choirs and congregations around the world for more than twenty-five years. Once again, the significance of a ministry in music gave the song leader equal billing with the evangelist. Earlier it had been "Moody and Sankey." Now it was "Torrey and Alexander" and "Chapman and Alexander." One is tempted to discount the laudatory reports of Alexander's conducting successes in newspapers of that day.

> Mr. Alexander is a conductor of the first order, and he exercises a curious spell over an audience. He drills a thousand people with the precision and authority of a drill-sergeant. He scolds, exhorts, rebukes, and jests. And the amusing feature is that the great audience enjoys being scolded and drilled . . . They seem at first an audience for whom music has ceased to have any ministry. But as the singing goes on, the tired faces relax, the eyes brighten, the lips begin to move . . . Music, as the servant and vehicle of religion has fulfilled its true and highest office. It has set a thousand human souls vibrating in gladness. No one need doubt that the gospel can be sung as effectively as it can be spoken.[20]

> I have watched the methods and the triumphs of the most famous baton-wielders of the time—Colonne, Nikisch, Mottl, Weingartner and Henry J. Wood. Never have I been so much impressed as I was by this bright-faced, energetic young evangelist. As the leader of a choir he has an amazing and almost magical influence, not only over the trained choir; he simply makes everybody sing, and sing as he wants them to. "Watch my hand!" he calls, and the men's unaccompanied voices rise and fall in crooning cadences with an effect any conductor might be proud of. Watch his hands? Why, we are watching every part of him; we cannot take our eyes off him; we are fascinated, hypnotized, bewitched . . .[21]

This kind of entertaining genius may help to account for the physical stamina which was demonstrated by audiences of that day. A "Festival of Song"—shared equally by congregation, choir and soloists—was expected to last for three hours. In a report of the meetings in Royal Albert Hall, London, it was said that the audience came at two o'clock in the afternoon and stayed until six. Torrey preached for about forty-five minutes and the rest of the time was consumed by song, with the audience calling for one favorite after another.

It is apparent that the revival choir was expected to share the prophetic/evangelistic ministry of the evangelist; its materials consisted of the "basic gospel" and it was seated with the evangelists behind the pulpit, not in a "divided chancel" or in the balcony in the tradition of Old World churches.

20. A statement by W. H. Fitchett, editor of *The Southern Cross,* describing a midday meeting in Melbourne, Australia's Town Hall. Quoted in *Charles M. Alexander: A Romance of Song and Soul-Winning,* pp. 51–52 (by Helen C. Alexander and J. Kennedy Maclean.)

21. Cited in Alexander and Maclean, op. cit., p. 106. The article is by H. Hamilton Fyle, music critic, in the *London Daily Mirror,* February 6, 1905, reporting on a meeting in Royal Albert Hall.

"Charlie" Alexander was responsible for one more secular innovation in revivalist music—the use of the piano. Earlier leaders had used the pipe organ when it was available, or else a harmonium, a reed organ. Alexander found that the percussive piano was more helpful in leading the livelier songs of his day. Robert Harkness[22] was his best known pianist, who also wrote a number of songs in a more distinctively "soloistic" style (e.g., "Why Should He Love Me So?") It is said that Harkness was recruited from a "music hall" before he was a committed Christian, and that Alexander led him to personal faith in Christ.

The Team of Billy Sunday and Homer Rodeheaver.

It is a popular misconception that "gospel music" did not change much from 1850 to 1950. Each generation has contributed its own theological, poetic and musical flavor. From 1890 to 1910, the scene was dominated by teachers and students of the Moody Bible Institute, where D. B. Towner had become the mentor of gospel music; songs of that period were intensely biblical and theological. Between 1910 and 1920, Billy Sunday came to the fore as an evangelist, with his songleader-soloist-trombonist, Homer Rodeheaver. Both men had gifts suited to the theater—Sunday the dynamic, compulsive, athletic spellbinder, and Rodeheaver the genial, suave, relaxed, joking "master of ceremonies." They brought a new level of secularism to evangelistic crusades, with crowd-pleasing mannerisms of entertainment.

> "Rody" was a master at getting people to sing. He used every gimmick at his disposal to break down the traditionally staid approach to religious music. Neither "Rody" nor Sunday would tolerate glumness in the Gospel, and the tabernacle crowds soon learned to expect the unexpected. Delegations that came were asked to sing their favorite song; railroaders, for instance, stood to sing "I've Been Working on the Railroad." College groups could count on a chance to sing their Alma Mater and give a victory cheer.[23]

Seafaring imagery was still around in those days because memories of the "Titanic" tragedy were still vivid.

> I was sinking deep in sin, Far from the peaceful shore . . .
>
> Love lifted me, love lifted me,
> When nothing else could help, Love lifted me.
>
> (James Rowe)

Other expressions were more serene, if not strongly theological!

> What a wonderful change in my life has been wrought,
> Since Jesus came into my heart;

22. Ibid., p. 55.
23. D. Bruce Lockerbie, *Billy Sunday*, p. 58.

I have peace in my soul for which long I had sought,
    Since Jesus came into my heart.
                                        (C. H. Gabriel)

The early 20th century had its own "physical" music, as well. I remember singing one in the 1920's that was obviously inspired by stories of the First World War.

    Over the top for Jesus, Bravely we will go,
    Over the top for Jesus, Routing every foe;
    Never delaying when we hear the bugle blow,
    We'll fight for the right with all our might
    As over the top we go.
                                        (Author unknown)

Radio Renewal.

During the "roaring twenties" mass revivalism went into a decline. It continued to be practiced in the local church, but there was no commanding evangelist-figure to capture the nation's attention for a period of almost 30 years. Southern Baptists showed the most interest in continuing the tradition in the local church or community, and their most gifted songwriter B. B. McKinney composed words and music of some of the most important gospel hymns of the period. For many, the interest in outreach shifted to the new communications/entertainment medium of radio. The music of "gospel radio" was colored by the demands and the traditions of the new medium. Like television 25 years later, radio contributed much to the "spectator complex" in the recreation habits of our culture, and undoubtedly it encouraged spectatorism in church life. Much of the new gospel music had been "special," never intended for congregational use. Undoubtedly the voicing (the ladies' trio, for instance), the choral and instrumental arranging techniques, and the more advanced harmonic and rhythmic patterns were all borrowed from the entertainment world.

At the historic, radio-conscious Chicago Gospel Tabernacle, Merrill Dunlop (b. 1905) wrote and published *Songs of a Christian*. He says that he was first inspired by the "different" harmonies and styles of Robert Harkness's songs. In his own advanced, jazz-related rhythm and harmony, Dunlop foreshadowed the present day. On one occasion he wrote a missions hymn in rhumba rhythm; to him this was perfectly logical because his special interest in foreign missions was South America. At about the same time and in the same city, Moody Bible Institute began gospel broadcasting in 1926; their radio director Wendell Loveless (b. 1892) wrote gospel songs and choruses in a pseudo-Broadway style.

Youth for Christ.

In the 1940's, evangelism was frequently associated with Youth for Christ, one of the parachurch organizations that have become so common on the evangelical scene. Traditionally YFC rallies met on Saturday evening for a pleasant blend of entertainment, fellowship and religious challenge. Their norm for congregational singing was the gospel chorus. This return to the campmeeting emphasis of the 1800's seemed to indicate that they agreed that the refrain was the only significant part of a gospel song, or that it was all the text that an audience could be expected to assimilate. When traditional gospel songs were sung, frequently the stanzas were completely omitted. In addition, many independent choruses were composed and collected in a huge proliferation of "chorus books."

> Into my heart, into my heart,
>   Come into my heart, Lord Jesus,
> Come in today, come in to stay,
>   Come into my heart, Lord Jesus.
>   Harry D. Clarke, 1922

Copyright Renewal 1952 by Hope Publishing Co.
Used by Permission

> Altogether lovely, He is altogether lovely,
>   And the fairest of ten thousand, This wonderful Friend divine;
> He gave Himself to save me, Now He lives in heaven to keep me,
>   He is altogether lovely, Is this wonderful Savior of mine.
>   Wendell P. Loveless, 1931

Copyright Renewal 1959 Hope Publishing Co.
Used by Permission.

In the late 1940's a new gospel hymn writer appeared, returning from his war service as an airforce pilot. John W. Peterson (b. 1921) first came to national attention about 1950 when his song "It Took a Miracle" began to be played on jukeboxes. His music was generally designed to be sung by soloists, choirs, and small ensembles, and only recently has begun to appear in hymnals. Peterson later found that he had a talent for composing "cantatas" for churches which had not traditionally used that form; he has now written more than a score of them and reportedly has sold some six million copies! In general, his lyrics show his strongly-biblical roots, particularly his post-war study at Moody Bible Institute in Chicago. His music varies from a typical gospel song style to an imitation of Broadway show tunes, and was sufficiently creative to capture the attention of a large section of the evangelical public.

The Era of Billy Graham.

The world-famous evangelist Billy Graham began his ministry with Youth for Christ, and in 1949, thanks to publicity by Hearst newspapers, he came to the attention of much of the world. The music of the Billy Graham crusades has largely depended on materials developed since

1850, borrowing some items from each period. A doctoral dissertation[24] recently completed at Southern Baptist Theological Seminary points out that, unlike its revivalist predecessors, the Graham ministry has neither produced nor promoted a large body of new musical material. This may be partly due to the fact that, unlike Sankey, Alexander and Rodeheaver, songleader Cliff Barrows is not a publisher. However, this unique phenomenon in the history of evangelism more likely reflects the "establishment" image which characterized revivalism in the mid-20th century. Dr. Graham evidently purposes to be conservative—fresh and appealing, but shunning the sensational and over-emotional. Consequently Barrows has used materials that have been already proven to be widely popular[25]—choosing them from Ira Sankey, Fanny Crosby, Charles H. Gabriel, Haldor Lillenas, Merrill Dunlop, John Peterson and finally, Bill Gaither. The new musical feature in Graham crusades has been the use of show-business talent like Johnny Cash and Norma Zimmer to attract the unchurched—as well as the best-known contemporary gospel singers.

Few of us who have lived through the past 30 years of Graham's ministry thought that we would see the day when John Peterson would be considered something of a sophisticate, an elitist in song-writing, but it has happened. In the typically "gospel song" style, it is Bill and Gloria Gaither from central Indiana who have captured the imagination and the approval of the evangelical public. The Gaithers write songs that are much less theological and overtly-biblical than Peterson's. They get their inspiration, they say, by listening to the latest secular "pop" songs, and then they compose a "religious" reply. There is just enough contemporary freshness in the title and the principal refrain-phrase to appeal to modern evangelicals whose favorite secular music is probably "country." (See "He Touched Me," "Get All Excited," "The King Is Coming," "Just Because He Lives," "The Old Rugged Cross Made the Difference," etc.)

As in all experience songs, the new "gospel music" reflects the thought patterns of our day. A modern person's need of God will not be expressed well in such frontier language as "I've wandered far away from God; Now I'm coming home," or "Would you be free from your burden of sin? There's power in the blood." Sin and lostness must be redefined for each succeeding generation. An individual's estrangement from God may be better described today in one of the favorite solos of Graham's "gospel singer," George Beverly Shea.

> Tired of a life without meaning,
> Always in a crowd, yet alone.
>
> Arthur Smith

24. George Stansbury, *The Music of the Billy Graham Crusades, 1947-1970*, pp. 311-312.
25. It must be acknowledged that the Billy Graham films have made their own contribution to contemporary music through the folk/ballad songs (e.g., "He's Everything to Me," and "The New 23rd") of Ralph Carmichael, who composed the musical scores for several releases. Pianist Tedd Smith has also written some very significant music.

In a time when psychologists remind us that love is sometimes best expressed in physical contact, it should not be surprising that Bill Gaither will ignore all the traditional fears of anthropomorphism (attributing to God the characteristics of mortals) and write these words:

> He touched me, oh, He touched me,
>   And O, the joy that floods my soul.
> Something happened, and now I know,
>   He touched me, and made me whole.

©Copyright 1963 by William J. Gaither.
Used by Permission

Both psychiatrists and sociologists tell us that the prevailing illness of our culture is loneliness. When "relational theology" is in vogue and we emphasize the "fellowship" aspect of Christian life and worship, it was inevitable that somebody would write about Christian fellowship:

> There's a sweet, sweet Spirit in this place,
>   And I know that it's the Spirit of the Lord;
> There are sweet expressions on each face,
>   And I know they feel the presence of the Lord.
>   Doris Akers, 1962

©Copyright 1962 by Manna Music, Inc., 2111 Kenmere Ave., Burbank, CA 91504.
International Copyright Secured. All
Rights Reserved. Used by Permission

Other Musical Styles

Of course, the gospel song has not been the only variety of witness music known in recent years. In the 1930's, perhaps recalling the heyday of barbershop quartet singing, the Stamps-Baxter "gospel quartet" emerged to present all-night "gospel sings," and to publish scores of small songbooks which became popular, particularly in rural churches of the South. Most of these "southern hymns" were "up tempo," combining the "call and response" techniques of spirituals with the word-repetition common to the quartet song. In later years, the singing groups have varied in size and in voicing (including women as well as men), have adopted several different musical styles, and communicate both in "sacred concerts" and on television.

Even more startling varieties of gospel music were yet to come! In the wake of "the Beatles" and Geoffrey Beaumont's *Twentieth Century Folk Mass,* "gospel folk" and "gospel rock" appeared in Great Britain in the early 1960's. It was quickly transported to America, where its first appeal was strongest in the liturgical and more-liberal ecclesiastical communities. It was heralded as a "renewal in communication" by churches whose attendance and financial support were falling off, and where young people were conspicuous by their absence.

The first reaction of the traditionally-evangelical groups was a little amusing, when one remembers their long-time heritage of "secular tunes for sacred purposes." We recall horrified protests that "this worldly, entertainment music is not worthy of the message of Christ." However, most evangelicals soon recovered their equilibrium, and their young people eagerly joined the crescendo of drums, guitars and voices. At first they were not allowed to indulge their new musical tastes in the church "sanctuary"; the folk musicals had to be performed in the "fellowship hall" or in an outside auditorium. But, in the last ten years, rock-and folk-gospel music has become common, and many other styles have been added. The movement is significant enough to require discussion in a later chapter. However, it is already apparent that we may have seen the most complete invasion of religious expression by secular forms in history, with the connoisseurs changing church styles almost monthly to keep up with the latest trends in secular popular music.

Summary and Evaluation

Much criticism has been leveled at modern day evangelism. What can we say then about the effectiveness of revivalism with its music in the history of America and of the world? Since we believe that the Holy Spirit has been present and creatively active in the world since Pentecost, we must acknowledge that the extra-ecclesiastical, personality-centered ministry of revivalists has contributed to the growth and the renewing of the church, from Francis of Assisi to John Hus to the Wesleys to D. L. Moody to Billy Sunday to Billy Graham and Barry Moore. Whatever their personal weaknesses, of character or theology or method, these individuals have been used of God to accomplish some of His purposes.

It would be difficult to separate the musical expression of revivalism from the preaching; the two seem to belong to each other, though both have tended to be anti-establishment. In 16th century Germany, Luther was both preacher and hymn writer, and it would be hard to prove that one role was more significant than the other in advancing the cause of the Reformation. In the history of Great Britain in the 1870's and 1880's, the names of Moody and Sankey are forever linked, for the musician seemed as important as the preacher in accomplishing God's work. It was the same with "Chapman and Alexander" and "Sunday and Rodeheaver." Furthermore, each period of renewal has been characterized by a flowering of new hymnody; it is as a result of these stimuli that hymnology textbooks are written!

The basic quality of modern evangelistic movements is a singleness and *simplicity of message*—that human beings are estranged from God, and that we can be forgiven, reconciled and transformed through the grace of God, because of the life, death and resurrection of Jesus Christ, a message of sin, grace and salvation. The atmosphere of the revival service is one of *joy, excitement* and *spontenaity*, because the creative God is present and is about to do His work in the human heart. There is also a sense of *urgency* (as expressed by Leighton Ford in *The Christian Persuader*)[26] for those who understand that man is really "lost" without God, and that believers are responsible to tell others what they themselves have found in Christ. As the Apostle Paul said:

> For we must all appear before the judgment seat of Christ, so that each one may receive good or evil, according to what he has done in the body. Therefore, knowing the fear of the Lord, we persuade men . . .
>
> So we are ambassadors for Christ, God making his appeal through us. We beseech you on behalf of Christ, be reconciled to God.
>
> (II Cor. 5:10, 11a, 20)

Because of this urgency, musicians (as well as evangelistic preachers) use their gifts to serve as God's "persuaders." They know that God will reach man's will only if human emotions are properly moved. Of course, they will face the accusation of "manipulation," and they should honestly evaluate both their motives and their methods. The faithful music leader or gospel singer knows that evangelism is primarily God's business. As Paul also says:

> All this is from God, who through Christ reconciled us to himself and gave us the ministry of reconciliation.   (II Cor. 5:18)

The final "persuader" is God the Holy Spirit, and the privilege of representing God should never be prostituted to satisfy the ego needs of the evangelistic musician or preacher.

If we remember this, we may just possibly escape the temptation to equate our human techniques and prejudices with success in evangelism. I recall once sitting on a panel and taking issue with a former president of the Southern Baptist Convention who insisted that "only absolutely-familiar music" should be used in revivals, particularly for the invitation hymn. I argued that the basic atmosphere of evangelism should reflect "newness and creativity" and that revivals had been the traditional birthplace of new song for the church. The well-known pastor probably did not change his mind until the presentation of the first folk-musical in his church in the late 1960's, when more young people responded than he had ever seen before!

On another occasion, in a Billy Graham crusade in Berlin in 1966, the pastor-sponsors expressed their fear that the repeated use of the closing hymn "Just As I Am" had an inordinate and hypnotic effect, causing folks to respond prematurely, without sufficient information or motivation. In response, Dr. Graham decided that we would not sing or play any invitation hymns. Night after night he gave the invitation, during which the organ, the choir, and the *posaunenchor* (brass choir) were abso-

26. See Leighton Ford, *The Christian Persuader*, pp. 11–40.

lutely still. But the inquirers responded, in as large numbers as ever. As might be expected, some critics suggested that this was due to that compelling, awful "quietness" broken only by the sounds of shuffling feet as individuals made their way to the front!

Even earlier, in May of 1961, I had my own comeuppance. The crusade in Manchester in North England was not an easy one. Billy Graham was ill for most of it, and the pulpit was occupied by substitutes. The weather was bitter cold in the outdoor football stadium, and we had heat lamps hanging over the piano and organ keyboards to try to keep fingers functioning. One night, to my dismay, songleader Cliff Barrows announced the hymn "Love Lifted Me" by C. Austin Miles, a song which has occasionally found its way into crusade song books, but which he had rarely used. It has never been a favorite gospel hymn of mine; the imagery is out of date, the message is not biblically strong, and the music has that pseudo-waltz rhythm which I don't care for. I was sure that the British audience would scorn it as an example of dubious American taste in church music.

Somehow we got through it and finished the service. Two or three days later the local crusade office received a letter from a woman who had attended the service. It carried this message, if not these exact words:

> The other night I attended the Graham service at Maine Road stadium. My father was with me. He is a seaman who is rarely home and hasn't been to church in years, but I persuaded him to come on this occasion. In that service, Mr. Barrows used a hymn which father had heard forty years ago, introduced by another evangelist from America. Hearing that song reawakened a commitment to God which he had experienced as a young man. Father went forward and rededicated his life to Christ as a result.

To my knowledge, Mr. Barrows has not used that gospel song since 1961. It is still not a favorite of mine, but I may be slow in expressing dislike if he should decide to use it again!

Perhaps the chief pitfalls connected with traditional evangelism are not actually related to the "revival" or the "crusade." It is rather that we have tended to take evangelism's pattern and style, the preaching and the music, and canonize them as the norm for regular church worship. Some churches which exult in their "evangelistic" reputation have done just this. Their worship pattern tends to be centered in a breezy, informal, personality-centered style. The sermon is invariably in the "sin-grace-salvation" cast, ignoring the responsibility to "teach and to disciple." Furthermore, the music is all of experience and Christian decision, with no opportunity to "see God as he is," to experience his transcendence and to worship him.

In one of his rare lapses from norm, Erik Routley once complimented a British Salvation Army group for their contemporary (folk-rock) expressions used in a BBC telecast. He admitted that there should be some room for "disposable church music," music that we use today and throw away tomorrow. Invariably, when a new secular-sacred music style appears in outreach activity, it will be argued "We don't intend this music for the worship of the church. It is just to reach the unchurched." But it never works out that way. We tend to sanctify and canonize the new evangelistic form and it makes its way into the regular worship experiences of the church community. Actually, the demurral is pointless. We should expect the new music to become part of the continuing worship material—*part, that is,* not the "alpha and omega" of the church's expression.

I believe that we need both the "transcendent" and the "immanent" in music, because that is the God we know—the God who is above all his creation, whom we cannot see except "through a glass darkly" (I Cor. 13:12), and yet One who dwells within the believer, closer than hands and feet. It is expressed well in one verse from the Old Testament:

> For thus says the high and lofty One who inhabits eternity, whose name is Holy: "I dwell in the high and holy place, and also with him who is of a contrite and humble spirit, to revive the spirit of the humble, and to revive the heart of the contrite.   (Isaiah 57:15)

This theological paradox seems to me argument enough for a dualism in church music. I am convinced that evangelicals require music that expresses the perfections of the "high and holy" God, and also the personal, religious experience of the "broken and humble."

Chapter IX

MUSIC AND WORSHIP IN AMERICA

When the early settlers came to America, beginning in the 16th century, they brought with them the worship traditions (including the hymnals and liturgical manuals) of their mother cultures. Many were seeking religious liberty, and they came with both the anxieties and the prejudices that were a part of their life in the Old World. In the new homeland some groups, like Roger Williams and his fellow Baptists in Rhode Island, experienced much the same persecution as before from the ruling Puritans.

Most of the first Americans came from humble backgrounds, and their aesthetic sensibilities were quite undeveloped. In the rugged frontier setting, their first musical achievements were very primitive. In the 18th and 19th centuries, revivalism was an important force in all religious life, and it continues to influence evangelical groups. This chapter will sketch the development of American worship and its music from those simple beginnings to the diverse practices and burgeoning activities of this late 20th century.

The Early Years

The very first colonists were Spanish Catholics who settled principally in the Caribbean Islands, in Florida and in Mexico; with them came the worship (including the music) of the Roman Catholic church, which flourished in Mexico (as well as in South America) in the 16th century, with music schools and choirs in many of the principal churches. In 1562 to 1565, a few Huguenot refugees established a short-lived colony in Florida, bringing with them the Genevan Psalter, and it is recorded that the French psalm tunes were taught to the Indians of that area.

The permanent settlers on the eastern seaboard were largely British (Anglicans, Presbyterians, nonconformists and Catholic refugees) with a sprinkling of Dutch Calvinists and French Huguenots. The English-speaking Protestants brought with them the Sternhold and Hopkins

145

psalter (the Old Version) from England and the Ainsworth Psalter, which the community of Pilgrims had produced at Amsterdam in 1612. In addition, the very first book printed in the colonies was the Bay Psalm Book (1640), which answered the widespread demand for a revision of the psalm texts. In most congregations, the psalms were "lined out" by the deacon or precentor, to aid those who did not have books, or who could not read. All the psalms were sung to a very few tunes; even those few suffered from desultory performance, because they were passed on to successive generations largely by oral tradition. Choirs and instruments were basically unknown until after 1700.

In the early 18th century, organs and choirs began to be common in larger American churches; they were both located in a rear balcony, along with a cello and possibly a woodwind instrument which provided accompaniment for the choral pieces. The choirs were trained in "singing schools" which were established by churches who were concerned about the poor quality of their congregational singing. The schools met in the evenings—often in the village tavern—and were led by talented musical amateurs who frequently traveled from town to village in their work.

Beginning in 1762, new "tune books" began to be published, which included additional psalm tunes, folk tunes of English origin, some "anthems" and the new "fuging" tunes (which were characterized by an opening homophonic phrase, a polyphonic imitative section, and a final homophonic phrase); the texts included many of the hymns of Isaac Watts. William Billings (1746–1800) was the most creative of the early composers, all of whom tended to imitate the Elizabethan folk melodies we now call "white spirituals"; because they had lost touch with British and European musical traditions, their works exhibit a rough-hewn quality that is both archaic and creative!

The 1700's saw new waves of immigrants coming to these shores, notably groups of German pietists; some of them allowed only unaccompanied congregational singing (of hymns as well as psalm paraphrases) and some had a more highly developed tradition. The most important of these were the Moravians who first migrated to Georgia in 1735 to do missionary work among the Indians, and in 1740 moved to Pennsylvania where they named their settlements Nazareth and Bethlehem. These *unitas fratrem* (united brethren) brought with them quite a sophisticated European musical culture, and they developed it to new heights in this land of freedom. Music was a part of everyday Moravian life and was associated with work and recreation, as well as with worship. In addition to the rich hymnic heritage of the old country (including the works of their leader and benefactor, Count Nikolaus von Zinzendorf), new texts were added by their American leaders, and were set to music by composers like John Antes, John Frederick Peter, John G. Herbst and Christian Gregor; these men also wrote fine anthem settings in the styles of J. C. Bach, Stamitz, Haydn and Mozart. Instrumental music also flourished; by 1780 a modest orchestra performed standard works of the European masters. A trombone choir (*posaunen-chor*) was also a regular feature of daily life, and was used to accompany congregational singing outdoors, and also to announce significant events to the community by playing from the church belltower. It is highly significant that the most and best music making in America, during the first years of the young republic, was not heard in concert halls, but in the normal community and worship life of the Moravian band.

> While Philadelphia may have led the country in its concert life toward the end of the 18th century, it did not begin to approach Bethlehem in the quantity and quality of its music-making.[1]

Revivalism in America

The Eighteenth Century.

As pietists—religious groups which emphasize the "personal experience of God"—the Moravians with their art music were quite apart from the normal pattern. William Warren Sweet[2] has pointed out that typical "revivalism" was introduced into the American colonies by other German immigrant groups of the late 17th and early 18th centuries. Its first expression in this country was a revival among the Dutch Reformed churches of New Jersey in the 1720's, led by Theodore J. Frelinghuysen, who was widely known for his impassioned preaching of the need of personal repentance and faith for salvation. Soon after, a similar movement broke out among the Scotch-Irish Presbyterians, centering in the leadership of William Tennent, a former Anglican who conducted a religious school at Neshaminy, Pennsylvania, derisively called the "Log College." As a result of this religious awakening, Presbyterianism had become the second largest religious body in the colonies (after the Anglicans) by the beginning of the Revolutionary War.[3]

In New England, beginning in 1734, the revival leader was the Congregationalist preacher Jonathan Edwards. Though he was a convinced Calvinist, Edwards believed in "personal religion" in which preaching to the emotions was very important. As he said:

> The heart of true religion is holy affection.
>
> Our people do not so much need to have their heads stored, as to have their hearts touched.[4]

No doubt the metrical psalms continued to figure largely in the services conducted by these leaders. At the same time, the hymns of Isaac Watts

1. Leonard Ellinwood, *The History of American Church Music*, p. 36.
2. William Warren Sweet, *Revivalism in America*, p. 25 ff.
3. Ibid., pp. 29–30.
4. Ibid. See also Ola Elizabeth Winslow, *Jonathan Edwards, 1703–1758*, pp. 162, 191.

and of Charles Wesley were beginning to be used. Watts' *Psalms* were first published in this country by Benjamin Franklin in 1729 in Philadelphia, and John Wesley released his first *Collection of Psalms and Hymns* in Savannah, Georgia in 1737.

Jonathan Edwards once wrote of the music in a series of meetings, indicating that the singing school training techniques were abetted by the spirit of renewal:

> Our congregation excelled all that I ever knew in the external part of the duty before, generally carrying regularly and well, three parts of music, and the women a part by themselves. But now they were evidently wont to sing with unusual elevation of heart and voice, which made the duty pleasant indeed.[5]

Perhaps the greatest contribution to the revival tradition was brought to the colonies by George Whitefield, the Calvinistic Methodist who was associated with the Wesleys in England. Whitefield was probably the first to encourage ecumenical cooperation in revivalism; he worked with every group in America that was open to him, including all the local evangelistic preachers. From 1738 to 1770 he made seven trips to these shores, preaching throughout the seaboard colonies. On many occasions, only the open air could accommodate the crowds of thousands which came to hear him; it is not surprising then that he developed a strong voice and clear enunciation. (Benjamin Franklin once estimated that he could be heard by as many as 25,000 people.)[6] He is said to have worn a robe while preaching, in the Anglican tradition, and to have used the prayer book, though he could also improvise prayer with great fluency and effectiveness. With the ministry of Whitefield, the singing of hymns became widespread in America, especially those of Isaac Watts.

Camp Meetings.

In the late 18th century, the revivalist emphasis shifted to the southern states, beginning with the Presbyterians in Virginia; the continuing movement centered, however, in the Baptists and Methodists. Presbyterians, Baptists and Methodists joined in the frontier camp meetings of 1800 and 1801, which broke out in Logan and Bourbon counties in Kentucky. The Presbyterian leader James McGready had sent invitations throughout all the backwoods country, and some families traveled as far as 100 miles in their horse-drawn wagons. The meetings were held in the open air, and the people lived in their wagons or in hastily-erected "brush arbor" camps. Perhaps because of the near-barbarism of frontier life, these revival characteristics were more spectacular and emotional than had heretofore been seen in the older settlements. The work of the Holy Spirit was evidenced in the number who "fell"—literally dropped

5. Quoted by George Hood, *A History of Music in New England,* p. 138.
6. Sweet, op. cit., p. 107.

to the ground under the influence of the intense emotion of "conviction of sin." Some also were moved to roll, to jerk, to dance and even to "bark." Understandably, the music of the camp meetings was highly spontaneous, and was frequently improvised. In chapter eight, we have described the emergence of the "spirituals" in this setting; they were no doubt vitally important in the development of the Sunday School hymn and the gospel song.

The "singing schools" continued to be popular in the 19th century, particularly in the frontier areas of the south and midwest. Oblong tune books continued to appear and were the source of the new material for both church and community gatherings; the most widely used were Davisson's *Kentucky Harmony* (ca.1816), William Walker's *Southern Harmony* (1835) and *The Sacred Harp* (1844), each of which had many successive editions. A principal feature of those southern books was the use of "shape notes" which designated the degree of the scale to be sung with each syllable of the text. At the same time, Lowell Mason (1792–1872) was most influential in the east, and he was assisted by other church musicians like William B. Bradbury and Thomas Hastings. Mason advocated the use of standard notation and developed the first program of music education in public schools of New England. He studied and traveled widely in Europe, introduced many continental melodies into American hymnals and at the same time wrote many hymn tunes and anthems himself.

The Finney Revivals.

Revivalism returned to the urban centers of the east coast with the advent of "The Second Awakening" under the "Arminian" Presbyterian, Charles Grandison Finney. The former-lawyer used his eloquence and his logic to lay a careful foundation of "closely reasoned truth" before addressing the emotions of his audience.[7] Because he ministered in the established churches of the Atlantic seaboard, he no doubt followed the standard order of worship prescribed by each church. A record of such a meeting held by Finney in the New Hartford Presbyterian Church in upstate New York in 1826 was recently uncovered, and the service was repeated in that church.[8] In its Directory of Worship, the General Assembly of the Presbyterian Church of that time declared:

> In time of public worship let all the people attend with gravity and reverence forbearing to read anything except what the minister is then reading or citing; abstaining from all whisperings, from salutations of persons present or coming in, and from gazing about, sleeping, smiling and all other indecent behavior. . . .

> It is proper to begin public worship in the sanctuary by a short prayer humbly adoring the infinite majesty of the living God, ex-

7. Ibid., p. 136.
8. Richard L. Manzelmann, "The Revival Heard Around the World."

pressing a sense of our distance from him as creatures and unworthiness as sinners, and humbly imploring his gracious presence, the assistance of his Holy Spirit in the duties of worship and his acceptance of us through the merits of our Lord.

It is apparent that a service of evangelism was expected to be also an experience of worship for the believers who were present. The following is the suggested outline of a Finney service, as it was conducted in the church.

Short prayer by the minister (possibly ten minutes long).
A psalm or hymn (e.g., Our God, Our Help in Ages Past, by Isaac Watts).
A "full and comprehensive prayer"—possibly as much as thirty minutes long, including "adoration, thanksgiving, confession of sin (both original and actual), supplication for pardon and peace with God, pleading and intercession."
Reading from Scripture.
Possibly a choir selection. (Thomas Hastings was associated with Finney in his ministry, led the music and edited revival hymnbooks.)
Sermon—the actual text consumed forty printed pages, and probably consumed two hours in its delivery.
A Congregational Hymn.
The Invitation (lengthy) delivered by an "exhorter"—sometimes a layman. In Finney's time, the seekers came forward to a "mourner's bench" (sometimes called the "anxious bench") where they were encouraged to "pray through" until they received assurance of their salvation.
Announcements and Closing Hymn.

The lengthy invitation marked the principal difference between Finney's campaigns and those of Edwards and Whitefield in the previous century. For the early Calvinist evangelists believed that revival comes, and that a sinner is converted, solely according to the will of God; men can do nothing except to preach the Word and wait for the "Spirit to fall." The Wesleyan (Arminian) emphasis of Finney held that believers could "pray a revival down" and that all persons may answer the gospel call of their own "free will"; the challenge then was to persuade as many as possible to respond. Almost all subsequent revivalism in America—including that conducted by moderate-Calvinist evangelists—has used invitation hymns and an "altar call."

It is interesting to note that the announcements included the notice that Mr. Finney would continue to minister night after night "as long as this revival season lasts." "Protracted meetings" were a feature of early revivalism in America; a campaign went on as long as the Holy Spirit was evidently blessing, and people continued to respond. The announcements also indicated that the trustees would meet after church to plan a remodeling of the church, because "the present location of seats and pulpit does not fit our new and necessary mode of worship." At that time the balconies were eliminated, a platform was built across the front with a center pulpit, the box pews were removed and simple benches were installed, obviously because preaching was henceforth to be the central activity of worship, and it must be easy for folk to respond to the invitation by "coming forward." From this heritage (which affected much of American Protestantism during the early 19th century) stem many of evangelicalism's 20th century practices and emphases in worship.

With regard to music, the Finney "awakening" seems to have been the beginning of a clearly-defined evangelistic music ministry. Thomas Hastings (1784–1872), a leading music teacher, conductor and author of that day, was associated with Finney in many of his campaigns, and compiled the first songbooks specifically planned for revival use.

Moody and Sankey.

The pattern of revivalism was well codified by the time that D. L. Moody and his soloist/songleader Ira D. Sankey came on the scene in 1873, when the remarkable response to their ministry in Great Britain brought them to the attention of the entire English-speaking world. The layman-evangelist, who had first been active in an urban ministry in Chicago, shunned the excesses of emotionalism which had characterized earlier movements; at the same time, his preaching was less polished, less theologically oriented, and also considerably briefer than that of Finney. A former businessman, Moody brought his gifts of analysis and planning to the ministry of evangelism and developed policies and procedures which have influenced revivalism to the present day; it is remarkable to note how closely the work of Billy Graham resembles that of Moody 100 years ago! Even more, the pattern of Moody and Sankey's services is still followed for corporate worship in certain evangelical churches. The larger services of Moody and Sankey were held in "secular" buildings, such as exhibition halls, or in "tabernacles"—temporary buildings erected for that specific purpose. In a recent definitive biography, James F. Findlay, Jr. reminds us that part of the revival atmosphere was created by the unusual surroundings.

> Decoration of the barn-like structures was practically impossible, although occasionally someone attempted to string the words of familiar Bible passages along the walls. These were rather pathetic efforts to create a church-like atmosphere. "Is it a religious service we are come to?" exclaimed one first-time visitor to a Moody service. "All around the hats are on; gossip is lively . . . These heads of households, followed by their 'all' (children); of what are they talking? To tell the truth, there is chiefly recognition of friends, hand-waving from arena to platform and box." The physical surroundings and the general attitude of the crowds usually contributed very little to feelings of spirituality as the services began. Such feelings would

have to be created, if at all, by other means, chiefly by those who led and partly by the other participants in the service of singing, worship, preaching, and praise.[9]

Moody and Sankey could be counted on to create those "feelings of spirituality." The evangelist's standard answer to the stock question "How can regular church services be improved?" was "Make the meetings interesting."[10] The materials of an evangelistic service were basic indeed—congregational singing, special music (by solo and/or choir), prayers, scripture reading and sermon. They were fitted together by the service leaders in what was obviously a thoroughly engaging and entertaining fashion that achieved the desired goals.

> There was a certain informality—a liveliness about which the evangelist often spoke, and which he never neglected in the services he directed—which set these proceedings apart from the ordinary Sunday morning service.[11]

> Moody had demonstrated in Illinois that as a leader of public meetings he possessed some sixth sense which enabled him to improvise and to rearrange the order of worship as he proceeded in order to bend the will of his audience to *his* desires. After much practice in the intervening years, he had refined this power of improvisation into a high art of subtle persuasion which cast its spell over almost every one of his giant revival gatherings.[12]

The services began with a full half-hour of congregational singing. The gospel songs used by Sankey were often introduced as a solo or a choir selection, and were contained in the hymnals he edited for the meetings. As a soloist, Sankey established many of the techniques which are still followed today—a concentration on the text that resulted in a sort of *sprechstimme* (vocal reciting), complete freedom of rhythm, rolling the ends of phrases and pausing for a moment between the lines of a song to assure that the attention of the listeners did not wander—a style which is and has long been common to popular singers of secular songs.[13] Sankey's own melodies have been judged to be some of the most creative of the period. In addition, he was supplied with a burgeoning supply of the new "gospel songs" by authors and composers, the best known of which are Fanny J. Crosby, Philip P. Bliss, D. W. Whittle, Robert Lowry, James McGranahan and George C. Stebbins. Their popularity is attested by a contemporary report in *The Nation*:

> Determine the pleasure that you get from a circus quick-step, a negro-minstrel sentimental ballad, a college chorus, and a hymn all

9. Cited by James F. Findlay, Jr., *Dwight L. Moody: American Evangelist, 1837–1899*, p. 207. The quotation is from *The Methodist*, p. 4, published in London, April 30, 1875.
10. Ibid., pp. 207–208.
11. Ibid.
12. Ibid., pp. 220–221.
13. Ibid., p. 210.

in one, and you have some gauge of the variety and contrast that may be perceived in one of these songs.[14]

Summary: Revivalism as an American Phenomenon.

The outstanding American church historian William Warren Sweet ends his thorough analysis of the characteristics and the techniques of historic evangelists with the ministry of Charles G. Finney. In his final chapter, "Revivalism on the Wane"[15] he describes D. L. Moody as the first of the "professional" evangelists who emerged with America's development as an urban society. He only mentions Moody's successors— Reuben Torrey, Wilbur Chapman, B. Fay Mills, Sam Jones, George Stuart, W. E. Biederwolf, and Billy Sunday—along with a host of diverse evangelistic enterprises which have appeared in the 20th century: the Student Volunteer Movement, the Salvation Army, the Oxford Movement (Buchmanism), and the "holiness" and pentecostal churches. Perhaps it is true, as he insists, that in our complex and growing culture, revivalism has a less-powerful impact on a smaller percentage of the population. Nevertheless, it has continued to be a vital and a conspicuous part of American church life. Billy Graham has proved to be the most durable evangelist on record and has undoubtedly preached to more individuals than any other person in history, using modern business techniques in crusade preparation, administration and "follow up." In recent times, evangelism has moved into "The Electric Church" of radio/television where it must be acknowledged to be the successor to the longtime revivalist tradition.

Many have asked why this particular technique has flourished so greatly in America. Its liturgical antecedent was the medieval "preaching mission" which grew out of the Prone service, and its simple format resembles the worship of English Separatists in the late 16th century. Its immediate ancestry has been traced to the pietist movements of Europe and the Wesleyan revival in England. However, revivalism has not continued to be a strong factor in European Christianity, probably because of the "state church" syndrome. In that tradition, even with the emergence of the Separatist bodies, one church (Anglican, Roman Catholic, Orthodox, or Reformed) is dominant in a country. Most individuals are "baptized into" the faith at birth, and though they may never attend church, it is a part of their culture which is not easily changed. Revivalism continues strong in the United States because of our historic separation of church and state. Furthermore, we have a more thoroughly democratic society than most, with each person free to make choices, without the restrictions and inhibitions that are part of a "class" or a "tribal" culture. This means that individuals are encouraged to make personal decisions, in matters of religious faith as in all others, and it is this freedom on which evangelism thrives. As a result, revivalism has

14. *Nation,* 22 (March 9, 1876), p. 157; quoted in Findlay, ibid., p. 211.
15. Sweet, op, cit., pp. 162-182.

been a fairly constant part of American church life for the past 250 years. There is no reason to expect that it will disappear in the near future, so long as it speaks to persons in each generation at the point of their ultimate spiritual concerns.

Many observers of the religious scene insist that in the past thirty years we have experienced a widespread "renewal of communication" in the American church, expressed in the use of contemporary words (new scripture translations, revised liturgies and new experience songs), contemporary art (architecture, furnishings, vestments and banners) and contemporary music (more emotionally-charged and based largely on use of stronger rhythmic devices.) It remains to be seen whether this "revival" movement has been genuine spiritual renewal or only an updating of symbolic languages of expression.

The impact of revivalism on our church life is seen not only in the recurring appearance of evangelists or of pietistic movements. As Sweet has pointed out, certain denominations have emerged as basically-revivalist in their normal patterns of polity and worship, and they are certainly identified with the "evangelicals" about whom this book is written. However, as older revivalist churches became more affluent and sophisticated, they tended to be dissatisfied with those simple worship patterns and to search for more developed service forms. We might argue that this proves that the effectiveness of historic "preaching missions" was due partly to the fact that they were *extraordinary* events, and that normal church life needs a pattern of worship which is less specialized and more complete. It is for such bodies that we offer a theological rationale and a broad outline of evangelical worship form in the next chapter. At the same time, our own generation has spawned new pietist groups (some even within the liturgical churches) which practice the same informal, spontaneous worship that has characterized earlier movements. It may be that this recurring sequence of freedom/structure/freedom is inevitable, even though it has been one of the divisive forces in church life.

Worship Forms and Music in Diverse Church Groups

It has already been noted that, in its frontier culture, early American worship practices were exceedingly primitive. Concurrent with advance in education and the arts, there was pressure in the older churches for the development and the standardization of worship forms. Following the War for independence, all Protestant bodies were independent of their Old World connections; nevertheless, worship design was frequently influenced by liturgical movements abroad as well as at home. At the same time, this interest in patterned worship came into direct conflict with the repeated outbreaks of revivalism. Through the years, there has been continuing tension between these two forces—formal worship versus freedom.

In the 20th century, we have seen "thesis, antithesis and synthesis" in the outworking of the struggle. Some groups are clearly "formal" or clearly "spontaneous" in worship habits. In other churches, a new interest in liturgy and liturgical symbolism has been coupled with a concern for Christian fellowship and a desire for spontaneity in worship. In the next few pages we will consider the historical developments in both the liturgical and the free churches, since they have tended to interact, sometimes in imitation and sometimes in reaction.

The Liturgical Communions: Roman Catholic.

The Roman Catholic church constitutes the only politically-monolithic religion worldwide. As a result, Roman worship in America is not appreciably different from that in other parts of the world, and it did not change its basic patterns from the Council of Trent (1562) until the Second Vatican Council (1962). Nevertheless, there has been considerable diversity in the music which accompanies the liturgy.

Little is known about Roman Catholic music in the thirteen colonies. In 1787, *A Compilation of the Litanies, Vespers, Hymns and Anthems As They Are Sung in the Catholic Church* was published in Philadelphia by John Aitken, containing litanies, historic hymns, psalms, anthems, a Mass of the Blessed Trinity, a requiem mass (in plainsong) and a Solemn Mass, with musical settings in both Latin and English.[16] In the 19th century, new waves of Catholic immigrants came to these shores, mostly from very humble circumstances in Europe; consequently their musical expectations were very limited, and in most churches there was no singing at all. In those which supported choral music, the preference was for 19th century operatic styles, in many instances performed by a quartet-choir. In a few dioceses, beginning in the late 19th century, the influence of John B. Singenberger (1848–1924) and his Cecilian Society led to musical reform. Like the parent Cecilian movement in Germany, this group espoused the revival of Gregorian chant, a return to a cappella polyphonic forms, and vernacular congregational singing. However, its influence was chiefly felt in the German communities of Cincinnati, Chicago and Milwaukee. Most Catholics in typical parish churches continued to favor the spoken mass, and singing occurred only in the popular novena services.

The Liturgical Communions: Lutheran.

Lutherans have brought many different national and regional traditions to this country. Those who found homes in the east lost their ethnic language and identity more quickly than those who settled later in the midwest; consequently, Lutheran worship (and especially its hymnody) along the Atlantic seaboard was more Anglo-American than Ger-

16. Ellinwood, op. cit., pp. 39–40.

man or Scandinavian. Many adherents had been identified with the Pietist movements within European Lutheranism, and in this country that influence was intensified by revivalist activity. In the mid-19th century, a growing disaffection with revival-influenced worship was fed by the sentiments of new European immigrants who shared the concern. The widespread desire to recover their confessional roots resulted in a conference of all Lutheran groups which adopted a Common Service in 1888, based on "the common consent of the pure Lutheran liturgies of the 16th century." Nevertheless, there continued to be considerable variation in Lutheran worship, since conformity was not obligatory. In the late 20th century, there seems to be a growing preference for a completely-vernacular version of Martin Luther's *Formula Missae* (described in chapter seven), as evidenced in the ecumenical *Lutheran Book of Worship,* 1978.

American Lutherans inherited the European preference for an ante-communion service; through the 19th century, the full eucharist was observed only a few times each year. In recent years, Holy Communion has been offered more frequently, and the historic Lutheran Matins service has also been used, perhaps once each month. In the 19th century, congregational singing was the musical norm; in the east, Anglo-American hymn traditions prevailed while the midwest churches perpetuated their German or Scandinavian hymnody. In recent years, Lutherans countrywide have shown a desire to share their unique ethnic traditions while preserving their common reformation heritage. In addition, thanks largely to the efforts of Concordia Publishing Company, choirs are using plainsong, as well as polyphonic styles, in singing the "propers" of the liturgy.

The Liturgical Communions: Anglican.

Established in the colony of Virginia in the early 17th century, the Church of England was organically united to the bishoprics of Canterbury and York. The church grew rapidly and by the time of the American Revolution, was the dominant religious force in this country. After the Declaration of Independence, Anglicans in the United States formed an independent Protestant Episcopal Church, linked only in heritage and in fellowship with the Anglican Communion worldwide. In colonial days, and even much later, Anglicans used the services of Morning and Evening Prayer almost exclusively, with Communion being observed only three or four times a year. The American Book of Common Prayer was based on Cranmer's Prayer Book of 1549, and was less Calvinistic than the 1552 and 1662 books which were commonly used in England.

According to Leonard Ellinwood, the music of colonial Anglican worship was scarcely different from that of the Puritans in New England, and consisted mostly of metrical psalms sung with the aid of a precentor.[17] Anglican chant was introduced during the last two decades of the 18th century, and its use became common within a short time. There is further record that organs began to be used in the 1700's, playing a "voluntary" following the "psalms of the day" and an "offertory" for receiving the collection. A few choirs (with boys singing the treble parts) also appeared during the 18th century. All of the extant music from that period is related to the services of Matins and Vespers.

In the mid-19th century the Episcopal church was influenced by the ideas of the Oxford Movement, which brought back much of Roman theology and liturgy into a number of British churches—reviving the ancient Greek and Latin hymns (in English translations), Gregorian chant, and the use of symbolism (in vestments, furnishings and liturgical action). This worship revolution, coupled with the advent of "liberal theology" in another group of Anglican churches, eventually resulted in the development of three Anglican "parties" in England in the late 19th century: (1) the Anglo-catholics, who were closest to Rome in theology and worship practice; (2) the Low churchmen, many of whom were strongly evangelical in emphasis, rejecting the Oxford movement as "popish", and (3) the Broad churches, who tended to be moderate in liturgy but liberal in theology, emphasizing social reform rather than personal salvation. In America, Episcopal churches have tended to be "high" or "low" in liturgy, but only a few would be as "evangelical" as their British counterparts.

After 1850, a number of American churches adopted the principles of the Oxford movement, using vested choirs (of boys and men) and substituting plainsong for Anglican chant. However, the quartet-choir was more common—a volunteer group of men and women led by four soloists, which often degenerated into just a quartet, singing mostly "romantic" Services and anthems by American, and later, European composers. The most-used compositions were written by such well-known musicians as Mendelssohn, Gounod, Gaul, Mozart, Boyce, Stainer, Parker, Shelley, Rossini and Buck, and others who are now forgotten—Hodges, Naumann, Larkin, Bridgewater, Hatton and Gilbert.

In the early 20th century, Anglican churches outside the United States experienced a musical renaissance under the influence of such men as Charles Stanford, Hubert Parry, Charles Wood, Ralph Vaughan Williams, Walford Davies and the Canada-based Healey Willan. Increasingly, their music (both Services and anthems) has also been favored in American Episcopal churches, along with the works of our own composers—Leo Sowerby, T. Tertius Noble, David Mck. Williams, Thomas Matthews, and others. During this century, the outstanding leader in Episcopalian church music has been Charles Winfred Douglas (1867-1944). An ordained priest in the church, he was long a member of the Episcopal Joint Commission on Church Music and the Hymnal

17. Ibid., p. 41.

Commission, serving as music editor for the denomination's hymnals of 1916 and 1940. A frequent lecturer on church music, he founded the Evergreen Conference in Colorado, and presided over its annual School of Church Music.

In very recent times, the Episcopal Church has adopted a new liturgy which, while retaining its essential "Anglican" character, has returned to the basic outline of the historic mass. For example, the *Gloria in excelsis* has been returned to the early part of the service, and much of the evangelical text of the eucharistic prayer has been restored.

Non-Liturgical Churches—Revivalist vs. "Pseudo-liturgical" Worship.

Even though many of the Calvinist and Wesleyan[18] groups in Europe and Great Britain followed traditional worship patterns, their American successors—Presbyterian, Methodist, Evangelical and Reformed—tended to adopt the freedom of the non-liturgical Congregationalists and Baptists. For some, this meant a "revivalist" format; others developed what I choose to call a "pseudo-liturgical" pattern. These two styles are still common in many American churches.

We have already narrated in detail the story of American revival movements and the resultant worship tradition which lingered in many churches. Following is their basic service outline, although the most significant feature was a sense of freedom and spontaneity generated by the leadership of "charismatic" personalities.

> Hymns (a group, often not related to each other or to the
>   sermon, led by a "songleader")
> Prayer (brief)
> Welcome and Announcements
> Special Music (choir, solo or small group)
> Offering
> Solo
> Sermon
> Invitation (Hymn)
> Dismissal (Benediction)

Revivalist free churches in the 19th century tended to favor gospel songs for congregational singing, with a sprinkling of traditional hymns from English and American authors. If the choir literature developed beyond those same hymnic boundaries, they tended to use "chorus choir" selections—two-page settings (found in the hymnal or songbook) in the style of extended hymns or abbreviated anthems!

18. Methodism in England resulted from an 18th century schism in the Anglican church, precipitated by the preaching of John and Charles Wesley. Worship among Methodists varied from group to group, from the "low church" style of the Church of England to the unstructured pattern of Baptists.

Other free churches evidenced a broader concept of worship, particularly as the influence of revivalism waned and liturgical movements abroad and at home came to their attention. They moved toward a pattern that has some kinship to the Ante-communion service of Lutheranism or the "Liturgy of the Word" in an Anglican eucharist, though we choose to call it "pseudo-liturgical." Ellinwood[19] gives the following outline of the dedication service held at the Broadway Tabernacle Church (Methodist) in New York City on March 5, 1905; it must be understood that such an occasion would result in a more highly developed ritual than the norm.

Salutation
Doxology
Invocation
Anthem: "Te Deum" in C, by Larkin
Commandments
Beatitudes
Responsive Reading (Psalter)
Apostles' Creed
Old Testament lesson
Hymn: "A Mighty Fortress"
New Testament lesson
Anthem: "Sanctus" from *Messe Solonelle* by Gounod
Prayer
Offertory Solo: "Lord, thy glory fills the heavens" from Rossini's *Stabat Mater*
Prayer
Hymn: "O God, beneath thy guiding hand"
Sermon
Service of dedication
Hymn of dedication (written for the occasion)
Prayer and benediction
Organ postlude: "Adoration" from Gaul's *The Holy City*

It will be noted that choral and solo literature in the early 20th century tended to fall into the same mold as that of Episcopal (and even Roman Catholic) churches of that period. Congregational singing was often limited to one or two selections in a service, and tended to use the standard hymns of British and American authors; gospel hymns were often standard fare on Sunday evening, for Sunday School and in other informal services. Until later in the 20th century, organists relied heavily on the music of romantic composers, including transcriptions of popular orchestral works.

The following may be a more typical "formal" service in an American non-liturgical church, and it is still followed faithfully by such historic congregations as that of Fourth Presbyterian Church in Chicago.

19. Ellinwood, op. cit., pp. 94-95.

Organ Prelude
Opening Hymn (Processional) or Doxology
Call to Worship (often choral)
Invocation
  (Response)
Hymn
Scripture Reading (the congregation participating)
  (Response) or *Gloria Patri*
Pastoral Prayer
  (Response) or the Lord's Prayer
Creed (Apostles')
Anthem
Offertory (choral or instrumental)
  (Response to Offertory Prayer)
Hymn
Sermon
Hymn
Benediction
  (Response)
Organ Postlude

It should be remembered that this is not an absolute and invariable pattern. Not all the items are included in all churches, though these are the basic components of traditional, sophisticated, "free" worship. Frequently this (or a similar) outline was included in the early 20th century hymnals or the worship manuals of a denomination. It is interesting to observe that this type of form is often labeled "liturgical" by churchmen who preferred the revivalist worship tradition. Actually, it usually denied the basic meaning of the word "liturgy" ("the work of the people"), since one of its principal characteristics was a large number of choral responses, and congregational participation was limited to the hymns and possibly the scripture reading. Like the liturgical fellowships, free churches tended to use the quartet-choir when their budget permitted it; their choices in literature were also similar. Instrumental music varied according to the size and affluence of the individual group: pipe organs with trained performers for the larger, wealthier congregations and reed organs and amateur organists for the smaller and less prosperous.

As the 20th century progressed, free churches have broadened the scope of their music—congregational, choral and instrumental—though there is marked variance within both "traditional" and "revivalist" groups. Hymnody now includes materials from the entire Christian heritage, American and European. Choral and organ performance covers the entire historic literature, from the Renaissance period through the contemporary. In addition, our century has encouraged the emergence of a large group of "functional" church music composers, who supply materials in every conceivable style for every possible taste. Nowadays only a few evangelical churches employ a quartet of professional singers, partly because of the high musical competence of many members in the congregation. In the early 20th century, following the example of revivalists of that day, pianos replaced the reed organ in small churches and joined forces with the pipe organ in the larger. With the advent of electronic organs beginning in 1935, many small congregations were financially able to add that sound to their worship experience for the first time. All in all, American churches today have more music activity—with more choirs and instruments, and larger budgets—than those in any other country in the world.

The Liturgical Movement

We have already mentioned the movements within Anglican and Lutheran fellowships in the 19th century, calling for a return to primal traditions in theology and worship practice. This trend was intensified in the mid-20th century, partly due to the influence of the "New Reformation." Along with a return to biblical authority (Barthian style), we have seen a revival of Reformation worship forms and practice, including even neo-baroque organ design. The total result is an accommodation which includes three traditions: the apostolic heritage, historic medieval contributions, and their own Reformation distinctives.

The movement includes a renewed interest in liturgical symbolism, especially in vestments, church design and furnishings. Many congregations have chosen to return to the basic design of the apostolic "house church," building "churches in the round" with the communion table in the center. A new Lutheran sanctuary in Chicago features a sloping roof (like a huge tent) as a reminder that the Hebrews worshiped in a transient structure, and an altar elevated on a stone foundation to typify "mount Calvary." A small chapel has a flowing stream of water in a floor channel to remind us that Jesus said, "I am the water of life."

The "liturgical movement" has had considerable influence on Calvinist and "free churches," some of whom have been guided by the same objectives mentioned above: to unite their own distinctives with the traditions of the apostles and the medieval church. To illustrate, the *Worshipbook* (1974) of the United Presbyterian Church contains a Communion Service which can be said to combine the early form of John Calvin with elements of eucharistic worship in earlier centuries. The text of the service is an amplification of Calvin's Geneva service of 1542. In the music section of the book, the historic songs of the mass (*Kyrie, Gloria, Credo, Sanctus, Agnus Dei*) are included so that they might be added to that service.

Though some evangelicals may doubt that they too have been influenced by the liturgical movement, these trends will be noted in many groups:

(1) Increased interest in more sophisticated church architecture and furnishings, whether or not it includes the consideration of theological principles in symbolism.
(2) Development of more complete worship forms, with more congregational participation.
(3) More frequent observance of the Lord's Supper. Many evangelicals do so once each month, rather than quarterly—the historic norm.
(4) Increased observance of the Liturgical Year, especially as related to Advent and Holy Week.

The Evangelical Influence of Vatican II

Eugene L. Brand describes "the liturgical movement" as "the label given to efforts across the breadth of the Western church to restore full and vital *corporate* worship that centers in a eucharistic celebration where Sermon and Supper coexist in complimentary fashion."[20] As such, much of its impetus came from encyclicals of Pius X and Pius XII, and from other church leaders both in Europe and America. The Second Vatican Council of 1962 marked the climax of the movement for Roman Catholics with the release of the *Constitution on the Sacred Liturgy*. All churchmen agree that the reforms have been "evangelical" in nature. These are some of the most significant:

1. Worship is to be social and rational, not personal and mystical.
2. A return to vernacular languages.
3. Full congregational participation, including "protestant" hymns.
4. Inclusion of several scripture readings from both Old and New Testaments.
5. Inclusion of a sermon on a regular basis.
6. "Concelebration" of the mass—the people *with* the priest.
7. A retreat from extremely-sacerdotal theology. (In common American missals, four versions of the eucharistic prayer are available; only one closely resembles the old Roman Canon).

Judging from the text alone, only a few portions of the mass can now be labeled non-evangelical—the references to prayer to the Virgin Mary and to the mass as a sacrifice, all in the Canon. As a result, there is now more similarity between the Services of Lutherans and Episcopalians (even of "liturgical" Presbyterians) and those of Roman Catholics, than there has been at any time since the Reformation.

As a result of their new freedom, many Roman Catholics now partici-

20. Eugene L. Brand, "The Liturgical Life of the Church," in *A Handbook of Church Music,* Carl Halter and Carl Schalk, eds., p. 53.

pate in the worship services of evangelicals. Some regularly attend small Bible study groups, and even extra-liturgical, charismatic worship services.

The New Pietism

What we identify as "celebration" today may be partly a reaction to the "liturgical movement" of yesterday. Laypersons who are expected to take a larger part in worship may well insist that it should consist of activities which they enjoy. For this reason we may call the contemporary style "The New Pietism" (the emphasis is on religious experience), or even "The New Worship Hedonism" (the emphasis is on enjoyable experience). As Dr. Brand has said, the liturgical movement has been diverted from its "preoccupation with history (what is proper?) to a more pastoral concern (what is relevant?)."[21]

Even so, there are other contributing influences which should be noted:

1. Existentialist philosophy—emphasis on the "now" experience which may sometimes be supra-rational.
2. McLuhan-ism—"the medium is the message." McLuhan signals the weakening of words as communicative symbols, and notes increased interest in audio-visual media.
3. "Secular theology"—a decline in the significance of traditionally-sacral expressions in the awareness that the church is sent forth "into the world."
4. Roman Catholic reforms—Vatican II encourages its communicants to be rational, social and joyful in worship.
5. Relational theology—the importance of our relationships with other persons, both in and out of the church.
6. The philosophy of "linguistics"—a consideration of the meaning of words.
7. A reappearance of the aesthetic concept of music as "revelation" (see Mellers, *Caliban Reborn*).
8. The growth of Pentecostalism.

The resultant expressions in contemporary worship can also be listed:

1. Emphasis on Celebration—a total experience in which there is appeal to all the senses, by means of new worship forms and expressions, more emotional music, multi-media, drama, new symbolism, physical movement, etc.)
2. Updated translations of scripture; fresh, more personal language in liturgy, hymns, prayers and sermon.

21. Ibid., p. 56.

3. Congregational participation, not spectatorism.
4. Renewed emphasis on Christian fellowship in worship (in the tradition of the "kiss of peace") and in daily life (remembering that we are all lay-priests and lay-pastors.)
5. Cross-fertilization of the sacred by the secular, in text as well as music.

"The New Pietism" appeared first among the liturgical and more-liberal communions, and its total impact may have been more revolutionary among them. After all, the movement simply validated our own evangelical heritage—of joy and enjoyment in worship and in fellowship with other persons, both supported by our service style, including our music. Furthermore, it was moving counter to the interest of some evangelicals who were seeking to develop a greater sense of reverence in public worship.

One of the first expressions of the new music in contemporary worship was Geoffrey Beaumont's *Twentieth Century Folk Mass,* which appeared in 1960. As a member of the Light Music Group of the Church of England, he stated their philosophy succinctly and boldly: Worship should include not only the "timeless" music of master composers, but also the popular styles of the day, which are so much a part of people's lives. Soon thereafter, youth musical ensembles were appearing among evangelicals in Great Britain, patterning their styles after those of the "Beatles" and other folk and rock groups. Their objectives were to communicate the gospel and to express Christian response in word/music languages that were comprehensible to young people, both inside and out of the organized church. Before long, liturgical churches and traditional denominational bodies in America were following these examples in an endeavor to make worship services more relevant and celebrative.

Among typical American evangelicals, popular expressions in witness music had not changed dramatically since the advent of the gospel song about 1850. To be sure, there had been modest variations in style in the mid-20th century—including "Southern quartet" forms, "western" hymns, a few songs in a mild Broadway-musical style, and the beginning of a "country ballad hymnody." But, by and large, evangelicalism had not shown great interest in new music since the days of Billy Sunday and Homer Rodeheaver.

There was, however, considerable awareness of the need of fresh expressions in the church, and considerable (but not universal) support for new translations of the Bible and new phraseology in prayer. Evangelicals used the available new scripture versions and even sponsored some of their own. The musical break-through came with a few gospel folk songs by Ralph Carmichael which appeared in Billy Graham films, and the youth musical, *Good News,* released by Southern Baptists in 1967. The latter was soon followed by a flood of similar works, written for various age groups, using contemporary popular music forms and frequently performed with the recorded accompaniment of a full professional orchestra.

Soon shorter musical works began to be published in the same idioms. Older titles (and even new works in older forms, like Bill Gaither's gospel songs) continued to appear, but usually in "up-beat" arrangements—with strong syncopated rhythms, a goose-bump-raising orchestration, and a series of "half-step-up" modulations—which added up to strongly-emotional expression.

In the last ten years, we have also seen an unparalleled rise in the number of professional performances of popular religious music by traveling artists. A large number of youth groups are on the road, like Re-Generation (with Derek Johnson) or the Continentals (sponsored by Cam Floria). Older professional singers (e.g., Hale and Wilder, the Bill Gaither Trio, Andraé Crouch, Ken Medema, Bill Pearce, Suzanne Johnson, Jimmy McDonald and Evie Tornquist) give full programs of music, sometimes in churches and sometimes in auditoriums. Many young performers write their own songs and perform them almost exclusively. All of this activity has been a great boon to the religious music publishing and recording businesses and has created a multi-million dollar market, centering largely in Nashville, Tennessee. It is safe to say that we have just witnessed the most significant new development in Christian witness music since Ira Sankey popularized the gospel song more than 100 years ago!

No doubt there is much that is good in the new spirit and expressions of worship. But, as in so much of life, every plus is a potential minus, if we do not maintain a healthy balance. It is well to give vent to emotional expression, providing it does not lead to emotionalism and irrationality. The new humanism is good when it helps us be more aware of ourselves and our neighbors in full-orbed worship/fellowship, but bad if we substitute transcendent human experience for a full understanding of the transcendence of God. The creativity which new forms offer may lead to a loss of meaning and identity if we forsake completely the historic expressions which are part of our religious roots. Finally, the "new enjoyment" may lead to a worship hedonism which is another form of idolatry—worshiping the experience instead of God.

Chapter X

THE DRAMA OF WORSHIP FOR CONTEMPORARY EVANGELICALS

In preceding chapters, we have narrated in some detail the practice of Christian worship from apostolic times through the medieval period and the Reformation, down to the present day, noting that evangelicals find their roots in the early church, feel a kinship to the reformers, and identify most with the pietist, revivalist and free church movements.

Our purpose has been threefold: (1) to show our commonality with the historic church, (2) to highlight the reasons for our uniqueness, and (3) to identify certain areas in which we should recover our lost heritage. All Christian worship is based on the biblical record, no matter how distorted it may have become during the Middle Ages by the continuation of Old Testament emphases in theology and in liturgy, or in the encrustations of non-biblical tradition. The medieval mass (which became standard for Roman Catholics worldwide with the Council of Trent in 1562) still retained the two types of worship common to the first century church: a Service of the Word and a Service of the Table. It continued to provide an opportunity (at least in stated rubric) for scripture reading, sermon, praise and prayer, even though the first two were often omitted and the public expression of the last two was limited to priests speaking a "foreign" language. The strongest argument for the decadence of medieval worship is found in the actions of the Second Vatican Council of 1962, in which some of the theological errors in the mass were corrected, and congregational understanding and participation were restored by the use of the vernacular, and the involvement of the laity in the hymns, the prayers, the creed, and the responses.

The renewing response of the Reformation churches was varied, though they all adopted the common languages and congregational participation. Lutherans and Anglicans retained many of the features of historic eucharistic and office services, and a "professional" choral ministry for larger churches and cathedrals. Calvinists dropped the choirs completely, and followed a simple service outline that was related to the medieval "preaching service" (the Prone). In some instances, Calvinistic churches have ignored the liturgical traditions of John Calvin, becoming essentially "free" in matters of worship design. In recent years, the leading representatives of the Reformation churches have tended to return to the essentials of both their Reformation and their Catholic heritage.

The reaction of pietists and of free churchmen to high liturgical worship was even more iconoclastic. In rejecting all manmade forms, they frequently eliminated all but the "bare bones" of worship—preaching, prayer and congregational song, with the simplest commemorative communion service occasionally added. Through the years, certain groups have gradually regained certain elements of their more sophisticated forebears (e.g., choirs, organs, more ornate worship structures), but often without consideration of their scriptural or theological significance. In recent times, some free, evangelical churches have tended to adopt the "pseudo-liturgical" outline of the American non-liturgical tradition, mentioned in the previous chapter. Some have added new captions for segments of the service, such as:

> Our Call to Celebrate
>> Our Quest for Understanding
>>> Our Confrontation with Today's Needs
>>> Our Response to God's Greatness

or:

> The Gathering
>> Taking Responsibility for What We Hear
>> Taking Responsibility for the World
>> The Scattering

In other places, there continues to be a good deal of prejudice against any set forms, such as responsive readings or litanies, and "read" prayers. The practice in some churches perpetuates the revivalist pattern: Opening songs, special music, announcements and offering, evangelistic sermon and invitation. Frequently some important essentials like scripture reading and prayer are given only cursory attention.

The most serious indictment of modern evangelicalism results from the almost-universal attitude that public worship is not important enough to plan carefully. Most of our seminaries and Bible colleges do not require courses in worship for ministers in preparation (except for studies in homiletics and preaching), evidently with the thought that to do so would deny the "free" tradition. As a result, most worship design and practice tends to be accidental, resulting from following the latest fad, or copying an "interesting" outline used by another church.

There is strength in the heritage of freedom, notwithstanding the fact that many pastors tend to be held in a worship straitjacket of their own choosing, following the same scant outline and frequently using the same poverty-stricken vocabulary week after week. We believe that evangelicals must understand thoroughly the biblical, theological and historical bases for corporate worship in their own fellowship, as well as the arts which are involved, if they are to include all the essentials, while exercising their freedom in planning experiences that are rich and varied.

The Drama of Worship

Worship is often referred to as a drama. In this chapter we will use that image to suggest certain considerations which may contribute to effective worship in the local evangelical church.

To begin, we are reminded that two types of activity take place on a stage. One is a vaudeville show, in which a series of basically-unrelated acts are held together by a "master of ceremonies"; logically, each successive act is acknowledged by the audience's applause. The other is a drama, in which a total "happening" takes place with a logical progression of scenes to convey a single message, and in which the audience participates in a total experience. It may be said that "revivalist" worship is most related to vaudeville; it is centered in the personality of a leader or leaders, and though there may be potential relationship between the "acts," it is often missed because of the intrusion of a personality. In a typical evangelistic service, the principal objectives are usually limited to the communication of the gospel message and the soliciting of an affirmative response; for these purposes, the person-centered medium may be argued to be effective. True worship, however, should be true drama, with a story continuity which moves to its *denoument* logically and effectively, and in which the actors communicate the "play," not themselves. We shall consider evangelical worship then as drama, with attention to (1) the cast, (2) the script, (3) staging, and (4) dramatic direction. In doing so, we expect to reinforce and amplify the positions taken in previous chapters, especially chapter five.

The Cast

In his book *Purity of Heart is to Will One Thing*, the Danish philosopher-theologian Søren Kierkegaard spoke of worship as a drama. In criticizing the non-involvement of many of the communicants in his own liturgical church (Lutheran), he insisted that in true worship the congregation are the actors, that ministers and choir are "prompters," and that God is the audience.

> In the most earnest sense, God is the critical theatergoer, who looks on to see how the lines are spoken and how they are listened to ... The speaker is then the prompter, and the listener stands openly before God. The listener, if I may say so, is the actor, who in all truth acts before God.[1]

1. Søren Kierkegaard, *Purity of Heart Is to Will One Thing*, p. 164.

Kierkegaard's argument was in keeping with the historical meaning of the word liturgy (Gr. *leitourgia*), "the work of the people." However, in the Middle Ages, though it was clear that God was intended to be the audience, the mass was essentially "the work of the priests"; the congregation were not even good spectators, since they did not understand the words, and in a large cathedral they could not even see the action!

In some evangelical situations, it also seems apparent that worship is the work of the minister and choir; the congregation is the "audience," which suggests that they function most as listeners. In many situations, they are never encouraged to speak a word in the service, in reading scripture or by participating in prayers (not even the Lord's Prayer). Of course, they are allowed to sing the hymns, though sometimes too few, and even this opportunity is ignored by many in some evangelical congregations. It is true that one can be involved in worship—one can even be speaking to God—without uttering audible sound, but we believe it is desirable to have maximum participation of the congregation in actual speech as well as song, and also in physical action.

We may not want to limit the worship cast as severely as did Kierkegaard. Because ministers and musicians are themselves worshiping as well as leading in worship, they might be considered to be both actors and "prompters." As we have said before, in the revelation and response of worship, they remind us what God has revealed about himself in his Word and his actions, and what our response to him should be.

Evangelical ministers (including musicians) need to continually reevaluate their roles as "leaders" of worship. Overt leaders announce their leadership, and as a result, frequently interpose themselves between the congregation (the actors) and God (the audience). "Prompters," we should remember, are offstage; they are only heard when they are needed. Ideally, worshipers will know the basic script well enough that subtle and almost imperceptible leadership will suffice.

This does not mean that the atmosphere of worship will be cold and impersonal. There is ample opportunity in the "welcome period" and in the sermon for the personality of the leader to express itself in warmth and even in humor. Even more, all the words and actions of the leaders should show the common joy of fellowship in Christian faith and action. It does mean that the leaders should not draw so much attention to themselves that the worshipers fail to "see God" and to fully experience true worship.

The Script

The inheritance of typical evangelicals is worship that is non-liturgical; that is to say, they reject all set forms or liturgies. Their worship drama then, is expected to have *no script*; it is to be improvised under the guidance of the Holy Spirit. Nevertheless, it invariably has a script, for the songs, announcements, prayers, special music and sermon add up to overall form and specific content, even though the final result may be a surprise to the leaders, for which the Holy Spirit may possibly not be responsible! Frequently, this unplanned and improvised form of worship fails to include some of the most significant bilbical-historical elements.

We are not suggesting that evangelicals adopt rigid service orders. We do insist, however, that there are essential actions in worship. In our corporate gatherings, these basic experiences have found expression in certain forms (speech, music, visual symbols, action), some of which have been traditional since apostolic times. Again, these forms need not be arranged arbitrarily in one prescribed pattern; nevertheless, there is logical order in terms of biblical example, human-divine propriety, and dramatic consistency, and that order is validated by the common practice of most Christians. Finally, the Holy Spirit may be more present in prayerful planning than in thoughtless improvising.

In this study, we are considering the regular pattern of Sunday morning worship, which may (or may not) include Communion. There are opportunities for unusual experiences of worship on festival days or on other occasions which are designated as "special." The greater challenge, however, is to use the regular hour in such a way that it contains both expectation and surprise. Part of the effectiveness of worship results from knowing that certain actions will take place in a service, and preparing for them. In addition, it is important that there be enough variety from week to week to give a sense of freshness and creativity.

The Basic Actions.

It has already been said that the basic actions of worship are revelation and response. Insofar as we are able to conceive and achieve it, there should be a *full revelation* of God, his actions and his will for us, and a *full response* by men and women, involving body, emotions, intellect and will. The following lists the broader aspects of revelation and response, and is based on the definitions of worship given in chapter five.

Revelation	*Response*
Who God is	What we become through God's grace
What God has done for us, What he is doing and will do	What we do in expressing our discipleship
What God says to us	What we say to God—in praise, confession, dedication, thanksgiving and petition

There is a concept of worship order held by some evangelicals, which sees "unity without diversity" as the guiding principle. If the morning sermon is about "faith," every hymn will support that subject—"Faith of Our Fathers," "Faith Is the Victory," "Have Faith in God," "O for a Faith that Will Not Shrink," etc. This practice reveals that the sermon and its response are the only significant acts of worship for those planners. The wise and humble pastor will acknowledge that on some occasions a praise hymn, or the prayer of confession or of intercession, or the choir anthem may meet the spiritual needs of some people more than the homily.

Revelation may be accomplished through all the communicative vehicles of worship—through words and other symbols, such as music and other arts, and actions. Response may be expressed in words (sometimes sung), and through actions (e.g., giving money, kneeling, and participating in the Communion.) However, we should always remember that true revelation and response is personal communication between God and each individual, and is possible only through the ministry of the Holy Spirit. It frequently occurs through the elements of the service, whether liturgical or unplanned, but it may happen totally apart from the service order!

Typical Forms and Materials

We have already noted that the barest outline of worship was followed by the first century church at Corinth (I Cor. 14:26) and by nonconformist groups in the late 16th century, both of whom were restricted by the persecution of civil and religious authorities. Probably few evangelicals believe that worship forms today should be limited to such a degree.

In chapter six, we reviewed the elements of worship activity which are recorded in the New Testament epistles. All these would probably be acknowledged to be lawful by modern evangelicals, whether or not their own particular worship practice includes them.

> Scripture readings
> A sermon
> A confession of faith (admittedly not favored by some groups,
> including Baptists)
> Singing (of various types)
> Prayers (of various types)
> A congregational Amen
> Almsgiving (a collection)
> Physical Action
> The Lord's Supper (including the following concepts):
> Thanksgiving
> Remembrance of the Lord
> Anticipation of Christ's return
> Expression of fellowship (the kiss of peace)

The Order of Worship.

If, then, all the above activities and materials are present in worship, can we be sure that we have provided amply for both revelation and response? Not necessarily, for there is a logical sequence in the denouement of the worship drama, which has both scriptural and historical validity. The basic concept is that revelation always precedes response; it is an evidence of God's grace that he always makes the first move in the divine-human encounter. This is expressed in worship design in two ways: (1) Each incidence of revelation is followed by its own response; and (2) The first part of the service is more revelation, and the closing is mostly response.

For the basic pattern of worship services, we refer again to Isaiah 6, where this progression is found: An Awareness of God in his transcendence and immanence ("I saw the Lord . . . high and lifted up," v.1); Confession ("And I said: Woe is me!" v.5); Forgiveness (" . . . your guilt is taken away, and your sin forgiven." v.7); God Calls to Discipleship ("Who will go for us?" v.8); We Respond ("Here am I! Send me." v.8); and We Pray in Petition ("Then I said, How long, O Lord?" v.11).

This pattern of worship is present in the following order which would be appropriate where the local church is not ready for much verbal participation, and where the music is limited to that of the gospel song tradition and is mostly congregational. This should demonstrate that true worship is not dependent on the use of a particular style of material.

Spiritual Actions	*Order of Worship*
An Awareness of God	Hymn, "To God Be the Glory" (Crosby-Doane)
Confession and Forgiveness	Opening Prayer (including Invocation, Confession and Assurance of Pardon)
	Greeting and Welcome
	Hymn, "Break Thou the Bread of Life" (Lathbury-Sherwin)
God Speaks	Scripture Reading
	Choir, "We Praise Thee, O God" (Mackay-Husband)
	Sermon
We Respond	Hymn (Invitation) "Stand Up for Jesus" (Duffield-Webb)
	Offering (Solo): "Wherever He Leads I'll Go" (McKinney)
We Celebrate Christ's Life, Death and Resurrection for our eternal Salvation	Prayer of Thanksgiving (including remembrance and words of institution) followed by "breaking the bread," "taking the cup," distribution and communion.
We Pray	Pastoral (the Congregation's) Prayer followed by a united "Amen"
	Hymn (Doxology)
	Benediction

The following commentary on this simple worship order will place the progression of actions in their biblical and historical contexts.

OPENING HYMN. One of the simplest ways to set forth the excellence of God is in a musical expression of praise. It can be found in many musical styles—a short anthem or motet, chorale, psalm, standard or gospel hymn, folk hymn, etc. "To God Be the Glory" is a gospel hymn by Fanny J. Crosby and William Howard Doane, but the text praises God for his actions in the Church universal and in our personal lives.

OPENING PRAYER. The minister may carry forward the theme of praise in his brief opening prayer, recalling the character and the providence of God, and "invoking" his blessing on the service. As in Isaiah 6, this awareness of God's perfections leads human beings to realize, deplore and confess their imperfections; in fact, they may not approach worship with any confidence until once again they have the assurance they are forgiven. This opening prayer should include that confession and evangelical assurance, using perhaps the words of I John 1:7, ". . . if we walk in the light as he is in the light, we have fellowship with one another, and the blood of Jesus his Son cleanses us from all sin."

GREETING AND WELCOME. It may be said that the pastor's greeting and a welcome to visitors is related to the historic salutation used by early Christians as well as their Jewish forebears, even though the modern extemporized version may not have the same spiritual quality, or the same opportunity for congregational response.

> Leader: The Lord be with you.
> Congregation: And also with you.

In many churches, this time in the service is limited to welcoming visitors and securing their registration. It may be a better practice to allow believers to express their love for each other as well as their welcome to visitors, if only by a handshake and a smile. When the congregation participates in this act, it may be said to perpetuate the traditional "kiss of peace."

SCRIPTURE READING. One of the more surprising characteristics of worship in certain evangelical churches is the scarcity of scripture reading. This is undoubtedly a carry-over from the heritage of revivalism, where the evangelist/minister simply takes a text (or reads a short passage) and then delivers a lengthy sermon on it. This pattern is clearly contrary to the example of the early Christians, who continued the synagogue practice of reading several passages from the Old Testament and singing the psalms, and who also read the letters of Paul which were circulated among the churches.

Evangelicals should pay particular honor to the Word of God, and this calls for more than holding the Bible in hand while preaching! In Jewish worship, the removal of the Torah from its "tabernacle" is a very solemn moment. In the Orthodox liturgy, the reading from scripture is preceded by a colorful processional through the congregation during which the Bible is held high. Some churches have recently adopted the custom of standing for the reading of scripture, to witness to its divine authority.[2] Special attention can be focused on the lection by preceding it with an appropriate hymn, such as "Break Thou the Bread of Life," or "Lord, Speak to Me that I May Speak." Reading should include Old and New Testaments when possible, to demonstrate the unity of scripture and the relationship of the two "covenants."

SERMON. Perhaps the greatest variance between this service outline and the typical norm of evangelicals occurs in the close relationship of the sermon to the scripture reading, and the delay of the pastoral prayer and the offering until later. It seems logical to follow the scripture passage quickly with its explanation; otherwise many worshipers lose the connection between the two. It is also appropriate for the minister to follow Calvin's example, by prefacing his homily with a "prayer for illumination." Such a prayer voices the same petition as the hymn "Break Thou the Bread of Life"—that God the Holy Spirit would make his Word known to both preacher and congregation.

This suggestion should not be taken to mean that there can be no break between "scripture read" and "scripture explained." This might be a good place for "special" music, ideally by an ensemble or choir,[3] which could be considered to be an offering of praise in thanksgiving for the word of God, or it might be related textually to the scripture and the sermon. It has long been the custom of many evangelicals (and this too stems from the revival tradition) to use a vocal solo at this point, with a text that is a testimony of personal Christian experience. In the context of evangelism, the practice may be meaningful, but it makes little contribution to the continuity of scripture and sermon in a worship service.

HYMN OF RESPONSE. The sermon has always been central in evangelical worship. It is God's continuing call to enlarged faith and the growing discipleship of forgiven and cleansed believers.

I remember the time (in midwest America, where an "invitation" was not common) when many evangelical pastors followed the sermon immediately with the Benediction. It seemed apparent that they were unwilling for anything to detract from that most important communication from God; they wanted folk to hurry home with it still ringing in their ears! However, that practice thwarts the possibility of response to God's self-revelation in the homily. There must be ample opportunity to respond, and the most logical expression is a hymn. In many churches, this part of the service includes an invitation to respond to the call of Christ for salvation, or to join the local fellowship of believers. This emphasis is also a continuation of revivalist practice, and there can be little quarrel

2. Liturgical churches traditionally stand for the "gospel reading," since that scripture records the life and the words of our Lord.
3. This may be said to follow the example of Anglican office worship, in which a Canticle (e.g., the *Te Deum*) follows scripture.

with it, so long as it does not limit the potential of preaching the "whole counsel of truth" and of a full response of *every* worshiper based on individual need. The doors of the church should be open wide; it should not be a difficult thing to join the community of faith and a regular opportunity is welcome. But this emphasis should not exclude the call to the larger group of worshipers to concentrate on the response they too should make to the Word of God, read and explained. Obviously, it is not appropriate to sing a typical "invitation hymn" (e.g., "Softly and Tenderly Jesus Is Calling" or "Let Jesus Come Into Your Heart") unless the sermon has been clearly addressed to the "lost." And a response for church membership (and even for initial Christian commitment) can take place with the singing of any good "discipleship" hymn, such as "Am I a Soldier of the Cross?" or "Take Up Your Cross, the Savior Said." Finally, the minister should make it clear in his remarks that *everyone* is expected to respond to the Word of God, in the hymn and in the offering which follows.

OFFERING. Placing the offering after the sermon and the response hymn will no doubt be startling to traditionalists. The explanation is that the offering is also "response" to God's Word, not just a perfunctory act to support the church budget or to show one's loyalty to the "program." We give our money to God in token of giving ourselves in a complete dedication. Contributing to the offering following the sermon is one way of saying "Amen" to God's will expressed in his Word, read and preached.

Many leaders question the effectiveness of an organ or piano offertory, because during its playing the individual worshipers probably do nothing more significant than admire the player's technique, "enjoy" wordless music, or let their minds wander. This is a place for vocal music, a "sacrifice of praise" that involves minds and emotions while we offer our sacrifices of self, symbolized by our money. Some churches in the Calvinist tradition combine the receiving of the offering with the response hymn following the sermon. When it follows that hymn, it can feature a choral piece or a solo (and possibly even a witness song, at that point in the service!)

Following the offertory, on appointed Sundays, the Lord's Supper may be celebrated. Since otherwise the outline is the same, we will proceed to consider the closing experiences of a non-eucharistic service, and then return to give special attention to the Communion.

PRAYERS. In the service outline above, the traditional title "Pastoral Prayer" was used for this part of the service, even though it encourages misunderstanding of the congregation's role in the prayer. In historical worship, this is correctly called the "Prayers of the Faithful" or "Prayers of the People," offered on their behalf by the pastor-minister. And what about its placement at the *end* of the service?

It may not impress the evangelical to know that it is the normal pattern of all Christian liturgies for the prayers of petition and intercession to follow the hearing of, and responding to the Word of God. It may be significant to note that this is the sequence of Isaiah 6 (and the point is missed by many expositors of the passage); the prophet hears the challenge to serve God, willingly responds "Here am I," but then returns to remind God of the problems encountered in his ministry, in the plaintive petition "Lord, how long?" (v. 11). Our argument for this order is twofold. First, God called the meeting to order to reveal himself and his will; it is simply good etiquet to "hear him out" and to offer a full affirmative response, before we break in on the conversation to remind God of our needs and those of others. Second, it is a moving experience for believers to pray together, to express their humanness and their needs, as the closing act of fellowship in worship.

Without doubt, even the "people's prayers" should be more than petition and intercession. They should include praise (an acknowledgment of God's transcendence) and thanksgiving (gratitude for his providence). The New Testament has given us specific instructions about intercessory prayer and all traditional worship forms have included them. In the evangelical church, they can be included by the minister even when the prayer is improvised:

> First of all, then, I urge that supplications, prayers, intercessions, and thanksgivings be made for all men, for kings, and all who are in high positions..." (I Tim. 2:1,2)

> Is any among you sick?... the prayer of faith will save the sick...
> (James 5:14,15)

> ... confess your sins to one another, and pray for one another, that you may be healed. (James 5:16)

It is a worthy hope that American evangelicals may one day adopt the practice of our brothers and sisters around the world, in following the statement of our common prayers by a united vocal "Amen"—"So be it, Lord, according to your will." The French Reformed theologian Richard Paquier[4] reminds us that it is pointless for the minister to add "Amen" to the prayer affirming what he has just said. The word "Amen" means literally "to be firm, true," and is connected with the verb "to believe."[5] When we voice it after a prayer spoken by another, we are saying "Yes, Lord, that's *my* prayer."

THE CLOSE OF WORSHIP. The service may close with a hymn or with a shorter expression of praise (e.g., the Doxology of Thomas Ken, "Praise God from whom all blessings flow, etc.") and a benediction (expressing the hope that God's "blessing" will attend each person in the departure to serve him in daily life.) It is customary to use the Aaronic blessing (Num. 6:24-26), one of the New Testament benedictions (II Cor. 13:14, Heb. 13:20-21) or a contemporary expression.

4. Richard Paquier, *Dynamics of Worship*, p. 63.
5. Ralph P. Martin, *Worship in the Early Church*, p. 36.

THE COMMUNION SERVICE. At the time of the Reformation, the "protesting" churches excised much that was evangelical along with the heterodox in the Communion service, and in recent years their successors have endeavored to recover what was good. The "dissenters and nonconformists" went even further, reducing the eucharist to the simple acts of eating and drinking, with the simplest prayer of thanks and repeating the "words of institution"—a relatively unimportant gesture at the end of a preaching service.

Such a limited (and limiting) experience is probably related to the refusal of some evangelicals to acknowledge that the Lord's Supper is a *sacrament* (a symbolic action which can be a "means of grace"), insisting that it is only an *ordinance* (something Christ commanded us to do.) Is it impertinent to inquire whether Christ would ask us to demonstrate our obedience with acts that have no spiritual implications? And is it not incongruous to insist that there is no potential of grace in the Communion, while talking about the sacrament of preaching, the sacrament of life, or the sacrament of pain?

For many evangelicals, observance of the eucharist is less than meaningful, because it is only a sketchy form, with words and actions that are not complete, tacked on to the end of a service. On the basis of scriptural reminders and historical precedent, the communion service should express:

> The historical instituting of the supper (the words of institution).
>
> The giving of thanks, as Christ set the example in his own upper room prayer, and because "thanksgiving" is the basic Christian response to his love for us.
>
> The idea of remembrance "until he comes," following his command. This includes more than "recalling his death and resurrection" as will be explained below.
>
> The concept of fellowship (communion) with God and with each other. A supper is a social occasion, and we demonstrate our mutual Christian love in such gestures as "the kiss of peace" or in passing the bread and the cup to each other.
>
> The act of "fraction" (breaking the bread) as Christ did to show visually that his body was to be broken for us, and of pouring out the wine, as his blood was poured out on our behalf.
>
> Our renewed dedication of ourselves to God, because we remember his love for us and the cost of our salvation.

Ralph P. Martin reminds us that The Lord's Supper is the "Christian Passover." When Jews repeat the story of the deliverance from Egypt, "it is not enough that the family . . . remember the past redemption; they must relive it in a most realistic sense."[6]

6. Ibid., p. 114.

Each member of the family was to regard himself as though he had been personally in bondage in Egypt and had been personally brought out by the Lord his God . . .

Likewise, at the Table of remembrance, the Church does not simply reflect (as a mental exercise) upon the Cross of Calvary, but relives the accomplished redemption, is taken back to the Upper Room and the Hill, shares in that saving work which it knows as a present reality—because its Author is the living One in the midst of His ransomed people.[7]

The problem with most "remembrance prayers" is that they do not tell the whole story. The chronicle of redemption does not begin at Calvary; that is the climax of the narrative! It begins with creation and God's purpose for humanity; it includes his dealings with his people through the centuries and the reasons for the incarnation; it ends with remembrance of the life of Christ, as well as his death and resurrection and the anticipation of his second advent. It may be argued that most folk remember the entire story while repeating only a small part of it. That is as fallacious as presuming that people know the Bible so we do not need to read it in church—only preach from it!

The following is a script for a complete communion service which would give evangelical worshipers the chance to recall and to place themselves in the center of the whole story! It can be improvised or read, and for the uncommitted present, it would present the gospel story in less than five minutes time.

Minister: This is the table of the Lord. We invite all who have trusted him as Savior and Lord to share in the supper which he has prepared.

Another minister, or deacon: Our Father, we thank you that you have made us in your image, and that you created the world in which we live. You have shown yourself to men and women throughout history, demonstrating your power, your love and your providence. We thank you that, when we rejected your love and went our own way, you sent your son Jesus, who lived among us and died and rose again that we might be reconciled to you and have eternal life. We look forward to his coming again, when we will celebrate this supper again in his kingdom.

We thank you for this bread, which reminds us that his body was broken for us, and for the whole world. Amen.

Minister: The Lord Jesus on the night when he was betrayed took bread, and when he had given thanks, he broke it, and said, "This is my body, which is broken for you. Do this in remembrance of me."

(Followed by distribution and partaking of the bread)

7. Ibid., pp. 118-119.

Minister (or deacon): Heavenly Father, we thank you for this cup, which reminds us that our Lord's blood was poured out for the remission of our sins, and not for ours only, but also for the sins of the whole world. We thank you that you constantly give yourself to us in fellowship day by day. We dedicate ourselves anew to you, to worship and serve you as long as we live. We dedicate ourselves also to each other, as fellow-believers. May we love each other as you have loved us. Amen.

Minister: In the same way also he took the cup, after supper, saying, "This cup is the new covenant in my blood. Do this, as often as you drink it, in remembrance of me." For as often as you eat this bread and drink the cup, you proclaim the Lord's death until he comes.

(Followed by distribution and partaking of the cup)

These prayers need not be written out and read. However, a pastor who entrusts them to his fellow ministers or to deacons should assume the responsibility to train these individuals in public prayer, and to help them make mental or written notes of the items each should include. The celebration of communion is not the time for "thoughtless improvising."

Since Christ and his disciples sang a hymn in the upper room, the eucharist service traditionally has included music that assists in the recall of Christ's life and atoning death. In medieval worship, some of the most glorious music was associated with the Liturgy of the Upper Room—the *Sanctus et Benedictus,* the *Agnus Dei,* and a Communion hymn. At the time of the reformation, Martin Luther encouraged churches to use John Hus's hymn *Jesus Christus, unser Heiland* (Jesus Christ, Our Blessed Savior) during communion. It was noted earlier that the very first hymn in the English tradition was written by the British Baptist minister Benjamin Keach for use in this service. Today, evangelicals frequently use congregational, choral or solo selections to make the experience more meaningful. A recent hymn "As We Gather Around the Table of Our Lord"[8] is a good presentation of the concept of "remembrance," and could be used to amplify that aspect of the prayers.

> As we gather around the table of our Lord,
>> We recall his humble birth in Bethlehem,
> As the angels sang, as the shepherds came,
>> Let us adore and worship the Lord,
>>> Let us remember him.
>
> As we gather around the table of our Lord,
>> We recall his agony upon the cross.
> There our Savior died, alone was crucified;
>> Let us adore and worship the Lord,
>>> Let us remember him.

8. *Baptist Hymnal* (1975), no. 251.

> As we gather around the table of our Lord,
>   We recall the empty tomb where he was laid.
> He is living still, our longing hearts to fill;
>   Let us adore and worship the Lord,
>   Let us remember him.
> Mark Blankenship

Copyright, 1975, Broadman Press. Used by Permission

Following the communion service, worship may conclude with the Pastoral Prayer (which may be somewhat briefer on this occasion), the Doxology, and Benediction.

Direction in the Worship Drama

We have thus far considered the actors and the basic script outline in the worship drama. But there is more to good theater than a competent cast and a good "book." We still need pacing and movement—a rise and fall of excitement—to make the script come alive as true drama. In achieving this objective, a period of silence may be as important as fast tempo or a high decibel level of music. Furthermore, because the drama is repeated week after week, the script needs to be varied from time to time to assure effective communication. This suggestion is made with full awareness that, in the worship drama, the congregation are the actors. Like actors in the theater, they need to feel that what they are doing is "dramatic."

The Church Calendar.

Historically, script variation has been accomplished mostly by following the emphases of the liturgical calendar, with changing lections, prayers and sermon themes for each day, as well as the extraordinary observances connected with festival periods. At the time of the Reformation, Calvin discarded the church year, and evangelicals have continued to ignore it until recently. As late as 100 years ago, Easter and Christmas were passed over in many churches. The scriptural support for this ban was Paul's indictment of those who insisted that Christians must also conform to the ancient Jewish cultic laws.

> But now that you have come to know God, or rather to be known by God, how can you turn back again to the weak and beggarly elemental spirits, whose slaves you want to be once more? You observe days, and months, and seasons, and years! I am afraid I have labored over you in vain. (Galatians 4:9-11)

To be sure, we all follow some calendar, though in some churches it may be only the "budget year." Yesterday's congregations, who sponsored spring and fall revivals each year, were inadvertently matching the two historic penance periods, Lent and Advent.

Increasingly, our churches are acknowledging the validity of the complete cycle of the year. A number have given more attention to Advent, perhaps to counter the excessive commercialism of our prolonged Christmas shopping season; the lighting of Advent candles is becoming increasingly common in Baptist churches and others. Still too few churches take full notice of Holy Week; no doubt this is a continued reaction against the observances of our liturgical neighbors, coupled with the idea that "every Sunday is Easter Sunday." But you cannot have a resurrection without a crucifixion, and you cannot properly celebrate Easter without remembering Christ's passion and death. Consequently, more churches are joining in a three-hour Good Friday remembrance, and/or conducting a Tenebrae service or a communion observance.

The day may yet come when the full shape of the Church Year (including Epiphany and Pentecost) will provide the framework for celebrating the entire history of God's revelation through Christ, and assure proper emphasis on all the doctrines of our faith.

Stage Directors for Worship.

In church the stage director role is filled by the worship planners, some of whom function also as worship leaders or "prompters." Communicating the direction of the worship drama is a unique problem since the cast never meets for rehearsal; it has only performances! Much of the directing is achieved simply by careful service planning, in which both unity and variety (which make for dramatic effectiveness) are the objectives. The worship planners/leaders carefully consider each element to insure that it fits into the script, and that there is a balance of faster and slower pacing, of loudness and softness, of sobriety and of humor, of ecstasy and reflection, of God-centeredness and self-consciousness.

The following suggestions list subtle methods of "directing" the drama while it is in progress.

1. The leaders/prompters should themselves appear to be worshipers, singing the hymns, speaking the responses, hearing the choir anthem and the sermon. Too many evangelical preachers apparently take a census of the congregation during the opening hymn and review their sermon notes during the choir selection.

2. The leaders/prompters should refrain from interpolating pleasant-but-irrelevant remarks in the progression of the drama. A typical example is "thanking the choir" after they sing; this is comparable to leading in applause following each vaudeville act. The choir sings as an offering to God, not for the praise of the congregation. It would be just as appropriate for the chairman of the deacons (or the clerk of the Session) to express appreciation to the minister following his sermon. There are proper occasions for the expression of support and gratitude to both minister and choir, but not in the middle of the worship experience.

3. The leaders/prompters can point to the significance of parts of the worship drama as it unfolds:

a. By indicating the subject of a hymn, as: "Our hymn of adoration is . . ."; or "To prepare us to hear the Word of God, we will sing . . ."
b. By leading from one act of worship to another, as from the opening praise hymn to the prayer of confession: "It is the perfections of God which remind us of what we want to be, but fail to achieve. Let us confess our shortcomings to God, and be reminded that we are accepted by him in Christ."
c. By relating the scripture to the sermon to follow, with a short explanation before the reading. (In days past, the Calvinist tradition allowed for verse-by-verse exposition of the scripture, in addition to the sermon.)
d. By encouraging the congregational Amen following prayers, by leading into it (in a fashion often used to indicate approval of a musical number): "And all God's people said . . . Amen." (Hopefully, after a period of such training, the "lead in" can be dropped, with the Amen continuing.)

John Skoglund[9] suggests that the choice and placement of music is one of the effective ways of achieving variety, adding emotional movement, "rise and fall" in free church worship. In our tradition, we are not required to use any particular hymns for choir or congregation; we may choose them as we please. Music may set forth the Word or respond to it. Music may substitute for speech. Music (like speech) may feature one voice, or a group, or the whole congregation.

In the following outline and commentary, a proposed service for New Year's Sunday is offered as an alternative to the simple worship pattern given earlier in this chapter, suggesting ways to vary the mood and pacing. We have included the most common, traditional forms which have the longest association with Judeo-Christian worship: the Salutation and *Sursum Corda*, the *Sanctus*, the *Gloria Patri* and the hymnic Doxology. Worship that uses these resources is not necessarily more complete than that which follows the simpler form. It is simply another possibility for experiencing the same essential spiritual actions, that may appeal to the evangelical church which has developed a more sophisticated taste in styles of speech and music.

Worship for New Year's Sunday
Service of the Word

An Awareness of God   Organ Prelude
                                   Choral Call to Worship
                                   Scripture Sentences
                                   Hymn of Praise, "O God Our Help
                                           in Ages Past"

9. John E. Skoglund, *Worship in the Free Churches,* p. 83.

Confession and Forgiveness   Prayer of Confession
                             Assurance of Forgiveness
                             Hymn, "God of Our Life, Through
                                All the Circling Years"

God Speaks   Old Testament Reading—Psalm 90
                                Gloria Patri
                                New Testament Reading—Eph. 5:14-21
                                Anthem or Hymn
                                Sermon: "The Gospel of Beginning
                                Again"

We Respond   Hymn of Invitation, "Moment by
                                          Moment"
                                Offering and Offertory: "Day by Day"
                                The Witness of Faith

                         Service of the Table

We Celebrate Christ's   The Call to the Table
   Life, Death and   Salutation and *Sursum Corda*
   Resurrection   The Prayer of Thanksgiving
                                Salvation history
                                   (*Sanctus*)
                                Remembrance
                                Dedication
                                Words of Institution
                                Distribution

We Pray   Prayers of Petition, Intercession,
                                Praise and Thanksgiving
                                Petition for the church worldwide
                                           for governments
                                           for all who suffer
                                           for local church needs
                                           for the unreached
                                The Lord's Prayer
                                Hymn (Doxology)

We Depart to   Benediction
   Serve and Worship   Organ Postlude

The following comments will offer variant possibilities in the service. It should be understood that no single service will include them all.

An Awareness of God.

The organ prelude has historically been considered as an opportunity to use characteristic sounds to aid the individual in personal preparation for worship. It has been described as a "curtain" which we draw to shut out life's pressures and distractions so that we may sense the presence of the numinous God. As modern worship theologians have reminded us, the purpose of worship is to bring the life and power of God to bear on those pressures and distractions, and that is the purpose of the scripture/sermon. But first, we need to be "quiet" and to focus on our relationship with God.

An effective communication of God's transcendence at the opening of the service is choral music. It may be quiet (as Vaughan Williams' "O Taste and See") or exultant (Norden's "Holy, Holy, Holy"), and it is good to vary the mood from week to week.

It is also possible to reveal God's person and presence early in the service through scripture. John Calvin began his worship order with the words of Psalm 124:8, "Our help is in the name of the Lord, who made heaven and earth." It is also good to involve the congregation in responsory reading.

> Leader: Blessed are those who hunger and thirst for righteousness, for they shall be satisfied.   (Matt. 5:6)
> Congregation: I was glad when they said to me, "Let us go to the house of the Lord!" My soul longs, yea, faints for the courts of the Lord; my heart and flesh sing for joy to the living God.   (Psalm 122:1; 84:2)
> All: Let the words of my mouth and the meditation of my heart be acceptable in thy sight, O Lord, my rock and my redeemer.   (Psalm 19:14)

The selected hymn of praise is very familiar, and is most appropriate to any service (like that on New Year's Sunday) which marks the passing of time. If a processional hymn is used, longer stanzas and more continuous rhythm are needed; a good choice would be "Another Year Is Dawning" (Havergal), to the tune AURELIA.

Confession/Forgiveness.

This prayer may include the acknowledgement of God's presence (the invocation) and may also take on the emphasis of the day, as is traditional for a "collect."[10] On this particular day the leader could begin: "Our Father, we thank you that, no matter how often we have failed you and others in the year that is past, today—and each day—we can begin afresh . . ." and then lead into the united confession.

The following prayer[11] is a bit longer than usual for this part of the

---

10. The title comes from the conviction that the minister speaks the "collective" prayer of the congregation.
11. This prayer was used by my pastor, Dr. J. Altus Newell, at St. Matthews Baptist. Church, Louisville, KY, on a Sunday in 1977.

service, but it contains the proper elements. The central paragraphs could be spoken (prayed) by the entire worshiping assembly.

O God of amazing grace and marvelous mercy, we come today thankful to be your people, to be alive in your world. Even with some hurts and pains, even with those things that may seem depressing, we have sensed an overcoming power. We pray today that this power might slip into our lives and that which would hold us back from experiencing life fully and living it abundantly might fade away and be cleansed from us.

Father, we come to you today asking that we might receive that refreshing of forgiveness. You've taught us to love people and use things, and we confess that too often we have loved things and used people and we need your forgiveness. Father, you have taught us to remember kindness and to forget slights, and we must confess that too often we have remembered slights and forgotten those who have expressed the kindness that comes from you. Lord, forgive us. We come today expressing our awareness that you have called us to be molded by the power of the coming age and we have been molded too often by the present world around us. Father, forgive us.

We come asking that as your cleansed and chastened vessels, as those who are loved by you without merit of our own, but because of the value that you place upon us, that you might help us to accept ourselves even as you love us.

And Lord, we come on behalf of our friends in this place and around the world and those persons unknown to us but known and loved by you, to pray that your redeeming mercy might be spread in persons' hearts beginning here in this sanctuary and extending wherever your word is preached and heard today.

Father, we ask that these moments might be times of spiritual growth. Speak to us through the hymn texts, speak to us through the word of scripture, speak to us through the proclamation of your word and speak to us through the response that we sense welling up in our hearts. For this is our hope in the precious name of Jesus. Amen.

God Speaks.

The hymn "God of Our Life" is clearly related to the emphasis of a New Year Sunday; the text (by Hugh Kerr) is contemporary in style, and the tune SANDON by Charles Purday is meditative. If this choice is not available, two other possibilities are "Now Thank We All Our God" (Rinkart/Winkworth-Crüger) or "Great God, We Sing That Mighty Hand" (Doddridge-Knapp).

It would be quite appropriate to use Psalm 90 for the Old Testament reading, even though the opening hymn of Isaac Watts is a paraphrase of that passage; for psalms, responsive reading is ideal because of their poetic structure.

Much scripture that is read by a minister falls on deaf ears because of the quality of the reading. It is well to treat the material as "poetically-dramatically" as possible to bring out its meaning. This can also be done by a group, in "choric speech."

Frequently, the "psalter" reading can be sung rather than read, by the congregation, by an ensemble, or as a solo. When this is done, it would be wise to label it as scripture, as Psalter: "God is My Shepherd" (Psalm 23)... Dvorak; or Psalter: "Bless Thou the Lord" (Psalm 103)... Ippolitov-Ivanov.

It may not be particularly appropriate to sing a *Gloria Patri* after a musical version of the psalter reading, unless the keys are closely related, or the organist is competent in improvising a modulation. However, it is strongly recommended when the psalm is spoken, following a tradition which reaches back almost to the first century.

The New Testament reading may be given by one of the ministers, or by a selected layperson, or it may be read by the congregation in unison. Following is an admittedly-startling reading of Luke 18:9-14 (New International Version) with interruptions by a "devil's advocate."

Reader: To some who were confident of their own righteousness and looked down on everybody else, Jesus told this parable: Two men went up to the temple to pray, one a Pharisee and the other a tax collector.

D.A.: A tax collector! An ordinary publican! Why, he was just one step below a child-molester in that society—collected taxes for the Roman governor, and cheated the people, at that—I'll bet he felt out of place in that holy and beautiful place!

Reader: The Pharisee stood up and prayed about himself: "God, I thank you that I am not like all other men—robbers, evil-doers, adulterers—or even like this tax collector. I fast twice a week and give a tenth of all my income."

D.A.: Man, what a record! A tither—even tithed his bank interest! You mean he fasted twice *every* week? No wonder he was considered to be a holy man by all his neighbors—God must have been proud to hear him!

Reader: But the tax collector stood at a distance. He would not even look up to heaven, but beat his breast and said, "God, have mercy on me, a sinner."

D.A.: Now, what kind of a prayer is that!? The man's not only a bounder—he should have his head examined! What a debasing and negative self-image for a mature man to have! He needs a psychiatrist.

Reader: I tell you that this man, rather than the other, went home justified before God. For everyone who exalts himself will be humbled, and he who humbles himself will be exalted."

D.A.:   Now, what's that supposed to mean? Come on, man, make sense!

On other occasions, scripture reading could become a mini-drama (or be presented with pantomime), or it could be sung. In the last instance, it should still be listed as the New Testament "reading": The Publican (Luke 18:10-14). . . . VandeWater. In the passage suggested above (Ephesians 5:14-21) the key phrase is "redeeming the time, because the days are evil"; however, many other New Testament passages could be chosen that relate to the particular emphasis of the sermon to follow.

If an anthem is used after the New Testament reading, it could be a setting of any of the hymn texts listed earlier; it could be another text related to the day or the sermon emphasis, or a general praise expression.

Since a New Year emphasis would come on the first Sunday of the month, many churches would be celebrating communion that day. If so, the homily might be called a "communion meditation." In the light of the topic "The Gospel of Beginning Again," the emphasis could be a call to penitence, forgiveness and renewing, through the atoning work of Christ.

On a communion Sunday, the sermon should probably be simple and brief. On other occasions, ministers may experiment with variations on the norm: A Sermon in Monologue (a one-man dramatization of scripture and exposition); A Sermon with Debate (in which a "devil's advocate" raises questions from the audience); the use of visual or audio aids (I once heard a sermon in which each point was introduced with a contemporary popular song); or a sermon-hymn combination (each point in the sermon is followed by an immediate hymn response).

We Respond.

The response hymn chosen is one of assurance, and would be appropriate for an "invitation."

> Moment by moment I'm kept in his love;
> Moment by moment I've life from above;
> Looking to Jesus till glory doth shine:
> Moment by moment, O Lord, I am thine.
>   Whittle-Moody

For the offertory in a church that is accustomed to experience songs in the morning service, a good possibility is the Swedish hymn "Blott en dag," translated by A. L. Skoog.

> Day by day and with each passing moment,
>   Strength I find to meet my trials here;
> Trusting in my Father's wise bestowment,
>   I've no cause for worry, or for fear.
> He whose heart is kind beyond all measure
>   Gives unto each day what He deems best—
> Lovingly, its part of pain and pleasure,
>   Mingling toil with peace and rest.
>
>   Sandell/Skoog-Ahnfelt

Another type of response to God's word which is favored by some churches is the reciting of a creed—"The Witness of Faith." After hearing God's message, we stand to state our beliefs. The preferred form among evangelicals is the short Apostles' Creed, which began to be used in the second or third century and achieved its present form about 650 A.D.

We Celebrate Communion.

The pattern for the Lord's Supper observance need not differ greatly from that which was suggested earlier in this chapter. Some churches use one extended prayer rather than two shorter ones, after which both bread and wine are served to the communicants; if so, the one prayer should contain all the elements that were divided between the two in the previous service.

When the traditional Salutation, *Sursum Corda* and *Sanctus* are included, the following might comprise the beginning of the communion service, following the "invitation to the table."

Minister: The Lord be with you.
People: And also with you.
Minister: Lift up your hearts.
People: We lift them up to the Lord.
Minister: Let us give thanks to the Lord our God.
People: It is right to give him thanks and praise.
Minister: Heavenly Father, we thank you that you have made us in your image, and that you created the world in which we live. You have revealed yourself to all people throughout history, demonstrating your power, your love and your providence. Great and wonderful are your works, Lord God almighty. Your ways are just and true. With men of faith from all times and places, we lift our hearts in joyful praise, for you alone are holy:

(Said or sung) Holy, holy, holy is the Lord of hosts; the whole earth is full of his glory. Glory be to God on high!
Our Father, we thank you that, when we rejected your love and went our own way, you sent your son Jesus . . . (continuing and concluding the prayer).

In recent days, some evangelical churches have become aware of the need to place greater emphasis on the communion service. One approach has been to dramatize the service, recreating the Leonardo da Vinci painting in a platform setting, with ministers and deacons repeating the words and actions of the upper room experience. This is not an inappropriate possibility, but it would not be effective more than once a year, perhaps on Maudy Thursday. It is even more important to be sure that each Sunday observance of communion is significant. In addition to the longer prayers which we have suggested, certain visual imagery might make a contribution.

The minister and deacons (or selected laypersons) could recall the first eucharist by surrounding the table, passing a loaf of bread around, and breaking off individual pieces; in the same way, a common cup could be shared. Communicants in the pew could express their understanding of the supper and their fellowship with others, by repeating the words "Christ's body was broken for you" or "Christ's blood was shed for you" as they pass the elements to each other. It is good practice for ministers themselves (as well as deacons and elders) to pass the bread and the cup to the seated congregation; while doing so they could repeat the above phrases, or others taken from scripture.

Jesus said: I am the bread of life. He who comes to me will never be hungry; he who believes in me will never thirst.

Jesus said: I am the vine, you are the branches. Cut off from me you can do nothing.

For God so loved the world that he gave his only Son, that whoever believes in him should not perish but have eternal life.

If we confess our sins, he is faithful and just, and will forgive our sins and cleanse us from all unrighteousness.

We Pray.

In leading the "Prayers of the People," the minister may consider the possibility of "bidding prayers." In this historic practice, the subject of prayer is announced (e.g., "governments"), each person is encouraged to pray quietly, and then the minister voices the collective prayer, mentioning the particular needs of the world, the nation, and the local community. The congregation may join in each petition with an Amen, following the word-cue "through Jesus Christ our Lord." It is desirable that these prayers be both general and specific; church members who are seriously ill or who have recently been bereaved should be mentioned by name. Finally, it is good to use the Lord's Prayer frequently to close the period of prayer; there are many new versions in the new scripture translations, and these could be printed in the order of worship.

Some churches have adopted unique practices to highlight the experience of corporate prayer. In some, the minister stands or kneels in the midst of the congregation to demonstrate that it is truly the people's prayer. In others, especially with our contemporary emphasis on relational theology, members of the congregation are encouraged to mention personal needs. In certain "Wesleyan" groups, including Churches of the Nazarene, worshipers with special concerns will kneel at the altar rail (in front of the platform) during the prayer.

Dismissal.

The close of the service may be as simple as that given earlier, with a Doxology and a Benediction. The organ postlude is generally exuberant in tone, reflecting thanksgiving for the experience of worship, and the movement of the congregation into the week of continuing worship, witness and service.

Staging the Worship Drama

In conclusion, the setting of the worship drama must also be considered. Just as the theater's stage, its acoustics and its properties affect the ability of the cast to communicate, the "worship stage" is important to the congregation in their perception of the drama in which they are the central characters. The worship stage is obviously the church sanctuary, and the "props" include all its furniture and decorations.

The medieval cathedral has often been said to symbolize the theology of worship in that period. The impressive and beautiful structure effectively conveyed the concepts of the majesty and glory of God, but also suggested his remoteness. Worshipers who were seated in the far recesses of the nave or the transepts could not clearly see or hear the awesome drama which was being enacted on their behalf. Some large evangelical churches (especially in the South) have built structures that pose the same challenge to effective participation. The worshipers in the rear are so far from the minister, the choir and the organ that they cannot really hear the sounds or follow the songleader. Often the acoustics (which are determined by the room's shape and surfaces) are so "dead" that congregational hymn singers feel as if they are soloists. Consequently, they participate timidly, if at all, because most nonprofessionals are a little afraid of the sound of their own voices in church!

Architecture, Decoration and Symbolism.

Early Christians, we remember, met in a "house church" around a communion table. In our day, some groups have become aware that fellowship is enhanced if worshipers see more than the back of each other's heads. Their new structures are built "in the round" or fanshaped, so that everyone is closer to the pulpit, organ and choir, and also more aware of each other's presence.

. The placement of ministers and choir has its own distinctive tradition in evangelical architecture. We reject a central "altar" since it suggests that God is present at a particular "holy of holies" in the room. We usually place the pulpit and the Bible in the center front of the platform to express the centrality of the scriptures and preaching; the communion table is usually located in front of the pulpit.[12] We often seat the choir behind the pulpit (probably from revivalism's traditions) because we associate their singing with the proclamation of the Word. Nowadays, some evangelicals are looking for an alternative arrangement that rejects the inference that the platform area is the stage, with the choir staring at the back of the minister during the sermon, and the congregation viewing the choir as a "backdrop" to the preacher. In some instances, the choir is placed toward the front, but off to one side. In this way, they can be visible when they are singing an anthem, and yet seem to be more a part of the congregation during the hymns and the sermon. This arrangement may also solve the problem of the placement of piano and organ; in a typical evangelical setting they are often located on opposite sides of the room at the front, so far from each other and from the director that "good ensemble" is difficult to achieve.

Evangelicals have traditionally been leery of the idea of symbolic expression in church architecture, furnishings and decoration. As a result, we are not alert to the possible incongruities which occur when our increasing affluence and a desire for beauty in worship encourage us to adopt erroneous symbolism. We reject the austere, noble, soaring lines of a Gothic cathedral and we are no longer willing to accept the plain "meeting house" of our forefathers. But what is the symbolism of a building that resembles an overgrown living room, with drapes and cushioned opera chairs or pews, pastel colors in robes, and thick carpeting wall to wall? As ministers, we oppose wearing the black Geneva robe of Calvinists (which is supposed to replace biblical "sackcloth" as a symbol of anonymity and humility), yet we occasionally don the splendor of academic regalia, perhaps on Christmas or Easter.

It is not necessary for evangelicals to adopt the stereotyped symbolism of older liturgical communions. Neither should we ignore the possibility of truly creative, evangelical symbolism, in the shape of our buildings, the placement of furniture and in decor. Liturgical banners, often with scripture texts, have been one recent feature of the "celebration revival." They are quite appropriate for all churches, and may be the beginning of beauty which truly represents holiness.

Acoustics.

The acoustical demands of a worship room are unique. The sound produced at the front needs to be projected to the back of the room. At the same time, the music and speech uttered in the chairs or pews needs to be heard well nearby (but without excessive reverberation), so that

---

12. In the First Baptist Church of Lincoln, Nebraska, the pulpit is large enough and so located that it also serves as the communion table. This expresses well the two-fold nature of full New Testament worship.

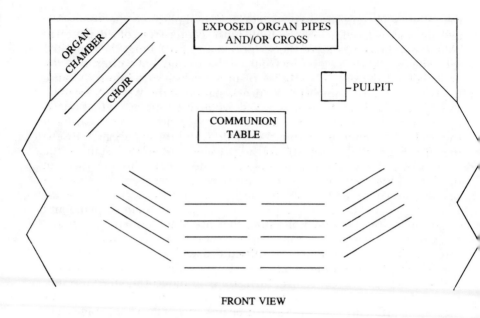

FRONT VIEW

worshipers are encouraged to join in the common hymns and prayers. The most crucial factor affecting acoustics is the construction of the sound-reflecting surfaces, both as to shape and material, especially those of the ceiling and walls. Ideally, the front of the auditorium (behind the pulpit and choir) will have a flat surface at the back with side walls sloping outward, a ceiling sloping upward as one looks from the choir loft toward the congregation. There should be no obstruction to the projection of sound above the platform, such as a proscenium arch. The ceiling line should ascend rather than descend, as it moves toward the rear of the room. It is also desirable that the side walls of the auditorium have irregular flat surfaces, to both reflect and "blend" congregational sound.

Surfaces at the front and sides of the church should be generally reflective (wood, brick or stone) and partially absorptive at the rear of

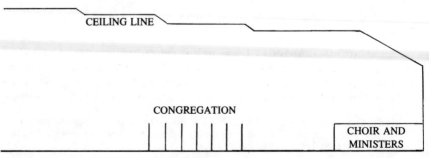

SIDE VIEW

the building (to prevent excessive "echo"). Many so-called "sound engineers" seem to be primarily interested in selling acoustic (absorptive) material; they construct a room in which there is no reverberation whatsoever, and then install an expensive electronic sound system so the congregation can hear what is said and sung. Good acoustics in a church will take advantage of natural reverberation to enhance the tonal colors of both organ and choir, and to encourage communal singing. It is true that the needs for ideal speech projection and ideal music sound are different. The church should seek a compromise that makes speech clearly audible, and music as tonally beautiful as possible.

Chapter XI

MUSIC IN SERVICES OF EVANGELISM AND FELLOWSHIP

It should not be surprising that within evangelical church life there is need for various forms of corporate worship experience, and that the musical requirements for each are unique. This has been true since the birth of the Church. At the time of Christ, Jews practiced sacrificial worship in the temple through sacerdotal rituals, and at the same time experienced congregation-centered services of instruction, praise and prayer in the synagogue. Early Christians continued to gather with fellow Hebrews in the synagogue, but met alone to celebrate their Lord's death and resurrection in the supper-service of remembrance and thanksgiving.

Medieval worship included both the eucharistic mass and the noneucharistic "offices," plus services which emphasized preaching, such as the Prone. Occasionally, prolonged "missions" were held in a church or a cathedral, featuring one of the many gifted preachers of history, such as Bernard of Clairvaux (ca.1090–1153). Sometimes these individuals took to the open air, particularly when the Holy Spirit breathed on the Church in a period of renewal; one such itinerant prophet was Francis of Assisi (ca.1182–1226), who has already been mentioned in connection with the unique music of his revival movement. In addition, the Middle Ages frequently offered services (often connected with pilgrimages) of penitence, which featured congregational song and prayers, including the historic responsive "litanies." Roman Catholics have also shared popular services of devotion, such as the novena, in which prayer was the central activity.

In the Reformation churches of the Lutheran and Anglican traditions there were at least three common forms of worship: (1) the eucharist; (2) the ante-communion service—a shortened version of (1) without communion; and (3) the offices of Matins and Vespers (Morning and Evening Prayer). The English-speaking "free churches" continued the Anglican office practice by scheduling basically-identical morning and evening services on Sunday; the form eventually developed into the

194

"pseudo-liturgical" pattern common in the more sophisticated American churches of the late 19th and early 20th centuries and described in a previous chapter. When communion was served, it was added at the end of the morning or the evening service.

We have already noted that evangelicals today exhibit wide variances in worship style, some following a variant of the "pseudo-liturgical" service of traditional free churches, others preferring the informal pattern which stems from 19th century revivalism, and still others combining elements from both traditions. Each church also tends to "add" the communion service at the end of its own customary worship form.

This book has expressed the conviction that a bonafide worship experience is important to all Christians, and earlier chapters have set forth the elements such a service should contain, and a possible order. At the same time, there is need for variety in our corporate services, especially in the church which offers more than one service each week. In this chapter we will discuss the variants in common use:

1. Evangelistic services, including "missions" (also called "revivals" or "crusades.")
2. Services of preaching/teaching/fellowship.
3. Services of prayer/fellowship.

Although these services are similar in style, each has its own objectives and consequently, its own requirements as to content, including music.

Services of Evangelism

In the broadest sense, evangelism is "bringing the whole gospel to the whole person," and as such, it may be said to include the total ministry of the church. In a narrower, more-typical use of the word, it denotes the initial, significant confrontation of the individual with his need of God and with the salvation provided through Christ; the objective is the individual's acknowledgment of need, acceptance of God's provision, and personal faith in, and commitment to Christ as Savior and Lord. Services of evangelism are planned for this distinctive purpose.

In the evangelical setting, it should not be necessary to justify the ministry of evangelism. It is inherent in the nature of the gospel that the "good news" will be shared by those who have themselves heard and experienced it. As it is frequently said, evangelism is one beggar telling another where he found bread! The methods of communication begin with the personal witness of each believer to those whom he contacts in everyday life. It is evident that the early church spread the gospel in this manner, and many Christian leaders believe that it may be the ideal method of evangelism for every period of history.

The New Testament carries the challenge of Jesus to his disciples in the closing words of three of the four gospels.

> Go therefore and make disciples of all nations, baptizing them in the name of the Father and of the Son and of the Holy Spirit, teaching them to observe all that I have commanded you; and lo, I am with you always, to the close of the age. (Matt. 28:19,20)

> And he said to them, "Go into all the world and preach the gospel to the whole creation. He who believes and is baptized will be saved; but he who does not believe will be condemned." (Mark 16:15,16)

> Then he opened their minds to understand the scriptures, and said to them, "Thus it is written, that the Christ should suffer and on the third day rise from the dead, and that repentance and forgiveness of sins should be preached in his name to all nations, beginning from Jerusalem. You are witnesses of these things." (Luke 24:45-48)

On the basis of this commission, the disciples carried the gospel to the far corners of the known world of the first century. Furthermore, the church has continued to demonstrate that this is one of the principal ways in which it shows its discipleship. The gospel of salvation has been preached within the regular liturgical forms of the church. In addition, specific ministries of evangelism have been held in the church, both in single services and in protracted series of meetings; many evangelical groups traditionally emphasized outreach in the Sunday evening service and in annual or semi-annual "missions." They have also been conducted outside the church, sometimes in the open air, and sometimes in so-called "secular" buildings or in temporary structures (tents or tabernacles) erected for that specific purpose. These series of services have also been called "evangelistic meetings," "revivals" or "crusades"; whatever the title, their character is reasonably predictable, because of their specialized purpose. Historically, a season of revival was often open-ended; the campaign continued as long as the Holy Spirit was evidently blessing, and people continued to respond. This pattern has persisted until recent times, and still exists in some rural areas. Although later campaigns have been more circumscribed in length, Billy Graham's 1957 crusade in Madison Square Garden in New York City ran for 16 weeks!

It is evident from Ephesians 4:11, that the early church expected that certain individuals would be ordained to the special ministry of evangelism. Throughout history this has continued to be true, and persons have been active as both preachers and musicians in this specialized ministry. The general characteristics of music in outstanding periods of renewal and evangelism have been outlined in chapter eight.

The Emphases and Their Communication.

The emphases of evangelistic services are centered in the simple *kerygma*, the gospel of God's love, of our lostness and estrangement from him, of his provision for our redemption, together with the urgent invitation to respond. Modern evangelists are frequently criticized for their "failure to preach the whole gospel." Dr. Billy Graham's response has been that his calling is a limited one—to be an evangelist who participates in some stage of the process in which an individual is new-born in Christ; he contends that it is the responsibility of others (pastors, teachers, etc.) to be more instrumental in their Christian maturing. Consequently, the preaching in evangelism is limited in scope, and it may be expected that the music would support that specific theological emphasis. The following examples are taken from 250 years of hymnic history. Some may be considered to be standard hymns; others employ the form, the simplicity and repetition of the gospel song or other related forms.

Sinners Jesus will receive:
    Tell this word of grace to all
Who the heavenly pathway leave,
    All who linger, all who fall!
This can bring them back again:
    Christ receiveth sinful men.
                    Erdmann Neumeister, 1718
                    Trans. Emma Bevan, 1858

And can it be that I should gain
    An interest in the Savior's blood?
Died He for me, who caused His pain?
    For me, who Him to death pursued?
Amazing love! how can it be
    That Thou, my God, shouldst die for me?
                    Charles Wesley, 1738

There is a fountain filled with blood
    Drawn from Emmanuel's veins,
And sinners plunged beneath that flood
    Lose all their guilty stains.
                    William Cowper, 1771

There's a wideness in God's mercy Like the wideness of the sea;
    There's a kindness in his justice Which is more than liberty.
There is plentiful redemption In the blood that has been shed;
    There is joy for all the members In the sorrows of the Head.
                    Frederick W. Faber, 1862

I lay my sins on Jesus, The spotless Lamb of God;
    He bears them all, and frees us From the accursed load;
I bring my guilt to Jesus, To wash my crimson stains
    White in His blood most precious, Till not a stain remains.
                    Horatius Bonar, 1843

Free from the law, O happy condition,
    Jesus hath bled, and there is remission;
Cursed by the law and bruised by the fall,
    Grace hath redeemed us once for all.
                    Philip P. Bliss, 1873

Would you be free from the burden of sin?
There's power in the blood;
Would you o'er evil a victory win?
There's wonderful power in the blood.

Lewis E. Jones, 1899

My hope is in the Lord Who gave Himself for me,
And paid the price of all my sin at Calvary.
For me He died, For me He lives,
And everlasting life and light He freely gives.

Norman Clayton, 1945

Worthy is the Lamb who died in awesome grief;
Worthy is the Lamb who saved a dying thief.
Worthy is the Lamb to make up for my fall;
Yes, worthy is the Lamb, praise God, He is all.

Stephen Leddy, 1967

The second emphasis of evangelistic services is a "pietist" one. The gospel is related to the personal cognitive-emotive *experience* of the individual—the immediate experience at the time of conversion, and continued experiences in everyday life as a believer. Though it must be admitted that gospel songs sometimes present a romanticized view of the Christian pilgrimage, the faithful have found encouragement in the promise of "love, joy and peace" which are the "fruits of the Spirit" in the present, as well as the "hope" in life which is eternal. Both are well expressed in songs which come from many periods of modern evangelical history.

When I can read my title clear to mansions in the skies,
I'll bid farewell to every fear, and wipe my weeping eyes.
There shall I bathe my weary soul in seas of heavenly rest,
And not a wave of trouble roll across my peaceful breast.

Isaac Watts, 1707

How happy every child of grace, who knows his sins forgiven!
"This earth," he cries, "is not my place; I seek my place in heaven;
A country far from mortal sight, yet, oh, by faith I see
The land of rest, the saints' delight, the heaven prepared for me."

Charles Wesley, 1745

O happy day that fixed my choice on Thee, my Savior and my God!
Well may this glowing heart rejoice, and tell its raptures all abroad.

Philip Doddridge, 1755

Amazing grace! how sweet the sound that saved a wretch like me!
I once was lost, but now am found; was blind, but now I see.
John Newton, 1779

My hope is built on nothing less than Jesus' blood and righteousness;
I dare not trust the sweetest frame, but wholly lean on Jesus' name.
Edward Mote, 1834

Jesus, my all, to heaven is gone;
    Jesus says he will be with us to the end.
He whom I fix my hopes upon;
    Jesus says he will be with us to the end.
Campmeeting Song (*The Revivalist,* 1845)

Redeemed, how I love to proclaim it!
    Redeemed by the blood of the Lamb;
Redeemed through His infinite mercy,
    His child, and forever, I am.
Fanny J. Crosby, 1882

I belong to the King, I'm a child of His love,
    I shall dwell in His palace so fair;
For He tells of its bliss in yon heaven above,
    And His children its splendors shall share.
Ida R. Smith, 1896

I stand amazed in the presence of Jesus the Nazarene,
    And wonder how He could love me,
    A sinner, condemned, unclean.
Charles H. Gabriel, 1905

O what a wonderful, wonderful day—Day I will never forget;
    After I'd wandered in darkness away, Jesus my Savior I met.
O what a tender, compassionate friend—He met the need of my heart;
    Shadows dispelling, with joy I am telling, He made all the darkness depart!
John W. Peterson, 1961

There's someone to whom I go and take my troubles to,
    He loved me and 'cause of this, long time ago He died.
    He's a friend, my friend.
Shout it out from every mountain, Spread it wide from sea to sea,
    Shine it bright from every lighthouse,
    He's alive! From sin we're free!
Tom Knighton, 1971

If there is significance in "personal experience" music, there is increased impact in a *personal* expression of this experience. It was this

truism which led to the emergence of the "gospel singers" in the 1840's and their continuing importance in evangelism. An individual—a layperson, if you please—gives witness to the truth which the evangelist is preaching, saying "it worked for me" in an emotional language which is convincing.

Congregational singing in evangelism affords many of the same opportunities that it offers in typical services of worship. For believers who are present, it allows them to join in a united and unifying expression of their worship of God, as well as of their common experiences in the life of faith. To the uncommitted, it serves to preach the gospel, as well as to witness to the experience which is available in Christ. It demonstrates the fellowship of the children of God, and tends to reach out with "arms of melody" to include those who are not already a part of the church. To be sure, since the music (like the preaching) emphasizes the ultimate realities of human life, it is replete with *emotional* expression. We have already considered the question of manipulation in connection with the use of music as a "gospel persuader." Though some will reject the validity of manipulation, none can deny the emotional impact of music in mass evangelism, especially in the songs of invitation.

Sinners, turn: why will you die? God, your Maker, asks you why;
   God, who did your being give, Made you with himself to live;
He the fatal cause demands, Asks the works of his own hands,
   Why, you thankless creatures, Why will you cross his love, and die?
                             Charles Wesley, 1741

Come, ye sinners, poor and needy, Weak and wounded, sick and sore;
   Jesus ready stands to save you, Full of pity, love and power;
He is able, he is able, He is willing; doubt no more.
                             Joseph Hart, 1759

Jesus calls us, o'er the tumult of our life's wild, restless sea;
Day by day his sweet voice soundeth, saying, "Christian, follow me!"
                         Cecil Frances Alexander, 1852

Whosoever heareth, shout, shout the sound!
   Spread the blessed tidings all the world around;
Tell the joyful news wherever man is found,
   "Whosoever will may come."
                           Philip P. Bliss, 1870

If you are tired of the load of your sin,
   Let Jesus come into your heart;
If you desire a new life to begin,
   Let Jesus come into your heart.
                         Lelia N. Morris, 1898

The Savior is waiting to enter your heart,
    Why don't you let Him come in?
There's nothing in this world to keep you apart,
    What is your answer to Him?
                            Ralph Carmichael, 1958

In this modern day we need God's Son,
    In this modern day He's still the One
Who can change our lives and set us free,
    And give us joy throughout eternity.
                            Jon Spong, 1974

On occasion, in the history of the church, the presence and power of
the Holy Spirit have been demonstrated by complete *spontaneity* in the
public services. In the Welsh revivals which have spanned more than two
centuries, the preacher would not be surprised to find himself inter-
rupted by an outbreak of song which might continue for a prolonged
period; sinners were moved to confession and faith more by spontaneous song than by prepared sermons. In other instances, a spirit of prayer
or of confession would sweep through a congregation for hours and
even days, so that prearranged orders of service and other normal activities were completely set aside. Remembering this tradition, revival services are often planned to leave room for such an intervention of the
Holy Spirit. It is partly for this reason that they often give the impression
of creativity and spontaneity.

"Pre-evangelism" and Evangelistic "Show Business."

It may be said that "mass evangelism" is religious theater or "show
business," and this should not be heard as a completely-derogatory
statement. It does imply that the evangelist and the gospel singer "project themselves"—using their gifts of personality and of communication
to present the gospel and to persuade. Of course, all communicators,
including preachers in a worship service, use all their resources of appearance, personality and of speech techniques to present their message.
This practice has been emphasized and sometimes exaggerated in historic
mass evangelism; no doubt this accounts for some of evangelism's effectiveness and also for much of the criticism it receives.

In early America, the advent of the local revival crusade brought a
good deal of excitement to a community which experienced little "entertainment." Like the traveling minstrels and the "medicine man," the
itinerant evangelist and musician could be counted on to attract the
unchurched by their dynamic preaching and singing. No doubt all

prophets and evangelists (whether Jeremiah, John the Baptist, the Apostle Paul, Francis of Assisi, Savanorola, John Wesley, Francis Asbury, D. L. Moody or Billy Sunday) possessed a high degree of charisma, and the same has been true of gospel singers—Philip Bliss, Ira Sankey, Homer Rodeheaver, George Beverly Shea or Andraé Crouch.

To be sure, professional evangelists have used theatrical techniques to accomplish their purposes, and no doubt some have misused them. Especially in our day, the methods and media of Madison Avenue have been applied to denominational, to local church and to revivalism promotion, in order to "pre-evangelize" the unchurched and to bring them under the hearing of the gospel. It should not be presumed that "show business" and sincere communication are incompatible. Contemporary actors and singers frequently use their talents and their art forms to promote political and social causes. Those who present the gospel of Jesus Christ should not be denied the same privilege, so long as the message is not compromised by its presentation.

Musical Styles in Evangelism.

We should expect that *new* musical styles will appear in periods of renewal and evangelism. This both demonstrates the creativity of the Holy Spirit at these times, and offers a fresh message for communicating the gospel. As noted in chapter eight, the history of revivalism has seen a repeated flowering of new sacred music forms which sprang from popular secular roots. The explanation is simple: musical sounds common to the secular world are effective in "pre-evangelizing" the uncommitted. Furthermore, this illustrates the incarnational character of the gospel, which uses ordinary human speech and music to communicate the divine message to human beings; in turn, the music and speech may be used by the Holy Spirit to transform ordinary, sinful people into members of the family of God!

Service Order in Evangelism.

Because of its limited objectives, the component parts of the evangelistic service are few, and their sequence may not be as important as it is in a full-orbed service of Christian worship. These elements are common, and this order is one possibility.

> Congregational Song
> Prayers
> Special Vocal Music—choral, solo or group
> Lay Witness, possibly with "entertainment communication"
> Offering
> Instrumental Music—usually prelude and offertory
> Scripture Reading
> Sermon
> Invitation

In the truest sense, the sermon is central in this type of service; all other elements should be evaluated by how they prepare for, support, or follow-up the preaching of God's Word. A salient characteristic is the informal, "reaching out" spirit which pervades the service, which is guided by the evangelist or the musician-in-charge, who acts as "master of ceremonies." The following is a typical outline, with comments and suggestions for effective planning.

Instrumental Prelude. The prelude has much the same function as in a worship service, providing an atmosphere of preparation for the service. It may be expected to be based on the music types which will characterize the meeting, and could feature piano and/or organ, or any other instruments. In a day when recorded accompaniment is common for use with both choirs and solos, a recorded orchestral prelude may be considered to be ideal; however, many individuals feel that "canned music" is mechanical and impersonal, and therefore inappropriate for guiding people in religious experience.

Congregational Song. In an evangelism setting, it is common to feature periods of singing in which a songleader may be used to good advantage—to announce the successive songs, to point out their relevance to the experience at hand, and to encourage the congregation to full and enthusiastic participation.

The scope of appropriate hymnic literature that may be used is quite broad. Every gathering of believers should be an opportunity for worship, and hymns/songs/choruses of praise and adoration should be included. Undoubtedly the specific message of God's purposes and provision of salvation in Christ should be emphasized, and such great hymns as "Depth of mercy! can there be" (Charles Wesley, 1740) or "Jesus, thy blood and righteousness" (Nikolaus von Zinzendorf, 1739) should be considered. It is always expected that hymns of personal experience will be used and they have appeared in every generation since that of Isaac Watts.

The evangelistic songleader should consider the possibility of: (1) combining hymns and songs related to a single theological emphasis, perhaps alternating congregational participation with that of the choir or soloists; (2) spontaneous singing (without books) of well-known and relevant hymns, folk hymns, songs, and choruses, sometimes without accompaniment; (3) introducing hymns with a scripture text, with a few words that focus attention on their central meaning, or with a narrative connected with their composing.

In historic evangelism, congregational singing was considered to be very important in laying a theological foundation for the preaching of the Word of God, as well as in uniting the congregation in corporate expression of their faith, their personal religious experience and their fellowship. More recently, "spectator music" by soloists and groups has tended to severely limit the time given to congregational song. We believe that in evangelism, as in worship, corporate participation is most important in encouraging a fruitful, mature response.

Opening Prayer. Once the attention of the congregation has been focused on the main purpose of the service through participation in song, there should be an acknowledgment of God's presence and sovereignty, through prayer. Because of the particular nature of the gathering, the scope of the prayer may be more limited than in a typical worship service. However, praise and thanksgiving should always be included, together with petition for the blessing of God on the ministry of his Word. It may be wise to eliminate the general prayer of confession for Christian believers, since this may detract from the opportunity for personal response in confession at the end of the service.

Choral Music. The choir in evangelism has many of the same functions that are common in traditional worship. It leads the congregation in its singing, and may have special significance in introducing the new songs which revivalism often emphasizes. Its offerings for congregational listening may not be expressions of praise as frequently as they are on Sunday morning. Historically, many American evangelical groups first introduced choirs in the revival settings of the 19th century, and the singers were considered to be an extension of the ministry of proclamation; for this reason they were usually seated in center platform behind the preacher. One of the best of older examples of choral preaching is found in a song of Dr. James M. Gray (1908), of which these are the first and last stanzas, and refrain:

> O listen to our wondrous story!
>   Counted once among the lost,
> Yet One came down from heaven's glory,
>   Saving us at awful cost.

Refrain:

(Women)	Who saved us from eternal loss?
(Men)	Who but God's Son upon the cross.
(Women)	What did He do?
(Men)	He died for you!
(Women)	Where is He now?
(Men)	Believe it thou!
(Together)	In heaven interceding.

> Will you surrender to this Savior,
>   To His scepter humbly bow?
> You too shall come to know His favor,
>   He will save you, save you now!   (Refrain)

Evangelism's choirs still emphasize the essential gospel of sin/grace/salvation in typical popular forms of the day—gospel, folk, country, pop and even rock. However, it is a cardinal error to believe that the gospel can only be communicated in these styles. Particularly in churches where traditional "functional church music" is the normal musical language, the choir director should search the library for materials in all styles. Many appropriate anthems and motets will be found, in addition to such standards as Stainer's "God So Loved the World," Roger C. Wilson's "Follow Me" (published by Lorenz), and settings of the folk hymn "What Wondrous Love is This?"

Lay Witness. In older days, we called expressions of personal witness "testimonies," and they were a central feature of 19th century Methodist "class meetings." As congregational experience songs are a corporate witness of the ways in which God's grace changes human life, a "lay witness" is a spoken, personal testimony of the same. Because we all share the frustrations and problems of our humanity and seek for answers to the same "ultimate questions," the narrative of human experience is profoundly interesting for us—far more so than the propounding of theoretical philosophy or theology. Christian believers are expected to give their witness whenever they have an opportunity; when it is accompanied with a life which exhibits the Christian graces, it may be the most effective means of evangelism. In an evangelistic service, presented prior to preaching, it announces: "This message is true! It worked in my life!"

In today's larger crusades, especially those carried on national television, it is common to bring well-known figures from public life—business, politics, sports and entertainment—for such a witness. In our hero-conscious culture, this practice may have some relevance. But we should not ignore the significance of the witness of ordinary men and women in the local congregation. Thoughtful seekers may be more impressed with the words of an individual whom they fully know and respect in the community. After all, response to the gospel does not guarantee that we will share the success of other famous persons; it does insure that we as ordinary people will be united with Christ and share in the life of the eternal God!

We have already acknowledged the entertainment element in both historic and modern evangelism. Certain individuals may be very successful in using their unique gifts—as humorists, as magicians, as puppeteers or as ventriloquists—in their personal communication of a Christian witness. Undoubtedly each of these modes will appeal more strongly to some people than to others, and their use may illustrate the Apostle Paul's *credo,* "I have become all things to all men, that I might by all means save some." (I Cor. 9:22)

Solo Song. The solo song is a personal witness set to music. For almost 150 years it has been shown to be the most powerful force in musical communication of the gospel. Particularly in our day, when musical-emotional possibilities are explored to the fullest, the impact of the solo witness song on the typical audience is almost overwhelming. For this reason, most evangelists usually schedule a solo just prior to the sermon. Many gospel singers add a personal verbal touch by preceding their singing with a spoken word of witness, or an introduction of the song.

In earlier days, the solo's accompaniment was exclusively offered by the pianist and/or organist. This was one of the opportunities to illustrate the spontaneity and creativity of "the Holy Spirit at work"—since most published gospel songs offered little but the melody and simple harmony, the instrumentalists developed remarkable gifts of keyboard improvisation. In more recent publishing, accompaniments are more fully developed, since they are often adapted from professional recording scores. In some instances soloists, groups and choirs perform with recorded orchestral accompaniments which are now widely available.

Soloists should not limit their offerings to one musical style. There are excellent choices in all the popular "personal" forms, and also certain arias and solos from the classics, such as "If with all your hearts" from Mendelssohn's *Elijah,* and "The Penitent" by VanDeWater.

Offering. One of the most criticized aspects of corporate evangelism services is the handling of the offering. In typical worship, the giving of money is best viewed as a response of believers in Christian stewardship. In an evangelistic effort, even though the motivation should be the same, the appeal has frequently emphasized meeting the expenses of the crusade. While the response of committed Christians may be positive, there is the possibility of misunderstanding by the unchurched folk who are present, because of the publicity given to the "money emphasis" of some professional evangelists.

In some church campaigns, the necessary funds have been provided in the annual budget, and no offerings are received during the meetings themselves. In other situations, believers are encouraged to respond and the "visitors" are "welcomed without participation"; however, this may be an affront to some—a premature "dividing" of the audience into "pro and con," before the message of the Word of God is presented. Those who are concerned about the future of mass evangelism will approach this matter with prayerful thought and planning.

With regard to the offertory music, I do not hold the same view that has been suggested for a typical worship service. Because the atmosphere is less structured and somewhat more "entertainment oriented," instrumental music may well be the norm. At the same time, it would be acceptable to use a solo or ensemble piece; however, some evangelists reject that possibility because vocal music is more intensely appealing, and may distract the attention of some who would otherwise contribute to the offering!

Scripture Reading and Sermon. The central feature of the evangelistic service is the spoken sermon. The decision to omit any discussion of it in these pages is testimony both to its significance, and to our limitation of space. There are many worthy approaches in both content and style, and they are discussed exhaustively in treatises on preaching and homiletics; there are also many published volumes of sermons by historic evangelistic preachers. All of the music suggestions we have made are expected to prepare for, to support, or to follow-up the message from God's Word.

It seems especially fitting that the scriptural basis of the sermon would be read by the evangelist at the beginning of the message. In the tradition of John Calvin, the reading may be followed by a brief prayer "for illumination."

The Invitation. Each church or each individual evangelistic team will have its own approach to planning the response to the evangelistic message. Some evangelical groups do not offer public invitations, possibly because of the fear of excessive emotionalism; individuals are encouraged to seek out the pastor at a later time if they want to respond to the gospel appeal. In the 19th century "holiness" campmeeting tradition, those who responded were expected to "pray through" publicly at the mourner's bench in front of the pulpit, accompanied by the ardent encouragement and counsel of the ministers and other "saints." D. L. Moody used the "inquiry room" technique, where seekers were counseled in private after the public service; this same basic approach is preferred by Billy Graham and many other contemporary evangelists.

If an evangelist expects to follow the sermon with a particular type of invitation to respond, it would seem to be fair and wise to announce that procedure at the beginning of the sermon. This puts the uncommitted on notice in advance that they will be encouraged to respond to the message, and reduces the possibility that they may complain of being "tricked" or "manipulated" by the subsequent sequence of events.

"Invitation hymns" have been a feature of evangelical church life since the mid-18th century. It is still common practice, in most evangelistic services, to use these hymns in extending the invitation. In a typical church situation, it is good to have the entire congregation sing the hymn. The prospective convert is thus surrounded by the encouragement of committed Christians, and is encouraged to join in singing such positive expressions as "Just as I am, I come," or "Lord, I'm coming home."

One of the matters in which evangelists and their musicians should use careful analysis and judgment is the length and the intensity of the invitation appeal. Undoubtedly, what is evidently effective in one culture or in a certain period of history, may not be as appropriate in another place or time.

Professional Music Evangelism

For the past 150 years, as in New Testament times, certain persons have been acknowledged to be "professional" evangelists. Following the campmeeting movement of 1800 and the eastern seaboard ministry of Charles G. Finney in the 1820's, revivalism became an important influence in American church life. It became traditional for many churches to conduct regular evangelistic services at least once each year, and they often lasted for a period of several weeks. Individuals were acknowledged to be gifted and called to a ministry of evangelism, and they gave full time to it, traveling from one community to another. Denominations frequently appointed professional evangelists. Other individuals worked independently, ministering in various churches as they were invited to do so.

With the advent of the "gospel singer" about 1840, it became possible for many people to devote themselves full-time to a ministry of music in evangelism. The first may have been Philip Phillips (1834–1895), "the Singing Pilgrim" who is known to have given programs of solo gospel music, in addition to assisting in the regular campaigns which were common in the 19th century.

Many of the first evangelistic singers, like Philip P. Bliss (1838–1876), began as itinerant "singing school" teachers. The typical individual functioned as both the song-leader and soloist (and often choir director, as well) and became essentially the "master of ceremonies," guiding the entire service until it was time for the evangelist's sermon. Frequently these musicians were song writers as well and they engaged in the compiling and publishing of gospel song books, used first in their evangelistic crusades, and then released to the larger church public.

The pattern was set by the time Dwight L. Moody (1837–1899) came on the scene. His own musician was Ira David Sankey (1840–1908) who may be considered to be the archetype of his profession—a singer, songleader (without waving his arms), composer and publisher. In the course of Moody's lifetime he gathered around him a group of evangelists, including Daniel W. Whittle, J. H. Brooks, W. G. Moorehead, A. T. Pierson, Dwight Pentecost and A. J. Gordon. Many of these individuals were hymn writers themselves, and worked with assisting musicians (e.g., Philip P. Bliss, James McGranahan, and William G. Sherwin).

In those days, musicians had no electronic equipment to help project the voice to large crowds. As a result, Sankey's voice quickly deteriorated from the strain, and other musicians were called to assist D. L. Moody in his later life (e.g., George C. Stebbins and Edwin O. Excell). One of these, Daniel Brink Towner (1850–1919), became a leader in the Chicago school founded by Moody (now called Moody Bible Institute) which specialized in training this type of musician.

During the first four decades of the 20th century, mass evangelism continued to flourish in this country, and a large number of individuals found full-time, lifetime opportunity in its musical activities. Since World War II, despite the publicity given to the large crusades of a few evangelists, interest in revivalism has declined at the level of the local church. As a result, fewer individuals have found such an opportunity for service. In the larger evangelistic teams, the trend has been toward greater specialization. The soloist rarely acts as songleader (because the latter activity can harm the singing voice), and frequently a third individual serves as choir director. Since the early 20th century, keyboard specialists have also found professional opportunities in this field.

Several factors have contributed to the decline of interest in mass evangelism in our day:

(1) The increasing tempo of ordinary life and the demands on the time of both the churched and the unchurched.
(2) A decline of interest in the total church program.

(3) The competition of other forms of "entertainment."
(4) A decline in confidence in professional evangelism. In more liberal churches, this was no doubt aggravated by a changing theology of evangelism. In evangelical churches, it was encouraged partly by a growing conviction that the traditional methods are not as effective in our day, and partly by personal and methodological failures on the part of evangelists.

One response to the distrust of oldtime techniques has been the increased use of "non-professionals"—pastors and traditional church musicians—who serve as evangelists in other churches of their fellowship for a short period (usually from four days to one week). This practice is particularly popular among Southern Baptists.

An alternative to church-related evangelism has been the use of mass media, both radio and television. Nowadays, almost all religious services on TV, except those sponsored by local churches or dioceses, are more geared to evangelism than to worship. Consequently these outlets have become the new opportunities for important evangelistic musicians, as well. It may be argued that television is "both stronger and weaker" as an evangelistic medium, as compared with a public gathering. The impact of the personalities of both evangelist and gospel singer is stronger because they come across bigger than lifesize in face to face confrontation with the individual viewer. On the other hand, the experience of identification with other believers and of actual participation (in congregational song, and in public response to the gospel message) is missed in the privacy of the home. Unless the programmers take great care to relate their ministry to that of local churches, they tend to create what has been called "The Electric Church," which is not really an effective part of the "body of Christ."

Services of Fellowship and Preaching/Teaching

Up to this point, this book has discussed two contrasting forms of services which are planned with different objectives. In the first, the church unites to worship God and to learn his will from his revealed Word; in the second, the church reaches out to win others to its faith and to welcome them to its fellowship. Of course, even when the principal objective is worship and *didache,* the evangelical church hopes that each service will clearly present the gospel and be used to "convict and convince" the uncommitted. Again, when outreach is the main focus, worship should still be experienced by all the believers present. Traditionally, many evangelical groups have used both these forms on Sunday—worship in the morning, and evangelism in the evening—and have named the services accordingly. In such an instance, the evening service will use the forms and techniques we have described for evangelistic crusades.

Admittedly, most folk attending evening services today are fully committed to Christ and the church. However, the same type of service style and material functions well as a medium for Christian fellowship/worship/teaching. While important elements of less-formal worship are always present, the prevailing spirit is one of "fellowship in the gospel." The traditional songs of Christian experience serve to recall the initial conversion experience, as well as to express the continuing episodes in the Christian pilgrimage. The informal leadership from the platform encourages the spirit of liberty and joy, and it may well be enhanced by spontaneous expressions of witness or prayer by members of the congregation. The preaching may be evangelistic on occasion, but it may more frequently emphasize a teaching ministry, centering in the Bible and directed toward believers; nowadays, a number of churches emulate the ancient synagogue tradition by free discussion of the morning sermon in the evening service.

Obviously, in services of this kind, music plays a very important part. A wide variety of styles and media are common—choral, solo and groups, both vocal and instrumental. It is an ideal time for emphasizing congregational song, using traditional hymns and teaching new materials; at this time a songleader can best use his talents in leadership and in pedagogy.

While the emphasis may be on experience music in both contemporary and traditional styles, it is advisable to use a good mixture of materials. This will encourage the concept that all types of musical language can express the Christian message, and discourage the idea that Sunday morning is "high brow, formal and dull" and that Sunday night is "low brow, informal and pleasurable."

Occasionally the Sunday evening service may be given over completely to "musical worship and fellowship," sometimes emphasizing "performance music" by choir and others, sometimes emphasizing congregational singing, and sometimes a combination of the two. A worthy possibility recalls the 19th century class meetings of Methodists and features the following spontaneous expressions which may be more or less guided by the service leader. If desirable, it may be the ultimate in informality, and may resemble the worship pattern of the early church described in I Cor. 14:26:

Congregational song—led by the musician, or chosen by members of the congregation, or even begun spontaneously by individual worshipers.

"Special Music"—planned by the musician and interspersed informally and "spontaneously," or even volunteered and performed by individuals in the congregation.

Scripture passages, brief expositions, prayers, prayer requests and personal witness, offered spontaneously by congregational members.

Services of Fellowship and Prayer

In churches where midweek prayer services are common, the same essential service pattern is usually followed. The service may emphasize Bible exposition or intercessory prayer, or include a combination of the two. Congregational singing predominates, with less attention to "special" music. Many of the simple, contemporary songs are appropriate, expressing praise, as well as petition, and the assurance that God hears our prayers.

> Lord, listen to your children praying,
> Lord, Send your Spirit in this place;
> Lord, listen to your children praying,
> Send us love, send us power, send us grace.
>
> Ken Medema, 1973

> For the one in need of your great love, we pray today.
> Lord, hear our prayer, hear our prayer.
>
> For our own lives, Lord, and the ones we touch from day to day.
> Lord, hear our prayer, hear our prayer.
>
> For those in need all around the world, give help, O Lord.
> Lord, hear our prayer, hear our prayer.
>
> Bill Floyd, 1969

> Sweep over my soul, Sweep over my soul;
> Come, gracious Spirit, Sweep over my soul.
>
> Harry D. Clark, 1927

Chapter XII

MUSIC IN SPECIAL SERVICES OF WORSHIP, INCLUDING WEDDINGS, FUNERALS AND BAPTISMS

In earlier chapters we have discussed the use of music in the traditional and regular services of the church, services whose central purpose was worship, evangelism or fellowship, or some combination of these activities. Music should also be considered in its relationship to special services of worship. Some of these focus on significant events in the lives of particular families in the congregation—such as weddings, funerals and baptisms. Others feature music as the central expression of worship, as in a seasonal cantata, an organ dedication recital or a Christian art festival.

Evangelicals have frequently shown the least concern for meaningful worship in those gatherings which mark the important occasions in the lives of individual believers and their families. As a result, we have often displayed considerable discrepancy between theology and practice at these celebrative and commemorative times. Particularly in marriages and funerals, we frequently deny the corporate nature of the church; in over-emphasizing the personal aspects of the occasion, we may give the family inordinate freedom in planning the service. Consequently, the occasion may fail to provide opportunity for the entire "body of Christ" to express itself, and may even deny basic tenets of our faith. We believe that Christians who marry should establish a truly Christian home; yet our wedding services often focus more on the bride than on Christ, more on human love than on the divine *agape* which truly consecrates a marriage and a home. We herald the Christian's hope of life eternal in the presence of God; yet our funeral services often include elements which exacerbate human grief, ignoring historic practices which would demonstrate Christ's victory over the grave and give strong comfort to the bereaved. Baptisms traditionally exaggerate the "aloneness" of the person who experiences the rite, and sometimes suggest either our self-consciousness about the "mode" used, or our conviction that it is not really a significant occasion.

These discrepancies are all the more glaring because, in distinction to typical Sunday services of worship, the evangelical minister invariably resorts to the use of a liturgy (a written or memorized outline of prayers and/or pronouncements) in certain parts of these services. In weddings and baptisms (though, admittedly the motivation is more practical than liturgical), he also wears a robe!

The primary issues to be faced in a discussion of this kind are:

1. The worship nature of the occasion.
2. The personal needs of the individuals involved, in relationship to those of the corporate fellowship of believers.
3. The ministers' responsibility to give leadership and exert authority at these times, in fulfilling their prophetic, teaching and pastoring roles.

Music in Christian Weddings

The scriptures teach that the home is an institution founded by God, and that there are certain spiritual principles involved in a Christian marriage. In the New Testament, the relationship of husband and wife is compared to that of Christ and the Church.[1] Consequently, few evangelicals are satisfied with a marriage ceremony conducted by a civil judge or a justice of the peace. However, during the first half of the 20th century, evangelical church weddings tended to be rather secular affairs with only minimal religious connotations, with secular love songs the musical norm, no sermon and no corporate expression of worship. It may be that this secularization of the marriage service was an over-reaction to the "marriage is a sacrament" theology and the lengthy services conducted in liturgical churches.

It has also seemed apparent that many ministers agree that a wedding is a private affair, and that the service may be planned largely according to the personal desires of the bride and groom, or of their families. In recent years, a number of significant changes have become the norm, and we can guess that these have been initiated by young people who have shared in the weddings of their friends in other (possibly liturgical) churches! Some of these changes have been healthy and actually more biblical and evangelical—less secular, more Christian expressions of Christian commitment to marriage in the wording of the wedding invitations, in the types and modes of music, in the involvement of the congregation, and in symbolic action. At the same time, some recent innovations have been less evangelical, as in the occasional instance where a "private communion" service is added.

1. See Ephesians 5:22-33.

It is time for the church itself to reassert its authority and assume its responsibility in guiding families and couples in the planning of wedding services. The occasion is conducted in the church as a "Christian" observance, presided over by the ministers and attended by many committed Christians. It should be approached like any other corporate worship service, except that the involved families are included in the planning. It may be well for the church to prepare a printed or mimeographed presentation of their understanding of the theology of marriage and an outline of an effective, acceptable corporate wedding service. Such a guide would explain the important acts of the service, listing the areas in which the participating individuals may make personal choices.

These basic principles and definitions would seem to be appropriate:

1. God is central in a Christian wedding. It is not merely a spectacle or a pageant centered around the bride and groom.
2. The various components of the wedding service should support the church's theology of marriage and of public worship. There should be ample opportunity within this rubric for shared planning by the families involved.
3. A Christian wedding is a service of corporate worship, in which a man and a woman are joined in wedlock and dedicate their newly-established home to God. Fellow believers witness and share the acts, and pledge to support the couple with their love and their prayers; they are also encouraged to renew their own commitment to their spouses, and the dedication of their homes to the glory of God in Christ.

Music.

Music has always played a large part in a wedding—one of the festive occasions of human life, closely related to our "tender affections." At the time of my own marriage in 1942, most Protestant weddings invariably included the love songs "O Promise Me" and "I Love You Truly"; in more sophisticated cultural settings we might have heard Grieg's art song "I Love Thee." On rare occasions the hymn "O Perfect Love" (words by Dorothy Gurney; music by Joseph Barnby) was used, but only as a solo.

Today's choices by young people often come from contemporary popular sources, and frequently they are just as objectionable as the old chestnuts, because of their emphasis on human love (sometimes even *eros*, with mention of the sexual act) rather than on divine love (*agape*). However, a growing number of couples have shown more discernment than their parents in choosing to use songs which speak of their sober dedication to each other and to God. A recent favorite comes from the Old Testament[2] and seems to be meaningful to many, though the original words were spoken by Ruth, a young widow, to Naomi, her mother-in-law.

2. Ruth 1:16–17, KJV

Entreat me not to leave thee, or to turn away from following after thee; for where thou goest, I will go; and where thou lodgest, I will lodge; thy people shall be my people, and thy God, my God. Where thou diest, will I die, and there will I be buried; the Lord do so to me, and more also, if anything but death part thee and me.[3]

Another new wedding song by Carol Melton combines an expression of human love with an acknowledgment of God and of love to others.

You have given me more than anyone has ever known,
    The sunshine of this hour as I'm standing here with you,
A promise of the future now I pledge in Him to you,
    The love of a lifetime to share.

I will love you every day in sickness and in health,
    I will love you every day in poverty and wealth,
More I could not ask you than to love me half as much as I love you—
    In the mornings, in the evenings, You every day of my life.

Let our love reach out to our friends away and near,
    For even as we gather He is present with us here,
Time will never change my feelings but to make them stronger than before—
    In the mornings, in the evenings, I will love you more and more.

Copyright©1974 by Agape.
Used by Permission.

It is fitting that some of the wedding music be "purely worship," and that some should emphasize God's love, which is the model for human love. The following classics are suggested, and similar texts are available in many different music styles.

J. S. Bach. My Heart Ever Faithful (Presser)
Bitgood. The Greatest of These Is Love (H. W. Gray)
Brahms. Though I Speak with the Tongues (from "Four Serious
    Songs")
Fetler. O Father, All Creating (Concordia)
Franck. O Lord Most Holy (Panis Angelicus) (G. Schirmer)
Handel. Thanks Be to Thee (J. Fischer)
Bender. Wedding Song (Psalm 128:1–4) (Concordia)
Peeters. Wedding Song (C. F. Peeters)
Schütz. Wedding Song (Chanty Music Press)
Willan. Eternal Love (Summy-Birchard)

It may be that both love songs and worship music can be featured in a wedding celebration. Some folk think that it is appropriate for tasteful love songs to be sung, but only before the service actually begins; certainly nobody will protest if they are sung at the reception following the service.

---

3. Musical settings are available by Black (G. Schirmer), by Gronham (Boston Music), by Gounod (C. Fischer), and by Gore (Concordia).

It is common to use instrumental music by the organ and/or other instruments in an extended prelude before the service actually begins; sometimes vocal music, solo or ensemble, will be used to intersperse the instrumental. It is my own preference that this music will assume the character of the best "festival music" used in worship services of that particular cultural group, from "classical" selections to settings of hymns, anthems, art songs, or folk-gospel music.

Much has been said about the appropriateness of the old "war horses" of processional and recessional—the "Pilgrim's Chorus" from the opera Lohengrin by Richard Wagner and the "Wedding March" from Midsummer Night's Dream by Felix Mendelssohn. It is not really relevant to argue that these pieces have secular, even mythological associations; much of our typical, effective church music comes from similar sources. One may question their "inevitability," for there was a time when no bride would feel properly married without them! There is little innately-religious connotation to their modern-day substitutes—the "Trumpet Voluntary" of Purcell[4] and the "Toccata" from Widor's Fifth Organ Symphony. Music is one area in which the bride and her participating musicians may demonstrate originality in selecting two of the many possible choices for marches, and the other music for organ, solo, ensemble or possibly even a choir. True creativity means that nothing is inevitable, not even Malotte's "Lord's Prayer," which would probably be better spoken by the congregation.

A corporate evangelical service should always include some congregational expression, and a hymn is an excellent possibility for weddings. Any fine text of praise or thanksgiving would express that Christian worship is the central focus of the ceremony. Certain hymns have frequently been chosen because of their references to God's providence, and to the home and marriage.

> For the Beauty of the Earth ("For the joys of human love")
> Now Thank We All Our God ("Who from our mothers' arms, etc.")
> O Perfect Love (the best-known wedding hymn)
> Great Is Thy Faithfulness (a favorite in Britain)
> O Happy Home, Where Thou Art Loved the Dearest
> Happy the Home When God Is There

Many volumes of excellent wedding music are available and the following are suggested. Note that some are simply lists of appropriate material, with publisher sources.

> *A Wedding Manual* (Abingdon)
> *Wedding Music,* by Regina Holman Fryxell (Augustana)
> *Music for Church Weddings* (Seabury Press)
> *Music for the Church Wedding* (Concordia)
> *Wedding Music, Part I,* Marches (Concordia)
> *Wedding Music, Part II,* Hymn Preludes (Concordia)

---

4. The one usually used and credited to him is actually the work of Jeremiah Clarke.

Wedding Blessings (12 songs) (Concordia)
The Parish Organist—Wedding Music (Concordia)
Wedding Music for the Church Organist and Soloist (Abingdon)
Organ Music for The Wedding Ceremony (Bradley)
It's Wedding Time, arr. by Fred Bock (Singspiration)
Music for the Christian Wedding (Lillenas)
Our Sacred Day (Hope)

Spoken Parts of the Service.

It is interesting to note that, although many evangelical ministers would never read a ritual or a prayer in a typical worship service, few fail to do so in weddings! Some might be a bit chagrined to learn that the traditional phrases are largely borrowed from the Episcopal *Book of Common Prayer.*

Current thought about the identity and the equality of the two partners has led to considerable revision of traditional acts and statements in the service, much of which has been adopted by evangelicals. For instance, the practice of "giving the bride away" may be a vestige of "arranged marriages" and it is possibly inappropriate when young people delay marriage until their late twenties. At the same time, it is now common to ask both the bride's and the groom's parents to express publicly their support of the young couple and the home they establish. In a recent service I attended, following the pronouncement by the presiding minister, the parents laid their hands on the heads of their children in blessing, saying "May you dwell in God's presence forever; may true and constant love preserve you."

Frequently today, wedding couples ask to write their own vows. This is appropriate and may help them to evaluate their commitment to each other. However, the presiding minister should have an opportunity to discuss the statements with the couple, perhaps in their pre-marriage counseling session. The following vows were prepared by one of my students for use in her wedding.

> Groom: I take you, (name), to be my wife, and these things I promise you: I will be faithful to you and honest with you, I will respect, trust, help and care for you; I will share my life with you, I will forgive you as we have been forgiven; and I will try with you better to understand ourselves, the world, and God; through the best and the worst of what is to come as long as we live.

> Bride: (Name), I take you to be my husband from this time onward, to join with you and to share all that is to come, to give and to receive, to speak and to listen, to inspire and to respond, and in all circumstances of our life together to be loyal to you with my whole life and with all my being.

It is also desirable that the congregation participate verbally as well as in song. They might join in repeating the Lord's Prayer or reading a scripture passage, or in a litany of dedication, or a pledge of support.

Minister (to Congregation): Will you who witness these vows do all in your power to prayerfully support and uphold this marriage in the years ahead? Will you pray for God's blessing and perfect will in their lives?

Congregation: We will.

Symbolic Actions.

Even though evangelicals employ little symbolic action in regular worship, they have invariably included it in weddings. The bride and groom usually enter separately and leave together. In some instances, the bride's father still "hands her over" to her spouse. Kneeling together for prayer is also common. In recent years, the "Ceremony of the Candles" has become a widely accepted practice. Two candles are lit (in addition to many decorative ones) at the beginning of the service, to symbolize the two personalities involved. After they are declared to be "husband and wife" each takes his/her candle and lights a central third candle, then extinguishes the first two, signifying that the "two have become one." A few individuals have objected to the symbolism, with the argument that neither person loses individual identity because they are joined in "holy wedlock." It would seem that they have two choices: to light the third candle and leave the other two burning, or to forget the entire ritual.

In a few instances, evangelical couples have asked that communion be served to them (and possibly to other members of the wedding party) as a part of their service. This may be an indication of their growing consciousness of the significance of the communion service, despite typical evangelical negligence. More likely the idea was born at a friend's wedding in a church with a different eucharistic theology. The tradition is rather clearly associated with the Roman and Orthodox doctrine that marriage is a sacrament that is celebrated with a private and votive communion. It is not a meaningful addition to an evangelical wedding. For us, communion is a meal that must be shared by the whole family of God in a service that is more completely congregational.

Music in Christian Funerals

It has frequently been pointed out that current American attitudes and rituals pertaining to death are unnatural, partly because technology and affluence provide medical care even after it is apparently pointless, and expensive "cosmetic" funeral arrangements that are determined more by salesmanship that plays upon guilt and/or grief feelings than on more significant realities. Today, most deaths occur in a hospital or a nursing home, removed from the familiar surroundings of the home and family. Most non-liturgical funerals are conducted in "funeral homes," not in the church where the individual celebrated all of his significant life experiences. In the service, the bereaved family is frequently shut off from the supporting family of God by a screen, or in an adjoining alcove. The music which is chosen majors on "favorites" of the deceased, further exacerbating the feelings of grief; it is invariably performed by a soloist rather than the congregation, with an organ which presents the poorest example of synthetic musical sound.

Even though it may seem to be in poor taste to criticize fellow evangelicals who fall prey to our cultural follies, such a funeral must be labeled "sub-Christian." It stands in sharp contrast to the narrative of practices in some mission situations.

> A former missionary tells how African Christians express their sympathy when death touches the home of a believer. Unlike some of us who glibly quote some Scripture verse and repeat certain cliches, they show their deep concern by sitting quietly with the bereaved family. Knowing that words are often empty and meaningless at a time like that, these Christians enter into the grief of their friends by tears and warm, understanding looks of love. But as the night shadows deepen, the mood changes. Instead of wild dancing and beating of drums, which was their custom before they became believers, they open their hymnals and begin to raise their voices in reverent singing. Every selection in the book, from joyous gospel songs of testimony to more subdued hymns of comfort and adoration, are rendered a cappella. This singing continues all night, and both young and old take part. By the time the last song is concluded, the sun has risen and the morning burial service takes place. Through the long hours of darkness, great blessings and spiritual help had been brought to the bereaved family. They had been pointed to the source of all comfort and reminded of the joys being experienced by their loved one in Glory.[5]

A Christian funeral is a service of corporate worship in which the participants praise a provident God who gives all life, both temporal and eternal; they also give thanks for the life which has just been ended, with its contributions to family and friends, to the church and to the community. It is a service conducted for the living, giving comfort in the midst of sorrow with the assurance that God is truly kind and loving. It is a reminder to everyone present that life at best is brief—an encouragement to believers to rededicate the remainder of their lives to the worship and service of our heavenly Father, and a call to the uncommitted to respond to God's love as revealed in Christ.

> The Lord gave, and the Lord has taken away; blessed be the name of the Lord.   (Job 1:21b)

It is interesting to note that one of Martin Luther's first hymnals was *Christliche Geseng, Lateinisch und Deudsch, zum Begrebnis* (Christian Songs, Latin and German, for Burials, published by J. Klug, 1542). Yet how few

5. Henry G. Bosch, in *Our Daily Bread*, reading for October 2, 1979.

evangelicals consider the possibility that a funeral should include congregational singing! There is no more significant time and no better way to encourage the bereaved and support the faith of the entire gathered congregation. The ideal hymns are those which remind us that God's "steadfast love endures forever"—"O God, Our Help in Ages Past," "Great Is Thy Faithfulness," "Praise to the Lord, the Almighty" or "Now Thank We All Our God."[6]

It may be argued that the plush living room setting of a funeral home is not conducive to effective congregational singing, especially when the music is supported only by a gasping electronic organ which invariably seems to be placed just outside the room! This is just one argument for the advisability of conducting the service in the church. Most large congregations have a smaller chapel which would accommodate the typical funeral gathering. In either setting, however, even a small group could follow the voice of a soloist in singing a hymn.

Of course, it is proper to sing hymns about heaven and our "blessed hope." But this theme need not dominate all the musical choices. One of the best memorial hymns, which expresses the ultimate triumph of the believer who dies in Christ, is William Walsham How's "For all the saints." We quote only a few stanzas here to demonstrate the best spirit of funeral hymnody.

> For all the saints who from their labors rest,
>   All who by faith before the world confessed
> Your name, O Jesus, be forever blest. Alleluia!

> You were their rock, their fortress, and their might;
>   You, Lord, their captain in the well-fought fight;
> You, in the darkness drear, their one true light. Alleluia!

> Oh, blest communion, fellowship divine,
>   We feebly struggle, they in glory shine;
> Yet all are one within your great design. Alleluia!

> The golden evening brightens in the west,
>   Soon, soon to faithful warriors comes their rest;
> Sweet is the calm of paradise the blest. Alleluia!

> From earth's wide bounds, from ocean's farthest coast,
>   Through gates of pearl streams in the countless host;
> Singing to Father, Son, and Holy Ghost: Alleluia!

As in weddings, funeral services have often been considered to be "family affairs." It should be acknowledged that it is sometimes difficult to sidestep the family's insistence that certain music be sung or played, even though some of the requests are outlandish. A longtime friend and

6. The last-named hymn of praise was written by Martin Rinkart (1586-1649) who lived and ministered in Eilenburg, Germany through the devastation and pestilence which followed the Thirty Years' War. It is said that during Rinkart's lifetime he buried more than five thousand people, and in the crucial year of 1637 frequently officiated at forty funerals a day.

organist once told me that for the funeral of a leading surgeon in Kansas City she was asked to play: On Wisconsin, Try to Remember, Lara's Theme (from *Dr. Zhivago*), No Other Love, *Santa Lucia, O Tannenbaum,* Sunrise and Sunset, Golden Days, Only a Rose, The Lord's Prayer, and "anything else by Sigmund Romberg."

The discerning pastor should consider his responsibility to help his flock face death in a thoroughly Christian manner. He can do this partly in his planning of funeral or memorial services. Undoubtedly, there are occasions when solo music must be included in the service. Yet it should be remembered (as mentioned in the discussion of evangelism's music) that solo "experience songs" are the most emotionally manipulative music we possess. If a song like "Face to Face" or "When We See Christ" (Esther Rusthoi) is included, it can be balanced by a solo setting of Psalm 23, or one of the great "providence" hymns mentioned earlier.

There are some occasions when a funeral service is best characterized as a "celebration," as when a well-known, faithful child of God "goes home" after a full life of service. At such a time, nothing could be a better musical choice than "Hallelujah" from Handel's *Messiah* or Luther's hymn "A Mighty Fortress." Whether played on a great organ or sung by a superb choir, it would be but a faint reminder of the music that John the Revelator describes as characteristic of "the new heaven and the new earth."

> Then I heard what seemed to be the voice of a great multitude, like the sound of many waters and like the sound of mighty thunderpeals, crying, "Hallelujah! For the Lord our God the Almighty reigns. Let us rejoice and exult and give him the glory . . . " (Rev. 19:6,7a)

Generally speaking, the music of a funeral (congregational, organ, solo or choral) should reflect the best styles common to the congregation, with texts that clearly voice the triumph of our faith, for "Death is swallowed up in victory." (I Cor. 15:54) Manuals and collections of funeral music are available, including these:

> *Funeral Music,* by F. A. Snell (Fortress)
> *A Manual for the Funeral* (Abingdon)
> *The Parish Organist,* Part X (Concordia)
> *A Collection of Funeral Music,* by Austin C. Lovelace (Abingdon)

Music in Services of Baptism and Child Dedication

Evangelicals show great diversity in the theology and the practice of baptism. Some favor "infant baptism" while others insist that the candidate must be an "adult believer." Some groups practice "sprinkling" or "pouring" and others baptize by immersion. Some groups emphasize that baptism is only "an ordinance" (commanded by Christ) and others will call it a "sacrament" ("a visible sign instituted by Jesus Christ to symbolize or confer grace.")[7] It is not our purpose to suggest that the theology or mode of baptism does not matter,[8] but to suggest ways in which any practice of a particular evangelical group can be enhanced, partly through the use of music.

Evangelicals who practice infant baptism probably do so within an acceptance of "covenant theology"[9] or simply as an act of dedicating the child to Christ and the Church. Implicit in either concept is the pledge of the parents and godparents to train children in the truth of the scriptures, so that they will later "confirm" that decision for themselves. Churches which do not baptize infants usually have services of "dedication of children." In either case, the whole congregation should join to pledge their support of and prayer for the child and for the involved adults, understanding that they too may share (possibly as Sunday school teachers or youth leaders) in bringing the child into a mature Christian commitment. It is well therefore for the congregation to join verbally in that pledge and in the dedication.

It has become customary for the organist to introduce these segments of a corporate worship service by playing some children's hymn while parents bring their children forward, either for baptism or for dedication. The musical effect could be heightened if the same hymn could be sung softly by the choir or the congregation—"I think when I read that sweet story of old," "Praise Him, all you little children," "I am so glad that Jesus loves me" or "Jesus loves me, this I know."

I cannot remember any occasion when hymn-singing has occurred in connection with an adult baptism. Obviously, this has been a historic practice, because most denominational hymnals still retain "baptism hymns." No doubt it would be a good thing to sing such a hymn, at least occasionally before a baptism, to allow the congregation to express its understanding of the rite. A good selection for such a purpose was written by the Mennonite minister, Samuel F. Coffman, and should meet the need of all evangelical groups, whatever the theology or the mode of baptism.

> We bless the name of Christ the Lord,
> We bless Him for His holy Word,
> Who loved to do His Father's will,
> And all His righteousness fulfill.

7. *The Random House Dictionary of the English Language*, 1966. No doubt most evangelicals would want to delete the words "or confer" from the definition. Notwithstanding, there are groups (e.g., Churches of Christ) who would come close to the definition of "evangelical" presented in our Introduction, who would insist that salvation requires personal faith, plus baptism.

8. I am personally committed to the baptism of "consenting" believers (those who are old enough to make an intelligent commitment to Christ) by immersion. It is commonly understood that the early church practiced immersion as a rite of initiation, and for present-day "immersionists" it symbolizes the subject's identification with Christ in death, burial and resurrection to new life. See Romans 6:4 and Colossians 2:12.

9. "Covenant theology" sees infant baptism as the New Testament circumcision—that as God's covenant to Israel was passed on from generation to generation as symbolized in that rite, so he covenants with Christian believers that their children will "come to faith," and this is symbolized in the rite of child baptism.

> We follow Him with pure delight
>> To sanctify His sacred rite;
> And thus our faith with water seal,
>> To prove obedience that we feel.
>
> Baptized in God—the Father, Son,
>> And Holy Spirit—Three in One,
> With conscience free, we rest in God,
>> In love and peace through Jesus' blood.
>
> By grace we "Abba, Father" cry;
>> By grace the Comforter comes nigh;
> And for Thy grace our love shall be
>> Forever, only, Lord, for Thee.

A large number of evangelicals practice adult baptism by immersion, and it may be that in this context congregational participation (including music) could be most meaningful. In some instances, churches have tended to minimize the significance of the observance by scheduling it before the beginning of the regular service while worshipers are still gathering, so that it cannot be fully shared by the whole congregation.

For this and other reasons, it is easy to get the impression that "immersionists" are just a little self-conscious about their baptismal mode. In a church I once attended, it was the practice to play the organ throughout the observance, and to improvise a grand crescendo when the candidate was actually immersed, in order to cover the sound. In retrospect, it seems to me that the most prominent sound of the occasion should be that of the swirling water! At best, it could only dimly remind us of the historic, dramatic moments when Christ was baptized by John, the Ethiopian eunuch was initiated by the witnessing disciple Philip, and our forefathers gathered at the closest river or lake for a most moving, corporate ceremony.

It has also seemed possible to me that the candidate might feel quite "alone on stage" at the time of his public baptism. Usually the lights of the church are turned down and spotlights are on the individual and the minister in the baptism waters. In my first church fellowship, the candidate was expected to improvise a testimony of Christian faith, and most of us repeated the shibboleths that we had heard from the pulpit or from older Christians. An improvised testimony is still a good idea, but young people should be encouraged to plan it, to make it brief, and to say it in their own words. This personal witness can also be expressed in a question and response which repeats one of the church's earliest and simplest creeds.

> Minister: (*Candidate's name*), who is your Lord?
> Candidate: Jesus is my Lord!

It would seem eminently fitting that on such an occasion, the church express its corporate nature in fellowship with the newly-baptized, perhaps in joining to sing a stanza of a witness hymn—"O Happy Day," "On Christ the Solid Rock I Stand," "Jesus, I My Cross Have Taken" or "O Jesus, I Have Promised." An excellent choice following the above question/response is a popular chorus, and it could be sung while the individual is still in the water.

> He is Lord, He is Lord,
> He is risen from the dead and He is Lord;
> Every knee shall bow, every tongue confess
> That Jesus Christ is Lord.   (Traditional)

Musical Worship Services

One of the important traditions of the church is the occasional use of services that are almost completely musical. Perhaps the oldest antecedent of this practice is the "sung mass" (*missa cantata*); when Gregorian chant was used, the entire mass was either sung or intoned. Since the 15th century, composed settings of the *Kyrie, Gloria, Credo, Sanctus et Benedictus,* and *Agnus Dei* have been common. In addition, the service of Vespers (the only office in the Roman tradition which permitted music other than plainsong) featured composed settings of the psalms and the *Magnificat.*

With the Reformation, musical works began to appear which are potentially still useful for evangelicals. The first of these, the vernacular Passions, were successors of an earlier Latin form that in turn may be traced to a 12th century "passion play" which helped medieval worshipers comprehend the suffering and death of Christ. Beginning in the 17th century, both cantatas and oratorios[10] were developed with the advent of the "new homophony" and the solo forms "aria" and "recitative." Cantatas have been both sacred and secular, and some oratorios have been planned for use in an auditorium, not a sanctuary; nevertheless, these extended forms have continued to be very important to the church. They appear under several generic titles (e.g., "Seven Last Words of Christ from the Cross," "The Christmas Oratorio"), and they tend to be associated with an important day of the Church Year (e.g., Christmas, Epiphany, Palm Sunday, Good Friday, Easter, Pentecost) or based on a particular theological concept (e.g., as in Bach's cantatas, or Gaul's *The Holy City*).

Oratorios, Cantatas, Musicals.

Evangelicals have not been averse to using historic works in this category where the available musical talent and cultural tradition have sup-

---

10. Willi Apel (in *Harvard Dictionary of Music,* 1964, p. 516) says "the history of the oratorio began in the mid-16th century when Filippo Neri inaugurated, in Rome, a special order called 'oratoriani' and founded a building called 'oratorio' (oratory, chapel) in which regular services of a popular character—similar in a way to those of the Salvation Army—were held. These included reading from the Scriptures, sermon, and the singing of *laude*. A special type of the latter were the 'dialogue-laude,' i.e., religious poems in the form of a dialogue between God and the Soul, Heaven and Hell, etc. . . . It is from these presentations . . . that the oratorio proper developed."

ported them; however, most churches have tended to stay with the "safe" choices—in our day, they are usually such compositions as Handel's *Messiah,* Dubois' *Seven Last Words,* Stainer's *Crucifixion* or Saint Saens' *Christmas Oratorio.* In the early 20th century, certain companies (notably, Lorenz Publishing Company, Dayton, Ohio) began to publish simple cantatas that were written especially for the small church; generally they adhered to the functional, "romantic" styles of the late 19th and early 20th century anthems sung in those same churches. In the 1960's, a new type of "cantata" appeared, which combined enlarged "gospel song" forms with some Broadway-style writing; the most popular composer of these "pop cantatas" was John W. Peterson. To be sure, his works were criticized by "serious" musicians, but they brought extended choral forms into churches which had never before sung a cantata.

The latest development in this field is frequently called a "musical," since it copies without apology the techniques of contemporary popular music—folk/rock rhythms, melodies, harmonies and instrumentation, as well as "modern language" lyrics, and frequently dialogue and dramatic action. Modern day musicals have appeared in versions for all age groups—adults, teenagers, subteens, junior choir, and even primary age voices!

Frequently, evangelical audiences are slow to respond to a serious cantata or oratorio because they do not perceive its theological significance. A choir director in a Presbyterian church in Baltimore has responded to this challenge with both written and informally-spoken comments that have helped to focus attention on the spiritual strength of a significant religious masterwork. With this educational approach, she has presented such music as Handel's *Messiah,* Mendelssohn's *Elijah,* Brahms' *German Requiem* and Vaughan Williams' *Hodie.* The following is the beginning of her written introduction to the *Requiem.*[11]

> The listener discovers almost immediately, in spite of the fact that it is named "Requiem," that here is music with one all-pervasive characteristic—JOY! . . . triumphant everlasting JOY!
>
> In sounds that progress from inward fervor to outward brilliance, set to a text that is wholly from the Bible, the composer has achieved a fitting-together of ideas and music which is unparalleled, and in the listening, as you experience the powerful Word of God washing over you in music of great nobility, you begin to sense a vision of celestial glory!

Lessons and Carols.

This traditional service of English origin combines Christmas carols (sung by choir and/or congregation) with scripture readings pertaining to the Christmas story, arranged in narrative fashion. Other variants

---

11. Lois Steigerwald, in the bulletin of April 29, 1979 of the Central Presbyterian Church of Baltimore, MD.

could feature Advent carols—which emphasize the anticipation of Christ's coming and the prophecies related to it—or Easter carols.

Some complete carol services of this kind are available in print.[12] Others can be planned, using a number of octavo carols or choosing some from such collections as the following:

> The Oxford Book of Carols (ed. Dearmer, Oxford)
> Carols for Choirs 1, 2 & 3 (three volumes, Oxford)
> Carols (InterVarsity Press)

Hymn Services.

Frequently, musical services concentrate on congregational materials, even though choirs may be featured in the presentation. The most common example is a Hymn Festival, in which a large number of hymns are presented, with possibly some "hymn anthems." It offers an opportunity to emphasize the meaning of hymns, and to feature a number of singing and accompanying techniques. The common plan for such presentations is related either to the calendar or to some theological concept. In the first instance, it is frequently the anniversary of the birth or the death of a hymn writer which is celebrated; in the second, all the hymns will be planned around a central theme, e.g., "The Love of God." Scripture readings, prayers, litanies, and even a sermon may be included.

Outlines of possible hymn festival services may be obtained from the Hymn Society of America.[13]

Choral Concerts.

A full-length service of music may be structured, using a number of shorter selections. As a general rule, this type of program features the more sophisticated literature known to the involved choir. It should also be pointed out that, unless it is carefully planned around a particular theme, such a presentation offers some potential for "mere entertainment," because of the lack of textual cohesion. It is because of this concern that Christians in Britain refuse to schedule "sacred concerts." For them a "concert" is a secular affair; a worship service of sacred music would more frequently be called a "Festival of Praise."

It has also been customary for choirs from church-related colleges, Bible colleges and seminaries to give programs in their supporting churches, usually touring at school vacation periods. This practice gives the school an opportunity to present its ministry in the church and

---

12. I have produced two collections of this type: *The Christmas Story in Candlelight Carols,* and *The Easter Story,* both released by Hope Publishing Company.
13. The current executive director and correspondent is W. Thomas Smith, Hymn Society of America, Wittenberg University, Springfield, OH 45501. Note that the January 1980 issue of *The Hymn* contains "A Commemorative Festival of Hymns for the Year 1980."

particularly to contact prospective students. It gives the group an added possibility for musical development, in repeating a prepared program many times. It affords the church an opportunity for growth in musical-aesthetic concepts, both because of the high quality of the singing and playing, and because of the extraordinary literature which is used. At the same time, it presents a pedagogical challenge. Frequently, evangelical churches have complained that the program presented by the visiting musicians was simply "over the heads" of the congregation; in time, they will respond to this by failing to attend. The wise director will be aware of this possibility and will vary his program (1) by including some simpler, more familiar music (2) by "teaching" the music to the congregation by adding narration between selections; or (3) by both procedures.

Instrumental Recitals.

The church owns two major musical instruments, an organ and a piano. They function mostly in accompanying the congregational singing and other music in the service, and it is well for them to be heard occasionally in full length recital. This will draw attention to their potential in leading worship in the regular preludes, offertories and postludes of the church service. It will also give an opportunity for musical self-expression by the regular instrumentalists of the church, and also by guests who may be invited to participate. Instrumental recitals are usually presented in Sunday afternoon hours. Occasionally, as in the dedication of a new instrument, they will take the place of a regular Sunday evening service.

In churches where art music is regularly offered, there is often no need to depart from a normal recital format. The congregation is acquainted with the literature, and finds meaning (including worship) in its performance. In other churches, particularly where a recital is an unusual observance, it may be wise to use certain educational procedures to improve the quality of the listeners' experience.

I play a large number of recitals in evangelical churches, usually in connection with the dedication of a pipe organ or a prestige-electronic instrument. Reasoning that many folk will attend for whom this is a "once in a lifetime" experience, I use a fair number of shorter, "listenable" pieces along with longer masterworks, including Mendelssohn sonatas, J. S. Bach preludes and fugues, works of Couperin, Langlais and Alain, and even the first organ sonata of Paul Hindemith. I also play a group of my own hymn preludes, as well as a "classical improvisation" on a hymn tune. Interspersing the program, I make comments on the registrations used, on the structure and the "meaning" of the historic music, and on the theology of the hymn texts which are associated with the featured tunes. Recently, at the close of a typical recital in a small rural church in central Illinois, the pastor thanked me for leading in a worship experience "that was also fun." The characterization was a bit of a poser, but I take it to be a compliment. Most non-concertgoers find our typical recitals to be dull, stuffy affairs; they are convinced that artists take themselves much too seriously. It is my hope that the one positive experience for typical churchgoers will pave the way for the playing of more serious music by the local organist, who has previously been limited to playing settings of gospel hymns, in some instances right out of the hymnbook!

Of course, the piano may be introduced and featured in the same way. Increasingly, it has come to be used as the "second instrument" in the church, frequently heard by itself as well as with the organ. When a new piano is purchased, especially if it is a good one, it should be heard in a solo recital. This may be the one opportunity for the church's regular pianist to play serious music for the home congregation. If desirable, an excellent pianist can be secured from the faculty of one of our evangelical schools. Some of them will also include settings of hymns or other church-related literature which will provide a road-to-understanding for the less-sophisticated listener.

Solo Vocal Recitals.

Vocal talent is possibly the most prominent musical asset in the local church. Many members of the choir have completed advanced study in their discipline; frequently the choir director is himself an accomplished soloist. Although they are heard regularly in the church worship services, it is possible that some singers should have the opportunity to provide a longer worship experience in a full recital.

Some churches will no doubt be able to support a traditional recital, including works in European languages and solo cantatas. Others will choose a "mixed" program, because of the need to "bridge" a cultural gap. A fellow faculty member recently presented a program of Psalms (translations of works of Heinrich Schütz), Hymns (sacred songs by Ralph Vaughan Williams) and Spiritual Songs (contemporary settings of "experience" words, of his own composing.)

In recent years, a full program by a guest soloist (who is also a recording artist) has become a common occurrence. Usually this individual uses mostly one style of music, often related to the contemporary mode of pietist expression; frequently the accompaniment is provided by "tape tracks" taken from recent commercial recordings. The singer often intersperses the music with "talk," sometimes just friendly banter, and sometimes a homiletical narration related to the words being sung. This custom has historical roots, to be sure; the phenomenon has become so common in today's culture that I deal with it more completely in chapter 17.

The Religious Arts Festival.

In a growing number of churches, the relationship of our faith to creativity in the arts is perceived so strongly and clearly that the group sponsors periodic art festivals. These activities include a large measure of music, but other arts are frequently involved. Sometimes these presentations occur within a comparatively short period of time—possibly a weekend—and sometimes they are spread over a year's calendar. Religious drama, poetry reading, dramatized choral works and solo recitals are possible, together with displays of visual arts such as sculpture, photography and painting. One Louisville church recently presented ten features over a period of four consecutive weekends:

1. A concert by the Murk Family (vocal-instrumental).
2. The Bible Hymnbook—A Service of Psalms (featuring the choir and congregation).
3. A Religious Art Exhibit (featuring three professional artists in paintings, etchings and sculpture).
4. A Piano Recital (featuring a church music assistant, who is completing doctoral study).
5. The Life of Christ Through Great Art Masterpieces (A slide presentation, with organ music; at the appropriate time in the sequence, a "silent communion" service was observed.)
6. A mini-concert by a visiting college choir, in a morning service.
7. An Organ Recital (by a former church member, now a professional organist and seminary teacher).
8. The Everyman Players (professional) in the drama "Romans by St. Paul."
9. A mini-concert by a guest singer, in the morning service.
10. A dramatized presentation of Mendelssohn's *Elijah*, with David Ford in the title role, the church choir, and semi-professional orchestra.

Chapter XIII

MUSIC IN FOREIGN MISSIONS

Foreign missions are best understood as a form of evangelism—transcultural evangelism in a country which is "foreign" to the missionary. The New Testament is a missionary book, the story of the first century propagation of the gospel throughout much of the known world. Nevertheless, in our day missions have been put on the defensive, and western nations have been asked to consider a "moratorium" on appointing missionaries. Obviously, we need to reconsider our apologetic for missions and our techniques of world evangelization.

Evangelicals believe in and promote world evangelization in order to glorify God, who is only perfectly revealed through Jesus Christ—his life, his death, and his resurrection. Secondly, they practice missions because it is the command of Jesus Christ.

> "Go therefore and make disciples of all nations, baptizing them in the name of the Father and of the Son and of the Holy Spirit, teaching them to observe all that I have commanded you; and lo, I am with you always, to the close of the age." Matthew 28:19,20.

Part of the criticism of traditional missions is based on the complaint that missionaries expected to hold the power in the newly planted church, and that they tended to preach a cultural as well as a religious conversion. For instance, the 19th century missionary invariably tried to communicate the gospel in translations of Anglo-American gospel hymns set to western tunes; these textual and musical styles remained to become the common worship song of the baptized believers.

As early as the mid-19th century, such missionary statesmen as Henry Venn[1] and Rufus Anderson[2] advocated the following principles for establishing national churches in foreign lands:

1. Self-government—the nationals make their own decisions, using their own approaches to organization and polity.

1. Henry Venn (1796-1873), General Secretary of the Church Missionary Society of London (Anglican).
2. Rufus Anderson (1796-1880), Corresponding Secretary of the American Board of Commissioners for Foreign Missions, Boston, MA.

2. Self-support—the nationals finance their own local ministry. (Exceptions are made in the case of such expensive projects as building hospitals and schools.)
3. Self-propagation—the nationals evangelize their own people.

The principle of "self-expression" is inherent in the adoption of the above, and in the context of this chapter it will be emphasized. This means that in worship the national church will use its own style of architecture and decoration, develop its own forms of liturgy (based on New Testament principles), and create its own musical expressions.

Regretably, it took evangelicals almost one hundred years to fully accept these principles. Until very recently they perpetuated the "missionary macho" image, arguing that the nationals were not capable of making the decisions. Eventually, the rising flood of nationalism forced the issue, and Christian congregations throughout the world have demonstrated that they are equal to the challenge.

In modern times, the evangelical missionary sees himself as a servant, a co-laborer, who works cooperatively and contextually with the indigenous church leadership. In the area of music, there is opportunity for a new breed of specialists, who will train nationals to develop their own hymns in their own ethnic styles of text and music, and will assist the local congregations in using music in worship, education and evangelism.

History of Music in Missions

The scriptures do not include any overt declaration that the early Christians used music in their propagation of the gospel throughout the then-known world. However, we noted earlier that the New Testament epistles contain many Christological hymns which were no doubt used to express the new faith and were possibly shared in Ephesus, Corinth, Colosse, and in other first-century congregations.

In *The Gospel in Hymns,* Albert Edward Bailey mentions[3] (but fails to document) that Niceta of Remesiana preached the gospel in southeastern Europe "chiefly by singing sweet songs of the cross." In the missionary expansion of the Roman Catholic Church during the 16th and 17th centuries, the Latin language and Gregorian chant followed the crucifix, not as an evangelistic technique, but as the official worship language and song. Similarly, with the colonial expansion of European nations between 1600 and 1800, Dutch Reformed, German Lutheran, and Anglican churches (as well as others) were established in urban centers around the world, and their worship included the traditional Calvinist psalms, the Lutheran Chorales and Anglican chants; these churches served the

---

3. P. 214; a statement attributed to St. Jerome.

needs of the white colonizers, but invariably a few nationals would be attracted to their message and be baptized into the fellowship.

The first bold missionary thrust of post-reformation protestants came with the Moravians. This group of 18th century pietists, from many different mid-European backgrounds, constituted a revival of the 15th century fellowship known as *Unitas Fratrem* (United Brethren.) Each member of the group was committed to spreading the faith as a "world pilgrim." To this end, they established colonies in North and South America, the West Indies, Asia and Africa. Moravians were among the first to evangelize the American Indians, settling first in Georgia. With them came their traditions of congregational part-singing, excellent choral music in the German style, and the brass choir (*posaunenchor*). That heritage still thrives in such Moravian centers as Bethlehem, Pennsylvania and Winston-Salem, North Carolina.

The modern Anglo-American missionary movement is acknowledged to have begun with the English Baptist William Carey (1761–1834) in the wake of the Evangelical Revival led by the Wesleys earlier in the 18th century. The movement spread to America as the revival came to these shores under Jonathan Edwards and George Whitefield, and the English-speaking countries have generally taken the lead in foreign missions since that time. Missionaries were rarely trained in music, but they instinctively packed their church's hymnal in their baggage along with other devotional books; eventually they translated the texts into the new language they were learning, singing the hymns to the tunes which were familiar to them. So it was that the early 19th century missionary hymnbooks consisted mostly of "Watts and Wesley," followed by a flood of the gospel hymns that were becoming so popular in both England and America at that time. As a result, Christian hymnals around the world have reflected the hymn-singing habits of each sponsoring mission board, with gospel songs forming the largest part of the hymnic diet. This constitutes probably the most widespread cross-cultural transfer of poetry and music the world has ever seen!

In some instances the aesthetic fertilization seemed to be eminently successful. One of America's first missionary efforts was directed to the Sandwich (Hawaiian) Islands. Congregationalists from New England arrived there in 1820. The Polynesian natives found the major harmonies of the missionary hymns quite suited to their own tastes and quickly learned to reproduce them on the ukelele, a four-stringed "chording" instrument which they had adapted from a form of the guitar introduced by Portuguese sailors. In three years' time, the missionaries had reduced the Hawaiian language to writing, and published their first words-only hymnal of sixty pages. In later years the last reigning monarch, Queen Liliuokalani (1838–1917), wrote many sacred songs, in which the texts expressed her love of nature as well as her faith, and the music bore strong resemblance to the tunes of Ira D. Sankey.

It must be admitted that the typical mission program of acculturation was based on a failure to appreciate the indigenous culture. Missionaries were no more prejudiced than any other group of travelers. It was the standard view until only recently that the cultures of primitive societies were innately inferior to those in the western tradition. Missionaries were tempted to add that they were more tainted by sin and probably even demonic. At the same time, they quickly discovered that primitive peoples were unusually curious and even captivated by their performance of gospel hymns. It served as a quick method of attracting attention, in the African bush or the South American village, so much so that they were tempted to call music a "universal language." Obviously, in using this slogan they meant "western" music, since they rejected the local ethnic expressions in rhythm and tone.

It never seemed to dawn on missionaries that the nationals were only curious about the strange sounds they were hearing, or that *they* might be "inferior" because they failed to appreciate the music of the indigenous culture. At any rate, it was common practice for the furloughed missionary to report that all the natives' songs were "in the minor key" until they were converted, when they began to sing "in the major key"[4]—forgetting that the new converts had learned the new major-key song only after painful, tedious drilling.

It has recently become apparent that the prejudice against indigenous culture was well-nigh a fatal one. Christianity has thereby been labeled a "western" religion. In a day of rising national and ethnic consciousness, the gospel of Jesus Christ has sometimes been rejected because it was associated with western economic and political structures, western dress and western art. Furthermore, it has become clear that the "cultural transfer" of western hymns was not so successful as it first seemed. When combined with "tonal" languages, the gospel song melodies often failed to conform to normal speech inflections, thus denying the text's meaning. In many instances, normal language rhythms were violated when they were forced into traditional western musical meters. In a broader sense, the sincere but misguided effort of the missionaries resulted in an unnatural expression of the gospel that greatly limited the effectiveness of both communication and response. It might well be compared to the Roman Catholic Church's use of Latin and Gregorian chant world-wide. Eventually it may communicate *something* based on the principle of association, but it would be foolish to expect it to become the universal congregational language of evangelical expression.

No doubt spurred by growing antagonism to their programs, and encouraged by rising worldwide interest in anthropology and ethnomusicology, missions have taken a new look at music in relationship to society, and are encouraging the use of indigenous modes and instruments where they are still a strong element in the local culture.

4. This statement reveals both misinformation and misconception. (1) The ethnic music was probably based on a non-western scale (e.g., pentatonic), not a typical minor or modal pattern. (2) It was only during the 200 years from 1750 to 1950 that the major mode was dominant in western church life; modern "sacred folk" music has tended to revert to the minor or modal.

The Modern Missionary Musician

In this last half of the 20th century, mission organizations are looking for professional specialists. In addition to the traditional evangelist and church planter, there is need for medical personnel, educators, agronomists, social workers, counselors and musicians, among others. Musician-specialists have several activities from which they may choose.

Institutional Music Education.

Occasionally, informal music education in "hospitality centers" serves as a tool in making contact with nationals, opening the door to a positive Christian witness. In a few instances (particularly in colleges and universities in societies where western music has become the norm) the missionary may be teaching music as a historic art and a cultural expression. More frequently, music educators will be appointed to a college, Bible institute or seminary, where they will train the future minister and his wife in singing, instrumental performance (piano, accordion, guitar, et al), in songleading, and music fundamentals, so that they in turn may give musical leadership in the churches they will serve.

Mass Communications.

Radio and television are used widely in foreign missions today, and many of the programs feature music. Trans-World Radio has major transmitters both in Monaco and in Bonaire, West Indies engaged in broadcasting to at least four continents in many different languages. Short wave and long wave transmitters of HCJB in Quito, Ecuador ("The Voice of the Andes") reach around the world. Radio ELWA of the Sudan Interior Mission specializes in reaching western Africa, and they are using a good deal of indigenous expression. The Far Eastern Broadcasting Association has studios in many parts of Asia and transmitters in the Philippines and in Korea. Some missions engage in broadcasting without maintaining their own transmission facilities; for instance, the Foreign Mission Board of the Southern Baptist Convention has production studios in many major cities around the world, and release their programs over national or international networks.

Musical Performance.

Some missionaries see themselves as performing witnesses to the gospel, either as singers, instrumentalists or conductors. Gene Jordan, my long-time friend and classmate at Northwestern University (Illinois), has spent his life of ministry in South America, playing settings of hymns on the marimba (especially appreciated in that society) and arranging/conducting choral music. A Baptist missionary couple in Kobe, Japan appear as vocal soloists specializing in "serious" sacred music, and the husband directs an inter-church chorus which presents major master-works of western sacred music and assists in evangelistic crusades.

An interesting development has recently taken place in France. Lead-ers of the Greater Europe Mission have encouraged the musicians in their school at Lamorlaye to form an International Congress of Christian Musicians. The purpose has been to encourage serious, young European and American evangelical musicians who find little opportunity to use their talent in the church, to give them training in their art and its relationship to Christian faith, and to help them communicate their witness through performances of sacred musical masterworks.

In the summer of 1979, the mission sponsored three musical groups—a 20-voice chorus, a small string orchestra and a woodwind sextet—which spent five weeks traveling to the tourist centers of France. It was my personal privilege to train the choir and to direct it during the first two tour weeks, singing music of J. S. Bach, Schütz, Sweelinck, Crüger, Gibbons, Brahms and Berger. Interspersing the selections was commentary which related the music to the gospel, and personal Chris-tian witness by the singers.

The primary objective of the effort was "pre-evangelism," since evan-gelical Christianity is very weak in France. The strategy was based on the hypothesis that Europeans have more interest in "art music" than most Americans. As expressed by Dennis Weber, dean of the European Bible Institute, who planned the enterprise: "Public concerts in the local (catholic) church are part of the cloth of village life. If the mayor and the general public recognize that the little group of protestants is offering some quality input, status has been achieved and bridges can be made to the unbeliever."[5]

It is interesting to note that, although this type of outreach activity adheres to our principle of choosing the proper musical language for a particular audience, in this instance it is not the musical language com-mon to evangelical worship in France. A typical small church would probably not have a choir; the principal music would be standard hymns and gospel hymns sung by the congregation. The same principle of music selection is also followed by the "Liberated Wailing Wall," a group of musicians sponsored by "Jews for Jesus." For witnessing to fellow Jews, they have developed Christian songs based on traditional Jewish folk music.

In certain situations, there has been increasing interest in the use of other national art forms related to music, for communicating the gospel. Bill O'Brien (now with the Foreign Mission Board of the Southern Bap-tists) participated in the development of a narrative ballet (with gamelan accompaniment) based on the historic ethnic dance of Indonesia. Students from Hong Kong Baptist College demonstrated national dance tra-ditions on the platform of the Baptist World Congress in Stockholm in 1975.

5. From a personal letter, dated February 27, 1978.

Music Development.

Music promotion or development includes a wide variety of approaches, all designed to assist local churches in developing their own musical expressions. In some instances, missions organizations have set up a "music office" for a specific country (e.g., Korea) or for a smaller area. A missionary-musician appointed to direct its activities functions very much like a state music secretary for Southern Baptists in the United States—planning workshops to teach basic music theory, vocal production, conducting, keyboard performance and worship—and also helping to publish music in the national language and in national styles.

Sometimes the individual in charge of music promotion will develop a "model choir" which will travel throughout the area to demonstrate what can be done in choral performance. In a few instances, a missionary has been "minister of music" in a local church. This latter activity is most successful where the musical culture most closely duplicates that "at home"—in churches that have a large number of westerners attending, or in countries (e.g, Korea or Japan) where western music has already become the norm. Usually, they are the largest and most prosperous churches in any country, and although the program has frequently been labeled a "pilot" for smaller congregations, it rarely functions to that end.

A number of music education approaches are copied from activities in the United States. In Puebla, Mexico, for instance, two-week music institutes are held at the Camp *Oasis de Agua Viva* (Oasis of Living Water) under the auspices of Samuel Smith of the Christian and Missionary Alliance. The institute is planned to help the amateur musicians in small, rural churches. The participants develop performance skills on instruments (e.g., piano, accordion, organ, guitar, clarinet) and attend classes in conducting, theory, music appreciation and chorus. In a recent institute, students made their first attempts to write hymns for use in their own congregations. Mr. Smith reports on the achievements of these short-course schools in a camp setting: "After four two-week institutes, many persons with no previous music study are now playing for services, leading choirs, and helping in evangelistic meetings."[6]

Perhaps the most successful music promotion is done by a missionary in an urban center who works with several national churches regularly. Dr. Michel Simoneaux has dedicated himself to this ministry as a Southern Baptist representative in Japan. He may function occasionally in congregational leadership, teaching the worshipers how to sing the correct notes and rhythms with "spirit and understanding." He will also seek to develop songleaders and accompanists within each congregation, and possibly soloists and choirs. Ideally, as a music tradition develops in the local church, the music missionary expects to "work himself out of a job" and move to another locale for a similar program.

6. From a missions report letter of October 19, 1978.

Ethnomusicological Research and Activity.

Specialized work in ethnic music is being done at two levels, professional and amateur. The first requires thorough research techniques and is usually preceded by acquiring an advanced degree in the field. The second can be performed by any alert musician who possesses a good ear and an open mind. The very first ethnomusicologists were amateurs and missionaries; a fairly large number continue to be active in the field.

In recent years it has become apparent that the missionary task will be shared by Christians in the "third world," who are themselves the product of missions. We can envision the time when urban nationals will be trained to use the ethnic music their culture has almost forgotten, in order to evangelize their own people in the rural, primitive areas that still exist. This kind of education would be supervised by a specialist trained in ethnomusicology.

Challenges and Needs

There are many purely-material needs and problems that beset the musical missionary. Modern hymnals and other music materials are expensive and difficult to produce. Frequently the missionary must make the translations and arrangements of new materials and then duplicate them for local churches; it would be ideal if a MusicRiter[7] (a notation typewriter) were available for this purpose. Music education materials are also not available unless they are produced by the missionary; several countries have translated and adapted the programmed course, *Fundamentals of Music* by William Hooper.[8] A good instruction manual in organ playing in the Japanese language has been produced by Jean Shepard, a Baptist Missionary. Musical instruments are also scarce and difficult to keep in good condition; to help meet this need, a Baptist congregation in Texas recently agreed to supply StroboConn piano tuners for all their missionary representatives in a certain part of the world.

The missionary musician will also face the challenge to adapt American pedagogical concepts to the needs of local culture. In many countries of the world, there is no democratic music instruction in public schools; what is done in the religious community must not depend on help from outside sources. Where there is an established tradition, techniques will differ from culture to culture. In Europe, sightsinging is taught by the *solfege* system (with a "fixed do"), while in America the norm is the "movable do." Notation systems also vary greatly; in many countries associated with the British commonwealth, choral singing is done from letter and punctuation symbols, not from notes and rests on a staff, as:

7. Available from Music Print Corporation, Boulder, CO.
8. Published by Convention Press, Nashville, TN, 1958.

$$: d.m \quad s \; ; \; -l \; : s : d^1 \quad d^1 \; : \; -l \; : \; s \; :$$
There   is   a   foun-tain filled with blood

In other countries, the music may be completely oral in tradition—there is no notation, no fixed tuning, and a high degree of improvisation is expected.

There is also the challenge of contrasting educational psychologies; most attitudes and techniques in non-American countries tend to be much more rigid and authoritarian than our own. Underlying thought processes and "life philosophies" in another culture seriously affect the missionary's ability to communicate in a teaching situation.

In general, the most important challenge remains the same from one generation to another—that the missionary will studiously refrain from superimposing American cultural values and patterns on a "foreign" people. One appointee to Japan reports that he was recruited "to develop the same church music program in Hiroshima that he had previously executed in South Carolina." Some Southern Baptist missionaries in the Philippines complain that their constituent churches are not as "free" in their worship patterns as they are in the United States; the truth is that many evangelical churches in those islands tend to be influenced by the prevailing Roman Catholic culture and its formal liturgy. In general, non-western groups seem to be relatively indifferent to musical *performances*, and more interested in functional music that is germane to its purpose and performed congregationally. Why then should we export our western sins of "spectator worship" under the pretext of helping them "advance" in their art?

Because "musical missions" is a relatively new concept in ministry, it should not be surprising that it involves a good deal of experimentation, of "trial and error." Even so, Southern Baptists now have 140 specialists working in this kind of activity the world around. I recently met with a group of musicians serving in East Asia in a conference in Taipei, Taiwan. In the final session, the group adopted this statement of their general purpose:

> In response to the call of God, the Music Missionary seeks to com-
> municate the Gospel, to discover and train national leadership to use
> their talents to glorify God and to minister to others, and to assist
> churches in establishing and improving their church music minis-
> tries:
> 1. Through developing and promoting a program of church
>   music, suited to the needs and opportunities of local Baptist
>   churches. This would include the development of appropriate
>   concepts and techniques of music in worship, discipling and
>   witnessing within the context of each particular culture.
> 2. Through providing training for congregations, pastors, lay
>   leaders and church musicians.
> 3. Through the preparation, publication and promotion of music

materials, and the encouraging of nationals to produce their own words and music.
4. Through musical performance to proclaim the Gospel, lead in worship and teach Christian truth.

Although the delegates insisted that no "sense of priority" be listed for the individual items in the statement, they did agree that the ministry to the local church should be placed first, and personal musical performance last. It was also refreshing to hear the frequent insistence that "music for worship" should be considered to be of first importance.

Indigenous Music in Missions

The question of western vs. indigenous music will have to be dealt with, country by country, and region by region. What the missionary began 150 years ago with the translation of Anglo-American gospel songs, has been continued by the onward march of Western industrialism, the portable transistor radio, and a broad spectrum of symphonic, operatic and rock music! Some non-western countries have become so thoroughly occidental in their musical tastes (e.g., Japan, Korea, Hong Kong, Taiwan) that it is almost unthinkable that they might return to their indigenous roots. The only major Asian country in which indigenous music is very much a part of missionary activity is Thailand, probably because that land has never been colonized.

Furthermore, non-westerners are as capable of developing prejudice for a more "advanced" communication language as anyone else. A missionary radio musician in Manila reports that it is difficult to persuade urban Christian Filipinos to sing in the provincial languages for purposes of outreach, because they consider them to be culturally inferior to English and the official "Tagolog" language. In East Africa the older national Christians, as well as some missionaries, oppose the use of the drum in worship, while the younger Christians desperately want to use the traditional native instruments. On the other hand, it is said that in Hong Kong the older Chinese Christians rather enjoy the settings of traditional Chinese melodies in the new Baptist hymnal, but the young people reject them as being "primitive and unsophisticated."

It has been suggested that there are three possibilities in resolving the issue of indigenous vs. western music, and that in some countries all three may exist side by side:

1. All western music, as in some churches in Japan and Korea.
2. All indigenous music, as in the hill country of Thailand, or with the remote Indian tribes of Ecuador.
3. A marriage of western and indigenous music, as in many parts of Africa, Asia and South America. In some instances western tunes

receive an indigenous treatment; in others, indigenous tunes are coupled with western-style harmonization, arranging and instrumentation.

Ethnomusicology and the Missionary

Ethnomusicology has emerged as a comparatively recent branch of musicology, the science of music. Historical musicology is older; it tends to analyze the art music of western culture and to compare the theory and the expression of music in one period with those of another, and even to compare the music of various composers within the same period (e.g., to compare the music of Bach, 1685–1750, with that of Haydn, 1732–1809, or to compare the music of Bach with that of his contemporary Handel, 1685–1757.) Ethnomusicology deals with the music of primitive cultures (e.g., in Africa and South America), the high Oriental civilizations (China and Japan), and folk cultures (the mountain peoples of Appalachia), to study its craftsmanship, its aesthetic worth and emotional power, and its function in that culture in relation to religion, politics, education and recreation.

An interest in ethnomusicology is strongly recommended for the music missionary, even the one who works largely with western styles. To begin, truly "cultured" persons are those who understand a broad spectrum of culture and as a result, see their own life-style in better perspective. Secondly, one of the principal requirements of a missionary is culture-consciousness. Even if an ethnic or a folk music culture is waning, to understand it is to better understand the people who sprang from it, particularly their thought processes, their sense of values and their emotional vocabulary.

A missionary has an opportunity to be a "conserver" of cultures, particularly of those that seem to be disappearing with the advance of industrialism. In the scramble for a better standard of living, many groups are tempted to make wrong decisions about cultural change. The missionary may want to help a group preserve its traditional culture so they may better understand their identity in an "increasingly homogenized" world. For example, the *anklang* of Thailand and *gamelan* of Indonesia have recently been adapted to the western scale pattern; in those societies, it would be wise for missionaries to use those musical instruments for education and worship, much as we use handbells in America.

A few years ago I received a letter from Rev. Alton J. Shea (brother of the gospel singer) who worked for seven years in the Gbendembu Recording Studio of the Wesleyan Church in Sierra Leone, West Africa:

> We are having a tremendous experience here in Africa. Indeed, we have had to sublimate our own musical tastes to promoting indigenous music in the churches and over the radio. Drumming is what touches the heart of the tribesman over here. But the young people

in school quickly pick up a liking for modern hits and western style harmony as it comes over the radio. The local station is playing the hit gospel songs and the kids are singing them.

Our studio has quite a library of tribal music in five languages and the music is fascinating to me. I am not a musician, but often hope that someone with interest will be able to analyze some of these patterns of singing.

Since *Roots*,[9] they say blacks in the United States are saying, "You look like a Mende tribe," or "You must be from Liberia, etc." Most slaves were from West Africa, and now they know who they are. I had a wild idea recently that some blacks in the United States might even be interested in hearing what their brothers are doing musically in the bush. . . .

This illustrates dramatically what we have been trying to say. American blacks are rediscovering their identity through the culture which they left behind in Africa! And modern-day radio missionaries have to wrestle with the question as to whether or not they should help perpetuate African ethnic culture, or whether they should encourage young Africans to reject it in favor of western "pop gospel"!

Much of the concern for ethnic music expression in missions has been voiced in the journals, *Practical Anthropology* and *Missiology*.[10] The individual who wants to work professionally in this field may receive training at such schools as New York University, Northwestern University and the University of California at Los Angeles.[11] General training in missions music and an overview of ethnomusicology is available at the Baptist seminaries in Fort Worth, Texas and Louisville, Kentucky and at Columbia Bible College, Columbia, South Carolina. Recently Professor Alan Lomax of New York released *Cantometrics: A Method in Musical Anthropology*[12]—a tool (with a manual and demonstration cassettes) for measuring the characteristics of ethnic folksong, which can be used by the professional ethnomusicologist and also by the talented amateur.

Summary

Nowadays, foreign missions is for all practical purposes the exclusive province of evangelicals, since traditional denominations have largely retreated from the challenge. All missions service involves a high degree

9. The widely-acclaimed book by Alex Haley (Doubleday, 1976), reproduced in a television series.
10. *Practical Anthropology* was published by the Society for Practical Anthropology from 1953 to 1963. It was succeeded by *Missiology*, the journal of the American Society of Missiology, 135 No. Oakland Ave., Pasadena, CA 91101.
11. An undergraduate curriculum in ethnomusicology was recently introduced at Wheaton College, Wheaton, IL.
12. Distributed by the University of California Extension Media Center, Berkeley, CA 94720.

of personal sacrifice, especially the requirement to live and work in a foreign land, removed from family and familiar culture. In addition, missionary-musicians will rarely be able to match the creative aesthetic experiences in traditional art music they would have had at home. However, in terms of witnessing and ministering, their opportunities are multiplied. People in other lands seem to find extraordinary pleasure in musical activity. Perhaps their ears have not been as "overloaded" as ours in America. Furthermore, the satisfaction found in Christian song is especially significant to overseas converts, because primitive non-Christian cults do not express the emotions of joy and freedom. The principal rewards of musical missionaries are those of educators. They see others develop their musical gifts, and entire congregations grow in their ability to respond in meaningful praise to God!

Recently, T. W. Hunt, a leading authority on music in foreign missions,[13] compiled a list of "Functions Music Has Served in Mission Outreach" which he had received from career missionaries throughout the world. Many of the functions mentioned are parallel with music's contributions to American churches. Some of them are unique to overseas activity.

1. Music is the most natural expression of Christian joy; all Christians sing.
2. Music has broken the barrier against women's expression in some cultures.
3. Music attracts population segments hostile to evangelical Christianity; the sung gospel often gives the preached gospel a chance to be heard.
4. Music has a *speed* factor in attracting attention; this is reported world-wide.
5. Music is an aid in *public relations* for the denomination and for evangelical Christianity. Music often breaks barriers nothing else can break. It also broadens the sphere of influence of local churches.
6. Music *integrates* the Christian message with daily life in most parts of the world.
7. Christian musical expression can supplant a heathen practice.
8. Music is adaptable to use in almost any sphere of mission effort (student work, medical work, teaching ministry, etc.) This is true because music is universal.
9. Music helps to express and to understand culture. Musical expression is one of the most significant and characteristic expressions of the nature of a given culture.
10. Music functions (a) as a mnemonic (memory-aiding) device, and (b) as a means of enhancing and deepening the meaning of a text.

13. Dr. Hunt is a professor at Southwestern Baptist Theological Seminary, Fort Worth, TX.

Chapter XIV

EVANGELICALS AND CONGREGATIONAL SINGING

Evangelicals have been known as "people of the Book." Actually, we are a people of *two* books, the Bible and the hymnal. It has been said that in the 16th century, Martin Luther "gave the German people in their own language the Bible and the hymnbook, so that God might speak *directly* to them in His Word, and that they might *directly* answer Him in their songs."[1] When our Pilgrim forefathers went to church, they carried two books, the King James Bible (which was then very new!) and the Bay Psalm Book, the very first volume printed in the colonies. When they returned home, both books became the basis for both family and private devotions.

In our own day, the hymnal seems to be one of our least-treasured possessions. In church, it may often be found lying on the floor. Occasionally it may prove to be really functional, propping up the lid of a piano, or providing "lifts" for the organ bench! It is possible that American economics have contributed to our profligacy. Partly because it is sold in large quantities, a hymnal will cost about one-fourth as much as a comparable-sized textbook. However, our carelessness in using the "physical" book—its pages and binding—is only symptomatic of our underestimation of its real value. The greater tragedy is that we do not prize what a hymnal contains; we do not really use it well.

For the central—and only indispensable—music of evangelical Christianity is congregational singing, the whole church demonstrating its priesthood in song. Singing in worship is not reserved for priests or for "singers"; singing is for believers. The crucial question is not "Do you have a voice?" but "Do you have a song?" As Luther said: "If any would not sing and talk of what Christ has wrought for us, he shows thereby that he does not really believe. . . ."[2] There have been times in history, as in the one thousand years before Luther, when the voice of the church's

---

1. Cited by A. E. Bailey, *The Gospel in Hymns*, p. 313.
2. Walter E. Buszin, *Luther on Music*, p. 6; from the foreword of the Babst *Gesangbuch* of 1545.

"first choir"—the congregation—was stilled. There have been other periods when Christians have neglected their heritage in favor of spectatorist worship; that non-evangelical practice was frequently demonstrated during the last generation of evangelical church life.

It has often been said that congregational singing is important because it provides an opportunity for a "united and unifying" response to the gospel. Actually, it can be both *revelation and response*, since great hymnody has always been "bathed in scripture," either quoting it directly or expressing our understanding of it. As Erik Routley says:[3]

> A hymn, basically, is an opportunity for a congregation to declare its experience and to rejoice in Christian doctrine corporately.

Evelyn Underhill has said that "transcendence" is expressed in evangelical (non-liturgical) worship largely in its congregational hymns.[4]

> ... those Christian sects in which the use of visible symbols is at a minimum, and the cultus has been deliberately stripped of sensuous appeal, seem to tend instinctively to hymns rich in concrete images and emotional suggestion—thus giving to the primitive layers of the worshiping mind the sensuous food that they need, by means of the ear instead of the eye.

Ms. Underhill's understanding of evangelical transcendence, it seems to me, is related to the involvement of the singers and the quality of their experience. First, the whole person is potentially involved: the body (in singing), the mind (in understanding what is sung), the emotional self (in "feeling" what is sung), and the will (in being changed by the singing). Second, human experience finds its "aesthetic transcendence" in both poetry (rhythm, rhyme, imagery, and structure) and music (the massed sound of voices, the melody-harmony-rhythm, and possibly the accompaniment of a great organ or a brass choir.) There have been times when I have found such an experience to be simply overpowering—as when I accompanied 2500 British ministers singing "Love Divine, All Loves Excelling" to the tune "Blaenwern" in London's Westminster Central Hall, or heard the Welsh congregation sing "Cwm Rhondda" in a church in Aberystwyth, or Korean Baptist seminary students "belt out" a hymn (with absolutely full voice and *lento* tempo) in their chapel in Taejon.

Of course, not all hymn singing measures up to this standard, and the fault usually lies in the poor quality of the material—which includes a good choice sung at the wrong time—or an ineffective performance. In this chapter, it is our purpose to trace the history of hymnsinging in America, and to suggest means of improving this "most evangelical" church music during the closing years of the 20th century.

3. Erik Routley, *Hymns Today and Tomorrow*, p. 18.
4. Evelyn Underhill, *Worship*, p. 41.

Hymn Singing in America

The first Americans sang metrical psalms only. It may be conjectured that Calvin's insistence on the exclusive use of psalms (which greatly influenced all English-speaking protestants) was an attempt to return to "scriptural" worship, discarding the postscriptural additions of the medieval church. The requirement of a metrical psalm was that it conform strictly to the content and order of the original scripture; forced into rhyme and meter, the resulting poetry was usually awkward in construction and unclear in meaning. During the ensuing centuries there were constant pressures for reform which produced several new English psalters, none of which showed great improvement.

In the middle of the 18th century, the English Methodist evangelist George Whitefield popularized the hymns of the Congregationalist minister Isaac Watts, "the Father of English Hymnody," in his meetings in the American colonies. It is interesting to note that, while the early Separatists in England rejected music completely, their successors on both sides of the Atlantic were responsible for breaking the bondage of psalmody and introducing "human-composed hymns." Calvin had essentially said that "only God's Word was fit to be used in God's praise"; by his actions, Watts indicated his agreement with Luther—that since it was *his* praise, it could be voiced in his own words. Furthermore, he argued, if psalms were used, they should be paraphrased—brought into the New Testament dispensation by the inclusion of Christian truth. It may be said, then, that in hymn singing the dissenters (or evangelicals) were more "liberal" than the Established Church. Baptists, Congregationalists and some Presbyterians quickly picked up the Watts tradition, while Episcopalians (and certain Presbyterians) stuck with the psalms until much later.

The Nineteenth Century.

In the late 18th and early 19th centuries, the hymns of Charles Wesley began to appear, and also those of Wesley's contemporaries—Thomas Olivers, John Cennick, William Williams, Augustus Toplady—as well as the later evangelical Anglicans, John Newton and William Cowper. America's first important hymnist, Timothy Dwight (1752–1817), president of Yale College, published a hymnal in 1800, which included compositions of all the above, plus some of his own hymns, among them a free paraphrase of Psalm 137, "I Love Thy Kingdom, Lord."

In the meantime, other ethnic groups (notably, German) had arrived in this country, bringing with them their own traditions of Moravian, Lutheran and Reformed hymnody. The Moravians preserved their own culture assiduously. However, once they became English-speaking, the others tended more to accept the English hymn traditions than to share their own with their neighbors in the New World. Most groups were influenced by the revivalist tradition of the 19th century, showing great interest in the "spirituals" of the campmeeting tradition and the new "gospel hymnals" that appeared with Finney's "Second Awakening," followed by the Sunday School songbooks of William Bradbury and Thomas Hastings. All of the early hymnal publishing in America was done by individuals, and many books were based on earlier versions (especially collections of Watts' hymns) in Great Britain. Copyright laws were not yet in effect, so that hymns of Watts, Wesley and their successors could legally be "pirated" once they appeared. When they were printed in this country, they were coupled with the campmeeting spirituals and the Sunday school songs, especially in the early compilations of Baptists.

Later in the century, denominational assemblies often adopted a certain privately-produced hymnal as "official" for their fellowship, and by 1850, many groups were editing and publishing their own. With each successive edition, they gradually added the new hymns which were pouring in from Great Britain, and also a number of works by budding hymnists in the New World. Episcopalians, of course, were most influenced by the "Old Country" and they adopted the "Romanticist" hymns of Reginald Heber (Holy, Holy, Holy), James Montgomery (In the Hour of Trial), Henry Hart Milman (Ride On in Majesty), Robert Grant (O Worship the King) and Christopher Wordsworth (O Day of Rest and Gladness), as well as all the fruits of the Oxford Movement—the translations of ancient Greek and Latin texts, as well as the original hymns of John Keble (Sun of My Soul), Henry Francis Lyte (Praise, My Soul, the King of Heaven), Samuel John Stone (The Church's One Foundation), John Samuel Bewley Monsell (Fight the Good Fight), John Henry Newman (Lead, Kindly Light), Frederick Faber (There's a Wideness in God's Mercy) and Matthew Bridges (Crown Him with Many Crowns). They also learned the hymns of American Episcopalian leaders: George Washington Doane (Fling Out the Banner; Let It Float), William Augustus Mühlenberg (Shout the Glad Tidings, Exultingly Sing) and Arthur Cleveland Coxe (O Where Are Kings and Empires Now). The more sophisticated urban churches of other denominations also included much of the same material in their hymnals.

Further away from the Atlantic seaboard, churches in the "evangelical" denominations were much more selective in adding "British" hymnody to their repertoire. A few individual works of the above hymnists were adopted, especially where they suited the theological temperament (e.g., Heber's "From Greenland's Icy Mountains.") Their preference, however, was for the hymns that came from the evangelical writers in the Church of England, or in the Free Churches, especially the Scottish: Charlotte Elliott (Just As I Am), George Croly (Spirit of God, Descend upon My Heart), Edward Bickersteth (Peace, Perfect Peace), Arabella Katherine Hankey (I Love to Tell the Story), Frances Ridley Havergal (Take My Life and Let It Be), Horatius Bonar (I Heard the Voice of Jesus Say), Elizabeth Clephane (Beneath the Cross of Jesus), George

Matheson (O Love That Wilt Not Let Me Go), and Sarah Flower Adams (Nearer, My God, to Thee).

Most American hymn writers during the 19th century would be called "evangelical." In marked contrast to their British contemporaries, they were not exceedingly prolific, and though their works were quickly accepted in this country and appeared in most hymnals, they are generally remembered for one significant hymn. American writers of "standard hymns" include Ray Palmer (My Faith Looks Up to Thee), Samuel Francis Smith (The Morning Light Is Breaking and My Country, 'Tis of Thee), Joseph Scriven (What a Friend We Have in Jesus), Elizabeth P. Prentiss (More Love to Thee, O Christ), George Duffield, Jr. (Stand Up for Jesus), John Henry Gilmore (He Leadeth Me), Edward Hopper (Jesus Savior, Pilot Me), Annie S. Hawks (I Need Thee Every Hour), Mary A. Lathbury (Break Thou the Bread of Life) and Jeremiah Eames Rankin (God Be With You Till We Meet Again).

To be sure, "liberal" hymns were written in those days, both in America and in England. Early in the 19th century, some of America's best-known authors wrote "theistic, humanitarian" poems which were later used as hymns—William Cullen Bryant[5] (Look from Thy Sphere of Endless Day), James Russell Lowell (Once to Every Man and Nation), Henry Wadsworth Longfellow (I Heard the Bells on Christmas Day), Oliver Wendell Holmes (Lord of All Being, Throned Afar), and Samuel Longfellow (Holy Spirit, Truth Divine). In general this group was liberal theologically; some of them were Unitarians, some "transcendentalists," and others "free thinkers." Their poetic "burdens" were the evils of their day—slavery, intemperance, and war. Their works were suited to the needs of the New England Unitarians, and they were generally added to other hymnals long after their writing. Those which have endured have been used by evangelicals in recent years, sometimes with a little "theological" laundering by slight revision of the text.

In a separate category we must mention John Greenleaf Whittier, whom Albert E. Bailey calls the "poet laureate of American hymnists"[6] on the basis of the high quality of his relatively-few hymns, and their universal appeal—to evangelicals as well as to Unitarians. Whittier, a Quaker, is remembered for O Brother Man! Fold to Thy Heart Thy Brother; Immortal Love, Forever Full; Dear Lord and Father of Mankind; and All Things Are Thine: No Gift Have We.

Later in the 19th century, the advent of "liberal theology" and the "social gospel" was accompanied by "suitable" hymns by both British and American writers. On the other side of the Atlantic, the "Broad Church" poets of the Church of England included Alfred Lord Tennyson (Ring Out the Old, Ring in the New), William Walsham How (O Word of God Incarnate), John Ellerton (God the Omnipotent! King Who Ordainest),

---

5. It must be mentioned that, late in life, after his wife's critical illness, Bryant confessed his faith in Christ and was baptized. After that, he revised some of his earlier hymns so that they conformed to evangelical doctrine.
6. Bailey, op. cit., p. 534.

and John Ernest Bode (O Jesus, I Have Promised). American "social gospel" hymnists also tended to reflect their concerns in their hymns: Ernest Warburton Shurtleff (Lead On, O King Eternal), Maltbie D. Babcock (This Is My Father's World), Henry Van Dyke (Joyful, Joyful, We Adore Thee), Washington Gladden (O Master, Let Me Walk With Thee), and Katherine Lee Bates (O Beautiful for Spacious Skies). These new hymns were generally accepted in the traditional denominations; this was possible, even when the church was strongly "evangelical" because they do not actually express anti-evangelical theology. Where they were condemned, it was more for what they "did *not* say" than for what they contained. It is interesting to note that, now that these particular individuals have ceased to be identified as theological "enemies," and especially since evangelicals are now generally agreed on the "social implications of the gospel," their hymns are at home in most evangelical (even fundamentalist) books.[7]

The Gospel Song Phenomenon.

Throughout the 19th century, the overwhelming majority of evangelical churchgoers were preoccupied with the popular hymnody which evolved from the campmeeting improvisations and the earlier "spirituals" that were sung to Anglo-American secular folk melodies. Typical examples first appeared in the 1840's as Sunday School songs, and they provided inspiration for that new, lay-centered Christian education movement. Because they were fully as popular with grownups as they were with children, the same style of music was used with somewhat more "adult" texts in what came to be known as "gospel hymns" or "gospel songs." It is difficult to overestimate the grip these simple experience songs, written by theological and musical amateurs, had on the general public. Millions of small, paperback books were sold for use in Sunday schools, "revival meetings," prayer services, "conventions" and home gatherings.

In the tradition of all earlier hymnbook production, gospel songs were published by individuals, not by church organizations. Eventually, some publishers developed large companies, each with its own "stable" of authors and composers. In this connection, it should be remembered that with the new hymn styles there emerged a new relationship of text and tune. In the British tradition, words and melodies were traditionally unrelated. A hymn writer was strictly a lyricist who wrote poems that

---

7. It is only fair to point out that, in some instances, we have failed to discriminate adequately. Some "social" hymns (e.g., We've a Story to Tell to the Nations, It Came upon the Midnight Clear) are obviously based on the post-millenial doctrine that the church will "bring in the Kingdom of God by the proclamation of the gospel," a theological position which is almost universally rejected nowadays. It may be argued that, on the principle of poetic license, you can ascribe a different meaning to the words of the Christmas hymn by the Unitarian minister Edmund Sears. But that kind of semantic "sleight of hand" will scarcely help the refrain of H. Ernest Nichols' missionary challenge!

were usually published first in collections, without music. The composer worked separately as well; he wrote tunes in the standard hymnic meters and, through the 18th century, they were also published separately. Consequently, in typical Anglo-American practice, any text could be, and usually was, sung to several different melodies. The "gospel song" tradition was quite different in that a text and a tune were (until very recently) forever wedded. Frequently the tune came first, and an author was commissioned to write words for it. It is from this practice that gospel songs were considered to be a unit of words and music, and had a separate "title" (e.g., Marching to Zion); in the earlier psalm and hymn tradition, the poem would be known by its first line (e.g., Come, we who love the Lord), and the tune would have a name of its own (e.g., ST. THOMAS).

Following is a list of the leading gospel song publishers of the 19th century, and the most prominent authors/composers associated with them.[8] The very first was William B. Bradbury (1816–1868), an associate of the renowned Lowell Mason, "father of American music education." Bradbury engaged Fanny Jane Crosby (1820–1915), the most prolific and successful of the writers, who produced possibly 9,000 poems, the majority of which were set to music. It is interesting to note that during the last five years, more than sixty years after her death, three new books have appeared that tell of the life and work of Fanny Crosby, the blind "Protestant saint"![9] In 1866, shortly before his death, Bradbury sold his business to The Biglow & Main Company of New York and Chicago. Along with the physical properties, Biglow & Main secured the continued services of Mrs. Crosby, and became the largest publisher of gospel songs in the 19th century.

 Biglow & Main Company, New York and Chicago
  Poets:
   Wm. J. Bradbury (Savior, Like a Shepherd Lead Us)
   Fanny J. Crosby (Rescue the Perishing)
   Philip P. Bliss (I Will Sing of My Redeemer)
   Daniel W. Whittle (Showers of Blessing)
   Anna Bartlett Warner (We Would See Jesus)
   Wm. O. Cushing (Under His Wings)
   Annie S. Hawks (I Need Thee Every Hour)
   Elizabeth P. Prentiss (More Love to Thee, O Christ)
   Lydia Baxter (Take the Name of Jesus with You)
   Robert Lowry (Low in the Grave He Lay)
  Musicians: (a number of the above wrote music also)
   Wm. Howard Doane
   James McGranahan
   George C. Stebbins

8. For an overview of one of the oldest traditions in gospel music publishing, see "The History of Hope Publishing Company and its Divisions and Affiliates," by George H. Shorney, pp. 1–21 in my *Dictionary-Handbook to Hymns for the Living Church*.
9. Bernard Ruffin, *Fanny Crosby;* John Loveland, *Blessed Assurance: the Life and Hymns of Fanny J. Crosby;* and Donald Hustad, ed., *Fanny Crosby Speaks Again*.

Ira D. Sankey
Chester G. Allen
Wm. F. Sherwin
Phoebe Palmer Knapp
Adoniram J. Gordon

John J. Hood Company, Philadelphia
Poets:
Eliza E. Hewitt (More About Jesus)
Lelia N. Morris (Let Jesus Come into Your Heart)
Musicians:
William J. Kirkpatrick
John R. Sweney
Henry L. Gilmour

John Church Company, Cincinnati
George Frederick Root (after 1871)

A large number of smaller companies also flourished, most of which concentrated on publishing the music of their owners, plus that of one or more lesser-known writers. Some of these publishers supported certain theological positions (e.g., that of the "holiness" groups within "Wesleyan" circles), or emphasized regional cultural preferences (e.g., the South). A few specialized in "custom" publishing.

A. J. Showalter Music Co., Chattanooga, Tennessee
James D. Vaughan Music Co., Lawrenceburg, Tennessee
Ruebush-Kieffer Music Co., Dalton, Georgia
Peter P. Bilhorn Company, Chicago, Illinois
Fillmore Bros. Music House, Cincinnati, Ohio
Adam Geibel Publishing Company, Philadelphia, Pennsylvania
Edwin O. Excell Company, Chicago, Illinois
Will L. Thompson and Co., East Liverpool, Ohio
Ralph E. Hudson Publishing Co., Alliance, Ohio

As we mentioned in chapters eight and nine, gospel songs were popularized in the waves of revivalism which swept America during the 19th century, notably in the meetings conducted by Moody and Sankey. They remained in the life of the community and especially of its churches, in books that were frequently placed in the pews alongside the larger denominational hymnal, and used in Sunday evening services, prayer meetings, and Sunday school gatherings. They were also integral to the activities of the permanent conferences which flourished during summer months as a perpetuation of the campmeeting tradition— including the Lake Chautauqua Assembly in New York, the Ocean Grove Campmeeting in New Jersey, and the Winona Lake Conference in Indiana. The tendency of many evangelicals who supported these revivalist and devotional activities was to limit their hymnic growth to this subjective material, while continuing to use the basic resources of

18th century English writers (Watts, Wesley, Olivers, Newton, Cowper), plus the devotional hymns of American writers and a few 19th century British hymns. Without denying the gospel song's contribution to evangelical worship, it must be apparent that many congregations suffered from an imbalance of the "objective" and "subjective" in Christian song, that persists in some quarters to the present day.

The Twentieth Century—the Total American Church.

In comparison with the productivity of traditional hymnists in the 18th and 19th centuries, the 20th century has to be seen as a comparatively "sterile" period. True, there were a few important contributors in both England and America but most of their emphasis was on the social aspects of the gospel. The outstanding preoccupation of mainline denominations in America had to do with (1) recovering their own unique heritage in hymnody (as demonstrated in the *Hymnal 1940* (Episcopal) and the *Lutheran Hymnal* (Concordia), 1941; and (2) expanding their hymnsinging resources along ecumenical lines, by adding the historic contributions of all Christian groups. As a result, most traditional denominational hymnals include representative examples of the following:

Greek hymns (through the 6th century)
Latin hymns (from the 4th century through the 19th)
German hymns (especially from the 16th to the 18th centuries)
Psalms (selected examples from the French, English and Scottish
    traditions)
British hymns of all periods (now including examples from the 17th
    century, originally written as a private devotional exercise)
American hymns (now including a large number of folk hymns from
    the 18th century, or earlier, and Moravian hymns)
Scandinavian hymns (from the Lutheran and the pietist traditions)
Some hymns from "foreign" sources (African, Oriental)

Interest in writing poetry has obviously diminished among English-speaking ministers and theologians. A number of individuals in Europe and America have written some material, but only a few are widely recognized as significant hymnists.

Frank Mason North (Where Cross the Crowded Ways of Life)
William Pierson Merrill (Rise Up, O Men of God)
Laura S. Copenhaver (Heralds of Christ)
Harry Emerson Fosdick (God of Grace and God of Glory)
Georgia Harkness (Hope of the World)
Ernest K. Emurian (We Thank Thee That Thy Mandate)
John Oxenham (In Christ There Is No East or West)
Albert Frederick Bayly (Lord, Whose Love through Humble Service)
Frederick Pratt Green (Rejoice with Us in God the Trinity)
Fred Kaan (Sing We of the Modern City)

The Twentieth Century—the Evangelical Scene.

Interest in the gospel song continued strong through the first two decades of this century, spurred largely by the evangelism crusades of Reuben A. Torrey, Wilbur M. Chapman and "Billy" Sunday, and their principal musicians, Charles M. Alexander, Robert Harkness, Homer Rodeheaver and B. D. Ackley. Both Alexander and Rodeheaver were active in publishing, and they were responsible for most of the new materials that were produced. By contrast, the Hope Publishing Company tended to bring together in their books the large body of gospel songs that had already become popular. These then were the leading independent publishers in the early part of the century:

> Hope Publishing Company, Chicago, Illinois (Eventually acquired the resources of the Biglow & Main Co., the Will Thompson Music Co., the E. O. Excell Co., and the Tabernacle Publishing Co.)
> James M. Black (When the Roll Is Called Up Yonder)
> Elisha A. Hoffman (Leaning on the Everlasting Arms)
> Mrs. C. H. Morris (Let Jesus Come into Your Heart)
> Wm. J. Kirkpatrick (music)
> Daniel B. Towner (music)
> Elton M. Roth (In My Heart There Rings a Melody)
> Henry Barraclough (Ivory Palaces)
> Wm. M. Runyan (Lord, I Have Shut the Door)

> Rodeheaver Hall-Mack Company, Winona Lake, Indiana
> Alfred H. Ackley (He Lives)
> George Bennard (The Old Rugged Cross)
> Charles H. Gabriel (He Lifted Me)
> C. Austin Miles (In the Garden)
> Oswald J. Smith (There Is Joy in Serving Jesus)
> Bentley D. Ackley (music)
> Homer Rodeheaver (music)

> Tabernacle Publishing Company, Chicago, Illinois
> Mabel Johnston Camp (He Is Coming Again)
> Avis M. Christiansen (Jesus Has Lifted Me)
> Harry D. Loes (All That I Want Is in Jesus)
> Haldor Lillenas (Wonderful Grace of Jesus)
> Paul Rader (Old Time Power)

> Charles M. Alexander, publisher in England, distributed in America by Hope Publishing Company
> J. Wilbur Chapman (Our Great Savior)
> Charles H. Gabriel (O That Will Be Glory)
> Robert Harkness (music)
> Charles M. Marsh (music)

As in the previous century, a number of writers created small publishing operations for the release of their own music, among them Grant C. Tullar (Tullar-Meredith Co.), Harry D. Clarke, Wendell P. Loveless

("Radio Songs and Choruses") and Merrill E. Dunlop ("Songs of a Christian"). Eventually their copyright holdings were controlled by larger companies. Some of these author-publishers developed sizeable businesses by including the works of other writers.

Robert Coleman Publishing Company
    B. B. McKinney (Wherever He Leads I'll Go)
    J. P. Schofield (Saved, Saved)
    L. B. Bridgers (He Keeps Me Singing)

Lillenas Publishing Company
    Haldor Lillenas (Wonderful, Wonderful, Jesus Is to Me)
    N. B. Vandall (My Home, Sweet Home)

Singspiration Company, Wheaton, Ill. (later Grand Rapids, Mich.)
    Alfred B. Smith (For God So Loved the World)
    John W. Peterson (Jesus Is Coming Again)

In the period from 1920 to 1950 (roughly between the end of Billy Sunday's important campaigns and the beginning of Billy Graham's), very little new congregational music was created by evangelicals. Evangelism moved to radio in those days, and musical interest turned to "specials"—solos, duets, trios, quartets, etc. The only exception to this "pause in creativity" occurred in the "Youth for Christ" movement of the 1940's, when interest in gospel choruses resulted in another flood of diminutive books filled with diminutive songs. It is interesting to note that the first new songs of John W. Peterson (and even of Bill and Gloria Gaither) were planned as specials; once they became popular, they began to be sung by the whole church, along with the best examples of the "lost generation" previously mentioned, which were first available in *Inspiring Hymns* (Singspiration, 1951) and *Tabernacle Hymns No. 5* (Hope, 1953).

Evangelicals also produced a number of "serious" hymnwriters during the 20th century, among them Thomas O. Chisholm (Great Is Thy Faithfulness), Joseph C. Macaulay (We Sing the Boundless Praise), Bryan Jeffery Leech (Let God Be God) and E. Margaret Clarkson (We Come, O Christ, to Thee), of Canadian heritage.

Publishing and Hymn Singing.

The 20th century witnessed the development of a number of new evangelical movements in the United States, many of them created by schism in major denominations over theological issues. When they left the parent body, they rejected all of its literature, including hymnals; all that was left for them to use in singing was the small, gospel song book which was never intended to provide all the singing materials. To meet this challenge, independent publishers tended to develop larger collections of gospel songs, and included with them a fair number of older, standard hymns. One of the first was *Gospel Hymns, 1-6 Combined* (Biglow

& Main), which was created by bringing together all the contents of the famous series edited by Ira D. Sankey and his associates; it was followed by the *Pentecostal Hymns* series and *Hymns of Praise 1 and 2, Combined* (Hope), the *Tabernacle Hymns* series (first by Tabernacle, later by Hope), and *Church Service Hymns* (Rodeheaver). Each of these books included the basic "standard hymns" which had been used by American evangelicals since the early 19th century, plus old and new gospel hymns. They were used by the new schismatic fellowships and by certain historic denominations which for one reason or another did not publish their own books (e.g., Cumberland Presbyterians and Southern Baptists). They were also selected by "more evangelical" churches within other major denominations who were dissatisfied with their group's major hymnal, because it contained few gospel hymns.

Evangelicals frequently tend to adopt new concepts and practices a generation or more after they appear in mainline churches. This was true of the emphasis on Christian education, and also in the matter of "eclectic hymn singing." Beginning with *The Service Hymnal* (Hope, 1935) and continuing with *Worship and Service Hymnal* (Hope, 1957) and *Great Hymns of Our Faith* (Singspiration, 1968), *Baptist Hymnal* 1956 and 1975, *Hymns of the Living Church* (Hope, 1974) and *Hymns for the Family of God* (Paragon, 1976), the interdenominational hymnals featured an increasing number of historic hymns. A notable addition unique to evangelicals was a group of pietist worship hymns of the English Keswick[10] tradition, which were first popularized by the InterVarsity Christian Fellowship (including Like a River Glorious, No Other Plea, Facing a Task Unfinished, O Breath of Life and Speak, Lord, in the Stillness); they have now been accepted by many groups.

Of course, not all evangelical hymnals have achieved so good a balance of objective vs. subjective hymnody. And not all the churches who have the stronger books are using their contents; in many instances, they purchase a new hymnal for the contemporary gospel/folk material it contains, but ignore the available resources of a larger selection of worship hymns. As a result, American evangelicals often exhibit a considerable gap between the materials they sing and the theology of their preaching. We confess to believe in a transcendent God who is above all His creation, yet sing few hymns which reveal Him in his excellencies. We insist on the "strong meat" of biblical theology in our preaching, but seem to be satisfied with "milk" or even lollipops in our hymns!

The Late Twentieth Century.

What then is the material used in hymn singing among evangelicals today? As in many aspects of this book's investigation, that is a difficult

10. The Keswick Convention is an inter-church conference which emphasizes Christian discipleship and the "deeper life," and meets each summer in the village of Keswick in the lake country of north England. Similar "Keswicks" have been held in many parts of the world.

question to answer, because there is much variation between different groups. A few (e.g., Mennonites) have sustained a strong ethnic heritage; others (in the South) sing completely from the shape-note Stamps-Baxter tradition. Some are still singing principally Sankey-Alexander-Rodeheaver-Hope gospel songs; still others have added the newer gospel songs of John Peterson and of Bill and Gloria Gaither, with some from their own denominational composers (e.g., B. B. McKinney and Wm. J. Reynolds for Southern Baptists). A few churches also sing a broad spectrum of standard historic hymns, particularly in the Sunday morning service. But for many evangelical groups, we suggest that "serious hymn" singing is little more than "tokenism" based on the convictions: (1) we must sing at least one worship hymn, and (2) it must be something that everybody knows, so it will go well! As a result, many congregations repeat the same ten, or fifteen, or twenty hymns over and over, Sunday after Sunday. From my observation of many different churches, I suggest the following titles as typical, listed roughly in the order of broad preference.

1. All Hail the Power of Jesus' Name
2. Come, Thou Almighty King
3. Holy, Holy, Holy
4. O for a Thousand Tongues to Sing
5. Love Divine, All Loves Excelling
6. O Worship the King
7. Crown Him with Many Crowns
8. Faith of Our Fathers
9. O God, Our Help in Ages Past
10. Come, Thou Fount of Every Blessing
11. Praise to the Lord, the Almighty
12. Guide Me, O Thou Great Jehovah
13. The Church's One Foundation
14. For the Beauty of the Earth
15. Praise, My Soul, the King of Heaven
16. Majestic Sweetness Sits Enthroned
17. Ye Servants of God, Your Master Proclaim
18. Rejoice, Ye Pure in Heart
19. All Creatures of Our God and King
20. Fairest Lord Jesus

It should be obvious that many evangelical churches use less than fifty percent of their hymnbook's contents, especially those whose "opening hymn" repertoire includes only one-half of the above list.

One musical phenomenon is characteristic of all evangelicals, except perhaps the most conservative. Beginning about 1965, as part of the continent-wide "renewal in communication" (new scripture versions, new language in prayer and preaching, new symbolism, multi-media), we saw a burgeoning of new music (new texts, new tunes, new rhythms) from many sources. Once evangelicals got past their frustration because "liberals and liturgical groups had stolen our traditional thunder," we too joined. The "new sounds" began to flood the market in all forms—musicals for choirs of all ages, books and octavos for soloists and ensembles, recordings to popularize them, and "tape tracks" to accompany them. In the mid-1960's Bill and Gloria Gaither appeared on the scene, popularizing their new version of the gospel song in public concerts, whereupon they were immediately accepted in many churches. Other composers wrote in more contemporary musical styles—Ralph Carmichael, Kurt Kaiser, Paul Johnson, Jimmy Owens, Andraé Crouch, Otis Skillings, Ken Medema, and many more.

The new music soon began to appear in another crop of paperback songbooks, planned for congregational singing, beginning with *A Time to Sing* (Hope, 1967) which John Wilson and I compiled for use at the InterVarsity triennial missionary convention for students, held at the University of Illinois at Urbana in late 1966. In the succeeding years, an almost endless supply of these books has continued to flow from every gospel music publisher, with such titles as "Reasons to Sing," "Sing 'n Celebrate!" "Folk Encounter," "Discovery in Song," "Folk Hymnal for the Now Generation," "A New Now," "Hymnal for Contemporary Christians," and "Dove Hymnal." One notable distinction from earlier paperbacks was evident when the material appeared in two sizes—a diminutive "pocket book" for singers and a larger copy for the accompanist. The music was first called "gospel folk," because some of it incorporated the harmonic and melodic styles common to both historic Anglo-American religious folk tunes (e.g., Poor Wayfaring Stranger and Wondrous Love) and the new secular "folk" style of the 1960's (with modal harmonies and guitar accompaniment) as popularized by groups like "Peter, Paul and Mary."

In subsequent editions the styles have multiplied. Some of the selections were borrowed from "musicals" or from earlier solo/ensemble pieces, and some was written specifically for congregational use. Some are extended in form, and some are as short as the earlier choruses. Some of it was obviously composed with great care, and some seems almost to have been improvised. In the latter category, we must mention a broad segment of "unsophisticated worship music" which may be described as a "repeated chorus with variations." Perhaps the best known is "Alleluia," and others include "God Is So Good," "Kum Ba Ya," "Peace Like a River," "I'm Gonna Sing when the Spirit Says Sing," "Glory Be to God on High," "Sweeten Me, Lord," and "Jesus in the Morning." It is apparent that this new emphasis is one of the strongest positive contributions of the movement. Earlier gospel songs and choruses were usually preoccupied with human experiences in faith. Many of today's texts are praise and adoration, and that's a plus, even though all of them are more simple than sublime. Another commendable feature of the new movement has been the recent preoccupation with scripture texts set to music. Both these trends should be applauded and must largely be credited to the work of charismatic groups in America, Great Britain and Australia.

Gospel/Folk Hymnody—Strengths and Weaknesses.

In chapter eight we listed the strengths of experience hymns in sustaining the faith of the evangelical community. Believing as we do in personal Christian experience, in a "know so, say so" faith (the assurance of the believer and our responsibility to give Christian witness to it), and in a consciousness of God's presence in everyday life, it should be expected that all this truth will find expression in song. At the same time, we must face honestly the criticisms which have been leveled at this hymnic heritage. Gospel songs have been around long enough to get the serious attention of some hymnologists, and a few have considered it necessary to "debunk" them.

It should be apparent that the new "folk pop" hymns are simply "up to date" successors of the gospel song, with many of the same textual concepts set to contemporary, popular music styles. This pop hymnody is obviously still in a state of flux, and it is not yet certain that any of it is going to remain long in the life of the church. Even though it has not been given the same careful scrutiny as its 19th century predecessors, no doubt it would be condemned with the same arguments.

1. "They are too personal in expression, too selfish." (e.g., "I belong to the King," "I know whom I have believed," "He touched me," "I'd rather have Jesus"). It should be pointed out that some gospel songs do use the first person plural—"Marvelous message we bring," "Dark was the night; sin warred against us," "Showers of blessing we need," "O Lord Jesus, how long ere we shout the glad song"—although they are a minority.

It is true that most worship hymns are expressed in the corporate "we," "us," and "our"—"Our song shall rise to Thee," "Help us Thy name to sing," "Lift up your voice and with us sing," "Joyful, joyful we adore Thee"; but not all—"My heart awaking cries," "Breathe on me, Breath of God," "Thee will I cherish, Thee will I honor," "O my soul, praise Him, for He is your health and salvation." The same forms are found in the Old Testament psalms, but with a preference for the *singular:* "The Lord is my shepherd" (23), "I will give thanks to the Lord with my whole heart" (9), "In thee, O Lord, do I take refuge" (71), "O come, let us sing to the Lord" (95), "It is he that made us, and we are his" (100), "Bless the Lord, O my soul" (103), "God is our refuge and strength" (46), and "Have mercy on me, O God, according to thy steadfast love" (51).

The accusation of self-centeredness seems rather weak on the basis of the scriptural example, and the proposition that personal salvation is a singular experience—God works with each person individually! So long as it is balanced by corporate expressions, and experienced personally in *corporate* gatherings, this type of song may well be in the singular, either first person or third.

2. "Some gospel/folk songs are not theologically sound."

"Pass me not, O gentle Savior, Hear my humble cry;
While on others Thou art calling, Do not pass me by."
F. J. Crosby, 1876

It is hard to believe that even the most dedicated Calvinist would argue that God could ignore the sinner who calls on Him "in deep contrition." This seems to be the anguished cry of one who has not yet come to faith—"Help my unbelief" (stanza 2). It may not be a strong hymn to use in public response to the gospel, because it is very, very personal. On the other hand, some of our contemporaries have suggested that worship should give opportunity for us to honestly express our doubts and even our anger toward God. Under that umbrella—and I'm not sure about the matter myself!—maybe it does have validity. A similar, but more serious, problem arises with the Carl Mueller anthem setting of "Create in Me a Clean Heart" taken from Psalm 51, which contains the words "Take not thy Holy Spirit from me." Evangelicals believe that the Holy Spirit has been resident in the Church (and in each believer) since the Day of Pentecost, and will remain "to the end"; yet this anthem is regularly sung and enjoyed in a large number of our churches.

> If Jesus goes with me, I'll go anywhere!
>   'Tis heaven to me, where'er I may be, if He is there!
> I count it a privilege here His cross to bear;
>   If Jesus goes with me, I'll go anywhere!
>
> C. A. Miles, 1908

In this instance, it may be argued that the reader must allow room for poetic license! Nowhere in the hymn does C. Austin Miles suggest the possibility that the Christian is asked to serve God without the sustaining presence of his heavenly Father. The true meaning (and everybody recognizes it, except the nitpickers) is "Since Jesus goes with me, I'll go anywhere!"

> If your heart keeps right, if your heart keeps right,
>   There's a song of gladness in the darkest night;
> If your heart keeps right, if your heart keeps right,
>   Every cloud will wear a rainbow, if your heart keeps right.
>
> L. DeArmond, 1912

> It will be worth it all when we see Jesus,
>   Life's trials will seem so small when we see Christ;
> One glimpse of His dear face all sorrow will erase,
>   So bravely run the race till we see Christ.
>
> E. K. Rusthoi, 1941

Probably most evangelical musicians categorize certain popular gospel songs as "unworthy," and I may reveal my own prejudices here. It seems to me that these examples express two contrasting excesses in expression. The first was Homer Rodeheaver's theme song during his songleading ministry in the 1920's with evangelist Billy Sunday. It expresses a "romanticism of optimism" that is not quite realistic. The second is a product of the affluent mid-20th century, when evangelicals were prospering numerically and financially; despite the optimism of the chorus quoted above, the stanzas (abetted by the tune) fairly reek of "feeling sorry for one's self." It is a "romanticism of pessimism." Again, it may be argued that as *personal* expressions of experience, "anything goes"; but that standard is not adequate when we choose music for corporate use. Personally, I can make a stronger case for the "overly optimistic" song than I can for the "pessimistic-optimistic." For the gospel is basically a romance—the greatest "fairy tale"[11] ever told—because it is true, and it does have a happy ending!

It seems to me that evangelicals have sinned most in the self-pity expressed in our "comfort songs." We might better learn and use the "cross and comfort" hymns of the early 17th century German writers, which expressed faith in a provident God at a time when living conditions were so difficult that death was seen as welcome release!

> If you but trust in God to guide you
>   And place your confidence in him,
> You'll find him always there beside you,
>   To give you hope and strength within.
> For those who trust God's changeless love
>   Build on the rock that will not move.
>
> What gain is there in futile weeping,
>   In helpless anger and distress?
> If you are in his care and keeping,
>   In sorrow will he love you less?
> For he who took for you a cross
>   Will bring you safe through every loss.
>   Georg Neumark, 1641. Trans., composite.

3. "They are sentimental." I have defined sentimentalism as "superficial emotion that is not based on full reality." The "nonreality" may be inherent in the song, or in its performance, or both.

It has been said that the 19th century, American frontier culture was one of the most sentimental the world has ever known. It should not be surprising that its gospel song composers, writing of human experience, produced some sentimental favorites, like "The Church in the Wildwood," "Just Before the Battle, Mother," "Beautiful Isle of Somewhere," and "Whispering Hope." During that "gospel song" era, these examples and others could be found in the paperback collections, along with "rally songs" for Sunday School, and Prohibition songs. They are seldom included in modern compilations, and even when they

---

11. On the basis of the *Random House Dictionary* (1966) definition: "An incredible . . . statement, account or belief."

are, they are rarely sung. In any period of "revivalist creativity," including the present one, a great deal of musical chaff is produced, along with a little "wheat." It seems that we must finally depend on the passing of time to do the necessary winnowing. Comparing the Sankey books of the 1870's with today's evangelical hymnals, it is evident that this has happened, though admittedly a little straw may still slip through!

It is one of my basic premises that only those within a culture are qualified to evaluate it. For that reason, this volume does not investigate the music practices of the most conservative evangelical sects. In the same spirit, I expect to be selective in accepting the criticisms of typical evangelical hymnody by those who reject our basic theology, or our understanding of human religious experience. I am personally very grateful to Erik Routley for the brilliant insights he has given on hymnody, as well as for his personal kindness in offering suggestions concerning some hymnic research I did in England in the 1960's. However, his advice will not always be helpful to evangelicals in the editing of hymnals.

> The question that must arise is whether it is wise often, or ever, to sing of God as somebody to whom one flies for refuge in life's dangers. (The reference is to "Rock of Ages" and "Jesus, Lover of My Soul.")[12]

> It may well be said that many sincere believers entertain serious doubts about the historical facts of the resurrection, the kind of facts which we are invited to accept as true in such hymns as "O sons and daughters," "Christians, to the Paschal victim," and certain lines of Charles Wesley's "Christ the Lord is risen today" . . . Easter is not only the season when we recall (if it be right to recall) the historic events. It is much more the season when our minds are directed by the church to the *principle* of resurrection, which is something much more fundamental.[13]

> . . . We must watch out for uses of such words as "Lamb" and "blood" and "sacrifice" in a manner that will encourage people to think sentimentally . . . The fact is that "Lamb" and "blood" and "sacrifice" can really be tolerated only when they are "dead metaphors." . . .
> > His blood can make the foulest clean,
> > His blood availed for me (Charles Wesley)
> may be just tolerable . . . but
> > There is a fountain filled with blood
> > Drawn from Emmanuel's veins (Wm. Cowper)
> is itself beyond the reach of any imagination now, except as a repulsive image.[14]

No doubt Routley is well qualified to establish hymnic criteria for certain church leaders, although, on the evidence that congregations are

12. Routley, op. cit., p. 31.
.13. Ibid., p. 58.
14. Ibid., p. 63.

more conservative than their ministers, I can guess that some of his suggestions would not be received with enthusiasm. It is up to evangelicals to establish the standards for "acceptable hymns" in their own circles. We need to do our own "demythologizing" of both gospel songs and standard worship hymns.

There are many of Routley's arguments in which evangelicals can concur. He is absolutely right when he contends that "there is no single influence in public worship that can so surely condition a congregation to self-deception, to fugitive follies, to religious perversities, as thoughtlessly chosen hymns."[15] We can also agree (1) that in a universal Christian church there is no excuse for hymns that speak of "snow" in connection with Christ's birth;[16] (2) that children's hymns have well left the "fear psychosis" of the 18th century and the "pedagogical preoccupation" of the 19th[17] ("Children are human beings and should be treated as such . . . with hymns embodying images and characters agreeable to the child's outlook . . ."; and (3) that we should have hymns which picture the Holy Spirit as the "rush of a mighty wind" and "tongues as of fire" as well as the more peaceful images of a dove or the "breath of God."[18]

Standards for Hymn Choices.

Evangelicals should evaluate their hymn-singing practices, using the following guidelines:

(1) Choose the best texts available in both worship hymns and experience songs. There are plenty to choose from. Skip the "possible" in favor of the best—true to our best biblical, theological and poetic heritage, challenging us to mature discipleship, and witnessing to our Christian experience. I have already suggested an alternative to traditional "comfort" hymns. We should be warned against the vaguely-religious song that is not a clear presentation of salvation truth. From my childhood, I remember the favorite solo "It's Real" (H. L. Cox), which talks about an "authentic" spiritual experience for four extended stanzas and a refrain, and scarcely mentions the basis of our faith or the name of Jesus Christ. A more modern ballad by Stuart Hamblen proclaims "It is no secret what God can do," but nowhere in the song is the secret revealed!

Writers of "pop hymnody" always need to guard against the temptation to be extreme in their expression of anthropomorphism—ascribing human attributes to God. It is true that we often fail to acknowledge (or even to believe) that Jesus Christ was fully human. But this is not remedied by the occasional irreverent musical expression which reduces him to a peer mortal, something less than the God/Man which he is.

15. Ibid., p. 22.
16. Ibid., p. 73.
17. Ibid., pp. 77–87.
18. Ibid., pp. 32–35.

From the past, we remember such blasphemous titles as "My Jesus Is a Livin' Doll." Today's lapses may be few because the preoccupation of much new music has been with "worship" more than with experience, but "Heavenly Father, We Appreciate You" does seem to fall short of the ideal. Human beings are tempted to hold two contrasting idolatrous attitudes. We may conceive of God as so transcendent—so far removed from our life experiences—that he has no claim on our actions "in the daily round"; or we may make of him the immanent Buddy-Buddy, imagining that we can somehow manipulate him according to our desires. While others may be guilty of the first sin, evangelicals may have a corner on the second!

(2) Use a song/hymn for its precise meaning. Admittedly, there are a number of hymns which can be interpreted in different ways. Charles Wesley's "Love Divine, All Loves Excelling" is a treatise on the Wesleyan doctrine of sanctification as a second, crisis-experience, "work of grace"; non-Wesleyans and many contemporary Methodists obviously find other meaning in it. However, other hymns have specific meanings which are obviously misunderstood. "Break Thou the Bread of Life" has no relevance to a service of communion; the author is talking about God's Word, the Bread of Life. Again, "Nearer, My God to Thee" and "Safe in the Arms of Jesus" are not really appropriate for funerals; the first speaks of the believer's close relationship with God *in life,* and the second teaches the "security of the believer" in Christ.

(3) Avoid practices which contribute to sentimental singing, especially the overuse of "favorite songs." This is a common practice, which has recently been demonstrated by the establishing of a "gospel hit parade" on certain radio stations! Perhaps the strongest negative contribution of the gospel song tradition stems from our temptation to make "classics" of these ephemeral expressions. They were originally published in paperbacks with the expectation that they would be shortlived; the publisher planned to return the following year to sell the newest batch! However, evangelicals tended to canonize them for all time, and in addition, allowed them to crowd out vital expressions of "standard worship and doctrinal hymnody." The problem is that, by and large they are too "light"—both as poetry and as theology—to survive that amount of repetition and still remain meaningful. Sentimental familiarity breeds intellectual contempt!

Erik Routley also reminds us that for at least ninety percent of worshiping singers "the pleasure of singing hymns is bound up with their music."[19] This is certainly true for gospel hymns, and also for the new folk-pop forms. When the words are considered to be unimportant, hymn singing will inevitably be a sentimental exercise.[20] In the last part of this chapter I will suggest how this may be avoided.

19. Ibid., p. 17.
20. Someone recently told the story of a service where favorite hymns were being requested and sung. One person called for a certain selection, and the leader said, "Fine! Let's sing it to a new tune." "No!" the individual objected; "I want the familiar tune."

Making Hymn Singing Exciting

When we read that Evelyn Underhill once said, as quoted earlier in this chapter, that "transcendence in free church worship" is most evident in the glory of their hymn singing, we may guess that she was comparing our evangelical tradition to her own Anglican heritage, or that hymn-singing has declined in more recent times. In the evangelistic crusades early in this century, the "song service" frequently lasted thirty to sixty minutes before the preaching began. This spirit carried over into the churches which supported the renewal movement, and that's the kind of full-throated, full-hearted singing I remember from my youth. Nowadays, by comparison, much congregational singing in evangelical churches is dull and lifeless, and probably much more is meaningless to the participants.

I am often tempted to believe that in recent years evangelicals have sold their birthright of believer-priest singing for the pleasure of spectatorist music, performed by choir, ensemble or soloist. It seems that people would rather be sung to, than to sing for themselves. Many church musicians have the same improper sense of values; they would rather lead choirs than congregations, and so, they do little to make hymn singing exciting. It all begins with attitude. If ministers of music really believe (1) that congregational singing is the most important, the only indispensable church music, and (2) that people should sing with enjoyment and with understanding, then they will use their imaginations and bend their energies toward achieving those goals. Too long we have held congregational singing in opposition to "special music." The remedy: *Make congregational singing special!* To that end, I offer a few suggestions and, at the same time, refer the reader to the more comprehensive material listed in the bibliography.[21]

Acoustics.

It is basic that a good acoustical atmosphere be provided, so that the amateur singer feels good in letting his voice be heard, at least by himself and his close neighbors! Much congregational singing suffers from low ceilings, or from too much carpeting and acoustic tile. The needs in building design have already been outlined in chapter ten.

Musical Factors.

Good hymn singing results from good leadership by the choir and the accompanying instruments. The choir's contribution to worship should

---

Chances are, it was the tune that was the "favorite." I have also noticed that, it you ask someone if he/she knows a certain hymn, an affirmative reply is often accompanied by humming or whistling the melody!

21. I recommend especially James Sydnor, *The Hymn and Congregational Singing;* William J. Reynolds, *Congregational Singing;* and Harry Eskew and Hugh McElrath, *Sing with Understanding.*

not be measured first by the anthem they sing, but in the contribution they make in leading the hymns. The instruments should be played with strong rhythm and sufficient volume to move the large congregation along with them. Variety, to add excitement and that "special" quality, can be added by the means of accompaniment—piano as well as organ, and certain orchestral instruments, especially brass. The organist should frequently change the registration, sometimes just for variety's sake, but more often to bring out the contrasting meanings of the hymn's stanzas. The congregation can sing in parts or in unison. Modulations and re-harmonizations, as well as descants by voices or instruments, can be used to achieve a climax in a "triumphal hymn."

What About Songleading?

Some quite-sophisticated churches have retained a vestige of the re-vivalist tradition in the use of a "songleader"—the choir director or another appointed individual—to lead the hymns. Other church musi-cians contend that the organ and choir really lead the congregation, and a visible, arm-waving songleader "gets in the way" of the individual worshiper, who should be thinking about the meaning of the hymn's words rather than trying to follow the gestures of a conductor. The first practice may seem to have support from some unusual traditions. I recently observed a mass at the Basilica of St. Clotilde in Paris (where César Franck once played), and a priest directed the congregational responses while standing in the center aisle of the nave! The eminent German choral conductor and church musician, Wilhelm Ehmann, is the author of a leading text on choral conducting, and has also published a booklet on "Leading Community Singing."[22]

My own preference is for no congregational songleading in a morning service of worship. Nobody can watch the director constantly and still read the words of the hymn, so that the actual "leading" is really done by the instruments and the choir. I really prefer that my singing springs spontaneously from my mind and emotions, rather than being "di-rected."

At the same time, good songleaders can serve well in other situations. They may be used to teach new hymns to the congregation during the period before the regular morning service begins, or at the midweek service, or in a church social hour. They may be very effective in leading a "song service" Sunday evening, since gospel songs offer the flexibility in which "song conducting" is most convincing. Other possibilities are introducing the hymns with an appropriate word or scripture to direct attention to the text, and perhaps "tying several hymns together" in an effective medley. I remember a few instances in which a gifted songleader has treated a congregation like a choir—rehearsing them thoroughly and leading them in many nuances of dynamics, tempo and

22. Wilhelm Ehmann, *Choral Directing.* Unfortunately, the booklet on leading community singing has not yet been translated from the German.

phrasing until the congregational hymn sounded more like a great anthem. This approach is certainly to be preferred to the repeated interruptions calculated to whip up flagging enthusiasm—"Sing it out now!" It could be the first step in breaking down the artificial separation between congregation and choir. Others can follow: (1) Use the choir antiphonally with the congregation on such hymns as "Are You Weary, Heavy Laden?" or "I Know Whom I Have Believed," and (2) Sing choral anthems that include the congregation, perhaps on the final stanza of the piece.

Can a New Hymn Be Exciting?

Many ministers and musicians are reluctant to use new hymns, because "they won't go well." Of course, they will always go *better* if they are well introduced, well played, and well supported by the choir. Many techniques have been suggested for expanding the hymnody of a congregation; one idea is to feature a "Hymn of the Month," introducing the tune first in an organ prelude, then with the words in a choir anthem setting; finally it is sung by the entire congregation.

It is probably true that we frequently allow the "need to succeed" syndrome to stand in our way in church life. Why must a hymn always be "sung well"? Is it possible that a congregation will pay more attention to a hymn's words when it is struggling to learn them, than they do after it is "over-learned"? In my experience, many congregations are more willing to learn new hymns than leaders are to teach them. Eventually, of course, after some repetition, they will sing them well. And the first excitement should be that which accompanies the awareness that the church is experiencing creativity—fresh expressions in song to keep pace with our new experiences in Christ!

Hymn Services.

Finally, the significance and excitement of hymn singing can be emphasized in special services of song. A Hymn Festival or a spontaneous service of congregational singing can do this most effectively. The first of these can be a fairly formal presentation, featuring also choral pieces, scripture, litanies and a sermon. The second can be built around the services of a songleader, but it can also provide a full experience of worship and fellowship. It is in such services that new hymns are easily taught. Because of the special hymnic emphasis, the congregation will expect them. Sandwiched between more familiar hymns, they provide welcome variety.

Making Hymn Singing Meaningful

There is one thing more important than emotionally-exciting hymn singing. That is meaningful hymn singing, in which the text effectively communicates a significant message to the singer, or expresses his thoughtful/emotional response in praise or prayer or witness. This kind of service experience rarely occurs unless pastors and music ministers feel strongly about the importance of hymn singing, understand the meaning of hymn texts, and make wise choices in the planning of worship services.

Frequently we underestimate the intelligence of a congregation. When a hymn is used simply because it has either "spirited" or "devotional" music, without careful consideration of the text, that rationale comes through loud and clear. On the other hand, if a hymn is chosen for a specific reason, even if a verbal explanation is not given, its significance is not lost on the congregation of average intelligence.

Hymns in Worship Design.

It will be remembered that Martin Luther composed a number of hymns to replace the traditional Latin songs of the mass—*Kyrie, Gloria, Credo, Sanctus* and *Agnus Dei*. Similarly, a free church minister should understand that the hymns he chooses relate to the different actions of worship—either as revelation or response, or both. The following types of hymns may appear, though probably no more than four or five would occur in a single service. The most common are marked by an asterisk.

  * HYMN OF PRAISE
     HYMN OF CONFESSION
  * HYMN OF MEDITATION (Preparation for scripture, prayer or sermon)
     HYMN OF SUPPLICATION (Preparation for, or response to prayer)
  * HYMN OF STEWARDSHIP (Preparation for offering, or offertory)
  * HYMN OF DEDICATION (Response to sermon)
     HYMN OF THANKSGIVING OR REMEMBRANCE (Lord's Supper)
     HYMN OF DISMISSAL (Doxology)

It should be obvious that not all the hymns should emphasize the theme of the homily, although to some ministers (who see worship principally as preaching) this seems to be the ideal. Some hymns should specifically amplify the sermon theme, and/or the significance of that particular day (e.g., Pentecost Sunday), but not all.

Sing the Entire Hymn (or all that is relevant).

Frequently the meaning of the hymn is declared to be irrelevant by the songleader who whimsically announces "we will sing the first and third stanzas," or worse, "We will sing only the first stanza. The attitude expressed seems to be "Twice through is enough of *any* hymn tune." A hymn is written to express a complete idea, with progression of thought from beginning to end. Frequently it has already been shortened (but carefully!) by the hymnal editors in acknowledgement of the fact that our services are not as lengthy as those of our forebears. When we further "cut" a hymn—and particularly, when we omit stanzas without a specific reason for doing so, we give the impression that the words are not important.

On Introducing the Hymn.

When a hymn is announced in the service, the songleader or the minister may outline its basic message in a single sentence of introduction, or by using a verse of scripture.

> We shall sing "Praise the Lord Who Reigns Above"—Charles Wesley's paraphrase of Psalm 150: "Praise the Lord! Praise God in his sanctuary; praise him in his mighty firmament! Praise him for his mighty deeds; praise him according to his excellent greatness!"

> Let us sing Bessie P. Head's hymn "O Breath of Life, Come Sweeping Through Us." These words speak of the Holy Spirit as the "Breath of God," and are based on John 20:22: "And when he (Jesus) had said this, he breathed on them, and said to them, 'Receive the Holy Spirit.'"

The minister may also direct attention to the meaning of a hymn *after* it is sung, by referring to it, either in the sermon or in a prayer.

Hymn Stories.

In the past, a large number of "hymn stories" have been published, and occasionally a songleader will use one to emphasize the meaning of a hymn. Frequently they are narrated, and recently some churches have used them as the basis of a dramatic vignette. The underlying supposition is that most every important hymn was written as the result of a moment of inspiration usually connected with some intense life experience. The concept has been particularly attractive to devotees of the gospel hymn, and it may be that those simple experience songs have more story associations than standard hymns.

> Civilla D. Martin wrote these words one Sunday afternoon in 1904, while her husband was on a preaching assignment and she remained ill in bed at home. Mr. Martin wrote the music when he returned that same day, and the hymn was sung in the evening.[23]

> > Be not dismayed whate'er betide,
> > God will take care of you;
> > Beneath His wings of love abide,
> > God will take care of you.

23. Adapted from my *Dictionary-Handbook to Hymns for the Living Church*, p. 143.

Occasionally this type of hymn introduction can be helpful, but it may give a wrong impression about serious workmanship in hymn composing. The truth is, great hymnists seldom wrote out of a "moving experience." Individuals like Charles Wesley or Isaac Watts simply made it a practice to write hymns almost every day; the inspiration may have been simply a scripture text or a single theological idea. For them and for many others, writing hymns was a way of life, and as a result, their craftmanship produced the best hymns in the English language. The same was true for the gospel hymn writer Fanny J. Crosby, who wrote perhaps nine thousand hymns, mostly during the quiet hours of the night. It is doubtful that she could have had that many notable experiences!

Hymn Sermons.

An excellent means for dramatizing the meaning of hymns is a "hymn sermon." There are two types. In the first, the congregation responds with a hymn after each item in a homiletical outline. Recently, in a sermon planned to draw attention to the meaning of music in worship, a Canadian minister explained the "psalms, hymns and spiritual songs" used in the early church, and the congregation sang "an example" of each.

> Sermon Topic: "Music in the Worship of God"
> Texts: Ephesians 5:19; Colossians 3:16
> 1. Psalms—"The Lord's My Shepherd, I'll Not Want" (Scottish Psalter)
> 2. Hymns—"Jesus! What a Friend for Sinners" (Chapman)
> 3. Spiritual Songs—"Alleluia" (contemporary chorus-song)

In the second example, the minister exegetes a hymn which is clearly based on scripture.

> Sermon Topic: "The Work of the Holy Spirit in the Believer"
> Hymn: Have Thine Own Way, Lord (Adelaide Pollard)
> Scriptures: Isaiah 64:8; Jeremiah 18:1–7
> 1. In Molding the Character
>   "Mold me and make me after Thy will"
> 2. In Cleansing the Life
>   "Whiter than snow, Lord, wash me just now"
> 3. In Enduement of Power
>   "Wounded and weary, help me, I pray!
>   Power—all power—surely is Thine!"
> Summary: Being "filled with the Holy Spirit"
>   "Fill with Thy Spirit till all shall see
>   Christ only, always, living in me!"

How about Hymnology Study?

A few music ministers have been bold enough to schedule basic hymnology courses for church members, sometimes as part of the adult education curriculum, and occasionally as part of a summer conference program. Undoubtedly, this activity is enjoyable and helpful for the few individuals who participate, but it is not an ideal approach to the understanding of hymns by the entire congregation. I recommend rather these types of *informal* education associated with the actual singing experience. There may also be merit in placing an occasional hymn analysis or story in the church bulletin.

The Hymnal as Devotional Material.

If, as has been suggested, the hymn singing diet of evangelicals falls short of their full theology and their best statement of Christian experience, what is the remedy? It must begin with the conviction of ministers that congregational singing is the central music of the church, and that a full range of excellent hymns must accompany the experiences of worship, of fellowship and of outreach. Even then, the church leaders must have personal knowledge of the content of standard hymns of the church, far beyond that which might be gained in a traditional course in hymnology.

It would be helpful if church musicians and preaching pastors (as well as other interested believers) followed the historic practice of using a hymnal as a resource for personal devotions. The hymnbook supplies expressions for every devotional attitude—adoration, meditation, confession, dedication, thanksgiving and intercession—and they come to us from our worship heritage of almost 2000 years. Worshiping individuals will discover that the words of our spiritual forefathers will stimulate the flow of personal prayer and, in the process, will learn the full meaning of the hymns, enabling them to make the best choices for public worship. The pastor who follows this advice will invariably find himself quoting the hymns in Sunday morning sermons.

The practice should begin with the local church hymnal, to be sure. Eventually, ministers may want to enlarge their repertoire of devotional hymnody, perhaps using one of the best denominational books, such as *Hymnal 1940, The Lutheran Hymnal* or the *Hymnary* of the United Church of Canada. When this happens, it will be easier for evangelical publishers to strengthen the hymnic content of their successive books, without wondering if they are flirting with bankruptcy!

The Pastor Should Sing Too.

Above all, ministers should set a good example in the matter of hymn singing. If they do not participate fully in the worship activities preceding the sermon, an observant congregation will assume that "joining in" is optional. To put it bluntly, such important pastoral chores as taking the roll of church attendance and reviewing the sermon notes should be done at some other time—not during the singing of the congregation or of the choir!

Hymns for the Future

In our day, questions are rife about the future of the church. Will it continue to exist in its present form? Will it grow? Will it become a "house church"? Whatever the answers, we can predict that tomorrow's church will have new expressions for worship, including new congregational hymns. The challenges that face the writers of that music, and also the editors of hymnals, are related to the forms and the language they will use.

Two contemporary movements have determined that some of the musical tradition we have heretofore experienced is being lost. The first is the burgeoning of "new witness music" during the last twenty years; the second is inherent in the recent worship revolution, the multiple versions of the Bible which have appeared, and today's tensions over the use of "sexist" language. We can dispose of the first problem quickly, because it has the "happiest solution."

It is quite apparent that the new wave of gospel/folk/pop songs has finally broken the hold of the Sankey/Alexander/Rodeheaver literature on evangelicals. "Gospel music" should be "fresh" in every generation; now that almost everybody is singing the new songs, we can expect that the large body of older material will begin to disappear from our hymnals. A few "classics" will remain, no doubt, and probably should be cherished as reminders of our heritage. But gradually, the more sophisticated congregations will forget "Leaning on the Everlasting Arms!" "Standing on the Promises," "Power in the Blood," and "Since Jesus Came Into My Heart," not because they have changed their theology, but because modern songs express the same truth in contemporary styles. Of course, changes come more slowly for some groups, and this prophecy will probably kindle their resentment. But *we all change,* and the comparison of any group's successive hymnbooks will prove this.

Thee-Thou-Thine Language in Hymns.

Most of the new scripture translations have changed the references to God from "Thee, Thou and Thine" to "You and Your," because the original Hebrew, Aramaic and Greek contain the intimate pronoun forms. Consequently, many evangelicals are insisting on the use of these words in prayer, as well. Since our hymnals are saturated with King James language, most traditional hymns use the 17th-century-intimate expressions "Thee, Thou and Thine," for Deity, and frequently for human beings as well.

There is certainly no excuse for continuing to sing the archaic forms which refer to humans. In many instances they can be changed easily. For example, in "Give to the Winds Thy Fears" (*Hymns for the Living Church*, no. 422), most of the problems are solved simply by changing "thy" to "your"; in the final stanza, "thou then shalt" becomes "you then shall." Similarly, "Praise Ye the Lord, the Almighty" becomes "Praise to the Lord . . ." and "Fight the Good Fight with All Thy Might" is changed to ". . . All Your Might." Note that this last example is most challenging, especially in the fourth stanza, but it can be worked out.

> Faint not nor fear, His arms are near,
> (changes)   (you are)
> He changeth not, and thou art dear;
> (you shall)
> Only believe, and thou shalt see
> (all, and all shall be.)
> That Christ is all in all to thee.

This answer, then, is categorical. When the "thou" form is used for human beings, change it, or find a substitute hymn.

The first reaction of hymnic experts to the pronoun changes in references to God tended to be, "We must alter all of our hymns." Perhaps the most conspicuous attempt was made in the new Presbyterian *Worshipbook* (1970). Most critics agree that the effort achieved minimal success, and that some notable incongruities resulted. Even if one doesn't object to "Come, You Almighty King," that hymn's third stanza offers the opportunity to gag on "You who almighty are." In many such instances, the mixture of 19th and 20th century language is less convincing than the original. Whether or not it was caused by the problems encountered, it is interesting to note that opinion has shifted on this matter. It is now generally agreed that making massive changes in historic hymns, which many people sing almost from memory, is less desirable than eliminating the hymns completely. This then is my advice:

(1) Where changes can be made while still preserving the author's "sense, style and scansion" (roughly, "meter")—the phrase is Erik Routley's—do it!

(2) Where change is not possible within the above rubric, sing the hymn as it is, or find a replacement.

It is now clear that the passion for this particular language change in hymns has subsided considerably. Since God is both transcendent and immanent to the believer, it may be that we can sing to Him as both "Thou" and "You."

Sexist Language in Hymns.

The latest bugaboo to raise its head is the matter of "sexist" language in hymns. As in all contemporary speech and literature, the "masculine-inclusive" language (e.g., "mankind," the use of "he" to denote a man or a woman, etc.) is judged by many to be discriminatory. Consequently, most speakers and authors are changing their habitual practice, some of us with great difficulty, even though we agree with the principle!

In this instance, decisions will relate more to the attitudes in the individual congregation.

(1) Where you can remove sexist language in an important hymn without ruining it, do so. For instance, "Good Christian Men, Rejoice" easily becomes "Good Christians All, Rejoice" or "Good Christian Folk, Rejoice."

(2) Where such changes would spoil the original, and if your congregation feels strongly about sexism in language, find a substitute, or omit the offending stanzas (where the sense allows it). Where nobody minds, sing it.

(3) In writing new hymns, avoid sexism in language. This rule creates no serious problem for the working poet.

In certain theological communities, the conviction concerning sexism in worship language is extended to the biblical images of "Father," "Son," "King" and even "Lord." These enthusiasts have already worked out some of the hymnic problems, according to their standards.[24]

> Praise to our God, the Almighty, the Source of creation!
> O my soul, fear not, for God is thy health and salvation!
> (Note that "thy" is still acceptable for mortals.)

> Dear Mother-Father of us all,
> Forgive our foolish ways . . .

> The church's one foundation is Jesus Christ the Lord;
> We are Christ's new creation by water and the word.
> From heaven Christ came and sought us, Christ's body true are we,
> Christ is the one who brought us the gift of liberty.
> (Note that the image of "bride" for the Church is also rejected.)

> Noel, Noel, Noel, Noel,
> Born is the Savior of Israel.

It is not our purpose to offer an apologetic for our refusal to go along with this extension of the "sexist" language problem. Suffice it to say that at this point evangelicals will part company with the movement. We are indebted to Erik Routley—with whom some of us are not completely in agreement on all points of theology—for sounding the alarm to the entire Church.

24. See *A Book of Hymns in Inclusive Language,* 1979, compiled by Perkins Women Students, Perkins School of Theology, Dallas, TX 75275; and *Because We Are One People,* 1974, Ecumenical Women's Centers, 1653 W. School St., Chicago, IL 60657.

... I think the excision of "man" for "humanity" is development, and the movement to remove "father" from God is heresy; that can be proved.[25]

New Biblical-Theological Language for Evangelicals.

In conclusion, I must mention briefly a much more relevant issue for evangelicals. We have never contributed our share of "worship hymns" that offer worthy hymn poetry and still contain our distinctive theology. Now that a single version of the Bible is no longer "standard," our challenge is to write hymns that are thoroughly biblical, even though there is no longer much point in using exact quotations.

I have seen enough hymnic efforts by evangelicals to believe that this is both a challenge and a harbinger of "better hymns to come." We have tended to be a people of "shibboleths," and we justified them with the argument that they were "biblical shibboleths." Now they are gone, and the "loss" may free our writers to do something really creative for the church. The following are two of the better examples I have seen in recent years.

(For Building a Church)

Let us build a house of worship
    To the God of heaven and earth,
Where His Church may bow before Him,
    Hear His Word and sing His worth.
Hearts and lives with bricks and mortar
    Gladly to our God we raise:
He will set His name forever
    On such building to His praise.

Let us build on God's foundation—
    Jesus Christ, whose blood atones;
Build with lives of grace and beauty—
    Gold and silver, precious stones.
Let us build for now, for ever—
    Build for those who live today,
Build for future generations
    Truth that triumphs, come what may.

Let us build to teach our children
    All the glories of God's grace;
Let us build to bring our neighbors
    God's good news for every race.
Let us build to tell all nations
    Life and health are theirs in God—
Jesus Christ is Lord and Savior!
    Sound His saving name abroad!

E. Margaret Clarkson, 1977

25. Erik Routley, "Sexist Language. A View from a Distance," p. 9.

Your cause be mine, great Lord divine,
    Your aim be my ambition:
For wasted is my greatest strength
    Unless it find expression
In love that gives itself away,
    In life responsive to obey
The terms of your commission.

Your cause be mine, great Lord divine,
    This be my life's vocation;
To seek the prize when life is done
    Your loving approbation.
Diminish pride, increase my love,
    O may your Spirit now remove
All selfish motivation.

Your cause be mine, great Lord divine,
    The world's emancipation:
To let your light invade the dark
    In every situation,
To prove you in a thousand ways,
    To serve you well with zeal ablaze
Through life's unknown duration.

Bryan Jeffery Leech, 1973

Chapter XV

EVANGELICALS AND INSTRUMENTAL MUSIC

Perhaps more confusion and conflict has centered about the use of instruments than about any other form of musical worship. The first pages of chapter four recount the progression of events which determined that instruments would not be used in the New Testament church, and the effect of this "accident of history" on the practices of Christians down through the centuries. We may guess that the recurring suspicion of instruments stems partly from the fact that they do not express cognitive ideas. Words are more easily recognized as either spiritual or demonic. Instrumental sounds are suspect, since they cannot be positively identified!

It is frequently difficult for the contemporary mind to understand this kind of prejudice against practices that—at the worst—we consider to be absolutely harmless. It may help to remember that in the mid-1960's many evangelicals opposed the use of the guitar in church, because at that time it was a symbol of the youth culture which practiced illicit sex and smoked "pot." To me, the frequently-explosive reaction seemed ridiculous, since I had grown up with Norwegian gospel music sung to guitar accompaniment. I consider myself to be "open" to all instruments in church—that is, all except saxophones. And that may be typical of most "liberal" attitudes!

But enough of negatives. In this chapter we will consider the positive contributions of instruments to the music of the church, and some of the questions that pertain to their use in evangelical life.

The Organ in Church

A Historical Overview.

Although the "pipes" mentioned in Psalm 150:4 may have been one of the earliest precursors of the modern organ, the first identifiable ancestor was probably the Egyptian *hydraulis* (3rd c., B.C.), in which the wind supply was controlled by water. Another form appeared in the Roman arena, and was possibly played as accompaniment to the massacre of early Christians! Tonally, it was no doubt a rather uncouth instrument, with great volume and little grace. Western European noblemen had organs in their palaces before the year 900, and in the tenth century Winchester cathedral in England boasted an instrument powered by twenty-six bellows pumped by seventy men! Apparently, the organ became known as "the church's instrument" largely because of its size; a great deal of sound—enough to fill a large sanctuary—could now be produced, and eventually many notes could be played by one performer.

Of course, early organs were extremely primitive, as compared with modern instruments. It was not until the 13th century that a keyboard was used; the first keys were three to four inches wide and were struck with the fist, dropping a distance of one foot. By 1361 a good-sized organ with a rudimentary set of pedals was produced in Halberstadt in central Europe.

During the Renaissance, organ building prospered most in north Germany and the Low Countries, where an instrument of three manuals and pedals rivaling some modern installations was produced before 1600. In other parts of Europe the progress was much slower; full organs with full pedals did not appear in England, France and Italy until the 19th century.

We do not have a clear idea of how the organ was used in the middle ages. Undoubtedly, it served to set the intonation for the singing of the chant, the polyphonic masses and motets. Modern musicology has proved that our common belief that all medieval music was sung *a cappella* is not correct; frequently voice parts were doubled or replaced by various kinds of instruments, including the organ. Up to the 17th century the organ was frequently used in what is known as *alternatim praxis*— "alternating practice"; sung sections of the mass were separated by sections (versets) which were played.

As we have noted in earlier chapters, the Reformation leaders of the 16th century were not enthusiastic about instrumental music in church, and organs were not at first used with congregational singing. In the 17th century, in Lutheran and Anglican practice, they began to be heard increasingly as accompaniment for the choir, and later for the commonly-sung hymns. In the German tradition, the chorale prelude emerged as an organ composition based on the hymn tune, to be played prior to its singing by the congregation; it is interesting to note that for some time, it was customary to play a "chorale prelude" and then to sing the chorale *without accompaniment*.

Early "Separatists" in Britain followed the example of Puritan Anglicans in rejecting instrumental music completely. Many of them continued this prohibition until well into the 19th century, both in Britain and America, especially among Calvinist groups. By the time smaller churches felt free to introduce a keyboard instrument in worship, the "reed organ" or harmonium was available. In size these instruments were comparable to the movable, *portativ* pipe organs which had existed since the Middle Ages, but the tones were produced by vibrating metal reeds, not by pipes. After 1850, they were common in those churches which could not afford a pipe organ. In the early singing schools and the later evangelistic missions of Moody and others, it was standard practice for the music leader to direct the congregational singing while playing such an organ, and also to accompany his solos in the same way.

Few 19th century churches would consider using a piano for its services—the piano was a secular instrument, and not suitable for sacred purposes![1] It was in the early 20th century revival campaigns in which songleader Charles M. Alexander was associated that pianos were first used. In the large auditoriums in which they met, if there was a pipe organ, it was not considered to be flexible enough to support Alexander's spontaneous choral and congregational directing! He solved the problem by installing two concert-grand pianos, played by strong fingers! As a result, that percussive, keyboard instrument was sanctified for church use, and it soon became accepted by evangelical congregations for worship in the local church. Nowadays reed organs are no longer available, and our most modest churches will use a spinet piano for accompaniment.

In the 1920's and 1930's, the same sanctifying process occurred (possibly with less desirable results) in certain churches which either inherited or purchased an organ from a movie-house which had discarded it. In those days, many evangelicals shunned the theater and its music, but they still found the tones of that uniquely-voiced instrument (with its strong tremolos) pleasing to their ears. Furthermore, the "theater sound" seemed to be amenable to the gospel song style with which the congregation was most familiar. Curiously enough, the inconsistency seemed to bother few ministers or churchgoers! These theater organs were used until they wore out, or until the church discovered that they were not really ideal for accompanying their full spectrum of music.

The first "electric" organ (the Hammond) appeared about 1935, and soon it was widely used by churches, as well as in radio broadcasting, in theaters and in bars! After all, it could be bought for a fraction of the cost of a traditional organ, and maintenance was minimal! Its sound only vaguely resembled that of a pipe organ, but it did produce sustained tones.

Since 1950, America has seen a revival in pipe organ design. In the wake of the *Orgelbewegung* (organ movement) in Germany, first heralded by Albert Schweitzer early in this century, we have moved away from the heavy, ponderous sounds of the typical English-American Romantic organ, which was at least distantly related to the theater's instrument. Some contemporary builders try to recreate the German baroque organ of the

---

1. It is interesting to note that when Erik Routley delineates the weakness of 19th century church music, he associates it with the dominance of the piano in the concert music of the period. See his *Words, Music and the Church*, pp. 91–107.

17th century. Others are producing eclectic organs which combine German, French and English (and sometimes even Italian and Spanish) characteristics in one instrument, so that it may more faithfully reproduce the music of all those traditions. Today's pipe organs are much more transparent and colorful in tonal design than those of the last generation, though in America's nonresonant church buildings, unless they are very carefully voiced, they sometimes sound overly shrill!

There has also been continuous and remarkable progress in the building of electronic organs. Certain companies have produced instruments which more nearly imitate pipe organ sound, and some have even combined pipes (usually for the principal chorus) with electronic components.

Choosing an Organ: Pipe or Electronic?

It is understandable that there would be argument about the validity of using an electronic organ in worship. After all, the tones are produced synthetically and its purpose is to imitate, not to produce a unique sound; in the opinion of many, this automatically disqualifies it as an authentic musical instrument. It must be admitted that no serious organist actually prefers an electronic instrument to a pipe organ. But many artists have played recitals in cities and in auditoriums where they could not have appeared without importing an electronic organ.

Invariably the discussion over whether a church should buy one instrument or the other centers in questions of cost—the original investment and the expense of maintenance. Many churches simply do not consider the possibility of a pipe organ, believing that it is not proper to buy such an expensive instrument when a cheaper substitute can be found. After all, they say, the typical parishioner "can't tell the difference." Of course, a trained organist finds a marked contrast between the two possibilities. Individual tones may be comparable, but the total ensemble of the best electronic instrument simply cannot duplicate the full, healthy sound of a pipe organ.

It is true that the initial investment for comparable specifications will be quite different; you may expect to pay up to three times as much for the most reasonable pipe organ as you will for the best electronic. But it is also true that an electronic instrument cannot deliver as much solid tone as a pipe organ with the same stoplist. You can get sufficient volume from even the smallest electronic device, if you have enough amplifiers and speakers. But the tonal definition—the clarity, beauty and variety of sound—will be markedly inferior.

One needs also to consider the probability of obsolescence. Up to this time, an electronic organ has usually needed to be replaced before it was fifteen years old. The science of electronics progresses so rapidly that even a good organ is outdated within that period. Many component parts of a pipe organ are usable for generations. In addition, recent advances in organ design give assurance that the traditionally high maintenance cost is a thing of the past. Certain companies are building "slider" chests (those used on a tracker organ) which are activated by electrical solenoids, so that there is no more need to replace electrical contacts and/or "leathers" periodically. "Combination actions" which change registrations are now using computer techniques (not to be confused with the electronic organ which advertises that it is a "digital computer"), and that will greatly reduce maintenance costs and improve reliability.

In other words, over a period of years, in churches where the sanctuary space is adequate,[2] installing one bonafide pipe organ may not be more expensive than purchasing several successive electronic substitutes. Invariably, the final decision must be made on the basis of which instrument best serves a particular church. If a congregation, working with its musical leadership, decides that a pipe organ supplies superior tone and will contribute to a better atmosphere in worship, and if it can make the necessary investment, that is what it should do. There should even be room for the concept that installing a costly, worthy instrument—like Mary's gift of "alabaster box" ointment[3]—may be a token of our love of Christ. On the other hand, if the church does not have that conviction—after its most knowledgeable musicians, including the organists, have been consulted—it should buy the best instrument it can afford.

One final caution! The decision to buy an electronic organ should not be made on the basis of a speech on electronic theory by a salesman. The church should buy the organ which *sounds best* (most like a pipe organ) and which will give the best service over a period of years. The decision as to tone should be made by a committee which includes trained organists who know what a good pipe organ sounds like. If the church does not have such a person in its membership, it would be wise to engage a consultant who can supply the necessary expertise. Average laypersons are not qualified to make decisions on the details of a church's electrical system or plumbing; neither should they be expected to make valid recommendations on what "organ sound" is most appropriate for the worshiping community.

Choosing an Organ: "Tracker" Action or Not?

Among organists, there is currently a lot of debate about pipe organ design. Builders of "baroque" style organs have tended to return to the "tracker" action of historic instruments, in which the player has direct mechanical control of the valves which admit air to the pipes. (By contrast, 19th and 20th century organs use either electrical and/or pneumatic devices). The arguments for "tracker action" are two: (1) There is less wear of fewer components and therefore, less maintenance cost and

2. It is generally thought that chambers are needed for the pipes and chests. However, many modern builders can "hang" an organ on the walls of the sanctuary.
3. Mark 14:3-9.

longer life; and (2) the organist has better control of the "speaking" of the pipe, because he actuates it directly with purely mechanical action, not through an electrical switch.

I enjoy playing a mechanical action organ, with the distinctive sounds and clarity of a truly "baroque" instrument, especially when it is located in a very "live" acoustical setting. It is unsurpassed in reproducing the German organ music of the 16th to 18th centuries. However, most evangelical churches choose a less specialized instrument, because their music literature is more varied. A tracker organ registration tends to be "purist," emphasizing the principal chorus; it will seldom include any large number of the softer flutes, and there are usually no strings or celeste stops that are so significant in accompanying typical gospel-folk music. Furthermore, mechanical action organs tend to shun "expressive" divisions, which allow easy control of crescendo-decrescendo dynamics; there may be one enclosed division with "swell shutters," but no more. Finally, tracker organs must have a direct link between console and pipe chests, which tends to limit the freedom to place the console where it is most convenient.

Organ Playing in Evangelical Services

The traditional uses of the organ in evangelical worship are these:

1. Leading the singing of the congregation.
2. Accompanying the choir, ensembles, and soloists.
3. Playing interludes or "background music."
4. Playing instrumental music, either as solo pieces or in ensemble with other instruments.

Leading Congregational Singing.

If congregational singing is the only "indispensable" church music, it follows that "leading that singing" is a very significant musical activity. I am convinced that it is best done by proper organ-playing. It is not possible for a congregation to watch a songleader constantly, and at the same time, read the words of the hymns and give proper attention to their meaning. Even though the choir also "leads" the hymns, in most churches the group is so small (and the acoustics are so unfriendly) that they cannot be heard when the congregation is singing. For these reasons, I believe that the organ should be allowed to fulfill its historic function—to play in such a way as to give sufficient pitch-and-rhythmic impulse, so that the congregation feels itself "carried along" in its singing. The first requirement is a good instrument, properly installed in a good acoustical setting. The second is a competent organist who will use proper registration and articulation, and employ valid techniques to control tempo, dynamics and rhythm.

The organ needs to be large enough and to have a full registration (including principals, mixtures and reeds) so that there is reserve volume—more than is actually needed to lead the hymns when the church is full. In the case of electronic organs, the number and placement of speakers is crucial. The instrument must be so located that it speaks into the auditorium with optimum efficiency. In the case of pipe organs, it is often advisable to consider the possibility of an "exposed" great division, with the pipes hanging on the wall of the church. In either pipe or electronic organs, an "antiphonal" section in the rear of the building frequently is of great help in boosting congregational singing. Obviously, acoustics are significant in projecting organ sound properly, so that it is well heard in all parts of the room. When a new church is being planned, an organ builder should be consulted, so that appropriate space and acoustic design can be provided for the instrument.

Techniques of playing for congregational singing are fully as important as the instrument itself. It is my opinion that many organists have been so intimidated by congregational and pastoral complaints, that they play too softly to effectively lead the hymns. The volume should be sufficient to allow the worshiper to "let out" his voice freely. At the same time, variety in dynamics is important. Some stanzas should be played with less sound, especially if the softer dynamic supports the meaning of the text. Later, especially in a concluding stanza, the instrument can lead to a brilliant climax. Experienced organists know that they can control the response of the congregation in considerable detail, by the level and the style of their organ playing.

Registration is most important. For congregational song, the organist should depend on the diapasons, mixtures and reeds. The stops which supply the upper tonal harmonics (4'2'1' III IV, etc.) will help the congregational singer to hear the pitches without excessive volume. Finally, differences of volume should be achieved by change of registration, not by use of the swell pedals.

Articulation (a break between successive notes) is the organ's only means of giving rhythmic accent. Organists should be competent in the traditional norm of articulation (i.e., every repeated note is articulated), but they should also be flexible, playing sometimes with more articulation, and sometimes with less. Above all, they should abandon the false idea—sometimes held by non-organists—that the organ is a *legato* instrument whose notes should be tied together as much as possible. Proper articulation is even more important than sufficient volume in helping a singing congregation stay together. Finally, I recommend a complete rhythmic, in-tempo phrase-break by the organ at the point of a congregational breath.

Normally, all "standard" hymn tunes should be played without tempo fluctuation, and the introduction should establish the tempo clearly. The final stanza of a hymn may be played at a slightly broader tempo, and the final phrase should probably have a marked cadence ritard.

It should be obvious from the above discussion that hymn accompaniments should be practiced carefully each time they are to be performed. In an organ workshop, I once heard the renowned pedagogue Mildred Andrews say that:

1. In practicing hymns, she plays each stanza. This suggests that different words may call for changes in phrasing, registration, etc.
2. While practicing, she also sings every voice part—soprano, alto, tenor and bass. Obviously, when this is completed, the hymn-tune will be well learned and it can virtually be played from memory.

Playing Accompaniments.

When organists accompany a choir, they are, in a sense, also "leading" them. Of course, the musical decisions are made by the director. But a skillful organist, by use of proper registration, articulation, dynamics and tempo, can help a conductor control the choir's response. I dislike the phrase which suggests that an accompanist should "follow" the director, the ensemble or the soloist, for this implies that the organ may be slightly behind! Rather, capable organists learn both the music and the performers' needs and desires so well, that they "anticipate" the trouble spots; they may actually assist in achieving a crescendo or a ritard, or in singing a phrase on a single breath, by the use of proper dynamics and articulation. Furthermore, organ registration should complement the group or the soloist, giving enough support and assuming its proper role in the ensemble. Some musicians forget that playing too loud is not the only accompanist-sin; playing too soft is just as bad!

Playing Interludes or Background Music.

It has become customary in many protestant churches for the organist to play interludes in the service, sometimes during the seating of latecomers, and sometimes simply to "tie parts of a service together." It may be that this practice stems from our electronic culture, in which every moment is filled with some kind of sound. In fact, it is particularly emphasized in a church which is broadcasting its worship service.

Apart from the needs of radio or television, we should be reminded that perpetual music may be fully as boring as no music at all! There are valid arguments for an occasional period of complete silence in the service, if for no other reason than to give contrast to sound, and to allow the congregation an opportunity for completely personal worship. At the same time, there should be no quarrel with occasional organ interludes, particularly for the purpose of seating individuals, and these are best improvised. The art of improvisation is just beginning to be considered seriously in American education—it has always been required of European church musicians—and capable organists should be able to base their creativity on melodies as well as on harmonies. The raw material for a good interlude may be derived from a preceding hymn or anthem, and the final product should occasionally be played "full or-gan." For the organist who is still learning to improvise, there are pub-lished collections of very short compositions or interludes.

It is also fairly common practice in evangelical churches to require the organist to play background music for prayers, sometimes even for a lengthy pastoral prayer. The hypothesis seems to be that the organ music helps people understand that they are speaking to God. What actually happens may be less than desirable, if it gives the congregation a vague, mystical-but-distracted feeling, while the minister talks to God! I would remind both pastors and organists that many people will hear the organ and not the prayer. If the organist uses a familiar hymn tune, the listener's attention may be directed to the words; if it is an improvisation (which seems to me slightly less objectionable), the musicians present may be following and evaluating the "instant composing." We need no background, "mood music" for talking to God; it really gets in the way of coherent and cognitive worship. If it is helpful to precede the prayer with a few moments of organ sound, well and good! But it should stop when the minister begins to pray.

Playing Instrumental Pieces.

The organ has frequently, if not always, been expected to contribute purely-instrumental pieces to the worship services. In earlier times the chorale prelude introduced Lutheran hymns, and the *alternatim* practice allowed the instrument to share certain portions of the liturgy with the choir. In the English tradition, the "voluntary" is defined as an "organ piece to be played in connection with the church service."

In typical American worship, the purely-instrumental music is usually limited to the prelude, offertory and postlude. The first of these is seen as a "preparation for worship"; frequently a church bulletin will carry the reminder, "The organ prelude can serve as a curtain to shut us in to the presence of God," or something similar. The individual worshiper is encouraged to use the time to pray and to prepare for the full experi-ence of worship. However, in many evangelical churches, the music is simply a background for the conversation of the congregation. It is time for us to face this issue squarely. Fellowship is one of the important aspects of church life; if it is the most significant activity preceding the worship service, it should not be hindered by irrelevant organ playing!

On the other hand, it is important to prepare for worship. In earlier times, a typical evangelical household began this preparation on Satur-day. All the important family needs related to clothes, food and personal grooming were taken care of in advance, so that Sunday could be de-voted entirely to rest and the worship of God. If communion was to be served in worship, a preparatory service was held on Saturday evening. In our hectic 20th century life, unless we are content to blunder into the presence of God, we must devise effective means of preparing for wor-ship. If organ music can help meet this need, it should be allowed to do so.

In some churches, where the conversation-prelude has been the historic norm, this challenge has been met in an interesting fashion. As they gather in the sanctuary, the congregation is allowed to visit or to remain silent, as they prefer. At about 10:50, the minister or his associate makes the important announcements for the week, closing with the admonition: "Now, let us worship God." The organ prelude follows, and the service moves on to its conclusion.

The question is frequently asked: "What type of music is proper for a prelude to evangelical worship?" Some organists follow the practice of using hymn tune preludes, and some simply play selections out of the hymnal. Others will always use "classical music"—not related to hymns—or chorale preludes (based on German hymn tunes) which are probably identified by the typical evangelical audience as "classical." To those who insist that the latter practice be followed exclusively, we would reply that when J. S. Bach used chorale preludes in his services, the tune was recognized by every member of the congregation. On the other hand, when the music is always based on a familiar hymn, we may be limiting the congregation's freedom in preparing for worship. Instead of allowing each person to use the time for whatever preparatory action is desirable, we are directing attention to the words of a specific hymn which may not be related to everyone's immediate needs. Once again, the question is whether a worshiper should be encouraged to chart his own best path to God in worship, or whether it is better to direct him in each action!

I believe that both types of music are potentially meaningful in worship meditation. On at least one occasion, our church experienced French baroque music *played on the piano* during the distribution of communion. At the same time, hymn tune preludes are a good possibility. Perhaps variety is the inevitable watchword. It is regrettable if an individual cannot have a valid worship experience apart from the "usual" medium of expression. Although we acknowledge that certain sounds become *ethos* symbols which help us worship, we should be able to come into God's presence with other sounds, or with none at all! This too is creativity!

In evangelical worship, the *offertory* is associated only with the "collection."[4] Ideally, the offering is a symbolic response to the Word of God, acknowledging that all that we are and have is his. Personally, I do not prefer an instrumental selection at this point in the service. True, it is possible for the players and the audience to offer a "sacrifice of praise" in musical sound, coincident with the offering of money and of self. But it is more probable that, for most worshipers it will be only a pleasant musical interlude, in which there is little or no spiritual action. A verbal "sacrifice" is preferable—a congregational hymn, a choral selection, or even a solo. The text may relate to the sermon topic, or it may be another expression of praise. Once the drama of worship begins, it seems to me

4. In liturgical churches, it often includes the offering of bread and wine for the eucharist, as well.

that it is doubtful wisdom to interrupt it for a period in which minds are encouraged to wander, or individuals are allowed to indulge their pleasure instincts in enjoying the work of a composer or the virtuosity of an organist. If an instrumental selection is inescapable—and, of course, the organ can be joined or even replaced by other instruments—it would seem wise to play a hymn tune setting, possibly one associated with words that express dedication or stewardship.

It should not be necessary to suggest that the *postlude* should reflect the mood of the close of the service. Normally, this can be a celebrative expression of the "church dispersing to worship and serve" in the world. On some occasions, however, it is possible that the congregation should leave in absolute silence, as at the close of a Tenebrae service (Maundy Thursday), or after a revival service where the Spirit of God has been present in evident power and conviction.

Other Uses of the Organ.

Of course, the church need not limit itself to these traditional instrumental expressions. The use of a true hymn prelude—i.e., one played *before* the congregational singing of the hymn—or of the *alternatim* practice (playing a setting in the middle of a hymn) might be considered, especially in a service which is given largely to hymn-singing. Frequently churches use the organ during the serving of communion. On those occasions, the literature and its performance should somehow intensify the meaning of the immediate experience.

Churches with fine instruments should also consider the possibility of presenting organ recitals. For believers, a concert of serious music can be an experience of divine worship. It also may serve as missions and as ministry, reaching out to others in the community.

Finally, churches should use their facilities to encourage their talented youth to study organ-playing. It is safe to say that many evangelical groups have better organs than organists. Many players are simply "converted" pianists; they have never taken the time to learn the distinctive techniques required by the organ. Competent church organists should become teachers, encouraging individuals in the congregation and in the larger community to study. Church boards should welcome this use of their instruments; most organs deteriorate more from rust than from wear! Those organists who feel that they are not yet competent should find a qualified teacher, in a local college or in another church. The standard techniques used by all capable organists are valid for use in evangelical worship and can be applied to our distinctive music literature.

The Piano in Church

Once the piano was found to be practical for the playing of gospel music in the evangelistic crusade of the early 20th century, it was also welcomed into the evangelical church which featured many of the same musical styles. It usually was played along with the organ, though sometimes it appeared by itself as an accompaniment for solos or ensembles. During the last two decades, in which highly rhythmic music has been introduced into the sanctuary, an increasing number of mainline churches have added the piano to their instrumental resources.

It must be remembered that pianists face a unique problem when asked to play the typical hymnal score at their instrument. The four-part harmony page is not in a pianistic style; if only those notes are played, the instrument's contribution is minimal indeed. Early revivalist pianists quickly met this challenge by developing improvisation styles that are similar to those of jazz musicians and others who play commercial popular music. "Playing by ear" it was called, and it probably originated with individuals like Robert Harkness and Henry Barraclough, both of whom played for the evangelism meetings early in this century in which Charles M. Alexander was songleader. Mr. Harkness authored a series of lessons in "Evangelistic Piano Playing" which he distributed as a correspondence course for many years; it was eventually published in a single volume.[5] In the fundamentalist community in which I grew up, it was expected that every pianist would play hymns "by ear." For the most part we were self-taught; our only outside help came from imitating each other's styles.

Some evangelical churches today use both piano and organ in all regular worship services. Others tend to restrict the piano to the evening service, where informal witness music is the norm. Obviously, the piano contributes musical effects that cannot be produced by any organ, and there is no reason why it should be excluded from worship use. At the same time, it may limit variety and flexibility if they are both used constantly, especially if they tend to play exactly the same notes.

In morning worship, the use of two instruments for the hymns means that a songleader is a "must"; otherwise, both players will be trying to lead the congregation, and they will probably not stay together. If a good organ is played well and "standard hymns" only are used, the piano adds very little to congregational singing. In the evening service, where songleading and informal hymns are the rule, both instruments may well be used. Even then, it is good judgment to use each instrument alone occasionally, and no accompaniment at times, as well as both instruments in ensemble. When the organist and pianist play together, if both performers can improvise, it may be agreed that on certain stanzas one will carry the burden of the tune and the other will add melodic, rhythmic, and even harmonic variety!

The same principles apply in accompanying a solo or a small ensemble. Especially when there is improvisation involved, even the best instrumentalists will need thorough rehearsal to stay together and with the solo/group; it may be better to use the organ sometimes and the piano on

5. Robert Harkness, *The Harkness Piano Method.*

other occasions. When using both instruments with a choir, there is no unusual difficulty, since a conductor is always involved. However, it is often self-defeating for both instrumentalists to play the "full score." Instead, the accompaniment should ideally be divided, with the piano taking the keyboard figures (e.g., arpeggios, repeated chords) and the organ supplying the more-sustained elements of the music.

In recent times, the art of "gospel piano" playing or improvisation has received a lot of attention through mass media and commercial religious recordings. In the years when radio was the principal electronic communication medium, most evangelicals could instantly identify the continuous-left-hand-octaves-style of Rudy Atwood, who played piano for the "Old Fashioned Revival Hour." Nowadays the distinctive creativity of Tedd Smith, Dino Kartsonakis, Kurt Kaiser, Don Wyrtzen, John Innes and Ron Boud are familiar to all. Their arrangements of hymn tunes can be purchased at the local book store, and used as prelude, offertory or postlude in the church, substituting occasionally for the organ. In addition, there is now available a large quantity of music written for the piano-organ ensemble, including accompaniments and re-harmonizations for congregational singing.

Evangelical pianists should also remember that they are no more restricted to hymn-based music than are organists. There is a great deal of standard literature which is appropriate: selected movements and pieces by Beethoven, Schubert, Mendelssohn, Schumann and Chopin, as well as of more recent composers, and a great quantity of *clavier* music from the Renaissance and Baroque periods, including J. S. Bach's chorale harmonizations. The use of this material in appropriate situations may be expected to contribute to both variety and maturity in evangelical worship.

Orchestral Instruments in the Church

The position of non-keyboard instruments in the church has been even more tenuous than that of the organ, the harpsichord and the piano. Only occasionally in history have they been so welcome as they are in this last part of the 20th century.

The Western Tradition Since the Middle Ages—an Overview.

History is unclear as to the use of these instruments in the Middle Ages. It may be that "strings" and "winds" were introduced as early as the organ (possibly the 10th or 11th century). It seems certain that with the appearance of the early polyphonic music, instruments were used to support or to replace the voice parts. By the 14th century they were quite at home in liturgical worship.

The Swiss Reformer Zwingli is said to have played many different instruments well; yet he banned all music from the reformation worship in 16th century Zurich, with the argument that Col. 3:16 teaches that God is interested only in the "melody in the heart," not that of the voice or of instruments! Luther played the lute, and he encouraged free development of congregational vocal music in the early 16th century; yet he was apparently indifferent about the use of organs or other instruments in church.

Modern stringed instruments of the violin family were developed in the early 17th century. Consequently, the Baroque period (17th and 18th centuries) saw a great flowering in the use of instrumental music, especially in orthodox Lutheran worship. Composers from Schütz to J. S. Bach used all the available musical resources in the performance of their "passions" and cantatas, and frequently instrumentalists outnumbered the singers in the choir loft! The instruments not only accompanied the voices, but also supplied preludes (overtures) and *ritornelli* (interludes) in connection with the music. In the Roman Catholic church of that same historic period, purely instrumental selections were also featured. "Epistle sonatas" (for organ and strings) were played before the reading of the epistle; Corelli's *sonata da chiesa* (church sonata) was a work of several movements, distinguished from the *sonata da camera* (chamber sonata) only by its smaller number of dance-related movements.

The Pietist movement in German-speaking countries emphasized a return to the simple worship of New Testament times, that is, without benefit of instrumental music. After the death of J. S. Bach, that movement eventually influenced all Lutheran worship and orchestral instruments tended to disappear from worship. Roman Catholics experienced something of the same reaction against "concert music" in church. The Cecilian movement of the early 19th century espoused a return to the style of the "golden age" (Palestrina, Victoria, Lassus); its leaders declared that *a cappella* singing was the ideal, on the basis of their conviction (however misinformed) that that was the standard 16th century practice. The "Cecilian ideal" was no doubt responsible for the dominance of unaccompanied choirs in American collegiate institutions up to 1940. In some instances, the tradition persists.

The American Scene.

One of America's first church music flowerings—that of the Moravians in the 18th century—strongly promoted instrumental music; the community supported full orchestra performances and the church used trombone choirs (*posaunenchöre*), especially in outdoor settings. In other 18th century protestant churches, long before organs were accepted, orchestral instruments (flute, oboe, clarinet, bassoon, trombone, cello, doublebass) appeared to support the singing. Only the violin was forbidden; since it was associated with the dance, it was called "the devil's fiddle." Once organs and harmoniums became common in the mid-19th century, the other instruments were generally put aside.

Significant Evangelical Developments.

In the late 19th century, the guitar appeared among Scandinavian immigrants, especially those of the free church tradition. Its use had been popularized in Sweden by Oscar Ahnfelt (1813–1880) who was the musical troubadour of the pietist revival in his country. Eventually Scandinavian evangelicals developed "string bands" which included mandolins and occasionally a doublebass, as well as guitars. They were used to accompany their own unique Scandinavian version of the gospel song.

At about the same time, the Salvation Army founded by William Booth brought brass instruments into their own in the service of the gospel. An English revival movement directed toward the needs of the working class, it was organized as a "Christian army" to fight sin and poverty. The leaders (pastors) were designated as "officers" and the members of the congregation were called "soldiers." The singing was, of course, led by an army band; that permitted the group to evangelize on city streets where no organ or piano would be found and where purely vocal music would never attract attention. After the street corner witness, the band led the way back to the "corps headquarters" and the full meeting continued. The Salvation Army movement soon spread around the world, and was especially successful in the United States. Army bands have continued to be a feature of their worship, evangelism and education activity to the present day. "In parade," modern Salvationist "lassies" even add a bit of modest choreography to their playing of tambourines.

During the early 20th century, Homer Rodeheaver came to the attention of the evangelical public, serving as soloist and songleader for evangelist Billy Sunday. Much of the time Rodeheaver played his trombone during the congregational singing; otherwise, he conducted with his right arm while the horn was draped over the left! Other evangelistic musicians during succeeding decades followed Rodeheaver's example, some with trombones, others with trumpets, and some even with violins and saxophones!

The historic Chicago Gospel Tabernacle, where the dynamic preacher Paul Rader held forth in the 1920's, sponsored a full concert band, which gained them a large following by appearing regularly on the new medium of radio. Concurrently, small orchestras became common in churches, featured especially in the Sunday School assembly or in the evening service. The larger gospel song books used in those meetings were usually available in orchestration form; the instruments accompanied the singing and also played selections for the prelude, offertory and postlude. My first salaried church position in 1936 included the responsibility to lead the Sunday School orchestra at the First Methodist Church in Oskaloosa, Iowa.

Today, in the late 20th century, there is almost no limit to the possibilities for using instruments in church. In many congregations, solo instruments and groups of all kinds appear frequently to accompany solos, choral ensembles and congregational singing, or to play purely-instrumental pieces. Since the baroque "recorder family" returned to popular use, and because acquiring an adequate playing technique is relatively easy, those instruments have frequently been substituted for flutes or other woodwinds. The Orff instruments, created principally for the music education of children, have also found their way into the church via the scores of published anthems. With the burgeoning of contemporary folk/rock/pop music, guitars, drums and various electronic instruments have also joined in.

The Significance of Orchestral Instruments in Church.

How then do evangelicals evaluate the proliferation of new musical sounds available to them? Is this perhaps another intrusion of a "musical concert" in the church (as in the 18th century mass) which will eventually be rejected in another "Cecilian" (no instrument) movement? I doubt it. Most church musicians see and treat these instruments as extensions of the keyboard and the console. A brass ensemble used with congregational singing simply amplifies the resources of the organ, and can help to give a new vision of the God transcendent; the same is true when it plays alone or with the organ in the service prelude on a festival Sunday. The Orff (and other) rhythm and pitch instruments are logical accompaniment for the singing of the younger-age choir, since the children use them regularly in their music-learning experiences. Handbells are an excellent aid in teaching rhythmic musicianship to both youth and adults, and they provide delightful sounds when heard alone or with voices. Perhaps most importantly, the use of instruments allows more individuals—those who play and may not be experts in singing—to offer their unique praise to God in the service of the church.

A contemporary Lutheran has expressed his approval of instruments which aid us to worship, in this way:

> Instruments can even play an important role in corporate worship. They can help us sing. They can help us dance. They can help us express our joy in the celebration of the Resurrection. They can help us experience a foretaste of that joy which awaits us when we shall one day celebrate with Christ the heavenly banquet.[6]

It is important to remember that certain musical expressions should be reserved for *special* occasions, and this is probably true of exotic instrumental sounds. Since they add greater intensity—greater emotion—to the experience, that intensity will tend to diminish if its inspiration becomes common or ordinary. I believe this applies both to big sounds (brass ensembles) and to small (handbells). It should also be reiterated that whenever instrumental accompaniment detracts from the text which it is supposed to support, it is expendable. That standard certainly

6. Reuben G. Pirner, "Instruments in Christian Worship."

applies to the sound of drums and guitars that are exaggerated by high-decibel electronic amplifiers!

Recorded Orchestral Accompaniments.

One more matter needs to be mentioned. In recent years, it has become customary for publishers to supply a full professional recording of new musicals, and even of anthems, for promotional purposes. In addition, the orchestrated accompaniment is made available on a tape "track" and can be used to accompany the singing group in public performances. More recently, certain companies have recorded accompaniments (in various key levels) to be used by soloists who present the latest gospel/folk/pop favorites in the church service, or in a sacred concert. Accompaniments of folk hymns for small worship groups (in the church or the home) have also been produced, and full symphonic orchestrations may soon be heard with congregational singing.

On the positive side, it must be said that the quality of performance on these accompaniment tapes is very high. They are recorded by the best professionals in Nashville, Chicago or Hollywood, and may set a standard for better instrumental performance by young musicians in the church. Undeniably, their use momentarily provides a technically-better background for the choir or the singer. At the same time, we must ask whether it supports true worship by individual believer-priests or whether it contributes to the blandishments of spectatorism. The next step might allow the entire service to be video-taped with more talented preaching and singing! But, of course, that is already being done, and some of the congregation stays home to watch the resulting performance of the "electric church" on television.

I contend that it is ill-advised to use taped accompaniments if the same talent is available in the congregation or the community. Even when it is generally agreed that they make a worthy contribution, their use should be carefully controlled. Otherwise, there will be little incentive for the development of instrumental musicians in the church.

Chapter XVI

EVANGELICALS AND MUSIC FOR CHOIRS

Choral music may be defined as ensemble singing by a group of individuals who have a certain degree of expertise, usually performed for an audience. Scattered throughout the earlier chapters of this book, a history of choral singing in Judeo-Christian worship may be traced. At the time of their deliverance from the Egyptians at the Red Sea, the prophetess Miriam led a group of Hebrew women in a song of praise. King David organized an enormous choir of singers (along with instrumentalists) who led the musical worship in the Jewish temple; in keeping with the sacerdotal character of their worship, the Levite priests provided almost all the music in that setting. It is believed that the early Christians favored congregational and nonprofessional music and that this was the continuing practice in the patristic period of the Church. Beginning in the fifth century, with the emergence of a highly developed, formal, priestly cult, choirs were given the responsibility of providing music for Christian worship. With the Reformation and its emphasis on believer-priesthood, choirs were either restricted in their activity or abolished. Early Separatists were especially vehement in denouncing them as "popish," and in certain parts of the world they are still considered to be unnecessary or even undesirable in evangelical worship.

Nevertheless, in American church life, choirs are very common, as has been emphasized in chapter ten. Most congregations consider that they are important to their worship, even when the quality of their performance may be questioned by outsiders. Choirs gained new acceptance among American evangelicals through their use in 19th century revivalism, when they were considered to be an extension of the pulpit ministry; they have remained to lead our worship, often assuming a major role.

In the early 20th century, the concept of a full-fledged church music ministry was developed in the Westminster Choir College, originally located in Dayton, Ohio. Many of our churches now support what is called a "fully graded choir program," which means that special music activity is provided for every age group. This possibility has become increasingly important, now that typical Sunday school activity does not include singing.

Functions of Choirs in Evangelical Churches.

What then are the functions of choir activity in modern evangelical church life? The following responses are valid, but must be evaluated for their relative importance.

(1) Choirs provide music for church services. This presupposes that there is validity in choral worship, first to help lead congregational singing, and also to provide special choral expressions. Choral music can provide an unusual musical experience which helps us apprehend the transcendent aspects of our faith.

(2) Choirs afford musically-talented persons an opportunity to offer their unique sacrifice of praise to God.

(3) Choirs are good promotion for the church. Folk who enjoy choral music and those who desire vocal training for themselves or their children, will be attracted to a church which sponsors a full music program. Parents will attend services in which their children are performing.

(4) Choirs provide an opportunity for the development of individuals in the church, as persons, as Christians and as musicians. However important the above (1–3) functions are considered to be, they are dependent on this last-named purpose, which is the primary function of a graded choir program in the church. Especially at the younger age levels, choral training is more important for its contribution *to* the choir members, than for its ministry *through* the choirs to the rest of the congregation. Consequently, in developing a choir program, the principles of music education and Christian education must be the focal emphases.

The Objectives of Music Education.

Typical music education in America is an integral part of the total program of democratic education, whose objectives are (1) a literate and well-informed citizenry and (2) equality of opportunity for each individual.[1] More specific objectives are stated in *The Purposes of Education in American Democracy,* published by the National Education Association, and they relate to the desired behavior of an educated person:[2]

(1) The objectives of self-realization (the person as an individual), e.g., the educated person appreciates beauty.

1. Charles Leonhard and Robert W. House, *Foundations and Principles of Music Education,* p. 10.
2. From "Policies for Education in American Democracy," National Education Association, Washington, DC, 1946, book III. Summarized in ibid., pp. 12–14.

(2) The objectives of human relationships (the person as a family member and social being), e.g., the educated person can work and play with others.
(3) The objectives of economic efficiency (the person as a producer), e.g., the educated producer knows the satisfaction of good workmanship.
(4) The objectives of civic responsibility (the person as a citizen), e.g., the educated citizen acts to correct unsatisfactory social conditions.

Based on these goals, Leonhard and House set forth in fifteen points the basic tenets of their philosophy of music education, from which eight are chosen as particularly significant in the church music context.[3]

(1) Aesthetic experience grows out of and is related to ordinary experience. Aesthetic quality is the source of man's highest satisfaction in living, and while all experience that is carried on intelligently has aesthetic quality, man's most valued experience is in connection with art objects consciously and feelingfully conceived and contemplated.
(2) All human experience is accompanied by feeling. Music bears a close similarity to the forms of human feeling and is the tonal analogue of the emotive life.
(3) The import of music is not fixed; it is subjective, personal and creative in the best sense of the word. We can fill the forms of music with any feelingful meaning that fits them.
(4) Every person has the need to transform experience symbolically and the capacity for symbolic experience with music.
(5) The only sound basis for music education is the development of the natural responsiveness that all human beings possess.
(6) Every child must be given the opportunity to develop his aesthetic potential to the highest possible level through expressive experience with music.
(7) Music education should be cosmopolitan, employing all kinds of music and giving recognition to the value of all kinds of music.
(8) While no type of music can be ignored in the music program, major attention should be given to providing musical experience that is educative in that it leads to an aesthetic response to great music, to the clarification of musical values, and to the development of musical independence.

Principles of Christian Education.

Roger L. Shinn defines Christian education as "the effort to introduce persons into the life and mission of the community of Christian faith."

3. Ibid., pp. 100-101.

He lists three components of Christian education:[4]

(1) The educational ministry of the church invites and incorporates persons into the life of the Christian community. It engages them in the characteristic acts by which this community responds to God.
  This community finds modes of expression that communicate and evoke faith . . . (1) worship, (2) Christian thought and (3) ethos (spirit of the community) and ethic (ethos in action).
(2) The educational ministry of the church is the appropriation of a heritage. It involves men in a past that significantly constitutes their present . . . Christian education requires the internalizing of a meaningful history.
(3) The educational ministry of the church is training in mission. It requires learning by service and for service of God in his world.

It should be readily apparent how music activity relates to these components of Christian education. Music is a primary mode of expression in worship, in conveying Christian thought (in the words of hymns and anthems), and in expressing the spirit of the community (the fellowship we experience in choir activities) and the ethic (we work together in mutual acceptance, cooperation and love, offering our musical gifts to God.)

The music program appropriates the heritage of God's acts in history with and through human beings. This heritage is conveyed in words which relate God's mighty deeds, and also in the verbal and musical art forms which have come down to us through the centuries.

Finally, the music program is a means of service, of mission. This concept is experienced by choir members in their regular service to a congregation and community (and perhaps in mission tours by youth choirs); it may even include a challenge to some individuals for lifetime service in a music ministry.

The Needs of Various Groups

In both music education and Christian education, a central requirement is awareness of the physical, cognitive and emotional development of the individual at each age level. Pre-school children have only limited physical capacity in producing sounds, limited aural and spatial-temporal imagery in identifying pitches and rhythms, and limited awareness of themselves as persons and of God. Experiences in choir education (both musical and theological) must match both their capacity and their interest at each age level, from pre-school to adult.

Church music educators (1) must identify the musical potential and the theological-psychological ages of each group with which they are

4. Roger L. Shinn, "The Educational Ministry of the Church," pp. 12–18.

working, and must choose techniques and materials adapted to their needs; (2) must be able to identify with each particular group,[5] i.e., to think as they think, to see God as they see him; and (3) must place all aspects of ministry in proper perspective. This last standard refers to the delineation of music ministries in chapter four; it implies that there will be a proper balance of "pastoral" concerns (singing the music that meets immediate needs and desires), with "prophetic" and "teaching" needs (presenting music and texts which encourage growth to Christian maturity.) The challenge to all ministers is to find the proper relationship between "comforting the afflicted" and "afflicting the comfortable."

The following principles apply especially to music education, and must be kept in mind by the church musician:

1. Some aspect of anything worth knowing can be taught at any age. In musical development, it is wise to start as early as possible, preferably at the age of four or five.
2. There is a logical expectation of achievement in musical knowledge and performing ability at each age. However, each level must be learned before the individual can proceed to the next step.
3. Vary the manner of presentation from activity to activity, rehearsal to rehearsal.
4. Work for parental involvement (particularly their understanding) in the educational process.
5. Make long-range plans, at least six months ahead.

The remainder of this chapter will be given to discussion of the theological and musical perspectives of various age groups in the choir program, and to the activities and materials which will meet their needs. The following questions will be considered:

1. At what ages can individuals "internalize" and duplicate certain melodic and rhythmic entities?
2. At what age do individuals read words? read music?
3. What is the vocal potential at different age levels? the degree of physical coordination?
4. How long is the attention span at each age level?
5. What are the psychological perspectives and needs of each age group?
6. What theological concepts can be assimilated at each level? What religious experiences are possible?

Each possible grouping will be considered though, admittedly, many churches could not provide individual training for each level. When different ages are combined, the leader would need to bridge the psychological and musical gaps between them. It may be possible in certain situations to unite advanced intermediates with high schoolers

5. This is yet another example of cross-cultural communication—using a musical language that is common to another age group, rather than one's own.

and even mature senior high voices with adults. At the same time, it must be acknowledged that there are limits to such combining; preschool children must not be included with the next-older group, and Juniors are best handled by themselves.

Pre-Schoolers.

There are almost no true monotones among children, providing their first musical experiences are pleasant. "Music activity" in church should start with the four and five-year-olds; however, they should not be considered to be a "choir." At this age, children do not really distinguish between song and speech, and the teacher begins by approaching singing as a variation of speaking, in which the child matches single pitches within a very limited range.

Teacher: Jimmy!

Jimmy: I'm here!

Teacher: Peggy Ann!

Peggy: Here I am.

The child begins to develop a sense of rhythmics through verbal chanting. It is also helpful to combine physical action with singing, sometimes matching rhythms and sometimes following the contour of a melody (up and down) with corresponding motions.

It has been said that the child has two voices, one for speaking (and yelling) and one (much lighter) for singing. With all young children, the music leader should present melodies with a "head voice." Male leaders often employ a falsetto to encourage imitation of that light, "floating" sound. The piano should be used very sparingly, so as not to force the young voices or to discourage children from singing. Finally, even the youngest child should be surrounded with quality sounds, including a good record player to provide background to the play time.

On a spiritual level, pre-school children should experience that the church is a good place to be, and that this means expanding horizons of learning as well as "having fun." This is a period when they become aware of themselves, and of their importance to the church and to God. Music for this age is the medium which brings them into contact with God's world and ours.

The Beginner or Primary Age.

Children from ages six to eight are rapidly gaining in muscular coordination and in cognitive comprehension. However, if they have not yet achieved the musical/spiritual awareness outlined for even younger children, those experiences must be assimilated before they can progress to the next level. This is a time of *action*—if children are not doing something under direction, they will be squirming and bouncing about on their own. Music with action—big sweeping movements of the arms and the whole body—is helpful. The primary child continues to match pitches, but over a broader range. *After experiencing* the organization of rhythm, they may learn to give it a name, and even to recognize the notation for it. At this age, children can become aware of the differences in the tone color of various instruments, and it is helpful to introduce them to the instrument's appearance (e.g., a flute, the tympani, or even the pipes of an organ).

The attention span is still very short, perhaps ten minutes at the most. Nevertheless, this is an age of clear thinking. Impressions are strong, but symbolic speech is meaningless. The six-year-old who sings "The B-I-B-L-E, I stand alone on the word of God" pictures an individual placing a Bible on the floor, and standing on it! One Sunday School teacher tried to explain that "This little light of mine, I'm going to let it shine" meant that we should try to live in an exemplary way, only to have the child retort, "If that's what it means, why doesn't it say so?" It is from such thoughtless use of music that children get the idea that church music is not expected to be cognitive, and perhaps retain that idea into middle age! I remember a time when our eight-year-old daughter came home from church school singing "The Word of God is like a hammer; it breaketh the rocks in tway" (sic). Hoping to encourage her to "make sense" of the song as well as to sing the words correctly, I asked what the words meant. "Don't be silly, Daddy," was her response; "It doesn't mean a thing; it's just a song!" Actually, all of these commonly-used choruses are not suited to this age, because of their figurative language.

Beginners are increasingly aware of their identity in relationship to others—their family, their school, their church and their world. They are also ready to perceive Jesus as a real person, though not as the "suffering Messiah"! Up to and including this age, children should not be expected to contribute to corporate worship; however, they may occasionally be allowed to demonstrate their musical/spiritual growth in the informal setting of the Sunday evening or the midweek service.

The Junior Age.

Some church musicians feel that the Junior span, ages 9 through 11, is the most exciting age to work with. They are no more little children, but *boys* and *girls* and (if you encourage it, which you shouldn't!) boys with boys, and girls with girls. Juniors are able to experience a personal worship of God. For this reason, and also because their musical potential is growing so rapidly, they may occasionally lead the congregation in a brief musical worship experience as the "Junior Choir." This suggests that they can and should become aware of music's function in worship, and should learn the meaning of other symbolism in the church. Children at this age can begin to sing the historic hymns; the leader should explain only the basic message of the words, knowing that the details can be filled in later.

Musically, Juniors have increased dramatically in their performance potential. They can distinguish and reproduce pitches that are close together; in fact, they can sing melodies (even in the tradition of contemporary atonality) that are difficult for adults who have developed "tonal prejudices"! It is well said that this group is limited only by the capacity of their adult leadership.

The child voice may be at its best at this age. It can cover a wide range of pitches with a lot of dynamic contrast, providing the volume is not forced. This age can learn that correct breathing and posture contributes to "support" that gives good tone and good pitch. Juniors are also beginning to read words and music for themselves; though they still sing a great deal in unison, two parts are possible, beginning with a unison plus ostinato, moving to canonic singing, parallel thirds, and finally adding a true descant; an alto part is not recommended since all children's voices are of equal range. It is often advisable to let this group accompany themselves with rhythm and/or pitch instruments—bells, drums, autoharps, and certain Orff instruments. Juniors are already "perfectionists," and can demonstrate a great deal of musical quality.

The Middle-Schooler (Junior High) Age.

Most church music leaders agree that it is most challenging to work with the Junior High group. It is imperative that at this age the musical experience be a positive one, lest the child be lost forever to the choir program, and possibly to the church. The problems encountered, in this transition period between childhood and maturity, are physical. Strange, wonderful things are happening to the body, and particularly to the voice. Even though both boys and girls have a "voice change," the experience is much more traumatic for the boy. Suddenly he can't control his singing, and his efforts result in breaks that can be compared to a yodel. It may be that some of the non-singing by adult males in church is the result of their embarrassment in trying to sing at the time of puberty. It is imperative that the young boy understand that this is a completely normal phenomenon, and that his new voice will be richer and fuller than the old. Nowadays, most experts agree that he should be encouraged to sing right through the voice change. To be sure, the range will be small, and it may seem to change from one week to the next. Most music sung by this age group is in one, two or three parts; in the latter, the "changing voice" may shift to either the alto or the baritone (tenor). It is also possible to buy music specifically written to include the *cambiata*, the changing voice. Many directors have also found it helpful to arrange their own music for this need.

The intermediate youth are sharpest in their assimilation of melodies. Their musical ears are keen, and their ability to duplicate complicated tunes is uncanny. Normal "pop syncopation" is quite natural for this group, but complicated rhythms pose difficulty; this is due to the fact that the body is not perfectly coordinated at this rapidly-growing-and-changing age. Variety is the watchword in working with the early teens.

They tire easily, both in voice and gangly body. They should be encouraged to sing lightly, using vocalises that stretch the range little by little.

Temperamentally, the Junior High person is mercurial; there is no possibility of predicting the quick changes from "serious" to "giddy." They are loyal members of the gang, and adults are "outsiders." The wise choral director will continue to demonstrate acceptance of them at those times when they don't seem to hear a word that is being said. The truth is, they are not missing a syllable, and the moment will come when the choir director becomes their new hero.

In spiritual experience, middlers continue to expand in awareness of their identity as persons and as Christians, especially in relationship to others, peers and nonpeers. For them, the Christian life should be presented as virile and heroic. This is a gang of hero worshipers, and Jesus Christ is the most logical hero-choice they could make. This group can fully understand the function of music in worship, and should occasionally contribute to services. Music which dramatizes or portrays biblical events is especially good to use, and this should include hymns and anthems as well as "musicals."

Junior high folk are open to fairly serious study of church music. They can learn the great hymns, and they are interested in the forms and the hidden meanings of poetry, as well as in the authors and composers who gave us our music. Basic theological concepts—the trinity, incarnation, the atonement—can also be understood by them. This age group is ready to make personal spiritual decisions, and wise church leaders have learned that it is best to encourage a positive response to the gospel without undue pressure. The latter often leads to imitation (to match one's peers) or conformity (to please one's parents or leaders) that may not be genuine commitment. Above all, apparent rejection should not become a reason for conflict. This is the period in which hostility to parents may be expressed in hostility to the parents' faith, and excessive confrontation should be avoided.

The High School Age.

If the intermediate group is the most challenging and difficult to work with, the senior high age may be the most rewarding. Mentally, these youth are at their peak. Vocally, they are just short of being adults. If music ministers will allow them to sing with a little lighter voice than fully mature persons, using music that is a little less demanding in range (both high and low), this age can give a truly exciting, artistic performance.

Now that the body has quite fully developed and physical coordination is at a high level, high school youth can respond to very intricate rhythms. This group welcomes the stiffest challenge and, like the junior age, is often limited only by the ability and imagination of their adult leaders. Mentally, the high schooler can reason like an adult, but lacks the knowledge and experience of older folk. Aesthetically, they respond to beauty in great poetry and music, and also to the natural, simple expressions of pop, folk and rock music; both historic art music and contemporary expressions should be included in their repertoire.

The musical interests of this age group are wide. Teens love to participate, to play all sorts of instruments (orchestral, pop—e.g., guitars and drums, Orff instruments, handbells), to lead singing, or to be an assistant to the choir director. They are interested in the stories of hymns and in the lives of hymn writers and other church musicians. They are able to understand most theological concepts, and to respond completely to the Christian challenge to discipleship, including stewardship of their talents. High schoolers can regularly lead in musical worship, and through this experience may be motivated to give their lives to the service of God, in foreign missions, in pastoring, in social work, or in church music. Many music ministers have capitalized on this readiness for challenge by taking youth choirs on mission tours, during which they assist struggling churches in summer vacation school outreach, in evangelism, and even by contributing physical labor in repairing, cleaning or painting church properties.

To be sure, temperamentally this group can be volcanic. They are idealistic, and keenly sensitive to the possibility of hypocrisy in their elders. They may seem to reject authority, but usually respond positively to firm, loving guidance. In our day, when discipline is said to be a problem in public schools, many music ministers are eminently successful in reaching and developing teenagers in the music program. This is partly true because music activity offers its own contribution to self-esteem, is an excellent safety valve for releasing excess energy and emotion, and encourages personal discipline through sound educational procedures.

During the past ten to fifteen years, the central focus of the music program in many churches has been the youth choir, possibly because there has been great concern about reaching and holding youth in the church. We live in a time when the teen culture is very strong, and many of the new music forms have developed from youth preferences. For this reason, many churches have majored in the contemporary styles (folk, rock, pop), especially in working with high schoolers. The first response was overwhelming; young people flocked to the youth choir who had never been interested in traditional music activity, either in the public school or in church. Now that the bloom is gone from this phenomenon, we can assess its contribution to the church.

Beyond a doubt, the new expressions are important because they use texts that communicate Christian truth in language that speaks to young people; furthermore, in the tradition of renewal music that springs from contemporary, secular forms, the use of contemporary sounds was inescapable. However, now that the interest in participation has diminished considerably, it becomes evident that many directors put too many eggs in that particular basket. Colleges and graduate schools report that the new generation of post-teens simply did not develop their vocal potential because their musical diet was too limited. Most youth did not learn to produce authentic vocal sounds, because they sang music exclusively in the pop style, which was projected—not by proper voice production and support—but by a microphone and a high-decibel sound system. Musically, they learned how to handle syncopated rhythms excellently, particularly when accompanied by drums and guitars, but other, more subtle rhythmics escaped them. The full range of voices was not developed and there was no incentive to emphasize good intonation, as would be required in unaccompanied music. All of this should remind us of the imperative of *balance* in music education. Teens should sing a fair amount of music in their popular idioms, but they should also learn to perform standard repertoire, including Renaissance motets, rococo anthems and contemporary serious styles. One of the objectives of education is to prepare individuals for the age groups into which they will move in the future. If the youth choir learns only how to sing in their presently-preferred styles, they will have little to offer the church when they get a little older, and lose their taste for the teenage literature.

The Adult Age.

Music education in the church does not stop at the teenage level. If there is validity in the music activities of the college, conservatory, university or seminary music department, there is obviously much yet to be learned by the adults in the church choir. Vocal development—good tone produced by proper phonation and support—goes on. Musicianship—intonation, rhythmics, articulation vs. legato singing, dynamic control, diction, phrasing—is the constant goal of the older choir. More difficult literature in all styles—renaissance, baroque, rococo, romantic, contemporary—offer new challenges week by week.

The senior choir may also need renewal in motivation. Many young adults drop out of the choir program, even though they were active as children and teenagers. Some who continue to participate have forgotten, or possibly never learned, the spiritual significance of their service to the church, and sing simply because they enjoy doing so. The call to give our musical gifts back to God who gave them to us—not in the rough form in which we received them, but developed and refined—is one that needs to be constantly reviewed in the adult choir.

The "Special People" and Music Activity.

In American society, "special education" denotes programs of training for the abnormal child, both the more talented and the handicapped. Music education for the first group must usually be obtained in "private lessons" or perhaps in such settings as the "Suzuki" string class. For the latter group, there is "music therapy" for which teachers may be specially trained at such schools as the University of Michigan.[6] This is

---

6. It is interesting to note that the blind composer/pianist/singer, Ken Medema, is a graduate of this program.

also a logical activity for the church musician to employ in ministry, although perhaps it falls more in the "pastoring" role than in "teaching."

Recently, I saw such a program in action in the First Baptist Church of Winter Haven, Florida. The church organist, who was herself a music teacher with an adopted, emotionally-crippled child, was leading a group of "special people" of various ages in "This Little Light of Mine" during the Sunday School hour. Some were accompanying the music with rhythm instruments—wood blocks, sticks, tambourines and a few handbells. Everybody was singing, with a physical and emotional gusto that may not have produced the best vocalism, but which revealed the intense involvement of each person.

It was obvious that, contrary to popular opinion, these handicapped persons can learn, and that music is a particularly effective educational tool. They were first allowed to listen to a song several times, either sung by the leader or played by a recording. Next, they repeated the words in rhythm, phrase by phrase, several times. Clapping the rhythms was also an effective learning device. Finally, the melody was added, and the entire song put together. Although purity of ensemble is not a strong feature of the resulting performance, these handicapped persons learn rather easily, and *never forget* what they have learned. Rhythmic, "up tempo" music is preferred, and words that tell about the love of Jesus, such as "What a Difference You've Made in My Life" and "Creature Praise" (with the significant phrase "Let everything that has breath praise the Lord.")

To be sure, music activity for the handicapped person is almost completely related to therapy and training, not to public performance. Nevertheless, the group mentioned above has appeared in an evening service in the sponsoring church, and received a standing ovation. In the "workshop shelter" at Lakeland, Florida, music therapy has produced a group of about twenty "special people" who regularly perform for various civic clubs and organizations to demonstrate the shelter's program. Wherever this kind of activity takes place, it must be seen as ministry. It is particularly appropriate that it be related to a church, where it expresses the love of God and of Christian believers to a group of individuals who are frequently shunned by society.

Music is one of the best means of communication to this group and of helping them to express themselves. The "stream of speech" differentiates the emotionally adjusted from the emotionally unadjusted. The language of music becomes a substitute for speech, and is particularly important because it is "the language of the emotions."

Senior Citizens and Music Activity.

It is usually expected that all music training will cease, once an individual retires from participation in a church's adult choir. In recent years, the importance of music activity for senior citizens has encouraged churches (especially in retirement areas) to develop therapeutic activity for them. In Winchester, Kentucky the LLL Club Band (Live Longer and Like It) sponsored by Central Baptist Church both sings and plays "noise instruments," and gives programs in hospitals, nursing homes, churches, civic clubs and state parks. The "Amazing Grace" Choir of Lynchburg, Virginia owns its own bus, which permits the retirees to combine their travel-recreation with the presentation of musical programs in many different places.

Evangelicals and Choral Literature

Adult Choral Music.

America's first important church music composers emerged in the 18th century. The oblong tune books of that period usually provided for all the music needs of a church, both congregational and choral; frequently the anthems appeared under pseudonyms or with no composer credit at all. *Kentucky Harmony,* 1816 ("A Choice Collection of Psalm Tunes, Hymns, and Anthems") includes:

> Anthem from Luke, 2nd chapter (Stephenson)
> Easter Anthem (W. Billings)
> Heavenly Vision ("French")
> Judgment Anthem (Grace)
> Rose of Sharon (W. Billings)
> Farewell Anthem (French)
> Redemption Anthem (no composer given)
> David's Lamentation (W. Billings)
> Funeral Anthem (no composer given)
> Prodigal Son (Josiah Moore)
> The Lover's Lamentation (A. Davisson)
> Bunkers Hill: An Ode (no composer given)
> Ode on Science (no composer given)

The Sacred Harp, 1844 ("A Collection of Psalm and Hymn Tunes, Odes, and Anthems") listed the following extended pieces in Part III:

> Christmas Anthem (no composer given)
> Ode of Life's Journey (E. J. King)
> Masonic Ode (no composer given)
> Baptismal Anthem (B. F. White)
> Reverential Anthem; 96th Psalm (E. J. King)
> Easter Anthem (Billings)
> David's Lamentation (Billings)
> Christian Song (no composer given)
> Ode on Science (no composer given)
> Claremont ("Vital spark of heavenly flame")
> Heavenly Vision (Billings)
> Rose of Sharon (Billings)
> Farewell Anthem (no composer given)

Stemming from this tradition, the early revival songbooks and later "revivalist hymnals" also included music for choral use, usually called "chorus choir selections." Much less contrapuntal than the "fuging tunes" and other anthems listed above, they usually consisted of two-page settings, which could be called extended hymns or gospel songs, or simplified anthems.

The publishing of what we know as "octavo" choral music began with the historic Novello and Company firm in London about 1844. These inexpensive editions of single choral pieces soon appeared on this side of the Atlantic, and began to be imitated by American publishers as well. One of the historic taboos of evangelical churches which promoted "free and simple worship" was directed against this new phenomenon of music produced especially for the choir. In some churches it still exists. If the music is printed in a book like the hymnal, the choir may use it; otherwise, it is forbidden!

In the late 19th century, E. S. Lorenz, a German immigrant, founded the publishing company that bears his name in Dayton, Ohio, and specialized in producing music for small church choirs. Stylistically, he attempted to bridge the gap between traditional anthems of the period and "gospel music." Through the years, the Lorenz Publishing Company has received a good deal of criticism from musicians with "more highly developed" musical tastes. Looking back, it is now difficult to discern much qualitative difference between Lorenz publications and the typical fare of American churches, even in the early 20th century: "Hark, Hark, my Soul" and "The King of Love My Shepherd Is" by Shelley; "Festival Te Deum" by Dudley Buck; "Praise the Lord, O Jerusalem" by Maunder; and "Springs in the Desert" by Jennings.

Many evangelical churches have continued their prejudice against typical anthems. Choral arrangements of hymns (hymn anthems) or of gospel songs have been the principal fare in many congregations. Nowadays, the prejudice against separate choral pieces has largely disappeared, but a large number of evangelical churches continue to follow the pattern in choral music which is typical of their hymnody: there is too little expression of objective praise, and too much preoccupation with pop music styles. It may also be argued that using the same melodies for the choir that are sung by the congregation contributes to the sentimentality-response which accompanies the "favorite tune" cult.

To be sure, many congregations have broadened their horizons by using contemporary and traditional anthems by gifted functional church music composers, like Austin Lovelace, Dale Wood, Fred Bock, Gordon Young, Carlton Young, Maxcine Posegate, Walter Ehret and Natalie Sleeth. This open attitude of many evangelicals toward more traditional choral styles is evidenced by the changes in the old-line publishers. Such companies as Lillenas, Word, Benson, Hope and Singspiration (as well as many others) now publish anthems in all styles for their constituents.

Larger choral works (cantatas, et al) have appeared in at least four styles: the standards (Handel's *Messiah*, Dubois' *Seven Last Words*, Vaughan

Williams' *Hodie,* etc.); the simpler imitations (as from Lorenz); more recently, the cantatas of John Peterson, which combine extended gospel hymn styles with modest solo recitatives and instrumental interludes; and the folk or rock musicals, like Buryl Red's "Celebrate Life" and John Wilson's "The Love Story." An even more contemporary version in the Peterson *metier* is found in the "happenings" based on songs of other modern-day composers (e.g., *Alleluia,* with Bill Gaither music). One of the principal features of this music is the use of contemporary styles in the arranging and orchestration, frequently done by such experts as Ron Huff, Ralph Carmichael, Otis Skillings, Jimmy Owens and Rick Powell. Accompaniment tapes are available so that a professional Nashville or Hollywood orchestra may be heard as accompaniment to the choir of any local church.

Choral Literature for Younger Ages.

Music for children has come a long way from the first efforts in the 18th century.

> (Song about Hell)
> There they lie, alas, how long!
>   Never can they hope release;
> Not a drop to cool their tongue,
>   Not an hour, a moment's ease;
> Damned they are and still shall be,
>   Damned to all eternity.

> (About the death of a scholar)
> A mourning class, a vacant seat,
>   Tell us that one we loved to meet
> Will join our youthful throng no more,
>   Till all these changing scenes are o'er.
> God tells us by this mournful death
>   How vain and fleeting is our breath;
> And bids our souls prepare to meet
>   The trial of His judgment seat.

> (On behaving in church)
> In God's own house for me to play,
>   While Christians meet to hear and pray,
> Is to profane his holy place,
>   And tempt the Almighty to his face.
> When angels bow before the Lord,
>   And devils tremble at his word,
> Shall I, a feeble mortal, dare
>   To mock, and sport and trifle there?

There were a few exceptions, like Charles Wesley's "Gentle Jesus, Meek and Mild," which may demonstrate that Arminian theology was more sensitive to children's needs than Calvinist thought.

Gentle Jesus, meek and mild, Look upon a little child;
    Pity my simplicity, Suffer me to come to Thee.

Lamb of God, I look to Thee; Thou shalt my example be:
    Thou art gentle, meek and mild; Thou wast once a little child.

It is little wonder that the 19th century welcomed the more winning expressions, both of the Sunday school movement and of British hymnwriters, even though some examples may have presumed too much theological understanding for children, and too much self-deprecation.

    The Sabbath school's a place of prayer,
        I love to meet my teacher there;
    They teach me here that everyone
        May find in heaven a happy home.
Refrain:
    I love to go, I love to go,
        I love to go to Sabbath school.
            (from *Sabbath School Wreath,* 1863)

Jesus loves me! this I know,
    For the Bible tells me so,
Little ones to Him belong;
    They are weak, but He is strong.
                    Anna B. Warner

When He cometh, when He cometh To make up His jewels,
    All His jewels, precious jewels, His loved and His own.

Little children, little children, Who love their Redeemer,
    Are the jewels, precious jewels, His loved and His own.
                    William O. Cushing

All things bright and beautiful, All creatures great and small,
    All things wise and wonderful, The Lord God made them all.

Each little flower that opens, Each little bird that sings,
    He made their glowing colors, He made their tiny wings.
                    Cecil Frances Alexander

In recent years, most of the creative planning of children's music has been done by denominational Christian education departments. Typical, independent evangelical publishers continued a heavy and unrealistic pedagogical bent which was illustrated in the choruses cited earlier in this chapter. Only recently has the situation been remedied somewhat by such Sunday school specialists as the David C. Cook Publishing Company. A large number of suitable junior choir pieces have also been released by all the church music publishers, including Chorister's Guild, who specialize in materials for this age group.

Nowadays, children find meaning in such poetic and mystical wonders as "Little Lamb" by William Blake (1757–1827).

Little Lamb, who made thee? Dost thou know who made thee?
    Gave thee life, and bid thee feed, By the streams o'er the mead;
Gave thee clothing of delight, softest clothing, wooly, bright!
    Gave thee such a tender voice, You make the vales rejoice.
Little Lamb, who made thee? Does thou know who made thee?

Little Lamb, I'll tell thee, Little Lamb, I'll tell thee:
    He is called by thy name, For He calls Himself a Lamb,
He is meek and mild; He became a child.
    I a child, thou a lamb, We are called by His name.
Little Lamb, God bless thee. God bless Thee.

In the early part of the 20th century, the Christian education movement directed attention to the needs of young people who are older than
children. At that time a large number of youth songs appeared, most of
them showing a self-consciousness which revealed that they were written
by adults who were quite detached from the youth mentality.

Serve the Lord in the days of youth,
    Learn His law and accept His truth;
Sing His praise with a ready tongue,
    While the heart is young.

Serve Him then, every youthful day,
    Choose His guidance without delay;
Waste no part of these precious years,
    Youth soon disappears.
                Edith Sanford Tillotson, 1917

I would be true, for there are those who trust me;
    I would be pure, for there are those who care;
I would be strong, for there is much to suffer;
    I would be brave, for there is much to dare.

I would be friend of all—the foe, the friendless;
    I would be giving, and forget the gift;
I would be humble, for I know my weakness;
    I would look up, and laugh, and love, and lift.
                Howard Arnold Walter

It has now become evident that young people (including high schoolers) are attuned to the truly aesthetic and poetic, and their favorites in
1980 are quite different.

Morning has broken like the first morning,
    Blackbird has spoken like the first bird.

Praise for the singing! Praise for the morning!
Praise for them, springing fresh from the Word!

Eleanor Farjeon, 1957

Be Thou my Vision, O Lord of my heart;
Naught be all else to me, save that Thou art—
Thou my best thought, by day or by night,
Waking or sleeping, Thy presence my light.

Irish; trans., Mary E. Byrne,
poem by Eleanor H. Hull

In the last ten years, extended works have been released for singing by
younger voices, and they are usually called "musicals" or "happenings."[7]
High school choirs were the first beneficiaries of the movement, and
they have performed such works as:

Good News, Bob Oldenburg (Broadman, 1967)
Tell It Like It Is, Ralph Carmichael and Kurt Kaiser (Sacred Songs,
1969)
Shepherds, Rejoice, John Wilson (Hope, 1968)
Now Hear It Again, Bob Burroughs (Broadman, 1970)
A Christmas Happening, John Wilson (Hope, 1970)
Come Together, Jimmy Owens (Lexicon, 1972)
Born! by John Wilson (Hope, 1973)
Celebrate Life!, Buryl Red (Broadman, 1972)
Backpackers Suite, Sonny Salsbury (Word, 1975)
Make It Clear, Bill Butterworth (Singspiration, 1976)
Angels, Cynthia Clawson (Triune, 1978)

More recently, the "subteens" received the attention of contemporary
composers:

The Story-telling Man, Ken Medema (Word, 1975)
All that Jazz Series, Herbert Chappell (Marks, 1971)
Zack, Jr., Jack Coleman (Lexicon, 1973)
Sam, Bobby Hammack (Lexicon, 1973)
Rock on the Head, Don Wyrtzen (Singspiration, 1974)

Finally, a host of material has been produced for the Junior Choir and
even for the primary group.

100% Chance of Rain, Horsley (Choristers Guild, 1972)
It's Cool in the Furnace, Buryl Red (Word, 1973)
Sunshine and Snowflakes, Clark Gassman (Lexicon, 1973)

7. A more complete list is given in Donald P. Ellsworth, *Christian Music in Contemporary
Witness*, pp. 203–207.

Jonah's Tale of a Whale, Robert Graham (Broadman, 1974)
A Night for Dancing, Hal Hopson (Choristers Guild, 1974)
They All Sang Jesus, Lee Turner (Benson, 1976)
The Music Machine, Jimmy Owens (Birdwing, 1977)
The Small One, John Wilson (Somerset, 1977)
Beauty and the Feast, Charles F. Brown (Word, 1977)
Barbecue for Ben, Donald F. Marsh (Agape, 1977)
Angels, Lambs, Ladybugs and Fireflies, Fred Bock (Fred Bock Music, 1978)
Babble at BAbel, Albert Zabel (Hope 1979)

Chapter XVII

EVANGELICALS AND MUSIC FOR SOLOISTS (AND SMALL ENSEMBLES)

About the time of the recent Liturgical Revival (ca. 1930–1960), the idea was widespread in "respectable" churches that solo song was unacceptable. "Worship is a corporate experience" was the argument. "The solo is too personal, and tends to draw attention to the singer rather than to the message."

Notwithstanding, performances by single individuals have a long heritage in the Judeo-Christian religion. The first reference to worship music in scripture follows the narrative of Israel crossing the Red Sea.

> And Miriam sang to them: "Sing to the Lord, for he has triumphed gloriously; the horse and his rider he has thrown into the sea." (Exodus 15:21)

We recall also the picture of the youthful shepherd David strumming his lyre while tending his father's sheep, and singing his personal experience and his praise of Yahweh—songs that were at least the prototype of the historic psalms. In the history of the synagogue, the solo cantor has been heard for possibly 2500 years! It has also been conjectured that the "spiritual songs" (Eph. 5:19, Col. 3:16) of New Testament times may have been improvised solos.

The solo tradition has been especially strong in secular music. The first recorded examples are those of the troubadours, the trouveres and the minnesingers in the 12th to the 14th centuries. One of the influences in the development of these forms was the adoration of the Virgin Mary; the songs of the minnesingers perpetuated this tradition and were very important in the development of the chorale. In the early and the medieval church, as well, the individual priest or deacon chanted portions of the liturgy, sometimes responsively with the choir.

In the 17th and 18th centuries, German Lutheran composers wrote solo cantatas for church performance. It is interesting to note that one early English Baptist leader[1] preferred to hear single voices in worship music, contending that certain individuals were given the "gift" of song, and fearing that in congregational singing, some might participate who were not true believers! In yet another tradition, the "precentor" in early British and American history "lined out" the psalms in solo voice, followed by the congregation.

In the late 19th century and extending into the 20th, the "quartet choir" in American churches was made up of four soloists. They sang four-part music as a group, but also traditionally functioned as soloists at other times in the service. In this tradition, certain solos were borrowed from cantatas and oratorios, sacred words were set to opera or operetta melodies, and new sacred solos were written in similar but simpler styles. These examples were very popular and are still being used today.

> Beside Still Waters (Bernard Hamblen)
> Great Peace Have They (James H. Rogers)
> How Beautiful upon the Mountains (F. Flaxington Harker)
> How Lovely Are Thy Dwellings (Samuel Liddle)
> My Redeemer and My Lord (Dudley Buck)
> O Divine Redeemer (Charles Gounod)
> Open the Gates of the Temple (Crosby-Knapp)
> The Holy City (Stephen Adams)
> The Lord Is My Light (Frances Allitsen)

In a recent article in a Lutheran magazine, Carl Halter makes a case for the validity of the solo in a modern worship experience.[2]

> But in a day which has seen the likes of Janis Joplin and Jimi Hendrix articulate in earthy howls the agonies of this time and has witnessed the sometimes frightening waves of mass identification which their performances (and others like them) have brought forth, perhaps we ought to take another look at how we can best speak to the kind of people who are stirred by Joplin and put to sleep by Josquin (des Prez).

He also argues, in recalling the recent prejudice against solos, that it is unfair to single out the vocalist while ignoring others.[3] The organist often functions as a soloist, and the preacher may also be said to be involved in "solo communication."

In this category of church music, American evangelicals have long ignored the opinions of the experts. Solo song has been one of the hallmarks of our worship and evangelism for almost one hundred fifty years. Philip Phillips (1834–1895) was the first of the acknowledged "gospel singers"; he was called "The Singing Pilgrim." We have already mentioned the giant of solo singing in the 19th century—Ira David

---

1. See Horton Davies, *Worship and Theology in England,* Vol. II, pp. 501–502.
2. Carl F. Halter, "The Case for the Soloist in Christian Worship."
3. Ibid., p. 1.

Sankey (1840-1908), who was chosen by the evangelist D. L. Moody to be his musical associate on the basis of his ability to lead a group in a hymn at a very early morning prayer meeting.[4] It was Sankey who most promoted the popularity of the gospel song in the late 19th century. In England, his published books were called *Sacred Songs and Solos;* the last edition is still in print one hundred years after the first appeared!

Many of the renowned solo gospel singers of the 19th century were also teachers of singing schools (conventions), and composers. They included these important individuals, many of whom were associated with the evangelists who moved in the "Moody circle."

> Philip P. Bliss (baritone) 1838-1876
> James McGranahan (tenor) 1840-1907
> Daniel B. Towner (baritone) 1850-1919
> Edwin O. Excell (tenor) 1851-1921
> Ada Ruth Habershon (soprano) 1861-1918
> Philip P. Bilhorn (tenor) 1865-1936
> George C. Stebbins (tenor) 1846-1945
> Elma Miller Stebbins (Mrs. G. C., soprano) n.d.a.
> May Whittle Moody (soprano) 1870-1963

It should be noted that, although America has the reputation of being the "revivalist" culture, gospel singers have also been known in other parts of the world. I have already mentioned Oscar Ahnfelt (1813-1882) who was the musical spokesman of the Swedish pietist revival. Well trained in serious music and all the arts, he began to write music for Lina Sandell's experience hymns, which he used in connection with his own preaching ministry. Jenny Lind (1820-1887), one of the world's renowned coloratura sopranos in opera and concert, financed the publishing of Ahnfelt's songs in several volumes of the *Andeliga Sånger.* When she toured America in 1850-1852 under the patronage of P. T. Barnum, the entertainment entrepreneur, "The Swedish Nightingale" often closed her performances with a simple gospel hymn.

In the 20th century, the first gospel solo singer to attract wide attention was Homer Rodeheaver (1880-1955), songleader for evangelist Billy Sunday. When I heard him sing late in life, Mr. Rodeheaver still possessed a warm, resonant baritone voice which was at its best when he sang his own song, "When Jesus Came."

The Ministry of Solo Song

In the modern era, the professional gospel singers are headed by George Beverly Shea (b. 1909) who began singing full-time in 1938 at the radio station of Moody Bible Institute (WMBI, Chicago), and is best

4. George C. Stebbins, *Reminiscences and Gospel Hymn Stories,* p. 202.

known for his association with evangelist Billy Graham. In his autobiography, *Then Sings My Soul,* Mr. Shea reminisces about the old family piano on which he wrote the music for his most famous song "I'd Rather Have Jesus."

> What a debt I owed that old instrument.
> Through it, Mother had transmitted to me her love of music and faith in God.
> Through it, I first learned to express those stirrings inside me which sought release.
> Through it, I found my life's work, a way to tell others of Christ.
> Through it and the sacred song, I have known the mute to speak, the deaf to hear, the blind to see.[5]

Shea's co-author ends the book with a quotation from Longfellow's poem "The Singers":

> God sent His singers upon the earth
> With songs of sadness and of mirth,
> That they might touch the hearts of men,
> And bring them back to heaven again.[6]

Those words express something of the genius of the solo ballad singer, whether he performs in the theater or in the church. John Denver sings of the anxieties of modern youth—their search for identity and security in a world threatened both by cybernetic anonymity and atomic Armageddon—and his songs become the shared expression of all the young folk within the sound of his voice. Johnny Cash sings of the hard and uncertain life of the working man—the truck driver, the farmer or the railroader—and his words and music express the "gut feelings" of every "blue collar" person in the audience. "Bev" Shea—or Ken Medema, Evie Tornquist, Andraé Crouch or Cynthia Clawson—sing of finding life's meaning in Jesus Christ, and every believer in the audience resonates with the truth and the emotion. Furthermore, nonbelievers hear in the song potential answers to their own search for ultimate meaning, and may become "seekers."

Part of the quest of contemporary worship leaders has been a search for means through which the individual may express his deepest hurts, his fears and his joys. Traditionally, we try to find meaning for ourselves in the expressions of others—in drama, in literature and even in visual-plastic arts. Of all the arts, music is one of the best means of articulating both the search and the discovery, and solo music may often be better than ensemble performance. This is person-to-person communication, not group-to-person. When the message is relevant to the listener, and the soloist is expressing it with apparent sincerity, the communication is convincing and gripping. If you doubt this, watch the ability of any good

5. George Beverly Shea, *Then Sings My Soul,* p. 176.
6. Ibid.

soloist—Joan Baez or Frank Sinatra or Frank Boggs—to get and to hold
the attention of an audience! Obviously, this is not purely a personal
experience, but rather one which is enhanced by the attention of the
whole group—it is intensely corporate. As Carl Halter says, in opposing
the recent taboo on solo singing in worship:

> The soloist has some advantages over the choir (as has the choir over
> the soloist) which ought to be used for the sake of the worship of all
> the people. These advantages relate mainly to that characteristic of
> solo performance which has customarily been viewed as its principal
> defect: its individualism.[7]

Following are a number of quotations from contemporary singers,
revealing that they see themselves as "ministers," particularly "musical
messengers"—in the exegesis of Ephesians 4:11–12, "prophets,
evangelists, pastors and teachers."

George Beverly Shea:
> ... I found my life's work, a way to tell others of Christ.[8]

Gloria Gaither:
Entry: (diary)
> After an already exhausting weekend we had to sing at a college
> tonight. We did our best to "feed the multitude." I think we knew
> how the disciples must have felt. So little to feed so many. But we,
> as they, just give God the little that we have, and trust that He can
> make it go around.[9]

Ken Medema:
> Commitment is not feeling you would like to do something. Com-
> mitment is not a promise and a tear. The conscious examination of
> risk considering all the issues, determining to make a specific
> choice and providing for yourself the wherewithal to follow
> through on the choice you have made—that is commitment. That
> means providing time, resources, thought-energy, money, what-
> ever is necessary. If we can somehow communicate these ideas
> then I think we will make tremendous strides toward a better
> understanding of what Jesus wants of his disciples. . . . Well, it's
> time to go on. They're dimming the houselights and they expect
> the singer to come walking on stage and touch those keys
> again. . . . I'll feel better about performing now that you know
> where I stand on these things.[10]

Claude Rhea:
> In all candor I had to admit God had endowed me with a talent. I
> had discovered while in the army that he had given me the ability
> to communicate through singing. . . . It was something beyond my
> ability—it was God's grace gift to me. It had to be used! And so,

7. Halter, op. cit., p. 4.
8. Shea, op. cit., p. 176.
9. Gloria Gaither, *Because He Lives*, p. 200.
10. Ken Medema, *Come and See*, p. 92.

calmly, rationally and in a conscious act of my will, I prayed . . . that God would take my gift and use it. I gave back to Him my music.[11]

Johnny Cash:

My message to the crowd had been simple. I told them, "I'm not here tonight to exalt Johnny Cash . . . I'm standing here as an entertainer, as a performer, as a singer who is supporting the gospel of Jesus Christ. I'm here to invite you to listen to the good news that will be laid out for you, to analyze it, and see if you don't think it's the best way to live."[12]

Anita Bryant:

I always shall remember Becky who blessed me in a way she didn't know. Only through unexpectedly leading a child to the Lord via a contemporary situation could I realize that *anything* we do can be necessary and perhaps even essential to God's purposes . . . I'd become somewhat unenthusiastic about pop songs because it's getting harder and harder to find really sweet ones. But pop music related to that little girl . . . God taught me once again—through her—that He can use anything we'll dedicate to Him. That night He took the pop music I looked down on, and used it to His glory![13]

Ed Lyman:

Remember the message we are telling. It is a love story, a song of deliverance, and melody of praise to our Lord. Our voices are channels through which the Spirit of God can bless others.[14]

Andraé Crouch:

The apogee of my day is when I'm really worshiping God on stage, playing and singing for Him and telling young people, "You've got to meet Him," or telling those who know Him, "Let's praise Him, let's have church."[15]

Solo Materials for Worship Purposes

In a typical worship service involving expressions of praise and adoration, a soloist might be expected to substitute for a choir. In small churches where a choir is not available, an individual (or small ensembles) may provide all the "special music." In other situations, the music of a soloist may be expected to supplement that of the choir, perhaps providing one of the two "special" selections in any particular service.

Much of the typical literature which was popular in the late 19th and

---

11. Claude Rhea, *With My Song I Will Praise Him*, p. 36.
12. Johnny Cash, *Man in Black*, p. 242.
13. Anita Bryant, *Amazing Grace*, pp. 35–36.
14. Ed Lyman, *Singing Your Song*, p. 21. Mr. Lyman has recently sponsored *Noteworthy*, "The Music Magazine for Communicating Christianity" (P.O. Box 220038, Charlotte, NC 26211), which emphasizes solo music.
15. Andraé Crouch, *Through It All*, p. 146.

early 20th centuries is still available, though it must be said to have outlived its usefulness in churches where the selections have already been heard for many years. When Stephen Adams' solo "The Holy City" is used nowadays (much as is true of the gospel song "The Old Rugged Cross"), we must guess that it is because of the congregation's (or the soloist's) sentimental attachment for it. Because of the decreased interest in solo worship music in recent years, comparatively little new material has been published. The major church music houses, however, have continued to release a few items. The following is a representative list of collections that are available, some of which depend largely on older materials recently rediscovered.

> *Fifty-two Sacred Songs You Like to Sing* (Schirmer)
> *Seventeen Sacred Songs* (Schirmer)
> *Solos for the Church Year* (Lawson-Gould)
> *Solos for the Church Soloist* (Lawson-Gould)
> *Anthology of Sacred Song* (Schirmer)
> *Sacred Songs from Schemelli's Gesangbuch,* J. S. Bach (Concordia)
> *Chorales for Lent,* Carl Schalk[16] (Augsburg)
> *Eight Chorale Settings from Opella Nova,* Johann H. Schein (Concordia)
> *The Morning Star Choir Book* (Concordia). Originally written for solo
>   voices, and may be sung in that form; three volumes, including
>   *Second Morning Star* . . and *Third Morning Star Choir Book*
> *Twelve Sacred Songs,* Oley Speaks (Schirmer)
> *100 Songs of the Seasons* (Singspiration)
> *Two Divine Hymns and Alleluia,* Henry Purcell (Boosey & Hawkes)
> *Charles E. Ives Sacred Songs* (Peer International)
> Dvorak's *Biblical Songs* (Associated Music Publishers)
> *New Testament Songs* (Hope)
> *Broadman Solo Collection* (Broadman)
> *Two Songs for Medium Voices,* Don McAfee (Abingdon)
> *Everything for the Church Soloist* (Hope)
> *The Sanctuary Soloist* (Fred Bock)

The soloist may also find a potential supply of material in hymnbooks, especially new hymnal releases. With the help of an organist who can improvise appropriate introductions and interludes, a worthy "sacred art song" can be created.

There are no strict rules about the placement of solo songs in worship services. They may substitute for a choral piece, though hardly for a "call to worship" or a "response," and perhaps ideally as an offertory. One traditional practice in some evangelical churches is disappointing—the use of a solo *experience* song immediately before the morning message. This idea is no doubt another vestige of the revival heritage, in which the soloist "prepares" for the "prophet" by announcing: "What this person will say is true; it worked in my life." In a worship service, the custom has

16. See Carl Schalk, "Solo Literature for the Liturgical Service" in which he gives a list of
    solo (and duet) material catalogued for the church year.

little validity, unless the homily is unashamedly evangelistic; otherwise, there is little thematic connection between song and sermon. In following the practice, a minister seems to acknowledge that a solo provides the best "mood" preparation for the congregation. The soloist may also serve to direct the audience's attention to the pulpit; having done so, the minister steps quickly into the spotlight!

Solo "Experience Songs"

In the early days of the gospel song (ca. 1850–1900) there was little to differentiate most solo music from that of the congregation. An existing Edison recording of Ira Sankey features the singing of "God Be With You Till We Meet Again" (Rankin-Tomer), and his account[17] of the introduction of solo song in Scotland in 1873 mentions "Free From the Law! O Happy Condition" (Words and music by P. P. Bliss), both of which we now consider to be congregational. At the same time, Sankey used (and wrote music for) some songs which were clearly soloistic, like "The Ninety and Nine" (Clephane-Sankey), "Flee As a Bird" (Dana-Spanish melody) and "In the Secret of His Presence" (Goreh-Stebbins). Others featured two solo voices (a duet) on the stanzas with the choir or congregation joining in the refrain, e.g., "Saved By Grace" (Crosby-Stebbins) and "I Surrender All" (VanDeVenter-Weeden). The typical congregational gospel song had a melodic range limited to one octave, very simple harmony and "dotted note" rhythms. The solo or duet had a slightly extended range and was "more flowing" in rhythmic quality. The "Spanish folk" setting of "Flee As a Bird to the Mountain" must have been quite an exciting exception to the rule, with its minor mode and range of eleven notes.

In the early 20th century, some composers tended to specialize in writing for solo or duet voices, continuing the style mentioned above, but with more harmonic variety. Robert Harkness (1880–1961), pianist for song-evangelist Charles Alexander, is remembered for such songs as "No Longer Lonely," "Why Should He Love Me So?" and "Gethsemane" (Into a garden went my Lord). B. D. Ackley (1872–1958), pianist for the Sunday-Rodeheaver campaigns, wrote tunes for these songs of Oswald J. Smith (b. 1889), all of which are considered to be solos or duets: "The Song of the Soul Set Free," "The Glory of His Presence," "God Is Waiting in the Silence," "God Is In the Shadows," "The Savior Can Solve Every Problem," "Beyond the Shadows," and "My Heart's Desire." These were only a few of the songs for which Ackley wrote music; his lyrics came from many author-sources.

From about 1920 to 1950, not many evangelical composers gave attention to writing congregational material. They were instead occupied with producing "performance music"—solos, duets, women's trios, male

17. Ira D. Sankey, *My Life and the Story of the Gospel Songs,* pp. 61–62.

quartets and choir material, and the styles tended to be influenced by the new evangelism medium of radio. Familiar names (in addition to B. D. Ackley, already mentioned) were George S. Schuler (1882-1973), Harry Dixon Loes (1892-1965), Herbert G. Tovey (1888-1972), Harry D. Clarke (1888-1957), Haldor Lillenas (1885-1959), Merrill Dunlop (b. 1905), Avis B. Christiansen (b. 1895), Wendell P. Loveless (b. 1892) and Floyd Hawkins (b. 1904). The solo materials of this era were quite different from the earlier examples; melodies had greater range and wider interval leaps. Increasingly, sacred songs copied the form of secular popular music, with very short stanzas and more developed refrains.

One exception to the above generalization was the Southern Baptist composer B. B. McKinney (1886-1952). In the period before 1940 he wrote a large number of gospel songs which received wide use in his denomination, including "Have Faith in God," "Holy Spirit, Breathe on Me," "Wherever He Leads I'll Go" and "Place Your Hand in the Nail-Scarred Hand." Although these songs were introduced as solos, they were in an older style and simpler. As a result (and also because they were published in fourpart settings), they soon were used principally as congregational material.

During each decade of the 20th century, the solo style continued to develop, with more florid melody set to more advanced harmony, quite different from the simple gospel hymns of Ira Sankey and Philip Bliss. Producing solo (and small ensemble) books was a large part of the business of the independent religious hymnal publishers; the best known in that period were the Rodeheaver Company, the Hope Publishing Company, the Lillenas Publishing Company, and the Robert Coleman Company. Some of the composers listed above released their own works (e.g., Schuler, Tovey, Loveless and Dunlop).

The first successful songs of John W. Peterson (b. 1921)—such as "It Took a Miracle," "No One Understands Like Jesus," and "So Send I You" (with words by Margaret Clarkson)—were solos, as were those of Bill and Gloria Gaither (b. 1936 and 1942, respectively). However, in the tradition of the early gospel song movement, many of the Peterson and Gaither songs have become favorites in congregational singing.

Contemporary Composing Performers.

I have frequently mentioned the centuries-long relationship between secular popular forms and their religious imitators. If John Peterson took his cues occasionally from Broadway, other recent composers borrowed their inspiration from "western" or "country" styles. During the early Billy Graham crusades a number of show business performers made professions of faith; in some instances their singing style and composing gifts were also brought "into the fold." So we have inherited a large and continuing tradition of country gospel music in the train of Redd Harper's "Tenderly He Watches Over Me" and Stuart Hamblen's "It Is No Secret What God Can Do."

With the coming of the new folk/soul/pop/rock styles of gospel music beginning in the 1960's, the writing and the publishing of solo (and ensemble) witness music has burgeoned. With very few exceptions, it was composed by singers for their own performing, and it has been promoted widely by the personal appearances and recordings of those composer-singers. Perhaps the best known of the new breed are Andraé Crouch (b. 1945) and Ken Medema (b. 1943). However, there must be scores, even hundreds of professional "gospel singers" who write their own music. Some of them are known only in limited circles, others more widely. These are a few recent examples, together with the title of a well-known song and/or recording for which they are responsible, and the sponsoring publisher.

> Sammy Hall (The Best to You, Paragon)
> Paula Diesel (The Lord Reigneth, Lillenas)
> Ted Sandquist (The Courts of the King, Word)
> Gary S. Paxton (More Songs from Gary S. Paxton, Alexandria)
> Bob/Jane Farrell (The Songs of Bob and Jane Farrell, Paragon)
> Don Francisco (He's Alive, Alexandria)
> John Fischer (Inside John Fischer, Lexicon)
> Stuart Hamblen (My Heart Can Sing, Gaither)
> Dan Whittemore (The Trumpet Song, Lillenas)
> Marijohn Wilkin (Isn't It Wonderful, Word)
> Carol Melton (From This Day On, Agape)
> Pat Hoffman (Little by Little, Butterfly Ministries)

The contemporary witness song shuns none of the styles which are heard in secular popular music; in fact, the time lapse between the appearance of the secular form and its "sacred parody" has almost disappeared. Furthermore, the lyrics of the new "sacred" songs are fully as "mod" and realistic. "On my new album I have references to V.D. and 'lezzies,'" says Gary Paxton. "This down-to-earth music is what I call Christian Grit."[18]

Apparently, the trend will be with us for a while. The January, 1980 edition of *Christian Bookseller* named these "New Stars of the '80s": James Vincent, Melodie Narramore (daughter of Clyde Narramore, Christian psychologist), Moose Smith, Keith Hawson, Jamie Owens-Collins (daughter of contemporary musicians Jimmy and Carol Owens), Dan Peek (former composer and lead guitarist for the pop group America), the Lanny Wolfe Trio, Terry Clark, Mark Heard, Craig Smith (one-time lead singer and drummer for a rock band), Bill Thedford, Denny Correll, and Karen Voegtlin.[19]

---

18. "The Death and Rebirth of the Outrageous Gary Paxton," an editorial in *Christian Life*, September, 1978. Mr Paxton has been billed as "astonishing, outrageous, amazing, incredible, unbelievable" in the published promotion of his music.
19. *Christian Bookseller*, Vol. 26, No. 1, pp. 58–63.

Solo Communication: An Evaluation

Singing Styles.

It should not be surprising that, just as there are differences between the composition style of the "serious" sacred song and that of the "witness" song (gospel, soul, country, folk, rock, or whatever), there may also be distinct differences in the style of vocal performance. Not many of the most popular professional singers handle both art and pop styles equally well. This is apparent to trained musicians (though the statement will certainly raise objections from "fans") when they hear a Barbra Streisand recording of a Debussy score or listen to Jerome Hines sing hymns (which he does frequently, giving sacred concerts for the benefit of certain foreign missions projects.) A few individuals do both convincingly, as perhaps Dean Wilder and Robert Hale, and some lesser-knowns like David Ford, Suzanne Johnson and Glenn Jorian. One of the most convincing singers in the dual role was the late John Charles Thomas (1891–1960), who had a long career in opera and concerts, and late in life appeared on radio and television, frequently singing hymns on his program. His preparation for gospel singing had been done well in advance, for he grew up singing with his minister-father in Methodist camp meetings!

The difference in singing style has much to do with the character of the text. The sacred art song ("solo anthem" might be a better title) is usually an expression of praise, frequently taken from scripture. Though it may exhibit more "personality" and more emotional projection than a choral selection, simply because it is a solo, it will be more reserved and less personal than a folk/gospel song. The message is praise to God, not a narrative of personal experience, and the singer does well not to allow his personality to intrude too strongly into the listener's attention. The performance should be personal and warmly expressive, but not pretentious, exhibitionist or even self-conscious.

On the other hand, the singer of a Christian "witness" is communicating mind to mind, emotion to emotion, soul-to-soul. It is important not only to communicate one's own convictions and experience clearly and with emotional persuasiveness; the singer must also identify with the beliefs and the life situations of the listeners, both in the texts chosen and in the manner they are sung.

It need not be said that the Christian musician should communicate with sincerity. But it is also important that the audience *hear* the singing as "sincere," because sincerity (like beauty) is in the ears and mind of the listener! I suggest that it is possible for an insincere singer to come across to an audience convincingly and for a devoted, pious believer to be heard as insincere, perhaps because of timidity or the lack of an adequate singing-communicating technique. "Communicating" can be learned—and that statement is not intended to be an excuse for the "phony" gospel singer.

It should also be remembered that it is not easy to evaluate or to communicate sincerity across cultural lines. Invariably, when my students visit a Roman Catholic mass or a Lutheran service, they report that the congregations just "go through the motions, without meaning." In the same way, devotees of the Speer Family singers would possibly question the validity of the religious experiences of Hale and Wilder, because they don't like those "opera voices." All of which is meant to say that potential singer-communicators (1) should develop a style to suit the group they expect to reach, or (2) they should expect to work within the group to whom their own preferred style is meaningful.

To be sure, singers of "witness" music often develop highly personal, stylistic traits of vocalization, just like secular "pop" singers—a certain vocal quality based on range or vowel coloration, control of the vibrato, glissando or *portamento* singing, *sprechstimme* (speaking-singing), rubato, and so forth. This happens because they are communicating a message partly by communicating themselves, and a distinctive vocal style helps to project a more sharply defined personal identity. (Admittedly, some concert singers may also do this even when the vocal style is "standard-concert." As an extreme example, it is a temptation for a brilliant tenor or a soprano to choose the songs which end on a high note, or for a bass to show off his low E flat!)

When then does the singer intrude himself and his vocal style to such an extent that the message is heard with uncertainty? Or to borrow a phrase from Marshall McLuhan,[20] when does the medium become the message, or better, when does the messenger become the message? And how do these questions relate to the words of St. Augustine, in his reference to another solo canticle, heard in a fifth century monastery, cathedral or parish church?

> . . . So oft as it befalls me to be more moved with the voice than with the ditty, I confess to have grievously offended: at which time I wish rather not to have heard the music.[21]

Recommended: The Eclectic Approach.

My advice to the middle-class evangelical church singer—those to whom most of the examples in this book make sense—is this: Develop a standard *bel canto* singing technique, and apply it with discrimination to a broad range of solo music, classical and folk/gospel, worship and witness. Within my lifetime, the appreciation of "trained vocalism" has increased within our culture, both at the solo and the choral levels. It is possible for an individual trained in such a way to sing the standard oratorio roles as well as Gaither songs, Dvorak's "Biblical Songs" as well as the Carmichael/Kaiser ballad, "It Only Takes a Spark." Since these

20. See Marshall McLuhan, *The Medium is the Massage* (sic).
21. Oliver Strunk, ed., *Source Readings in Music History,* Vol. I, p. 74.

styles will also be heard side-by-side in the choral program of the church, it is advisable for soloists to be able to handle both adequately.

It is recommended that the informal witness song be performed from memory. Only then will the personal communication be completely convincing, coming "from the heart" rather than from the book. Obviously, the phrasing and diction should be carefully planned and rehearsed, since the song's essential communication lies in the text. What about gestures? Not many singers can use them convincingly in the church. "Posturing" is not desirable; "modesty" seems to be preferred.

It may be even more challenging to present a sacred artsong believably in an evangelical situation. For the communication must be just as sincere and personal, even when the words are objective praise rather than subjective experience. Anything that smacks of "vocalizing," operatic "make believe" or exhibitionism will undoubtedly fall short of its goal to communicate, to lead a congregation in worship.

The Sacred Solo (or Small Ensemble) Concert

One of the growing phenomena among today's evangelicals is the sacred concert, featuring a popular religious singer or group, sometimes held in a church but frequently in a large community auditorium. In the latter instance (and sometimes in the former) tickets at standard theater prices are sold, and the artists or their representatives remain after the program to sell their recordings and sometimes their music. The performances follow a fairly consistent format. The singers intersperse their songs with a running "patter" that is folksy and entertaining, occasionally with a devotional commentary on the songs. The amount of humor and/or "spiritual" material will vary according to the gifts and the convictions of the performers. Accompaniment is usually provided by "tape tracks" of orchestrations, or by the singers themselves playing piano or guitar, or by other "live" instrumentalists.

The idea of uniting entertainment with a spiritual message is not a new one.[22] George Stebbins reports that at the time Ira Sankey joined D. L. Moody's ministry in 1870, the gospel singer "had under consideration a proposition to accompany Mr. (Philip) Phillips to the Pacific Coast to assist him in sacred concerts, for which he was offered flattering pecuniary rewards."[23] A certain John A. Hultman (1861–1942), a Swedish-American, became known as the "Sunshine Singer" in the early 20th century, traveling back and forth across the Atlantic to give sacred concerts in both Sweden and the United States; Hultman also wrote music and published sacred song books.[24]

22. Actually, the earliest antecedent may well have been the medieval minnesinger who sang devotional lyrics in praise of the Virgin Mary—not in church, but in the castles of the noble families of that day. There was one notable difference: the ancient bards were of titled birth, and probably were not tempted to commercialism!
23. Stebbins, op. cit., p. 221.
24. Donald P. Hustad, *Dictionary-Handbook to Hymns for the Living Church*, p. 262.

In our own day, professional sacred music performance has become big business in evangelical circles. Many of the artists are represented by talent agents, and in some cases the fees charged rival those of Nashville, New York City and Hollywood singers. In fact, the talent roster has been augmented by a number of opera and entertainment stars who regularly sing religious music, apparently with personal conviction and dedication, e.g., Pat Boone, Debbie Boone, Anita Bryant, Natalie Cole, Roy Rogers and Dale Evans, Norma Zimmer, Carol Lawrence, the Lennon Sisters, Jerome Hines, Irene Jordan, Robert Hale and Dean Wilder. According to Noel Paul Stookey (converted member of "Peter, Paul and Mary" folk singers), the latest to join the swelling chorus of witness voices is none other than Bob Dylan, the leading bard of pop music during the last generation.[25] Following is a list of musicians promoted in the *Christian Bookseller*[26] in four issues of 1979-80.

Randy Adams	Rick Foster
Doris Akers	Don Francisco
Albrecht, Roley and Moore	Bill Gaither Trio
Archers	John and Mary Giger
Jerry Arhelger	Happy Goodmans
Tammy Baker	Amy Grant
Les Baxter	Keith Green
Birdwing	Janny Grein
Frank Boggs	Hale and Wilder
The Boones	Larry Hart
Stephanie Boosahda	Pamela Deuel Hart
Scott Wesley Brown	Tramaine Hawkins
Brush Arbor	Judy Herring
Eddie Burton	Benny Hester
Pete Carlson	Hinsons
Chalice	Dallas Holm
Cynthia Clawson	Ron Huff
Rick "Levi" Coghill	Imperials
Continentals	Isaiah Air Freight
Ken Copeland	Janny
Andraé Crouch	Gordon Jensen
Bob and Joy Cull	Jeremiah People
Andrew Culverwell	Kathie Lee Johnson
Dixie Melody Boys	Paul Johnson
Jessy Dixon	Vernard Johnson
Bob Dylan	Dino Kartsonakis
Mike Douglas	Phil Keaggy
Dale Evans	Kids of the Kingdom
Family	Lille Knauls
Farrell and Farrell	Lamb
John Fischer	Carey Landry
The Followers of Christ	J. J. Lee

25. Noel Paul Stookey, "Bob Dylan Finds His Source."
26. Published by Christian Life, Inc., Wheaton, IL 60187.

Erv Lewis	The Henry Slaughters
The Living Sound	Morse Smith
Maranatha! Music	Thurlow Spurr
Maranatha Singers	Statler Brothers
Barry McGuire	David Stearman
Gary McSpadden	B. W. Stevenson
David Meece	Lynn Sutter
Len Mink	Sweet Comfort Band
Tom Netherton	B. J. Thomas
Michael Omartian	Thrasher Brothers
Leon Patello	Evie Tornquist
Gary Paxton	Veltz, Veltz and Housenecht
Dan Peek	Wall Brothers Band
Rick Powell	Matthew Ward
Billy Preston	Mike Warnke
Dottie Rambo	Koger Wiles
Reba Rambo	Flech Wiley
Resurrection Band	Kelly Willard
Nedra Ross	Sister Miriam Therese Winter
St. Meinrad Archabbey	The Wondering Souls
Kol Simcha	Word of God Chorus and Orchestra

It should be obvious from the above list that in all our discussion of "solo singers" we are including the small ensemble—a group of soloists who sometimes sing alone and sometimes together. Here too the church has copied secular entertainment patterns. Yesterday's women's trio and male quartet have been joined by all sorts of variants today, from two singers (Hale and Wilder) to ten (Regeneration).

Nor is this rage limited to "big time" performers. Every evangelical community supports talent that is available to local churches for special services, sometimes without compensation, and frequently on a free-will offering basis. As in secular show business, the amateur hopes to become a professional, and the local performer hopes to make the "big time."

An Evaluation.

It has recently been reported that, in certain evangelical training schools, young musicians are much more interested in preparing for a career in sacred concerts than a ministry in the local church. For them, I offer a summary of the pros and cons, as I see them. This may also be of some help to the local church in determining how much time and money it will devote to this type of programming.

1. *Pro:* It is a satisfying activity for the performer, who is allowed to develop and use personal musical gifts, and to experience the sense of self-esteem which comes from being accepted by an audience.

Con: In any "show business" context, positive audience response may be ephemeral, particularly in a day when stylistic preferences change so frequently. Furthermore, a "star" performer is subject to the "ego temptations" that are unique to show business, which sometimes lead to the disintegration of personality, and a resulting deterioration of family relationships.[27]

2. *Pro:* It offers an opportunity for the artist to offer to God a personal "sacrifice of praise."

Con: The singer must be sure not to equate personal satisfaction with "doing the work of God." A gospel singer once admitted to one of my students that she chose revivalism instead of opera, because an opera singer faces an audience only occasionally, and the gospel artist could do so every night.

3. *Pro:* It may be a means of livelihood, if one is able to earn a living or to augment income in this way. In earlier generations, there were many calls for singers to be associated fulltime with traveling evangelists; now that that opportunity has greatly diminished, the concert ministry is a possible substitute.

Con: The prospective gospel/folk artist should be reminded that continuing professional possibilities depend on the whim of audiences (they can be faithless!), on one's continuing ability to sing well, and on the state of the national (and the church) economy! Furthermore, the individual must be one who finds satisfaction in an itinerant ministry, and in a transient and distant relationship with mass audiences, whom you never get to know personally!

4. *Pro:* It obviously gives pleasure to the listener-audience, and pleasure is one of the valid meanings of music, including sacred music.

Con: It may be that for some, pleasure is the only meaning in the musical experience. There are devotees of gospel-quartet or country gospel music, who do not support the organized church in any way, and for whom the Saturday night "gospel sing" is their only worship activity. The concert experience (sacred or secular) is very much like that of a worship service; however, in that setting, the object of veneration may be the experience or the performer, not God!

5. *Pro:* As an intense means of communication, it may provide a unique opportunity for worship and for spiritual decision by the listener who identifies with, and responds to the music.

Con: The spiritual experience in such a case may be truncated (especially when it occurs outside a church sanctuary), because it is principally spectatorist, and because it is separated from other significant worship acts, such as scripture reading, preaching, prayer, hymn singing and offering. (It is difficult to see the admission fee as a replacement for the latter!)

Furthermore, the experience may "prejudice" other musical worship experiences in a more normal setting. Participants may be encouraged to

---

27. I have often wondered why this is apparently more of a potential snare to the Nashville/Hollywood artist than to the opera star or concert performer. My guess is that the serious musician may have more opportunity for personal maturing through the intense discipline of professional preparation, and may possibly learn some humility from the "transcendent" literature which is being studied and performed. The pop singer (and the gospel vocalist) is working with simpler stuff. If the performance is (to the audience) still "transcendent," the singer may well take most of the credit!

expect the same personality-centered, spectatorist, semi-entertainment atmosphere in the regular Sunday morning service.

6. *Pro:* It may provide an opportunity to minister to the unchurched in evangelism, if they are attracted to such a musical performance, and if, after proper response to the musical message, they are directed into the full life of a local church.

Con: Everyone rejoices when this happens, and it frequently does. However, I have often seen members of a crusade audience applaud such stars as Johnny Cash as they left a stadium, even while Billy Graham was earnestly trying to "give an invitation." I must guess that, for those individuals, the singer was the message.

Re-reading the last paragraphs, I am aware that many folk will hear them as "mostly negative." But that is not my intention. Ray Robinson, president of the prestigious Westminster Choir College, has often spoken positively about contemporary "religious entertainment"; this is not too surprising, since he grew up in the evangelical community and was once a part of the music life of "Youth for Christ." I have experienced myself the satisfaction which comes from personal performance, both as a soloist and an accompanist. I am also convinced that "special music services" are a unique ministry, and that there is validity in a solo recital or concert, as well as in a choral cantata.

My plea is for balance. I must admit to some unhappiness when a church regularly spends large sums for guest performers, but will not adequately compensate a director for developing the musical talent in the local congregation. I am disappointed in gospel singers who profit financially from evangelical audiences, yet develop a personal religious cult, refusing to appear in church-sponsored gatherings and pointedly criticizing the institutional church in their concerts. To insure the strongest possible spiritual emphasis, it would be wise to sponsor musical programs in the local church, rather than to encourage attendance in secular auditoriums. In addition, the church should patronize those guest performers who bring the best-balanced and most coherent biblical message in song, and present the best role models in Christian commitment and humility. It may also be argued that "guest talent" should be presented only occasionally; most of the church's "special music" should originate in the local congregation. In some of our neighbor congregations in the rural near-south, the pastor regularly invites volunteers to present an impromptu, personal sacrifice of praise. In a typical Sunday evening service in a small church, this sometimes results in performances by representatives of almost every family present.

To the prospective Christian artist, I would say, "If you feel constrained to pursue such a ministry, you will be wise to set up safeguards against the perils of the personality cult." In this regard, the gospel song composer John Peterson has given good advice.

> Throughout the evangelical world there is a kind of star system, just as there is in every other sphere of life. Human nature is human nature, and despite the grace of God and every good intention

people *will* put you on a pedestal if you achieve some measure of success. This is especially true where the performing arts and the mass media are involved. The element of entertainment—of show biz—is always present. In a religious telecast or concert. In a Billy Graham crusade. Even in a small-town evangelistic meeting. Why pretend otherwise?

The crucial thing is to keep this element in perspective. If the Lord is using and blessing someone's fame, fine. If it becomes an end in itself or a means to glorify the person, it's another matter. Since the limelight is the inevitable result of a ministry like mine, I have to try to view it through the eyes and understanding of people far wiser than I. How do some of the old catechisms put it?—the chief end of man is to glorify God and enjoy Him forever.[28]

28. John W. Peterson, *The Miracle Goes On*, pp. 80–81.

Chapter XVIII

POSTSCRIPTS

At the end of a book like this, there are often a few items left over which apparently need to be added as postscripts. Generally, they constitute a final look at the present situation, and our hopes (or fears) for the future.

The Renewal-in-Communication Movement

The present pietist (experience-centered) emphasis, which introduced a new level of emotional expression into the contemporary church, has been a part of evangelical life now for almost fifteen years. In the broader church, it began with Geoffrey Beaumont's *Twentieth Century Folk Mass* in 1960. Since it has affected church music in all branches of American Christianity, in both its serious and popular expressions, it may be judged to be the most revolutionary movement since the gospel song appeared more than 150 years ago.

There are those who insist that what has happened has all been wrong, and that the movement is another sign of the decadence of the church in our day. While admitting that the secular-becoming-sacred cycle has been a fact of history, they contend that today's situation is different. They argue that there is a qualitative difference between the German folksongs which Luther borrowed in the 16th century and the music of the Beatles in the 20th, and that, while what Luther did was good, what contemporary evangelicals have done is bad. My response is twofold: (1) Inferior new music is better than *no* new music, because our expressions must be fresh and creative; and (2) We really had no choice, since we are obliged to use the forms of the world in which we live, if we are to communicate with our generation.

Occasionally someone raises the plaintive cry, "Why must the church get its new forms from the world around it? Why can't it create its own fresh forms?" An intriguing suggestion, but not very practical in a day of mass advertising and democratic church life! For if those forms used a musical language that is essentially different from that of the secular music around it, they would not be received either by the individuals within the church or the uncommitted outside. In the final analysis,

I believe that the church must use *some* of the forms of the culture in which it exists.[1] In our day, the choices are (as they have always been) between serious contemporary music (jazz-related, electronic sounds, high dissonance, tone clusters or aleatory techniques) and popular contemporary sounds (pop, folk, soul, gospel, rock, or whatever.)

It must be admitted that much contemporary music is more elemental, more physical and more primitive than its predecessors, because it depends more on rhythmic qualities than on melodic. This definition of a "limited intrinsic meaning" in music has been confirmed by E. Thayer Gaston in one of his early studies of the use of music in therapy; at the same time, he argues that melody added to rhythm tends to sublimate its primitive influence.

> In brief, then, rhythm or pulse is the driver, the physical stimulant, while melody is the more apperceptive, the more integrative, and in the long run, the more satisfying. Witness a tango or rhumba; first, there is developed that surging, unique pulse and rhythm which stimulates and demands action. Then superimposed, one hears the attractive melody which acts as a counter influence on the primitive and physical intent of the rhythm.[2]

Admittedly, today's contemporary gospel music is stronger rhythmically than that of Charles H. Gabriel in the 1920's, which in turn was stronger than that of P. P. Bliss and Ira D. Sankey in the 1870's. But at what point do we say, thus far we will go and no further? All music is rhythmic, and even Calvin's psalm tunes were called "Geneva Jiggs." Now that we have lived through perhaps the most provocative examples, it can be said that there are few forms which are incapable of any valid religious expression. Buryl Red's "He Is Alive" in *Celebrate Life* is convincing illustration that resurrection truth can be well spoken for today's youth in a rock beat.[3]

Of course, it is not necessary to choose the most extreme pop forms of our day. A few churches will be more attuned to contemporary serious music, and will use some of the creations of Daniel Pinkham, Gyorgy Ligeti or Richard Felciano, notwithstanding the fact that atonal, electronic and aleatory music would be heard as "demonic" by many evan-

---

1. The only historical exception to this pattern lies in the chant tradition which has been associated with Jewish and Christian worship, but has never been a part of evangelical life. At the present time, its future among Roman Catholics seems even to be in doubt.
2. E. Thayer Gaston, "Psychological Foundations for Functional Music."
3. I must add one parting shot at the idea of music's ethos, and the argument that contemporary music contributes to drug addiction and illicit sex. One of the latest careful examinations of this idea is recorded by Richard D. Mountford in an article, "Does the Music Make Them Do It?" (*Christianity Today*, Vol. 23, No. 15, pp. 20-23) His final paragraph includes the statement, "The music could have its effect only if the person desired to let it affect him." This confirms that music's meaning is given to it by the culture which uses it. It may be assumed that the same effect could be produced (if the individual desired it) with any kind of music—jazz, folk, waltz, Bach or even Gregorian chant!

gelicals. Some will choose contemporary folk rather than rock, and some will select "soft rock" (like Tedd Smith's "There's a Quiet Understanding") rather than "hard rock."

We must also admit that for some professional church musicians the new music has been nothing but "bad news" which they could not tolerate. A few persons with that conviction have been able to survive in certain urban churches where the art music tradition is sufficiently strong. I even know one music minister in rural western Kentucky, who has been able to convince his youth choir to sing music mostly in traditional styles, but he is an exception to the rule. For a fairly large number of musicians, the present day has offered little joy and they have simply left the profession of church music. One such example had served in a leading Baptist church in Louisiana for 23 years, and departed to seek a position in higher education. When he resigned, his pastor acknowledged his sincerity and courage in doing so.

> The important point is not whether _____ was correct in his critique of contemporary church music trends. That is a very complicated question into which we need not enter here, involving as it must such factors as history, aesthetics, theology, and personal taste. Rather the point is that _____ knew who he was and what he believed and he refused to squander those bedrock realities for that fickle illusion called "success." Humanly speaking, I am sure that _____ wanted always to have large choirs and grateful congregations singing his music with gusto. But what mattered most was integrity, the integrity of the music and of the musician alike. And so he chose a course consistent with his vision, and pursued it as fashions waxed and waned, and goes from us to finish it as God shall continue to lead him.[4]

I recently viewed a telecast in which young Israeli students asked Artur Rubinstein, the eminent nonagenarian pianist, what he thought of contemporary music. The venerable maestro replied that he was convinced that the new music (and he was including most composers of the 20th century) communicated something of value. However, it did not speak to him, and so he was content to stay with the literature of 19th century Romanticists. Clearly, Rubinstein had that right, and with his pianistic gifts, he was able to pull it off. So does the church musician who finds that the new sounds are not satisfying; albeit, among evangelicals, it will be difficult to find a church today which does not indulge in them to some extent. But I must also commend the musicians who, though they do not prefer the prevailing contemporary forms, use them because they minister significantly to others.

One of the reasons why I personally applaud the new "renewal in communication" movement is that it includes concern for an increasingly-cognitive experience to match the increasingly-emotive musical expressions. New versions of scripture and fresh worship language,

4. William E. Hull, "In Praise of a Good Man."

together with new texts in anthems and in folk musicals, have insured that there should be increased rational understanding along with higher emotional impact. A few persons insist that the new words don't say anything that is theologically worthy; I contend (hopefully with grace) that they are not able to separate 17th to 19th century language from eternal truth, or that they have not looked at enough present-day material. In the burgeoning new publications, there is admittedly a fair amount of textual trivia. At the same time, for those who painstakingly choose the best available materials, there is a freshness of language that expresses our praise, our theology and our experience in up-to-date language that is "real, not romantic."

Contemporary Worship

One of today's foremost preoccupations is with "creative" worship, and that is good, providing that the emphasis is on a full-orbed experience, rather than just being "creative." The latter may lead to a cult of novelty which becomes another form of idolatry. A good standard is *total worship*, using *total means* to minister to the *total person*, and extending to the *total congregation*.

"Total means" is usually taken to mean the use of multi-media—correlating speech, music, audio-visual aids, movement, drama, architecture, furnishings—in order to involve through the senses the total person—body, intellect, emotions and will. A principal concern of the church should be the planning and leading of the regular week-by-week services, in order that they may be continually effective in the life of the congregation. This book has outlined worship that is complete, scripturally and theologically, and also suggested a form, together with certain variants, to help achieve that goal.

"The total congregation" includes everyone who regularly meets together for worship. It may be said that this inclusive concept is demonstrated in the music program, when each age group, juniors through adults, contributes from time to time to the corporate services. But total worship for the total congregation should mean more than that. Each group should be acknowledged by the material of worship. Attention should at one time be directed to the 10-year-olds, and on another occasion to retired persons, as well as to young and mature adults. Furthermore, representatives of each group should at times be allowed to participate in worship leadership, perhaps (after some training) in reading the scripture lesson, or leading in a litany. I am sometimes embarrassed that Roman Catholics are more liberal in recognizing laypersons in worship service leadership than my own Southern Baptist fellowship, where such action is limited to ordained deacons and to ministers.

"Creative worship" has now been with us long enough to take a tentative measure of its impact on evangelical life. By now, it has lost much of its self-consciousness. Interest has dwindled in the "far out" services which blossomed ten to fifteen years ago. Most churches have settled down to a norm which shows one or more of the following characteristics, without much uniformity between churches even in the same denomination:

1. More congregational participation, in calls to worship, scripture readings, prayers, litanies.
2. More use of contemporary language in both words and music, as well as in related arts.
3. More expressions of Christian fellowship between worshipers.
4. Greater variety in music styles, often within a single service.
5. More functional room and furnishings design.

By and large, it is difficult to see any sweeping change in typical Sunday worship. The expectation that traditional preaching-singing-praying patterns would give way to revolutionary communicative methods has just about disappeared. Some would guess that this is another evidence of the "conservatism" of the established church, which sees the opportunity to realize new vistas of experience, but retreats even within sight of the Promised Land! I would guess that it is rather due to the realization that the historic forms, which had enough strength to persist for 1900 years, may yet last for a few more! For evangelicals, the conviction that traditional "preaching" is God-ordained in the New Testament witness, will probably discourage any rapid departure from the customary norms. Then too, there is the nagging conviction that, in the final analysis, true worship depends on anticipation (knowing what's coming) and contemplation (thinking it through personally), rather than on sense-storming novelty and manipulation.

Of course, there will be opportunities for "special" worship experiences that are more exotic, but they will only serve to expand the meaning of regular worship. It is in this pattern that cantatas are now often transformed into "operas" or "musicals" and that religious drama is increasingly used, even by evangelicals, whose pietistic tradition has often shunned the theater. Interpretive movement (worship ballet) will have scant acceptance in our culture, though some evangelicals in Canada and in Europe have been bolder than we in the United States. It may be that the use of sign language for the deaf will be the first step for some churches in coming to the realization that the body can be expressive without committing sin! In the Berlin Congress on Evangelism in 1966, one of the most moving moments was the communication of "The Lord's Prayer" in Indian sign language by "Sonny" Claus. That too is religious dance, and its counterpart—the art of ballet—can be far more meaningful than the "chorus line" formulae which have accompanied some of the youth musicals in recent years.

An Exciting Exception and Example.

If most evangelicals have been reluctant either to study worship carefully or to engage in sweeping revision of traditional practice, there are a few notable exceptions to the rule whose example might well be followed. We will consider just one.

The essence of life and ministry at the College Hill Presbyterian Church of Cincinnati, Ohio has been characterized by its pastor[5] as (1) Joyous worship, (2) Strict teaching from the scriptures, and (3) a Call to radical obedience to God's Word. To become a member of the church, one must attend an Inquirers Class of ten sessions. These meetings explore what it means to be a Christian and a Presbyterian; how to grow as a Christian; what it means to worship and to minister in the church; the doctrines of our faith; how to discover one's spiritual gifts and to use them in Christ's work in the world through the local church; and how to share one's faith and lead others to Christ. Upon completing the class, those who have made a profession of faith and are baptized[6] become members and are placed in "Discovery Groups" (led by seasoned laypersons), to help them mature as Christians and learn how to plug in their gifts and skills to the Body of Christ.

Services at College Hill are planned by the Worship Team, a group of laypersons who have studied worship in depth and feel called to the "worship ministry"; some of the team are professional artists who bring particular expertise to the experience, whether in drama, speech, graphics, dance or music. The group meets twice a month with the Minister of Worship and Music, first of all to worship together, with the understanding that this experience will best prepare them to lead others in worship. Individual team members are assigned to a particular service; they meet with the pastor who preaches on that occasion, to pray and to discuss the sermon topic, brainstorming ideas as to how full-orbed worship could best be encouraged. The completed service is then coordinated with the musical selections and given to the Minister of Worship and Music for final approval.

Sunday morning worship tends to emphasize the vertical relationship with God more than the horizontal relationship between believers. There are three services, the first two being identical, with a full choir. At 12 o'clock there is a specially planned family service, in which the music is mostly congregational (led by a soloist), with a "revised version" of the sermon-of-the-day that is more easily understood by children. Holy Communion is celebrated once a month at the earlier services, and *every week* at the noon hour. In addition, there are regular monthly "Body Life" services in the evening, which emphasize the experiences and concerns of the Body of Christ—with testimonies, prayer requests, and other congregational participation in the pattern of I Corinthians 14:26.

Although worship at College Hill contains all the elements discussed in chapters five and ten, there is no *regular* worship order; in successive weeks, a liturgical form may be followed by a relatively "free" design.

5. Dr. Jerry Kirk leads a team of ten professional "pastor-enablers" in a remarkably democratic fashion.
6. Immersion is encouraged, but other modes are acceptable.

Each service is planned with the aim of communicating the Word for that day in the best possible manner. The "Preparation for Worship" (following the announcements of church activities) may feature the choirs or congregational song, instrumental music (possibly played by members of the Cincinnati Symphony Orchestra), or the organ (or piano!) alone. This music is always related to the theme of the day; if it is instrumental, the bulletin (frequently designed by graphic artists to reflect the emphasis of a season or a special day) will contain an appropriate scripture verse or a reference to a hymn which will help to focus on worship.

The major choir at the church is considered to be the congregation, and Sunday morning repertoire runs the gamut from historic hymns and chorales to Gaither songs and scripture choruses. Often verses of praise hymns are joined together by modulations in a medley of praise. If the congregation knows the morning anthem (or even the solo), they may sing along. Responses are often sung by the congregation rather than by the "smaller choir" seated in the chancel.

To be sure, there is a fully graded choir program at the church, and more: "Desert Rain"—a 25-voice auditioned ensemble, vocal soloists, a brass choir, and many professional instrumentalists from the University of Cincinnati and the Cincinnati Symphony; all persons contribute their talents to the church as their personal "ministry." Many types of accompaniment are used, including synthesizer, string quartet, drums and cymbals. Musical offerings by the adult Chancel Choir include gospel and folk styles, as well as such masterworks as J. S. Bach's *Christmas Oratorio*, Fauré's *Requiem*, and Honegger's *King David*. Other art forms are used, with care to insure that they are biblically based— audio-visual aids, drama and dramatic reading, and visible symbols such as bread, grapes, and a crown of thorns. On some occasions, after careful education of the congregation and thorough review by the worship committee, interpretive movement may be used with such musical works as Vaughan Williams' *Magnificat*.

It is apparent that the music/worship leadership at College Hill Presbyterian Church works to strike a balance between artistic media and styles, between form and freedom, between meticulous planning and spontaneity. Lay speakers or readers (sometimes including children) will be carefully coached by the ministers and rehearsed in the sanctuary, using the public address system. At the same time, in a period of prayer, members of the congregation might be asked to call out attributes of God the Father, after which they join to sing a chorus like "Father, I Adore You"; the same would then be done in reference to God the Son and God the Holy Spirit.

Of course, not every evangelical believer would feel at home in the services at College Hill. But the church must be commended for taking worship and its music seriously. Furthermore, the care which is given to achieving a balance of forms and styles should forestall a preoccupation

with either aestheticism or worship hedonism, and help to prevent the
"rut-ualism" which can beset both liturgical and "free" churches.

Evangelicals and Commerce

One of the important factors in evangelical life today stems from our
statistical strength, as it is linked to American business techniques. Our
churches have thrived numerically and prospered financially. Relating
this fact to the proliferation of new music and of "religious entertainment," we should not be surprised that "evangelical business," especially
in publishing and recording, has boomed. Some observers are wondering if we can stand this kind of success.

Religious music business is not a new thing. It is said that the new
hymns of Martin Luther were published in "broadsheets" and hawked
on the streets of 16th century Europe. Money earned by selling
evangelistic songbooks during the 19th century Moody-Sankey campaigns was used to finance a number of philanthropic efforts, including
the building of a Bible Institute and "Tent Hall" in Glasgow and Car-
ruber's Close Mission in Edinburgh, all in Scotland. Many religious
music publishers came into existence as a result of the revivalism of that
period in American history.

Religious music publishing today is a multi-million dollar business.
"And what's wrong with that?" many will ask. "If you have something
good, do you not have the right and even the obligation to share it with as
many folk as possible?" It is not my intention to belabor the issue, but it
is wise to examine our "Madison Avenue" culture even though we are all
a part of it. Suffice it to say that we should be alert to the temptations
inherent in commercialism. It is just possible that the "most popular"
item advertised might not make the strongest contribution to our church
life, and that creating a religious "hit parade" may encourage a
homogenization of our church life culture that is not the best approach
to the creativity which the Holy Spirit would bring into the church.

One example may suffice to demonstrate our temptations. The October 1978 issue of *Christian Bookseller* featured an article, "Jesus Tee-
Shirt Fad Sweeps the Nation—What to Do About It." The lead-in
paragraph follows.[7]

> Some call it religious pop art, others call it a type of Christian free
> press, a "silent witness." Whatever your definition, be a part of the
> booming Christian tee shirt business expected to total $5 million in
> sales this year.

If that isn't enough to encourage us to question our taste and sense of
propriety, a later paragraph should do it.

7. Jan Lokay with Bill Bray, "Jesus Tee Shirt Fad Sweeps the Nation."

A Christian "canine force" is the latest wrinkle in the world of marketing "born again" religious products. Supplying puppies with "doggies for Jesus!" uniforms is Windy Distributors, one of the major wholesalers of Jesus tee shirts and contemporary Christian music.[8]

It may be that the more stringent economic situation facing us today will determine that less money will be spent on foolish fads and gimmicks. But, in buying music, the church will always need to be careful to get the best for its money, rather than the most popular.

The Electronic Church

We must also take a brief look at another contemporary phenomenon which has a profound effect on our church life, including its music. It might be expected that the "outreach theology" of evangelicals would encourage them to turn to radio and television as the most efficient communication media in our day. As a result, according to the *New York Times,* the "electronic church" (also called "electric") has flourished.

Over the past 15 years, membership in the National Religious Broadcasters, an umbrella organization for television and radio evangelical groups, has risen from 104 to 900; one in eight of the nation's radio stations now carries at least 14 hours of religious programming; 600 of them offer it full time; religious broadcasting represents a $1 billion yearly business; religious radio stations are being founded at a rate of one a week, television one a month.[9]

We should all applaud a sincere concern to communicate the gospel and rejoice in the genuine results which have accrued, when individuals have come to biblical faith and been brought into the total life of the local church. It is also clear that the electronic church performs a vital function in bringing worship to shut-ins.

We must be concerned, however, if the electronic experience becomes a substitute for the "church gathered to worship and sent forth to serve" in the world. Television-watching is not the biblical pattern for discipleship. Admittedly, this accusation has not been proved to be true, since The Electronic Church appeals mostly to evangelicals, whose services are crowded these days. At the same time, every church has many folk on its rolls who rarely occupy their pews, and some leaders suggest that these drop-outs make up a large number of the TV "worshipers." If this is true, there must be an immense underground church hiding in homes who need to be marshaled for full service in the kingdom of God!

It is also proper to express concern about the influence of this phe-

8. Ibid.
9. Kenneth A. Briggs, "The Electronic Church Is Turning More People On."

nomenon on more-typical worship. Beyond much question, electronic worship caters to the demand for religious entertainment and is limited by the medium which it uses. The newspaper article mentioned earlier also commented on an evaluation by Rev. Charles Swann, a Presbyterian minister, who is himself manager of a "religious radio station."

> ... He argues that most television preachers consciously imitate the "entertainment" aspects of the television medium because the audiences for such programs "will choose the one which is more entertaining to them."

> "... Magic solutions are the norm of expectations from television. ... Television cannot handle complicated material or challenging ideas very well; therefore theology becomes very simple-minded."[10]

It may be anticipated that many church members will expect their own churches to imitate the message and the techniques of the electronic media. Without subtracting from the good which is done by gospel radio and television, it is safe to say that, like revivalism, most programs present a "limited gospel." The emphasis is a "message of compassion, concern and interest in their (audience's) problems," according to Pat Robertson, who produces and stars in "The 700 Club," seen on 140 television stations.

> We are doing what we can. The attention span of the modern audience is terrible. You've got to say what you have to say in five minutes or less. You may not like it but that's the way it is.[11]

It seems to me that it would be preferable for religious radio and television to be more closely related to established churches and local congregations. It may also be hoped that more centrist evangelical groups will participate in The Electronic Church; at the moment, much of the sponsorship seems to come from one theological segment, which promotes only one aesthetic approach.

There is also room for more imaginative use of the media, incorporating the arts which are best communicated by them. One of the soundest approaches to religious television has been made by the Lutheran Church-Missouri Synod. Their dramatic series "This is the Life" effectively relates the gospel of Christ to real-life situations, without compromising the norms of worship in their own churches. Furthermore, it is paid for by members of local churches, not through appeals to listeners.

Finally, electronic communication should be approached as an end in itself, not as a means to the end of promoting other ministries, either of individuals or of organizations. It is a hard, cold fact that if radio and TV

10. Ibid.
11. Ibid.

were not "money making" they would not long survive. This fact encourages competition between the media sponsors which leads to some of the excesses in "entertainment" programming. As we have learned in secular radio/TV, audience appeal is not always the best measure of the quality of programming.

Religious journals have recently reported[12] a conflict between religious broadcasters and publishers, which witnesses that both groups understand the commercial aspect of their professions, and that both are motivated partly by the condition of their balance sheet. The American Association of Religious Broadcasters have objected to paying for "performance rights" on music produced by evangelical publishers, as is required by ASCAP, SESAC and BMI, who license the copyrights for the purpose of collecting performance royalties. In response to the publishers' argument that they deserve a fair return on their properties, the broadcasters countered that it was their promotion of the music which helped sell it, and that they should not be asked to pay additionally for putting certain composers and publishers on the evangelical hit parade!

The Future

And what lies ahead? These words are being written at a time when the political and economic future of our world seems as unpromising as at any time I remember. We are living, to quote a phrase I have often heard from Billy Graham, "either just prior to Armageddon, or in one of God's terrible springtimes." There is no possibility of predicting the future of the church in a time when it is difficult even to categorize the present *status quo,* which (as I once heard a black preacher say) "is Latin for the mess we're in." I dare say present conditions are not as rosy as evangelical statistics would suggest, or as gloomy as some of the indicators which have been cited in this chapter.

Nevertheless, as Christian believers we live "in hope," that is, the assurance that God is working out his purposes in the world and in the church. It may be that the troublous days ahead will provide the refining which the church needs in order to "serve the present age." My own hope is bolstered by harbingers which appear like the first flowers of spring.

I believe that evangelicals will continue to grow in maturity in theological education. We have seen evidence of this in the increasing enrolments in our seminaries, and in the rising standards set by our scholars. We have grown in our awareness of the relationship of our faith to our world—in meeting social needs and even relating to ecology. Let us hope that our maturing will include awareness of the theology, sociology, psychology and aesthetics of corporate worship, and that appropriate

12. Editors, "Discord and Rising Decibels over Broadcasting Religious Music."

studies will be a regular part of theological curricula, in our seminaries and Bible colleges.

Let us also pray that evangelicals will mature in their use of all the arts and the media in communicating the gospel, both within the church structure and outside. I do not dream that the church may reform the aesthetic tastes of our total society, or that we could or should create an elitist cultural "refuge" within our sanctuary walls. I hope only that we may approach music, as well as all the arts, with understanding of its true function in our lives and our worship, and that we may choose the best that our talented artists can produce, in order that it may truly serve God and the church. When that happens, we will live out the meaning of a new hymn by F. Pratt Green.

> When, in our music, God is glorified,
> And adoration leaves no room for pride,
> It is as though the whole creation cried:
>   Alleluia!
>
> How oft, in making music, we have found
> A new dimension in the world of sound,
> As worship moved us to a more profound:
>   Alleluia!
>
> So has the Church, in liturgy and song,
> In faith and love, through centuries of wrong,
> Borne witness to the truth in every tongue:
>   Alleluia!
>
> And did not Jesus sing a Psalm that night
> When utmost evil strove against the Light?
> Then let us sing, for whom he won the fight:
>   Alleluia!
>
> Let every instrument be tuned for praise!
> Let all rejoice who have a voice to raise!
> And may God give us faith to sing always:
>   Alleluia!
>
>   F. Pratt Green

GLOSSARY

Aesthetics—a study of what is beautiful at a given time or place in history.

Agape—the love of God for human beings; or the brotherly love which believers express toward others.

Agape Meal—a "love feast," a fellowship meal, observed by early Christians, which was at times associated with the Lord's Supper. The custom has been continued by later Christian groups, e.g., the Moravian Church.

Alternatim Practice—the custom in the late Middle Ages, in which the organ alternated with the choir, in performance of the mass music.

Anglican—of, or related to, the Church of England. Since the Revolutionary War, the Episcopal Church in America has been organically separated from the Anglican Church, but is part of the worldwide Anglican fellowship (communion).

Anglican Chant—the harmonized chant used in the Church of England (and the Episcopal church) for the reciting of psalms, canticles and other non-poetic texts.

Ante-communion—a worship service which is identical with the church's eucharistic service, except that communion is omitted. Such services have been common in Lutheran and Anglican practice, and are essentially the same as a "missa brevis" (short mass).

Anthem—a form which originated in the Church of England, in which an English text is set for choral performance, generally with organ accompaniment. The anthem is the counterpart of the motet in Latin-language worship.

Anthropology—a study of the nature, the cultural development, social practices and beliefs of humanity.

Anthropomorphism—a conception or representation that ascribes human form or attributes to a deity.

Apocrypha—the group of 14 books included in the Roman Catholic Bible, but not considered to be canonical by most Protestants.

Apocryphal—of doubtful authenticity and/or authorship.

Arminianism—a theological emphasis supported by John and Charles

341

Wesley (in opposition to Calvinism). In the context of this book, its most significant tenet was "free grace," which held that salvation was available to all persons, not only to "the elect."

Atonality—a principle in music composition which appeared in the 20th century, in which there is no discernible key, or tonal center.

Barthian Theology—the theological system which originated with Karl Barth, sometimes called neo-orthodoxy or neo-reformation theology. It featured a renewal of the concept of divine revelation through scripture, and was accompanied by renewed interest in Reformation worship forms (especially among Lutherans), and even historic German organ design.

Bidding Prayers—historically were the formal prayers of petition in worship. In modern practice, the term can be used to mean the invitation to silent (and later, spoken) prayer, beginning with the words, "Let us pray for . . . ."

Bluegrass Music—a form of country music that is often polyphonic in character, using unamplified instruments for accompaniment—guitars, violin, banjo and "washtub bass."

Broad Church—a party in the Anglican Church which emphasizes social implications of the gospel and approaches liturgy with an emphasis on ecumenical participation.

Calvinism—the teachings and theology which stem from John Calvin. The significant concepts (in the context of this book) are predestination, the sovereignty of God, and the "irresistibility of grace."

Canon—the main part of the eucharistic prayer in the Roman mass, that section between the *Sanctus* and the distribution of the elements. In music composition, a canon is a note-for-note imitation of one melodic line by a second, which begins after the first.

Cantillation—chanting, or intoning, in religious services, usually a single melody or tone (monody).

Cantor—in this book, refers to the solo singer who chants prayers and leads the worship in a Hebrew synagogue.

Cathedral—the central church of a diocese, with which a bishop is associated.

Chorale—the hymn tunes of the German (Lutheran) Church. The title is used to include the text, as well.

Chorale Prelude—an organ (or keyboard) composition based on a chorale or hymn tune.

Collect—(a) brief prayer (or prayers) which occur(s) early in the worship of a liturgical church, and which usually reflects the emphasis of that day in the liturgical calendar. It has been said to bring together (or "collect") the prayers of the congregation to be spoken by the worship leader.

Collegiate Church—a leading church in the liturgical tradition, with which canons (ministering dignitaries) and a dean are associated, but not a bishop.

Common grace—the idea that God endows all individuals with natural gifts, irregardless of their faith in, or commitment to, him.

Country Music—also called country-and-western, denotes a ballad style in lyrics, and simple (usually major mode) music, accompanied by guitars and double-bass, etc.

Descant—a melody which accompanies a principal theme, and usually appears above it.

Didache—the teaching of the entire body of Christian doctrine. *The Didache* refers to an early Christian treatise discovered in 1875, which is considered to have been written in the second century; it is also called *The Teaching of the Twelve Apostles.*

Dissenters—those individuals and movements which rebelled against the authority of the established (state) church in a country or region. (See also "Non-liturgical churches.")

Dogma—a system of doctrinal tenets, particularly of a church or a denomination.

Ethnomusicology—the study of folk music and primitive music, and the relationship of each type to the culture which produced it; sometimes called "comparative musicology."

Ethos—the "ethical character" of each of the ancient scales (modes). It was assumed that each mode expressed certain concepts or qualities, and affected human behavior accordingly.

Eucharist—the service of Holy Communion, the Lord's Supper.

Evening Prayer—also called Vespers, is the evening non-eucharistic service of the Anglican (and Episcopalian) Church, consisting of psalms, canticles, scripture readings, prayers, and possibly a sermon.

Flagellants—persons who scourge themselves for religious discipline. In the Christian tradition, flagellation was practiced by various groups, principally from the 12th to the 16th centuries.

Free Churches—see Non-liturgical Churches.

Graded Choirs—a program of music education in the local church, in which the singers are divided into age-maturity groups such as Preschoolers, Beginners, Primary, Juniors, Intermediates, Senior High, Adults, etc.

Gregorian Chant—the liturgical chant of the Roman Catholic Church.

Hedonism—the conviction that pleasure is the greatest good.

Heterophony—refers to music in two parts, in which the second is characterized by slight variations of the first.

High Church—a movement within the Anglican (or Episcopal) Church which emphasizes church authority and the historic liturgies and symbolism of worship.

High Mass—the celebration of the complete Roman Catholic mass, in which there are two assistants (a deacon and a subdeacon) and the liturgy is sung (or chanted) rather than spoken.

Holiness Theology—is an aspect of Wesleyan doctrine which emphasizes the experience of "Christian holiness" as a "second work of grace" that follows the experience of "the new birth." The experience is also called "entire sanctification."

Homophonic—refers to music which has one predominant melody, usually supported by a harmonic (chordal) accompaniment.

Hymns of human composing—hymn texts not taken directly from scripture (God's "composing").

Icon—a picture, often a painting of some ecclesiastical personage, e.g., Christ, the Virgin Mary, or a saint.

Iconoclasm—the spirit which encourages an attack on established beliefs and traditional practices, as being based on error.

Illuminated—when used to describe a page in an ancient manuscript, refers to the decoration of a painted design in gold, color, etc.

Indigenous music—music that originates in, and is characteristic of, a certain region, or culture.

Intonation—or incipit, consists of the opening words or phrase of a liturgical text, delivered by one or two singers. When organs began to be used in worship, they usually played the music of the intonation in advance, to set the pitch.

Jazz—a type of instrumental popular music which originated among black musicians in New Orleans early in the 20th century, and features complex rhythmic patterns, polyphonic ensemble playing and improvisation.

Jubilus—a melismatic prolongation of the final "a" of "Alleluia" immediately before the Gospel reading in the mass.

Kantorei—refers to groups of amateur singers who supplied music for their communities, including their churches, following the Reformation in Germany.

Kerygma—the preaching of the central aspects of the gospel of Christ.

Keswick Hymnody—is so called because it originated in connection with the Keswick Convention, a religious conference which meets each July in the village of Keswick in the lake country of north England. Keswick meetings emphasize "the deeper life" for Christians, and the hymnody is pietistic (experiential) and devotional.

Kodaly Music Education—educational concepts and techniques originated by the Hungarian composer-educator Zoltan Kodaly (1882–1967).

Lection—a passage of scripture, to be read in a worship service.

Lectionary—the list of scripture readings scheduled to be read throughout the Church Year in liturgically-oriented churches or institutions. At the present time, the trend is to use a three-year cycle which includes much of the Bible.

Lessons and Carols—usually refers to a Christmas service which is characterized by scripture readings of the Christmas story interspersed by traditional carols or hymns, sung by the choir and/or the congregation. The same pattern can be followed for a service in Advent, or in the Holy Week/Easter season.

Levitical Music—worship music performed by the professional priest-musicians in ancient Hebrew life. They were members of the tribe of Levi.

Liberal Theology—a late 19th century movement in protestant life, which attempted to restructure traditional beliefs in the light of scientific concepts. Liberalism frequently emphasized that salvation comes through education or social betterment.

Litany—a form of ceremonial public prayer, in which a series of petitions are followed by a repeated response, which is usually spoken by the entire congregation.

Liturgical church—one which follows set forms for worship, e.g., Eastern Orthodox, Roman Catholic, Lutheran or Anglican (Episcopalian).

Liturgy—a form of public worship.

Low Church—a movement within the Anglican (or Episcopal) Church which emphasizes evangelical religion and downgrades church authority and historic (medieval) worship traditions.

Low Mass—a mass with little ceremonial form, in which the words are said, not sung, and in which the celebrant is accompanied by a single assistant (server).

Macrocosm—the representation of a particular small phenomenon by a larger, or a universal one.

Mass—the eucharistic service of Roman Catholics. The word is also used to denote the musical setting of the five historic songs of the service—*Kyrie, Gloria, Credo, Sanctus* and *Agnus Dei.*

Matins—see Morning Prayer.

Melisma—an expressive or ornamental phrase, consisting of several notes sung to one syllable of text, as in certain types of chant (e.g., Gregorian).

Meters, Hymn—a poetic measure which indicates the number of syllables per line, and is used to match a poem with a tune. In the English metrical psalm tradition, certain meters became standard: Common (8,6,8,6), Short (6,6,8,6) and Long (8,8,8,8), etc.

Metrical Psalm—a literal versification of the biblical psalm, intended for singing. (By contrast, a psalm paraphrase is a freer version.)

Microcosm—the representation of the world by a smaller portion of the same. In this volume, a worship service is presented as a microcosm of God's revelation of himself and man's positive response in all of history.

Modal—refers to music which is based on one of the medieval scales, other than major or minor.

Morning Prayer—also called Matins, is the morning non-eucharistic service of the Anglican (and Episcopalian) Church, consisting of psalms, canticles, scripture readings, prayers, and possibly a sermon.

Motet—a choral composition on a sacred prose text. Generally, the title is applied to unaccompanied, polyphonic works with Latin texts.

Musicology—the scholarly study of music. In this volume, the word will generally refer to "historic musicology"—the study of western art music.

Non-conformist Churches—see Non-liturgical Churches.

Non-liturgical Churches—churches which have no regular forms of worship and are free to develop patterns as they see fit.

Novena—a series of services or private devotions on nine consecutive days, usually in honor of a particular saint, to request his/her intercession on behalf of the worshiper.

Oblong Tune Books—the oblong-shaped volumes which appeared in America in the late 18th and early 19th centuries, characterized by the inclusion of new tunes (including "white spirituals") for traditional as well as new hymn texts.

Octavo Music—a phrase now understood to mean the publishing of a single anthem in a size about 6 by 9 inches. The name is derived from the original practice of folding a typical printing sheet so that it created a booklet of eight (an octave of) sheets, or 16 pages.

Offertory—in the context of this book, usually refers to the musical selection which occurs during the receiving of the offering (collection). In certain liturgical churches, it refers more to the offering of bread and wine for the eucharist.

Office Worship—also called the "Services of the Hours," is the non-eucharistic worship which developed in monastic life in the early church. It is perpetuated in Roman Catholic and Orthodox life, and also in the Matins and Vesper offices of Anglicans and Lutherans.

Ordinance—the word used by certain free church groups to characterize the Lord's Supper and Baptism. They prefer it over "sacrament," because it indicates that these sign-acts were commanded by Christ, but do not automatically confer spiritual grace on the recipient.

Ordinary—the parts of a liturgy (e.g., the mass) which remain basically the same each time it is repeated.

Orff Music Education—educational concepts, techniques, and instruments originated by the German composer-conductor Carl Orff (b. 1895).

Oxford Movement—also called Tractarianism, was a renewal movement in the Anglican Church beginning in the 1830's, which emphasized the concepts of the early church fathers, as well as historic catholic practices. Successors of the movement are the High Church party within Anglicanism.

Parachurch—pertaining to an organization or activity which purports to support or supplement the work of the church, though it is not considered to be part of the church.

Passion—a musical account (in the style of a cantata or oratorio) of the sufferings of Christ, which usually follows the narrative of the last days of his life, beginning with Palm Sunday.

Patristic—pertaining to the (early) church fathers, especially those of the first four centuries after Christ.

Pietism—a religious movement which stresses personal piety above institutionalized theology and worship practices.

Pietist Hymns—hymns produced by pietist movements.

Polyphonic—refers to music consisting of two or more voices (or parts), each having melodic independence and importance.

Precentor—in the uses of the word in this book, refers to the individual who led the psalmsinging in free churches in the 17th and 18th centuries, sounding the starting pitch, and frequently "lining out" the psalm phrase by phrase, with each phrase repeated by the congregation.

Prone—a "preaching service" which was inserted in the mass during the medieval period, and which was the model from which John Calvin developed his Reformed worship pattern.

Propers—the parts of a liturgy which change with the particular day or festival of the church year.

Revivalism—the tradition of promoting renewal in the church by use of personality-centered, entertainment-related activities.

Revivalist Worship—the tendency to use revival techniques for regular worship services.

Rock Music—a short name for "rock-and-roll," refers to a type of popular music related to blues and folk music, which has a heavily accented beat.

Rubric—a rule (or directive) for the conduct of a religious service, or the administration of the sacraments.

Sacerdotal Worship—worship conducted by priests.

Sacral—pertaining to sacred rites or usage.

Sacrament—a visible sign-act instituted by Christ to symbolize or confer grace (e.g., baptism and the Lord's Supper).

Salutation—an expression of mutual greeting between minister and congregation (versicle and response), common to Jews and Christians since early times.

> V: The Lord be with you.
> R: And also with you.

Schola Cantorum—the choir school of the Roman Catholic Church. The title can also be used for a local ecclesiastical choir or choir school.

Social Gospel—a theological emphasis which appeared in the 19th century, that sometimes reduced the gospel to "social betterment." Frequently, however, and increasingly among evangelicals, it rather emphasizes the "social implications" of the gospel.

Spirituals, Negro—the religious folk music of blacks in America, which originated in the late 18th and early 19th centuries.

Spirituals, White—usually refers to the tunes and/or the text of experience hymns which appeared in the American colonies prior to the 19th century. The tunes were frequently adapted from secular folk song brought to this country by settlers from Great Britain.

Sursum corda—a versicle and response between minister and congregation. It is usually preceded by the Salutation, and introduces the Eucharistic Prayer.

> V: Lift up your hearts.
> R: We lift them up to the Lord.
> V: Let us give thanks to the Lord.
> R: It is meet and proper to do so.

Tenebrae—the office service of matins-lauds conducted during the final days of Holy Week, in which candles are gradually extinguished to commemorate the crucifixion of Christ. In modern free church practice, the office liturgy may not be strictly followed.

Therapy, Music—the treatment of disease (especially emotional) or the promotion of health, by the use of musical sounds or music activity.

Tracker Action Organs—also called "mechanical action" organs, are characterized by a direct mechanical link between the player's fingers and the flow of air through organ pipes, with no electrical switches or pneumatic devices involved.

Versicle—a short sentence or phrase, usually from the Psalms, spoken by the worship leader and followed by a congregational Response.

Vespers—see Evening Prayer.

Votive Mass—a mass said for a "special intention" (e.g., the soul of a deceased person). In the medieval period, votive masses were frequently offered with only the celebrant present.

SUPPLEMENTARY READINGS

Chapter I—Music: God's Gift to Us

Leonard Bernstein, *The Joy of Music*.
John Dewey, *Art as Experience*.
Irwin Edman, *Arts and the Man*.
Leonard B. Meyer, *Music, the Arts, and Ideas*.
Bruno Nettl, *Theory and Method in Ethnomusicology*.
H. R. Rookmaaker, *Modern Art and the Death of a Culture*.
Jane Stuart Smith and Betty Carlson, *A Gift of Music*.
Dale Topp, *Music in the Christian Community*.
Walter Wiora (trans. by M. D. Herter Norton), *The Four Ages of Music*.

Chapter II—Church Music: A Functional Art

Joseph N. Ashton, *Music in Worship*.
Walford Davies and Harvey Grace, *Music and Worship*.
Donald P. Ellsworth, *Christian Music in Contemporary Witness*.
Carl Halter, *God and Man in Music*.
———— *The Practice of Sacred Music*.
Robert H. Mitchell, *Ministry and Music*.
Kenneth W. Osbeck, *The Ministry of Music*.
William J. Reynolds and Milburn Price, *A Joyful Sound: Christian Hymnody*.
Johannes Riedel, ed., *Cantors at the Crossroads*.
Erik Routley, *Church Music and the Christian Faith*.
———— *Music Leadership in the Church*.
Dwight Steere, *Music in Protestant Worship*.
Gunnar Urang, *Church Music—for the Glory of God*.
John F. Wilson, *An Introduction to Church Music*.
Paul W. Wohlgemuth, *Rethinking Church Music*.

Chapter III—Music Languages: Communication and Conflict

Donald P. Ellsworth, *Christian Music in Contemporary Witness*.
Robert H. Mitchell, *Ministry and Music*.
H. R. Rookmaaker, *Modern Art and the Death of a Culture*.
Erik Routley, *Church Music and the Christian Faith*.
John F. Wilson, *An Introduction to Church Music*.
Paul W. Wohlgemuth, *Rethinking Church Music*.

349

Chapter IV—Authority and Leadership in Evangelical Church Music

David P. Appleby, *History of Church Music.*
Kenneth W. Osbeck, *The Ministry of Music.*
C. Henry Phillips, *The Singing Church.*
Erik Routley, *The Church and Music.*
Lynn W. Thayer, *The Church Music Handbook.*
Federal Lee Whittlesey, *A Comprehensive Program of Church Music.*
John F. Wilson, *An Introduction to Church Music.*

Chapter V—Christian Worship: A Definition and Some Implications for Church Music

Andrew W. Blackwood, *The Fine Art of Public Worship.*
Peter Brunner (trans. M. H. Bertram), *Worship in the Name of Jesus.*
Gaines S. Dobbins, *The Church at Worship.*
Cheslyn Jones, Geoffrey Wainwright, Edward Yarnold, eds., *The Study of Liturgy.*
Anne Ortlund, *Up with Worship.*
Richard Paquier (trans. by Donald Macleod), *Dynamics of Worship.*
Franklin M. Segler, *Christian Worship, Its Theology and Practice.*
John E. Skoglund, *Worship in the Free Churches.*
Geoffrey Wainwright, *Doxology, The Praise of God in Worship, Doctrine, and Life.*
James F. White, *Introduction to Christian Worship.*

Chapter VI—Music and Worship in the Bible

A. W. Binder, *Biblical Chant.*
Carl Halter and Carl Schalk, eds., *A Handbook of Church Music.*
A. S. Herbert, *Worship in Ancient Israel.*
A. Z. Idelsohn, *Jewish Liturgy and Its Development.*
Ralph P. Martin, *Worship in the Early Church.*
C. F. D. Moule, *Worship in the New Testament.*
Alfred Sendrey, *Music in Ancient Israel.*

Chapter VII—Christian Worship from the Second Century through the Reformation

David P. Appleby, *History of Church Music.*
Ford Lewis Battles, ed. and trans., *The Piety of John Calvin.*
Friedrich Blume, and others, *Protestant Church Music.*
L. W. Cowie and John Selwyn Gummer, *The Christian Calendar.*
George M. Gibson, *The Story of the Christian Year.*
Carl Halter and Carl Schalk, eds., *A Handbook of Church Music.*
Theodor Klauser (trans. by John Halliburton), *A Short History of the Western Liturgy.*
Edwin Liemohn, *The Chorale through Four Hundred Years.*
——— *The Organ and Choir in Protestant Worship.*
——— *The Singing Church.*
Kenneth R. Long, *The Music of the English Church.*
Ralph P. Martin, *Worship in the Early Church.*

James Hastings Nichols, *Corporate Worship in the Reformed Tradition.*
C. Henry Phillips, *The Singing Church.*
Johannes Riedel, *The Lutheran Chorale.*
Erik Routley, *The Church and Music.*
Carl Schalk, ed., *Key Words in Church Music.*
Russel N. Squire, *Church Music.*
Bard Thompson, ed., *Liturgies of the Western Church.*

Chapter VIII—Music and Renewal in the Church

Leonard Ellinwood, *The History of American Church Music.*
Donald P. Ellsworth, *Christian Music in Contemporary Witness.*
Carl Halter and Carl Schalk, eds., *A Handbook of Church Music.*
William Loyd Hooper, *Church Music in Transition.*
Phil Kerr, *Music in Evangelism.*
D. Bruce Lockerbie, *Billy Sunday.*
Ellen Jane Lorenz, *Glory, Hallelujah!*
Robert H. Mitchell, *Ministry and Music.*
Kenneth W. Osbeck, *The Ministry of Music.*
Homer Rodeheaver, *Twenty Years with Billy Sunday.*
Erik Routley, *Music Leadership in the Church.*
Paulus Scharpff (trans. Helga B. Henry), *History of Evangelism.*
E. O. Sellers, *Evangelism in Sermon and Song.*
James R. Sydnor, *The Hymn and Congregational Singing.*
Paul W. Wohlgemuth, *Rethinking Church Music.*

Chapter IX—Music and Worship in America

David J. Beattie, *The Romance of Sacred Song.*
Mandus A. Egge, ed., *Worship: Good News in Action.*
Leonard Ellinwood, *The History of American Church Music.*
Carl Halter and Carl Schalk, eds., *A Handbook of Church Music.*
Stanley High, *Billy Graham.*
William Loyd Hooper, *Church Music in Transition.*
Ellen Jane Lorenz, *Glory, Hallelujah!*
John Pollock, *Billy Graham.*
Johannes Riedel, ed., *Cantors at the Crossroads.*
Erik Routley, *Music Leadership in the Church.*
Ira D. Sankey, *My Life and the Story of the Gospel Hymns.*
John E. Skoglund, *Worship in the Free Churches.*
George C. Stebbins, *Reminiscences and Gospel Hymn Stories.*
James F. White, *Christian Worship in Transition.*

Chapter X—The Drama of Worship for Contemporary Evangelicals

James C. Barry and Jack Gulledge, eds. and cplrs., *Ideas for Effective Worship Services.*
Fred Bock and Bryan Jeffery Leech, *The Hymnal Companion.*
Donald J. Bruggink and Carl H. Droppers, *Christ and Architecture.*
L. W. Cowie and John Selwyn Gummer, *The Christian Calendar.*

Harry Eskew and Hugh T. McElrath, *Sing with Understanding.*
George Ferguson, *Signs & Symbols in Christian Art.*
Paul W. Hoon, *The Integrity of Worship.*
Alton H. McEachern, *Here at Thy Table, Lord.*
Anne Ortlund, *Up with Worship.*
H. Boone Porter, Jr., *Keeping the Church Year.*
James R. Sydnor, *The Hymn and Congregational Singing.*
John T. Wayland, *Planning Congregational Worship Services.*
James F. White, *Christian Worship in Transition.*
———— *Introduction to Christian Worship.*
———— *New Forms of Worship.*
Stephen F. Winward, *The Reformation of Our Worship.*

Chapter XI—Music in Services of Evangelism and Fellowship

John R. Bisagno, *The Power of Positive Evangelism.*
Robert Harkness, *The Harkness Piano Method of Evangelistic Hymn Playing.*
John F. Havlik, *The Evangelistic Church.*
Donald P. Hustad, "Music and the Church's Outreach."
———— "Music in Today's Crusades."
Phil Kerr, *Music in Evangelism.*
Terry Lindsay, *How to Build an Evangelistic Church Music Program.*
Edwin McNeely, *Evangelistic Music.*
Kenneth W. Osbeck, *Singing with Understanding.*
———— *The Ministry of Music.*
William J. Reynolds, *Congregational Singing.*
John F. Wilson, *An Introduction to Church Music.*

Chapter XII—Music in Special Services of Worship, including Weddings, Funerals and Baptisms

Cheslyn Jones, Geoffrey Wainwright, Edward Yarnold, eds., *The Study of Liturgy.*
Ralph P. Martin, *Worship in the Early Church.*
John E. Skoglund, *Worship in the Free Churches.*
Geoffrey Wainwright, *Doxology, The Praise of God in Worship, Doctrine, and Life.*
James F. White, *Introduction to Christian Worship.*
William H. Willimon, *Word, Water, Wine and Bread.*

Chapter XIII—Music in Foreign Missions

Vida Chenoweth, *Melodic Perception and Analysis.*
Marion Fred Ellerbe, "The Music Missionary of the Southern Baptist Convention: His Preparation and His Work."
Donald P. Hustad, "Must the Aucas Sing Our Songs?"
Alan P. Merriam, *The Anthropology of Music.*
Bruno Nettl, *Theory and Method in Ethnomusicology.*
Henry Weman, *African Music and the Church in Africa.*

Chapter XIV—Evangelicals and Congregational Singing

Paul Baker, *Why Should the Devil Have All the Good Music?*
Fred Bock and Bryan Jeffery Leech, *The Hymnal Companion.*
Harry Eskew and Hugh T. McElrath, *Sing with Understanding.*
Donald P. Hustad, "Shall We Demythologize Our Hymns?"
_____ "Apocalyptic in Contemporary Hymnody."
_____ "The Hymnbook and Your Quiet Time."
Bob Larson, *Rock.*
Cecil Northcott, *Hymns in Christian Worship.*
Kenneth W. Osbeck, *Singing with Understanding.*
William J. Reynolds, *Congregational Singing.*
_____ and Milburn Price, *A Joyful Sound: Christian Hymnody.*
Erik Routley, *Hymns Today and Tomorrow.*
George H. Shorney, Jr., "The History of Hope Publishing Company and Its Divisions and Affiliates."
James R. Sydnor, *The Hymn and Congregational Singing.*

Chapter XV—Evangelicals and Instrumental Music

Mildred Andrews and Pauline Riddle, *Church Organ Method.*
Louis Ball, *Hymn Playing* (piano).
Henry Coleman, *The Church Organist.*
James W. Good, *Church Organist Kit.*
Carl Halter and Carl Schalk, eds., *A Handbook of Church Music.*
Robert Harkness, *The Harkness Piano Method of Evangelistic Hymn Playing.*
Hans Klotz, *The Organ Handbook.*
Gerhard Krapf, *Liturgical Organ Playing.*
Edwin Liemohn, *The Singing Church.*
Austin C. Lovelace, *The Organist and Hymn Playing.*
William Stephan Mathis, *The Pianist and Church Music.*
James Ode, *Brass Instruments in Church Services.*
Phillip C. Posey, *Strings and Things.*
Harold Pottenger, *Instrumental Handbook.*
Erik Routley, *The Organist's Guide to "Congregational Praise."*
Carl Schalk, ed., *Key Words in Church Music.*
Samuel Walter, *Basic Principles of Service Playing.*

Chapter XVI—Evangelicals and Music for Choirs

Frances W. Aronoff, *Music and Young Children.*
Paul Bobbitt and Gerald Armstrong, *The Care and Feeding of Youth Choirs.*
Leonard Ellinwood, *The History of American Church Music.*
A. Oren Gould and Edith J. Savage, *Teaching Children to Sing.*
Carl Halter and Carl Schalk, eds., *A Handbook of Church Music.*
Stephen E. Hilson, *What Do You Say to a Naked Spotlight?*
Alvin Juliette, *Music for the Handicapped Child.*
Edwin Liemohn, *The Organ and Choir in Protestant Worship.*
_____ *The Singing Church.*
Alfred E. Lunde, *Christian Education thru Music.*
Robert H. Mitchell, *Ministry and Music.*

Ruth Nininger, *Growing a Musical Church.*
Carl Orff, *Music for Children.*
Kenneth W. Osbeck, *The Ministry of Music.*
C. Henry Phillips, *The Singing Church.*
Festus G. Robertson, *Church Music for Adults.*
Mabel W. Sample, *Music Making with Older Children.*
Carl Schalk, ed., *Key Words in Church Music.*
Federal Lee Whittlesey, *A Comprehensive Program of Church Music.*
John F. Wilson, *An Introduction to Church Music.*
James D. Woodward, *What to Do in Case of a Choir Rehearsal.*

Chapter XVII—Evangelicals and Music for Soloists (and Small Ensembles)

George Beverly Shea, *Then Sings My Soul.*
———— *Songs That Lift the Heart.*
Ethel Waters, *To Me It's Wonderful.*

Chapter XVIII—Postscripts

Paul Baker, *Why Should the Devil Have All the Good Music?*
James C. Barry and Jack Gulledge, eds. and cplrs., *Ideas for Effective Worship Services.*
Eugene Brand, *The Rite Thing.*
George Ferguson, *Signs & Symbols in Christian Art.*
Henry E. Horn, *Worship in Crisis.*
Donald P. Hustad, "Fellow Artists in Celebration."
———— "Jazz in the Church."
Bob Larson, *Rock.*
Kenneth G. Phifer, *A Protestant Case for Liturgical Renewal.*
H. Boone Porter, Jr., *Keeping the Church Year.*
John A. T. Robinson, *Liturgy Coming to Life.*
Ross Snyder, *Contemporary Celebration.*
William H. Willimon, *Word, Water, Wine and Bread.*

BIBLIOGRAPHY

Alexander, Helen C. and Maclean, J. Kennedy. *Charles M. Alexander: A Romance of Song and Soul-Winning.* London: Marshall Bros., 1920.

Andrews, Mildred and Riddle, Pauline. *Church Organ Method.* New York: Carl Fischer, Inc., 1972, 1973.

Appleby, David P. *History of Church Music.* Chicago: Moody Press, 1965.

Aronoff, Frances W. *Music and Young Children.* New York: Holt, Rinehart and Winston, Inc., 1969.

Ashton, Joseph N. *Music in Worship.* Boston: The Pilgrim Press, 1943.

Bailey, Albert E. *The Gospel in Hymns.* New York: Scribners, 1950.

Baker, Paul. *Why Should the Devil Have All the Good Music?* Waco, TX: Word Books, 1979.

Ball, Louis. *Hymn Playing* (piano). Nashville: Broadman Press, 1979.

Baptist Hymnal. Nashville: Convention Press, 1975.

Barrows, Cliff, ed. *Crusade Hymn Stories.* Chicago: Hope Publishing Company, 1967.

Barry, James C. and Gulledge, Jack, eds. and cplrs. *Ideas for Effective Worship Services.* Nashville: Convention Press, 1977.

Barzun, Jacques. *Music in American Life.* Garden City, NY: Doubleday, 1950.

Battles, Ford Lewis, ed. and trans. *The Piety of John Calvin.* Grand Rapids: Baker Book House, 1978.

Beattie, David J. *The Romance of Sacred Song.* London: Marshall, Morgan & Scott, Ltd., 1931.

Bernstein, Leonard. *The Joy of Music.* New York: Simon and Schuster, 1959.

Best, Harold. "Toward a Biblical Perspective on the Arts." *InForm*, Wheaton College, Wheaton IL, April, 1979.

Binder, A. W. *Biblical Chant.* New York: Philosophical Library, 1959.

Bisagno, John R. *The Power of Positive Evangelism.* Nashville: Broadman Press, 1968.

Blackwood, Andrew W. *The Fine Art of Public Worship.* Nashville: Abingdon Press, 1939.

Bloesch, Donald G. *The Evangelical Renaissance.* Grand Rapids: William B. Eerdmans Publishing Co., 1973.

Blume, Friedrich, and others. *Protestant Church Music.* New York: W. W. Norton and Company, Inc., 1974 (translation).

Bobbitt, Paul and Armstrong, Gerald. *The Care and Feeding of Youth Choirs.* Nashville: Convention Press, 1975.

Bock, Fred and Leech, Bryan Jeffery. *The Hymnal Companion.* Nashville: Paragon Associates, Inc., 1979.

Bosch, Henry G. *Our Daily Bread.* Devotional readings published by Radio Bible Class, P.O. Box 22, Grand Rapids, MI.

Brand, Eugene. *The Rite Thing.* Minneapolis: Augsburg Publishing House, 1970.

Briggs, Kenneth A. "The Electronic Church Is Turning More People On." *New York Times,* Feb. 10, 1980.

Bruggink, Donald J. and Droppers, Carl H. *Christ and Architecture.* Grand Rapids: Wm. B. Eerdmans Publishing Company, 1965.

Brunner, Peter (trans. M. H. Bertram). *Worship in the Name of Jesus.* St. Louis: Concordia Publishing House, 1968.

Bryant, Anita. *Amazing Grace.* Old Tappan, NJ: Fleming H. Revell, 1976.

Buszin, Walter E. *Luther on Music.* St. Paul: North Central Publishing Company, 1958.

Cash, Johnny. *Man in Black.* Grand Rapids: Zondervan Publishing House, 1975.

Chailley, Jacques (trans. by Rollo Myers). *40,000 Years of Music.* London: Macdonald & Company, 1964.

Chenoweth, Vida. *Melodic Perception and Analysis.* (A Manual on Ethnic Melody). Ukarumpa, Papua New Guinea: Summer Institute of Linguistics, 1972.

Coleman, Henry. *The Church Organist.* London: Oxford University Press, 1955.

Cowie, L. W. and Gummer, John Selwyn. *The Christian Calendar.* Springfield, MA: G. & C. Merriam Co., 1974.

Crawford, G. A. "Louis Bourgeois," *Groves Dictionary of Music and Musicians,* 5th ed., Vol. I.

Crouch, Andraé. *Through It All.* Waco, TX: Word Books, 1974.

Davies, Horton. *Worship and Theology in England,* Vol. II, 1603–1690. Princeton, NJ: Princeton University Press, 1975.

Davies, Walford and Grace, Harvey. *Music and Worship.* London: Eyre and Spottiswoode, 1935.

Dewey, John. *Art as Experience.* New York: G. P. Putnam's Sons, 1934, 1958.

Dobbins, Gaines S. *The Church at Worship.* Nashville: Broadman Press, 1962.

Editors, "Back to That Old Time Religion," *Time,* Vol. 110, No. 26 (December 26, 1977).

Editors, "Discord and Rising Decibels over Broadcasting Religious Music." *Christianity Today,* Vol. 24, No. 6, pp. 46–48 (March 21, 1980).

Edman, Irwin. *Arts and the Man.* New York: W. W. Norton & Company, Inc., 1928, 1939.

Egge, Mandus A., ed. *Worship: Good News In Action.* Minneapolis: Augsburg Publishing House, 1973.

Ellerbe, Marion Fred. "The Music Missionary of the Southern Baptist Convention: His Preparation and His work." Unpublished thesis, 1970; available from University Microfilms, Ann Arbor, Michigan.

Ellinwood, Leonard. *The History of American Church Music.* New York: Morehouse-Gorham Company, 1953.

Ellsworth, Donald P. *Christian Music in Contemporary Witness.* Grand Rapids: Baker Book House, 1979.

Eskew, Harry and McElrath, Hugh T. *Sing with Understanding.* Nashville: Broadman Press, 1980.

Ferguson, George. *Signs & Symbols in Christian Art.* London: Oxford University Press, 1954.

Findlay, James F., Jr. *Dwight L. Moody: American Evangelist, 1837–1899.* Chicago: University of Chicago Press, 1969.

Ford, Leighton. *The Christian Persuader.* New York: Harper and Row, 1966.

Gaebelein, Frank E. "Toward a Biblical View of Aesthetics." *Christianity Today,* Aug. 30, 1968.

Gaither, Gloria. *Because He Lives.* Old Tappan, NJ: Fleming H. Revell, 1977.

Garrett, T. S. *Christian Worship.* London: Oxford University Press, 1961, 1963.

Gaston, E. Thayer. "Psychological Foundations for Functional Music," *American Journal of Occupational Therapy,* Vol. 2, No. 1 (Feb., 1948).

Gibson, George W. *The Story of the Christian Year.* Nashville: Abingdon Press, 1955.

Good, James W. *Church Organist Kit.* Nashville: Convention Press, 1980.

Gould, A. Oren, and Savage, Edith J. *Teaching Children to Sing.* Dubuque, IA: Kendall Hunt Publishing Company, 1972.

Haley, Alex. *Roots.* Garden City, NY: Doubleday, 1976.

Halter, Carl. *God and Man in Music.* St. Louis: Concordia Publishing House, 1963.

_____ "The Case for the Soloist in Christian Worship," *Church Music 71-2.*

_____ *The Practice of Sacred Music.* St. Louis: Concordia Publishing House, 1955.

_____ and Schalk, Carl, eds. *A Handbook of Church Music.* St. Louis: Concordia Publishing House, 1978.

Harkness, Robert. *The Harkness Piano Method of Evangelistic Hymn Playing.* Kansas City: Lillenas Publishing Company, 1941, 1962.

Harvard Dictionary of Music, 2nd Edition. Cambridge, MA: Harvard University Press, 1964.

Havlik, John F. *The Evangelistic Church.* Nashville: Convention Press, 1976.

Helmholtz, Hermann (trans. Alexander J. Ellis). *On the Sensations of Tone, 1862.* New York: Dover Publications, Inc., 1954.

Herbert, A. S. *Worship in Ancient Israel.* Richmond: John Knox Press, 1959.

High, Stanley. *Billy Graham.* New York: McGraw-Hill Book Company, Inc., 1956.

Hilson, Stephen E. *What Do You Say to a Naked Spotlight?* New York: Belwyn and Mills, Inc., 1972.

Hood, George. *A History of Music in New England.* Boston: Wilkins, Carter and Company, 1846.

Hoon, Paul W. *The Integrity of Worship.* Nashville: Abingdon Press, 1971.

Hooper, William Loyd. *Church Music in Transition.* Nashville: Broadman Press, 1963.

Horn, Henry E. *Worship in Crisis.* Philadelphia: Fortress Press, 1972.

Hull, William E. "In Praise of a Good Man." *The Church Chimes,* Vol. 58, No. 51. Published by First Baptist Church, Shreveport, LA (August 28, 1976).

Hustad, Donald P. "Apocalyptic in Contemporary Hymnody," *Review and Expositor,* Vol. 72, No. 3 (Summer 1975).

_____ *Dictionary-Handbook to Hymns for the Living Church.* Carol Stream, IL: Hope Publishing Company, 1978.

_____ "Fellow Artists in Celebration," *Review and Expositor,* Vol. 71, No. 1 (Winter 1974).

_____ "Jazz in the Church," *Eternity,* Vol. 17, No. 4 (April, 1966).

_____ "Music and the Church's Outreach," *Review and Expositor,* Vol. 69, No. 2 (Spring 1972).

_____ "Music in Today's Crusades," *Moody Monthly,* Vol. 63, No. 7 (March, 1963).

_____ "Must the Aucas Sing Our Songs?", *Eternity,* Vol. 18, No. 2 (Feb., 1967).

_____ "Shall We Demythologize Our Hymns?", *The Asbury Seminarian,* Vol. 19, No. 2 (June, 1965).

_____ *The Christmas Story in Candlelight Carols.* Carol Stream, IL: Hope Publishing Company, 1964.

_____ *The Easter Story.* Chicago: Hope Publishing Company, 1969.

_____ "The Hymnbook and Your Quiet Time," *Moody Monthly,* Vol. 64, No. 8 (April, 1964).

Hymns for the Living Church. Carol Stream: Hope Publishing Company, 1974.

Idelsohn, A. Z. *Jewish Liturgy and Its Developments.* New York: Holt, Rinehart and Winston, Inc., 1932.

James, William. *The Principles of Psychology.* New York: Henry Holt and Company, 1896.

Jones, Cheslyn; Wainwright, Geoffrey and Yarnold, Edward, editors. *The Study of Liturgy.* London: Oxford University Press, 1978.

Juliette, Alvin. *Music for the Handicapped Child.* London: Oxford University Press, 2nd ed., 1976.

Kerr, Phil. *Music in Evangelism.* Grand Rapids: Singspiration Publishing House, 1952.

Kierkegaard, Søren. *Purity of Heart Is to Will One Thing.* New York: Harper Brothers, 1938.

Killinger, John. *Leave It to the Spirit.* New York: Harper and Row, 1971.

Klauser, Theodor (trans. by John Halliburton). *A Short History of the Western Liturgy.* London: Oxford University Press, 1969.

Klotz, Hans. *The Organ Handbook.* St. Louis: Concordia Publishing House, 1969.

Kostelanetz, Richard, ed. *Esthetics Contemporary.* Buffalo: Prometheus Books, 1978.

Krapf, Gerhard. *Liturgical Organ Playing.* Minneapolis: Augsburg Publishing House, 1964.

Kuyper, Abraham. *Lextures on Calvinism.* Grand Rapids: Eerdmans Publishing Company, 1931.

Lang, Paul Henry. *Music in Western Civilization.* New York: W. W. Norton and Company, 1941.

Langer, Susanne K. *Mind: An Essay on Human Feeling.* Baltimore: Johns Hopkins Press, 1967.

_____ *Philosophy in a New Key.* Cambridge: Harvard University Press, 1942, 1951, 1957.

_____ *Feeling and Form.* New York: Charles Scribner's Sons, 1953.

Larson, Bob. *Rock.* Wheaton, IL: Tyndale House, 1980.

———— *Rock and the Church.* Carol Stream, IL: Creation House, 1971.

Leonhard, Charles and House, Robert W. *Foundations and Principles of Music Education.* New York: McGraw-Hill Book Company, Inc., 1959.

Lewis, C. S. "On Church Music," *Christian Reflections.* Grand Rapids: Eerdmans Publishing Company, 1967.

Liemohn, Edwin. *The Chorale through Four Hundred Years.* Philadelphia: Mühlenberg Press, 1963.

———— *The Organ and Choir in Protestant Worship.* Philadelphia: The Fortress Press, 1968.

———— *The Singing Church.* Columbus, OH: The Wartburg Press, 1959.

Lockerbie, D. Bruce. *Billy Sunday.* Waco, TX: Word Books, 1965.

Long, Kenneth R. *The Music of the English Church.* New York: St. Martin's Press, Inc., 1971.

Lorenz, Ellen Jane. *Glory, Hallelujah!* (The Story of the Campmeeting Spirituals). Nashville: Abingdon Press, 1978, 1979, 1980.

Lovelace, Austin C. *The Organist and Hymn Playing.* (Revised) Carol Stream, IL: Agape, 1981.

———— and Rice, William C. *Music and Worship in the Church.* Nashville: Abingdon Press, 1976, rev. ed.

Lunde, Alfred E. *Christian Education thru Music.* Wheaton, IL: Evangelical Teacher Training Association, 1978.

Lyman, Ed. *Singing Your Song.* Winona Lake, IN: Rodeheaver Hall-Mack Company, 1955.

Manzelmann, Richard L. "The Revival Heard Around the World." Published by Auburn Theological Seminary, 3041 Broadway, New York, NY, 1975.

Martin, Ralph P. *Worship in the Early Church.* London: Marshall, Morgan and Scott, Ltd., 1964.

Mathis, William Stephan. *The Pianist and Church Music.* Nashville: Abingdon Press, 1962.

Maxwell, William D. *An Outline of Christian Worship.* London: Oxford University Press, 1936.

———— *John Knox's Genevan Service Book, 1556.* Westminster: The Faith Press, 1931, 1965.

McEachern, Alton H. *Here at Thy Table, Lord.* Nashville: Broadman Press, 1977.

McLuhan, Marshall. *The Medium is the Massage.* New York: Bantam Books, 1967.

McNeely, Edwin. *Evangelistic Music.* Fort Worth: Seminary Hill Press, 1959.

Medema, Ken. *Come and See.* Waco, TX: Word Books, 1976.

Mellers, Wilfred. *Caliban Reborn.* New York: Harper & Row, 1967.

Merriam, Alan P. *The Anthropology of Music.* Evanston, IL: Northwestern University Press, 1964.

Meyer, Leonard B. *Emotion and Meaning in Music.* Chicago: University of Chicago Press, 1956.

———— *Music, the Arts, and Ideas.* Chicago: University of Chicago Press, 1967.

Mitchell, Robert H. *Ministry and Music.* Philadelphia: The Westminster Press, 1978.

Moule, C. F. D. *Worship in the New Testament.* Richmond: John Knox Press, 1961.

Mountford, Richard D. "Does the Music Make Them Do It?" *Christianity Today,* Vol. 23, No. 15, pp. 20-23.

Nettl, Bruno. *Theory and Method in Ethnomusicology.* London: Collier-Macmillan, Ltd., 1964.

New English Bible, The (NEB). Oxford University Press and Cambridge University Press, 1961, 1970.

Nichols, James Hastings. *Corporate Worship in the Reformed Tradition.* Philadelphia: The Westminster Press, 1968.

Nininger, Ruth. *Growing a Musical Church.* Nashville: Convention Press, 1969.

Northcott, Cecil. *Hymns in Christian Worship.* Richmond: John Knox Press, 1964.

Ode, James. *Brass Instruments in Church Services.* Minneapolis: Augsburg Publishing Company, 1970.

Orff, Carl. *Music for Children.* (English adaptation by Doreen Hall and Arnold Walter). Mainz: B. Schott's Söhne, 1957.

Ortlund, Anne. *Up with Worship.* Glendale, CA: Regal Books, 1975.

Osbeck, Kenneth W. *Singing with Understanding.* Grand Rapids: Kregel Publications, 1979.

———— *The Ministry of Music.* Grand Rapids: Zondervan Publishing House, 1961.

Paquier, Richard (trans. by Donald Macleod). *Dynamics of Worship.* Philadelphia: Fortress Press, 1967.

Perkins, Jocelyn. *Westminster Abbey: Its Worship and Ornaments.* Quoted by Horton Davies, *Worship and Theology in England,* Vol. II, 1603-1690. Princeton, NJ: Princeton University Press, 1975.

Peterson, John W. *The Miracle Goes On.* Grand Rapids: Zondervan Publishing House, 1976.

Phifer, Kenneth G. *A Protestant Case for Liturgical Renewal.* Philadelphia: The Westminster Press, 1965.

Philipson, Morris, ed. *Aesthetics Today.* New York: The World Publishing Company, 1961.

Phillips, C. Henry. *The Singing Church.* Hamden, CT: Archon Books, 1969.

Pirner, Reuben G. "Instruments in Christian Worship," *Church Music 70-1.*

Pollock, John. *Billy Graham.* London: Hodder and Stoughton, 1966.

Porter, H. Boone, Jr. *Keeping the Church Year.* New York: Seabury Press, 1977.

Posey, Phillip C. *Strings and Things.* Nashville: Convention Press, 1974.

Pottenger, Harold. *Instrumental Handbook.* Kansas City: Beacon Hill Music, 1971.

Prall, D. W. *Aesthetic Analysis.* New York: Thomas Y. Crowell Company, 1936.

_____ *Aesthetic Judgment.* New York: Thomas Y. Crowell Company, 1929, 1967.

Ramm, Bernard. *The Evangelical Heritage.* Waco, TX: Word, Inc., 1973.

Randolph, David James. *God's Party.* Nashville: Abingdon Press, 1975.

Reese, Gustave. *Music in the Middle Ages.* New York: W. W. Norton Company, 1940.

Reynolds, William J. *Congregational Singing.* Nashville: Convention Press, 1975.

_____ and Price, Milburn. *A Joyful Sound: Christian Hymnody.* New York: Holt, Rinehart and Winston, Inc., 1978.

Rhea, Claude. *With My Song I Will Praise Him.* Nashville: Broadman Press, 1977.

Riedel, Johannes, ed. *Cantors at the Crossroads.* St. Louis: Concordia Publishing House, 1967.

Robertson, Festus G. *Church Music for Adults.* Nashville: Convention Press, 1969.

Robinson, John A. T. *Liturgy Coming to Life.* London: A. W. Mowbray & Company, Ltd., 1960, 1963.

Rodeheaver, Homer. *Twenty Years with Billy Sunday.* Winona Lake, IN: The Rodeheaver Company, 1936.

Rookmaaker, H. R. *Modern Art and the Death of a Culture.* London: Inter-Varsity Press, 1970.

Routley, Erik. *Church Music and the Christian Faith.* Carol Stream, IL: Agape, 1978.

_____ *Hymns Today and Tomorrow.* Nashville: Abingdon Press, 1964.

_____ *Music Leadership in the Church.* Nashville: Abingdon Press, 1967.

_____ "Sexist Language: A View from a Distance," *Worship,* Vol. 53, No. 1, pp. 2-11 (Jan., 1979).

_____ *The Church and Music.* London: Gerald Duckworth & Company, Ltd., 1950.

_____ *The Organist's Guide to "Congregational Praise."* London: Independent Press, Ltd., 1957.

_____ *Words, Music and the Church.* Nashville: Abingdon Press, 1968.

Rudolph, Otto. *The Idea of the Holy.* London: Oxford University Press, 1923, 1925.

Ruffin, Bernard. *Fanny Crosby.* Philadelphia: United Church Press, 1976.

Sample, Mabel W. *Music Making with Older Children.* Nashville: Convention Press, 1972.

Sankey, Ira D. *My Life and the Story of the Gospel Songs.* New York: Harper and Brothers, 1906.

Schalk, Carl, ed. *Key Words in Church Music.* St. Louis: Concordia Publishing House, 1978.

_____ "Solo Literature for the Liturgical Service," *Church Music 71-2.*

Scharpff, Paulus (trans. Helga B. Henry). *History of Evangelism.* Grand Rapids: Wm. B. Eerdmans Publishing Company, 1966.

Segler, Franklin M. *Christian Worship, Its Theology and Practice.* Nashville: Broadman Press, 1967.

Sellers, E. O. *Evangelism in Sermon and Song.* Chicago: Moody Press, 1946.

Sendrey, Alfred. *Music in Ancient Israel.* New York: Philosophical Library, 1969.

Shea, George Beverly. *Songs That Lift the Heart.* Old Tappan, NJ: Fleming H. Revell Company, 1972.

_____ *Then Sings My Soul.* Old Tappan, NJ: Fleming H. Revell Company, 1968.

Shepherd, Massey H., Jr. *The Worship of the Church.* New York: The Seabury Press, 1952.

Shinn, Roger L. "The Educational Ministry of the Church," *An Introduction to Christian Education*, pp. 12-18. Nashville: Abingdon Press, 1966.

Shorney, George. "The History of Hope Publishing Company and its Divisions and Affiliates," *Dictionary-Handbook to Hymns for the Living Church*, pp. 1-21. Carol Stream, IL: Hope Publishing Company, 1978.

Skoglund, John E. *Worship in the Free Churches*. Valley Forge, PA: The Judson Press, 1965.

Snyder, Ross. *Contemporary Celebration*. Nashville: Abingdon Press, 1971.

Squire, Russel N. *Church Music*. St. Louis: The Bethany Press, 1962.

Stebbins, George C. *Reminiscences and Gospel Hymn Stories*. New York: George H. Doran Company, 1924. Reprinted AMS Press, Inc., New York, NY, 1971.

Steere, Dwight. *Music in Protestant Worship*. Richmond: John Knox Press, 1960.

Stookey, Noel Paul. "Bob Dylan Finds His Source," *Christianity Today*, Vol. 24, No. 32.

Strunk, Oliver, ed. *Source Readings in Music History*, Vol. I. New York: W. W. Norton and Company, 1965.

Sweet, William Warren. *Revivalism in America*. New York: Charles Scribner's Sons, 1944.

Sydnor, James R. *The Hymn and Congregational Singing*. Richmond: John Knox Press, 1960.

Temple, William. *The Hope of a New World*. New York: The Macmillan Company, 1942.

Terry, Lindsay. *How to Build an Evangelistic Church Music Program*. Nashville: Thomas Nelson, Inc., 1974.

Thayer, Lynn W. *The Church Music Handbook*. Grand Rapids: Zondervan Publishing House, 1971.

Thompson, Bard, ed. *Liturgies of the Western Church*. Cleveland: The World Publishing Company, 1961.

Topp, Dale. *Music in the Christian Community*. Grand Rapids: Wm. B. Eerdmans Publishing Company, 1976.

Underhill, Evelyn. *Worship*. New York: Harper & Row, 1936.

Urang, Gunnar. *Church Music—for the Glory of God*. Moline, IL: Christian Service Foundation, 1956.

Vantoura, Suzanne Haik. *La Musique de la Bible Reveleé*. Paris: Dessain et Tolra, 1978.

Wainwright, Geoffrey. *Doxology—The Praise of God in Worship, Doctrine, and Life*. New York: Oxford University Press, 1980.

Walter, Samuel. *Basic Principles of Service Playing*. Nashville: Abingdon Press, 1963.

Waters, Ethel. *To Me It's Wonderful*. New York: Harper & Row, 1972.

Wayland, John T. *Planning Congregational Worship Services*. Nashville: Broadman Press, 1971.

Wellesz, Egon. "Early Christian Music," *The New Oxford History of Music*, Vol. I. London: Oxford University Press, 1957.

Weman, Henry (trans. by Eric J. Sharp). *African Music and the Church in Africa*. Uppsala, Sweden: Lundequistska bokhandeln, 1960.

Werner, Eric. "Jewish Music," *Grove's Dictionary*, 5th ed., Vol. IV. New York: St. Martin's Press, Inc., 1954.

———— *The Sacred Bridge*. New York: Schocken Books, 1970.

White, James F. *Christian Worship in Transition*. Nashville: Abingdon Press, 1976.

———— *Introduction to Christian Worship*. Nashville: Abingdon Press, 1980.

Whittlesey, Federal Lee. *A Comprehensive Program of Church Music*. Philadelphia: The Westminster Press, 1957.

Williams, Peter. *Bach Organ Music*. London: British Broadcasting Corporation, 1972.

Willimon, William H. *Word, Water, Wine and Bread*. Valley Forge, PA: Judson Press, 1980.

Wilson, John F. *An Introduction to Church Music*. (Revised) Carol Stream, IL: Hope, 1981.

Winslow, Ola Elizabeth. *Jonathan Edwards, 1703-1758*. New York: The Macmillan Company, 1940.

Winward, Stephen F. *The Reformation of Our Worship*. London: The Carey Kingsgate Press, Ltd., 1964.

Wiora, Walter (trans. by M. D. Herter Norton). *The Four Ages of Music*. New York: W. W. Norton and Company, 1965.

Wohlgemuth, Paul W. *Rethinking Church Music*. (Revised) Carol Stream, IL: Hope, 1981.

Woodward, James. *What to Do in Case of a Choir Rehearsal.* Nashville: Convention Press, 1972.

Woodward, Kenneth L., Barnes, John and Lisle, Laurie. "The Year of the Evangelicals," *Newsweek,* Vol. 88, No. 17 (Oct. 25, 1976).

Young, Carlton. "HSA Convocations: Back to the Basics!" *The Hymn,* Vol. 28, No. 4 (Oct., 1977).

INDEX